D. Yenni

A Grammar of the Latin Language

Salzwasser

D. Yenni

A Grammar of the Latin Language

1. Auflage | ISBN: 978-3-84604-974-7

Erscheinungsort: Frankfurt, Deutschland

Erscheinungsjahr: 2020

Salzwasser Verlag GmbH

Reprint of the original, first published in 1869.

A GRAMMAR

OF THE

LATIN LANGUAGE.

BY

REV. D. YENNI, S. J.,

PROFESSOR OF GREEK AND LATIN IN SPRINGHILL COLLEGE.

Quo minus sunt ferendi qui hanc artem ut tenuem cavillantur, quæ nisi oratoris futuri fundamenta jecern quidquid superstruxeris, corruet: necessaria pueris, jucunda senibus, quæ vel sola ex omni studiorum genere plus habeat operis quam ostentationis.

Quintil. de Inst. Orat., L. I., c. 4.

NEW YORK:

JOHN G. SHEA, PUBLISHER,

1869.

CONTENTS.

CHAPTER V.

THE VERB.

CHAPTER VI.

PARTICLES.

SYNTAX.

CHAPTER I.

THE FOUR CONCORDS.

CHAPTER II.

CHAPTER III.

SUBSTANTIVES.

CHAPTER IV.

ADJECTIVES.

CHAPTER V

PRONOUNS.

CHAPTER VI.

THE VERB.

CHAPTER VII.
PARTICLES.

APPENDIX.

PROSODY.
CHAPTER I.

CHAPTER II.

INCREMENTS.

CHAPTER III.

CHAPTER IV.

INTRODUCTORY REMARKS.

1. The present Work is the fruit of the Author's thirty years' experience as a Classical Teacher, in Germany and in America. In this country, he has found the chief obstacles to solid Classical acquirements to be: first, the hasty and consequently superficial study of Grammatical elements, and secondly, the imperfection and deficiencies of Grammatical treatises. On the one hand, the Student is hurried forward to translation, before he has mastered the rudiments; on the other, the Grammars that are given to his use, are either beyond his capacity because they are too learned and philosophical,—or too extensive, embodying all possible minutiæ of words and forms of no real and practical use,—or, again, too short and defective, passing over in silence matters of paramount importance, such as the rules of gender, the perfects and supines of verbs, and treating, if at all, many questions of Syntax in a very superficial and desultory manner.

2. To present to the friends of Latin Literature a Grammar, as far as possible, free from these inconveniences, it has been our main effort to combine brevity, comprehensiveness, and method. We have discarded, with that view, a number of preliminary remarks, definitions, divisions, and subdivisions, and all matters, in fine, which, belonging to General Grammar, are justly presupposed to be familiar to the Student from a previous study of his own language, or which, if peculiar to the Latin Tongue, may easily be supplied orally by the teacher himself. The present Work thereby gains the advantage, that it adapts itself to any preceding stage of learning and method of instruction, and the fresh energies of the beginner, instead of lingering at the very outset, are at once started into full play.

3. The declensions, as well as the conjugations, have been placed side by side, in order to produce a stronger and more lasting impression on the eye and mind of the pupil, and to render a reference to them as easy as possible.—To the Paradigms both of the declensions and adjectives, vocabularies have been added which should be carefully committed to memory and recited, at the rate of ten or fifteen words every day. The same practice of learning the Rules of Gender and the Perfects and Supines of Verbs, we most earnestly recommend. Experience teaches how successful this practice is, and how the young Latinist feels encouraged, when in the course of a few weeks, he finds himself, by means of the stock of words thus acquired, capable not only of translating short narratives into his own native Tongue, but of framing by himself simple Latin sentences, without a continual, irksome recourse to the dictionary. Mindful of Seneca's : *Longum est iter per praecepta, breve et efficax per exempla,*—we have with unsparing hand collected in the Syntax a great variety of Classical examples, which exhibit each rule in its various shades and lights, and supply the Student not only with exercises for translation, but chiefly with models for imitation. A short example, in heavier type, has been prefixed to every rule of the Syntax, according to Lhomond's method, so that, when called upon to account for some case, construction, or form, the pupil may, instead of reciting the rule at full length, equivalently express it by merely quoting the Heading.

4. In preparing the Grammar here presented to the public, we have availed ourselves of the labors of the very first Grammarians and Lexicographers of Germany, England, France, and Italy, incorporating with borrowed materials such observations and arrangements as the experience of so many years has suggested. It is, therefore, not originality that is claimed for the present Work, but utility. No new system has been invented; no new method introduced. The work thus compiled we intend not only for Students actually going through a regular course of Classical studies in Schools and Colleges, but for such also as may deem a private review of the Latin Grammar available. We intend it equally for both the Higher and Lower Classes : for we do not share the opinion of those who require a Latin Primer for beginners, and a Quarto Grammar for adepts, as a necessary condition of a successful Classical education. We rather think that Grammar best calculated to insure final success, which provides equally

for all, which goes with the child and the youth, from year to year, from Class to Class, as a dear companion and trusty guide. In this *vade mecum*, the more talented pupil will have a treasure from which to store his mind and fit himself for a superior Course, while the less talented pupil will have a Mentor to clear up his doubts,— and both will be benefited gradually, naturally,—as the constant perusal of the same book will, by strengthening local memory, render its use more agreeable. " The force of first associations," wisely remarks B. A. Gould in his Preface to Adam's Latin Grammar, "renders it almost impossible to use a different Grammar from that first learned, with the same readiness. The page, the situation on the page, the type, and other circumstances connected with it in the memory, all contribute to facilitate the turning to any rule or observation desired. And no small loss of time is occasioned by the confusion which results from having learned two or three Grammars of the same language."

5. In order to prevent an incorrect pronunciation on the part of the learner, several Grammarians on this Continent have thought it, if not necessary, at least expedient, to make use of accents and other signs of Prosody. Indeed, the Author himself has occasionally employed them, though for the most part in the case of such words only as are of less frequent occurrence, e. g., *perbrĕvis, trucīdo, infīdus,* etc., or such as, having some derivative in English, may easily mislead the pupil in his accentuation, e. g., *confīdens, instīgo, irrīto, suffŏco* (Engl., cónfident, ínstigate, írritate, súffocate), etc.— In general, however, we believe that the best, and perhaps the only means of imparting a correct pronunciation, is the *vox viva magistri* together with the teacher's constant, persevering care that every word shall be correctly uttered and, whenever a fault has been committed, that the learner shall repeat the word properly. Where this attention is wanting, all signs and marks will prove, if not utterly useless, at least of very little avail : they will serve only to fatigue the eye, confuse the mind, and impede an easy, fluent diction. We appeal to experience for the fact.

6. To many teachers, a regular series of exercises, such as are found in several of the modern Elementary Books, will doubtless seem to be wanting in this Volume. After mature deliberation, the Author has deemed it unadvisable to insert any besides the examples illustrating the Rules. And this for several reasons : (1.) not to render the Work too voluminous and costly ; (2.) to

place the different matters of both the Elementary and Syntactical Parts, in close, uninterrupted connection, before the eyes of the Student; and (3) because he is fully convinced that far greater advantage is derived from those exercises, which the teacher himself carefully prepares beforehand and skilfully adapts to his own previous explanations, as well as to the capacity and the advancement of his scholars, than from those which of late are met with in several so-called First and Second Latin Books.—These Books will, no doubt, be of use in the hands of a skilful master, who is able to change any sentence at will, to adapt the same example now to this, now to that rule, and to include such difficulties, as the state and progress of his pupils may require or permit: but, as Text-books, the Author thinks, that, so far from forming solid and thorough Latinists, they are more apt to paralyze the activity of both teacher and pupil.

7. Yet, although averse to such books, he is far from being opposed to the writing of exercises; nay, he would most earnestly recommend them and urge their daily practice. And, indeed, what are lessons, rules, theories, but a preparation for the more important task of composition? From the very outset, therefore, the pupil should be directed to form Latin sentences by means of the declension or declensions he has already mastered, together with a few forms of *sum, esse,* or of any other verb, either previously explained or dictated, at the time, in the required person, number, tense, and mood. In the General Directions and Cautions (§ 84), both teacher and pupil will find, even before entering on the study of Syntax, ample and more than sufficient matter for a variety of exercises, during the Course of the first year.

8. Two kinds of exercises should every day keep pace together: viz., translating from Latin into English, which, for brevity's sake, we call VERSION (written translation), and translating from English into Latin, which we call THEME (written Latin exercises). Which of the two is the more important, we will not decide. One thing is certain, that the Theme shows the real proficiency of a Student, as there is less room for mere guess-work. On the other hand, the Version is the best preparation for the Theme, as it furnishes to the thinking scholar Latin forms, original expressions, which may enable him to imitate successfully the Roman models of History, Poetry, and Eloquence. It has, besides, this unparalleled advantage, to which we call the special attention of pupils, parents, and

directors, in this our commercial age and country, that it is by far the best, almost the only way to learn one's own language scientifically and radically, first, by the knowledge of derivatives, and then, by the endeavour to exhibit in a modern dress the blended strength and beauty of the Original,—an effort, which, to be successful, must be renewed again and again, and which, if continued with patient constancy, will far better and sooner than a mere English course of study, lead to literary preeminence.

9. The Author would, moreover, call the attention of every Classical teacher to another kind of exercise, calculated to produce immense fruits in a very short time. This exercise is called *Prælectio* (Explanation). It is the teacher's own. Let him every day read to his pupils ten or twelve lines from one of the best Latin authors, and, having given first a literal translation, make on every leading word all the grammatical, literary, and miscellaneous observations of which it is susceptible, ending his explanation with a fluent translation in the best English possible ; let him, in fine, require of the students, for the next day, after committing to memory the passage, to give an oral repetition of what he himself has said, with such additional remarks of their own, as reflection or research may have suggested. It is incredible how much this exercise, even alone, can achieve, if properly performed : but when the *Prælectio* is daily gone through, and that for several years, together with the *Version* and the *Theme*, a thorough knowledge of Latin must be the happy and natural result. The Student, enriched with an abundant stock of Classical words and phrases, and encouraged by the example of his teacher, will soon begin to express confidently and boldly, in Classical diction, his own thoughts and feelings, and free himself from that embarrassment in speaking Latin which even Scholars, otherwise proficient in the study of ancient authors, are often unable to overcome.

10. Thus do we understand Classical training : thus was it understood for centuries. But where the method of f r e q u e n t composition united to a constant and p r o g r e s s i v e reading of the best Latin authors is wanting, where both teacher and pupils content themselves with a cursory, often but o r a l, perusal of some p r i n t e d exercises, there results no improving influence on national literature, and no solid, no lasting fruit of Classical education can be expected. Though we may be ranked among the *laudatores temporis acti* of Horace, still we fear not to assert that

fifty years ago Latin was much better and more solidly known than now-a-days, despite the progress and inventions of the age. How often have we met with Students, who, after having spent several years at school, when they applied for admission into College, being questioned concerning their previous studies, boldly answered : "We have read so many books of Cæsar—so many of Virgil—so many Orations of Cicero, etc.,"—but who, when more closely examined, not indeed on Philosophy, not on intricate Syntactical questions, but on the very first elements of Grammar, on the conjugations, and even the declensions, were not able to answer, still less to arrange five or six words into a simple, but complete and correct Latin sentence !

11. This sad experience is well depicted and justly lamented by a man of highest authority in these matters,† in the following passage : " *De scholis inferioribus quid dicam ? Omne studium in eo positum, ut quam plurima pueri discant, discant autem quam* brevissimo tempore *et quam* minimo labore. *Belle sane. Sed ista tam multarum rerum disciplinarumque varietas, quas summis labris attingunt potius adolescentuli quam hauriunt, illud scilicet efficit, ut sibi quidem multa scire videantur et aliquando semidoctorum turbam, scientiis æque ac reipublicæ, si qua est alia, perniciosissimam augeant ; at nihil vere ac solide sciant.* Ex omnibus aliquid : in toto nihil. *Ut percursis brevi tempore humanitatis studiis, ætate tenerrimi, ingenio etiamnum rudi, ad gravissima philosophiæ superiorumque scientiarum studia accedant, ex quibus cum emolumenti veri capiant ferme nihil, tum majoris libertatis usu capti in vitium præcipites rapiuntur, futuri mox doctores, certe, ut lenissime dicamus, immaturi. Quod autem methodi usque faciliores excogitentur, id si quid habere videtur commodi, habet certe et illud incommodi non parum, quod primum quidem quæ sine labore comparantur, levissime etiam mentibus adhæreant, et brevi tempore acquisita brevi oblivione deleantur ; deinde, quod quidem gravioris longe damni est, licet fortasse minus a plerisque cogitetur, quod ille deperdatur puerilis institutionis fructus vix non præcipuus, ut a teneris annis ad seriam animi applicationem, et ad laborem non sine vi aliqua sibi illata tolerandum assuescant ; quod quantum valeat in omnem deinceps ætatem ad pravos animi motus compescendos, et ad imperandum sibi, quotquot fuere sapientes homines intellexerunt, et*

---

† Rev. J. Roothaan, S. J.

Spiritus Sanctus docet, ubi ait: Bonum est homini, si portaverit jugum ab adolescentia sua."

12. To conclude:

With a sincere desire of promoting Classical studies in this country, and a hope of having contributed our mite to encourage the youthful scholar in his rugged ascent to literary eminence, this Work is respectfully submitted to the friends of Education.

THE AUTHOR.

SPRING–HILL COLLEGE, near MOBILE, Ala.
March 19, 1869.

ELEMENTARY PART.

CHAPTER I.

SUBSTANTIVES.

§ 1. In every substantive four things are to be observed: *gender, number, case,* and *declension.*

The cases are six in each number: the *nominative, genitive, dative, accusative, vocative,* and *ablative.*

The NOMINATIVE answers to—*who* or *what* placed before the finite verb: as, "Paul excels." *Who* excels? Paul.—"The battle rages." *What* rages? The battle.—"Paul" and "The battle" are the nominatives.

The GENITIVE answers to the question *whose?* or, *of whom* or *what?* asked in connection with a noun; as, Cæsar's legions conquered? *Who* conquered? The legions. *Whose* legions? Cæsar's.—"Legions" is the nominative; "Cæsar's," the genitive.

The DATIVE answers to the question—*to whom* or *what?* as, "A misfortune has happened to me." *What* has happened? A misfortune. *To whom?* to me.—"A misfortune" is the nominative; "to me," the dative.

The ACCUSATIVE answers to—*whom* or *what* placed after a verb transitive; as, "God rules the world." *Who* rules? God. Rules *what?* the world.—"God" is the nominative; "the world," the accusative.

The VOCATIVE is the case of direct address; as, "My son, fly from the wicked."—"My son" is the person addressed, and is, therefore, put in the vocative."

The ABLATIVE answers to—*when? where? from (with, by) whom* or *what?* as, "The body is hardened by labor." *What* is hardened? The body. *By what?* by labor.—"The body" is the nominative; "by labor," the ablative.

§ 2.—There are five declensions, distinguished by the ending of the

genitive	1	2	3	4	5	singular.
	æ	i	is	us	ei	

To the *first* declension belong all substantives that make the gen. sing. in *æ ;* to the *second* belong those that make the gen. sing. in *i,* and so on.

To the *fifth* declension belong those that end in *es* and make the gen. sing. in *ei.*

GENERAL REMARKS.

1. The *voc.* is throughout like the *nom.,* except in words in *us* of the second declension, which make the voc. sing. in *e.*

2. The *dat.* and *abl.* plur. are alike in all declensions.

3. *Neuter* nouns occur only in the 2d, 3d, and 4th declensions. They have three cases alike: the *nom., acc.* and *voc.,* and these cases in the plural end always in *a.*

		I.	II.	III.	
	Rosa (f.) *a rose*.		**Slave.** (m.)	**Realm.** (n.)	**Lion.** (m.)
S. N.	ros-a,	*a rose,*	serv-us,	*regnum,*	leo,
G.	ros-æ,	*of a rose,*	serv-i,	regn-i,	leon-is.
D.	ros-æ,	*to a rose,*	serv-o,	regn-o,	leon-i,
A.	ros-am,	*a rose,*	serv-um,	*regnum,*	leon-em,
V.	ros-a,	*O rose!*	serv-e,	*regnum,*	leo,
A.	ros-a,	*with a rose,*	serv-o,	regn-o,	leon-e,
P. N.	ros-æ,	*roses,*	serv-i,	*regna,*	leon-es,
G.	ros-arum,	*of roses,*	serv-orum,	regn-orum,	leon-um,
D.	ros-is,	*to roses,*	serv-is,	regn-is,	leon-ibus,
A.	ros-as,	*roses,*	serv-os,	*regna,*	leon-es,
V.	ros-æ,	*O roses!*	serv-i,	*regna,*	leon-es,
A.	ros-is.	*with roses.*	serv-is.	regn-is.	leon-ibus.

First Declension.

§ 4.—Nouns of the I. Declension end in *a*, and are of the feminine gender.

ærumna, *hardship.*	galea, *a helmet.*	rana, *a frog.*
ala, *a wing.*	gallina, *a hen.*	regina, *a queen.*
alauda, *a lark.*	gemma, *a jewel.*	rima, *a chink.*
ancilla, *a maid.*	gratia, *a favor.*	ripa, *a bank.*
aqua, *water.*	gutta, *a drop.*	rixa, *a quarrel.*
aquila, *an eagle.*	habena, *a rein.*	rota, *a wheel.*
ara, *an altar.*	hasta, *a spear.*	ruga, *a wrinkle.*
aranea, *a spider.*	herba, *an herb.*	sagitta, *an arrow.*
arena, *sand.*	hora, *an hour.*	sapientia, *wisdom.*
arista, *an ear of corn.*	hostia, *a victim.*	sarcina, *a burden.*
aula, *a hall.*	injuria, *a wrong.*	scintilla, *a spark.*
aura, *a breeze.*	inopia, *want.*	semita, *a path.*
avia, *a grandmother.*	insula, *an island.*	sententia, *an opinion.*
barba, *a beard.*	invidia, *envy.*	silva, *a wood.*
calumnia, *slander.*	ira, *anger.*	simia, *an ape.*
campana, *a bell.*	jactura, *loss.*	socordia, *sloth.*
candela, *a candle.*	janua, *a door.*	spina, *a thorn.*
catena, *a chain.*	lachryma, *a tear.*	spuma, *foam.*
causa, *a cause.*	lana, *wool.*	stella, *a star.*
cera, *wax.*	lima, *a file.*	superbia, *pride.*
charta, *paper.*	lingua, *the tongue.*	tabula, *a board.*
ciconia, *a stork.*	luna, *the moon.*	tegula, *a tile.*
cœna, *a supper.*	macula, *a stain.*	tela, *a web.*
columba, *a dove.*	memoria, *memory.*	terra, *the earth.*
corona, *a crown.*	mensa, *a table.*	turba, *a crowd.*
culina, *a kitchen.*	mica, *a crumb.*	turma, *a troop.*
culpa, *a fault.*	mora, *a delay.*	ulna, *an ell.*
cura, *care.*	musca, *a fly.*	umbra, *a shade.*
epistola, *a letter.*	nebula, *a mist.*	unda, *a wave.*
fabula, *a fable.*	ora, *a coast.*	ungula, *the hoof.*
fama, *fame.*	pecunia, *money.*	uva, *a grape.*
femina, *a woman.*	pagina, *a page.*	vacca, *a cow.*
fenestra, *a window.*	pluvia, *rain.*	venia, *leave.*
fistula, *a pipe.*	porta, *a gate.*	via, *a road, way.*
formica, *an ant.*	præda, *booty.*	vindicta, *vengeance.*
fossa, *a ditch.*	procella, *a storm.*	virga, *a rod.*
fovea, *a pit.*	pugna, *a fight.*	vita, *life.*

Decline together : *Barba longa—causa justa—columba timida—gemma pretiosa. Regina pia et benigna—formica sedula et laboriosa—turba perfida et tumultuosa,*—and the like.

Five Latin Declensions.

	Head. (n.)	Step. (m.)	Horn. (n.)	IV	V. (Sing. c., Plur. m.)	
	caput,	grad-us,	corn-u,		di-es,	a day,
	capit-is,	grad-us,	corn-us,		di-ei,	of a day,
	capit-i,	grad-ui,	corn-u,		di-ei,	to a day,
	caput,	grad-um,	çorn-u,		di-em,	a day,
	caput,	grad-us,	corn-u,		di-es,	O day!
	capit-e,	grad-u,	corn-u,		di-e,	on a day,
	capita,	grad-us,	cornua,		di-es,	days,
	capit-um,	grad-uum,	corn-uum,		di-erum,	of days,
	capit-ibus,	grad-ibus,	corn-ibus,		di-ebus,	to days,
	capita,	grad-us,	cornua,		di-es,	days,
	capita,	grad-us,	cornua,		di-es,	O days!
	capit-ibus.	grad-ibus.	corn-ibus.		di-ebus,	on days.

Second Declension.

§ 5.—Nouns of the II. Declension end in *us* and *er* (masc.) and in *um* (neuter.)

acervus, *a heap.*
aculeus, *a sting.*
agnus, *a lamb.*
amicus, *a friend.*
angulus, *a corner.*
animus, *the mind.*
annulus, *a ring.*
annus, *a year.*
asinus, *an ass.*
autumnus, *the autumn.*
avus, *a grandfather.*
campus, *a plain.*
cervus, *a stag.*
cibus, *food.*
clavus, *a nail.*
coquus, *a cook.*
corvus, *a raven.*
cumulus, *a heap.*
cuneus, *a wedge.*
cuniculus, *a rabbit.*
digitus, *a finger.*
dolus, *deceit.*
dominus, *a lord.*
equus, *a horse.*
famulus, *a servant.*
figulus, *a potter.*
fluvius, *a river.*
focus, *a hearth.*
fumus, *smoke.*
fundus, *a farm.*
gladius, *a sword.*
hædus, *a kid.*
hamus, *a hook.*
herus, *a master.*
hortus, *a garden.*
humerus, *a shoulder.*
juvencus, *a bullock.*

laqueus, *a noose.*
lectus, *a bed.*
legatus, *a legate.*
ludus, *a game.*
lupus, *a wolf.*
malleus, *a hammer.*
medicus, *a physician.*
mendicus, *a beggar.*
modius, *a bushel.*
modus, *a manner.*
morbus, *a disease.*
mundus, *the world.*
murus, *a wall.*
nidus, *a nest.*
nodus, *a knot.*
numerus, *a number.*
nuncius, *a messenger.*
oculus, *the eye.*
populus, *a people.*
porcus, *a hog.*
pugnus, *the fist.*
pullus, *a chicken.*
puteus, *a well.*
radius, *a ray.*
ramus, *a branch.*
remus, *an oar.*
rivus, *a rivulet.*
sciurus, *a squirrel.*
somnus, *sleep.*
sonus, *a sound.*
taurus, *a bull.*
tumulus, *a hillock.*
urceus, *a pitcher.*
ursus, *a bear.*
ventus, *the wind.*
vicus, *a village.*
vitulus, *a calf.*

argentum, *silver.*
aurum, *gold.*
anxilium, *help.*
bellum, *war.*
brachium, *an arm.*
collum, *the neck.*
damnum, *loss.*
donum, *a gift.*
ferrum, *iron.*
folium, *a leaf.*
furtum, *theft.*
gaudium, *joy.*
ingenium, *genius.*
initium, *a beginning.*
lignum, *wood.*
lucrum, *gain.*
membrum, *a member.*
mendacium, *a lie.*
negotium, *business.*
odium, *hatred.*
oppidum, *a town.*
ovum, *an egg.*
periculum, *a danger.*
præmium, *a reward.*
pratum, *a meadow.*
pretium, *a price.*
proelium, *a battle.*
signum, *a sign.*
somnium, *a dream.*
tectum, *a roof.*
telum, *a weapon.*
venenum, *poison.*
verbum, *a word.*
vinculum, *a chain.*
vinum, *wine.*
vitium, *vice.*
vocabulum, *a word.*

Decline together : *Cervus timidus—annulus pretiosus—donum pretiosum—templum magnificum. Puer modestus et verecundus—bellum longum et perniciosum,*—and the like.

THIRD DECLENSION.

§ 6. Nouns of the III. Decl. end variously, and generally increase in the genitive.

☞ In this declension special attention must be paid to the Stem, from which, by the addition of the respective endings, all the cases are formed.

The Stem of any substantive or adjective is obtained by dropping the ending of the genitive.

(m.)	(f.)	(n.)
flos, oris, *a flower.*	concio, ōnis, *an assembly.*	funus, ĕris, *a funeral.*
mos, oris, *a custom.*	ratio, onis, *reason.*	fœdus, eris, *a covenant.*
ros, oris, *dew.*	oratio, onis, *a speech.*	genus, eris, *a kind.*
pedes, ĭtis, *a footman.*	suspicio, onis, *mistrust.*	latus, eris, *the side.*
eques, itis, *a horseman.*	arundo, ĭnis, *a reed.*	munus, eris, *a gift.*
fomes, itis, *fuel.*	formido, inis, *fear.*	onus, eris, *a burden.*
gurges, itis, *a whirlpool.*	hirundo, inis, *a swallow.*	opus, eris, *a work.*
limes, itis, *a limit.*	valetudo, inis, *health.*	pondus, eris, *a weight.*
trames, itis, *a path.*	caligo, inis, *darkness.*	scelus, eris, *a crime.*
homo, ĭnis, *a man.*	fuligo, inis, *soot.*	sidus, eris, *a star.*
turbo, inis, *a whirlwind.*	origo, inis, *an origin.*	ulcus, eris, *an ulcer.*
caupo, onis, *an innkeeper.*	rubigo, inis, *rust.*	vulnus, eris, *a wound.*
carbo, onis, *a coal.*	virgo, inis, *a virgin.*	agmen, ĭnis, *a troop.*
crabro, onis, *a hornet.*	vorago, inis, *a gulf.*	acūmen, inis, *acuteness.*
latro, onis, *a robber.*	mater, tris, *a mother.*	carmen, inis, *a poem.*
præco, onis, *a herald.*	mulier, ĕris, *a woman.*	crimen, inis, *a crime.*
prædo, onis, *a robber.*	lex, legis, *a law.*	culmen, inis, *a summit.*
pulmo, onis, *the lungs.*	vox, vocis, *the voice.*	volūmen, inis, *a volume.*
sapo, onis, *soap.*	fax, facis, *a torch.*	gramen, inis, *grass.*
pavo, onis, *a peacock.*	pax, pacis, *peace.*	limen, inis, *the threshold.*
sermo, onis, *discourse.*	crux, crucis, *a cross.*	lumen, inis, *light.*
tiro, onis, *a beginner.*	lux, lucis, *light.*	flumen, inis, *a stream.*
aquilo, onis, *the north wind.*	cervix, īcis, *the neck.*	fulmen, inis, *lightning.*
frater, tris, *a brother.*	radix, īcis, *a root.*	nomen, inis, *a name.*
pater, tris, *a father.*	laus, laudis, *praise.*	numen, inis, *the Deity.*
aër, ĕris, *the air.*	fraus, fraudis, *deceit.*	discrīmen, inis, *a danger.*
agger, eris, *a mound.*	salus, ūtis, *safety.*	specīmen, inis, *a model*
anser, eris, *a goose.*	virtus, ūtis, *virtue.*	ebur, ŏris, *ivory.*
asser, eris, *a pole.*	æstas, ātis, *the summer.*	robur, oris, *strength.*
carcer, eris, *a prison.*	ætas, atis, *an age.*	fulgur, ŭris, *a flash.*
passer, eris, *a sparrow.*	bonitas, tis, *goodness.*	guttur, uris, *the throat.*
calor, ōris, *heat.*	brevitas, tis, *brevity.*	murmur, uris, *a noise.*
color, oris, *color.*	civitas, tis, *a state.*	fel, fellis, *the gall.*
clamor, oris, *a cry.*	jucunditas, tis, *delight.*	mel, mellis, *honey.*
decor, oris, *grace.*	paupertas, tis, *poverty.*	corpus, ŏris, *a body.*
olor, oris, *a swan.*	pietas, tis, *piety.*	decus, oris, *honor.*
dolor, oris, *pain.*	probitas, tis, *honesty.*	dedĕcus, oris, *disgrace.*
lepor, oris, *wit.*	potestas, tis, *power.*	facinus, oris, *a deed.*
pastor, oris, *a shepherd.*	sanitas, tis, *health.*	frigus, oris, *cold.*
pudor, oris, *shame.*	satietas, tis, *satiety.*	littus, oris, *a shore.*
rubor, oris, *a blush.*	veritas, tis, *truth.*	pectus, oris, *the breast.*
stupor, oris, *amazement.*	ubertas, tis, *fertility.*	pecus, oris, *cattle.*
sudor, oris, *sweat.*	voluntas, tis, *will.*	pignus, oris, *a pledge.*
timor, oris, *fear.*	voluptas, tis, *pleasure.*	tempus, oris, *time.*

Decline together: *Homo ingeniosus—labor continuus—virtus heroica—crimen horrendum. Pastor fidus et intrepidus—lex impia et funesta—opus arduum et periculosum,*—and the like.

CHAPTER II.

I.—Exceptions in declension. II.—Rules of Gender. III.—Some particulars about Substantives. IV.—Declension of Greek words.

I.—EXCEPTIONS IN DECLENSION.

FIRST DECLENSION.

§ 7. The words *dea*, a goddess; *filia*, a daughter; and occasionally *domina*, a mistress; *anima*, the soul; *liberta*, a freedwoman; *serva*, a female slave; *equa*, a mare; *mula*, a she-mule; and *asina*, a she-ass, form the Dat. and Abl. plur. in *-abus* instead of *-is*, to distinguish them from the corresponding masculine forms in *-us*; as, *diis deabusque, cum filiis et filiabus*.

When this distinction, however, is clear from the context, the regular form in *-is* is always preferred; e. g., *cum ambabus filiis*.

SECOND DECLENSION.

§ 8. Proper names in *ius*, as *Antonius, Caius, Pompeius*, and also *filius*, a son, and *genius*, a tutelar spirit, drop in the Voc. sing. the final *-us* of the Nom.; as, *O Antoni! O Cai! O Pompei!* But the proper name *Pius*, Greek proper names in *ius* (from ιος), as *Arius, Darius*, and all common nouns and adjectives, as *nuncius, gladius, impius, egregius*, together with the adjectives derived from proper names, as *Delius, Cynthius*, are regular, and make the Voc. in *e*; as, *O Pie!* etc.

Deus, God, has in the Voc. *Deus*; and *meus*, my, has *mi*. Hence: *O mi Deus! O fili mi!*

Deus, in the plur. is thus declined: *dii*, deorum, *diis*, deos, *dii*, *diis*.

The genitive plur. in *-orum* is often contracted in *-um*, as *virum, deum, nummum, modium, sestertium*, instead of *virorum, deorum*, etc.

§ 9. Words in *-er* of the second declension make the Voc. sing. like the Nom. They are thus declined:

N.	puer	puer-i	N.	ager	agr-i
G.	puer-i	puer-orum	G.	agr-i	agr-orum
D.	puer-o	puer-is	D.	agr-o	agr-is
A.	puer-um	puer-os	A.	agr-um	agr-os
V.	puer	puer-i	V.	ager	agr-i
A.	puer-o	puer-is	A.	agr-o	agr-is

Like *puer*, "a boy", are declined: *Liber*, Bacchus; *gener*, a son-in-law; *socer*, a father-in-law; *vesper*, the evening; and *liberi, -orum*, children.

The following drop *e* before *r*, and are declined like *ager*, "a field:" *aper*, a wild-boar; *arbiter*, an umpire; *auster*, the south-wind; *cancer*, a crab; *culter*, a knife; *liber*, a book; *faber*, a workman; *magister*, a teacher; and *minister*, a servant.

THIRD DECLENSION.

§ 10. ACCUSATIVE SING.—In the accusative sing. have *im* instead of *em*: 1. *securis*, an axe; *sitis*, thirst; *tussis*, a cough; *vis*, violence; and commonly also *febris*, a fever; *pelvis*, a basin; *puppis*, the stern; *restis*, a rope; and *tur-ris*, a tower. 2. Many parisyllables in *-is* denoting cities and rivers; as, *His-palis* (Seville), *Neapolis*, *Tiberis*, *Albis*.

§ 11. ABLATIVE SING.—In the ablative sing. have *i* instead of *e*: 1. Those words that have *im* in the accusative; 2. The names of months, and occasionally also

avis, *a bird.*	classis, *a fleet.*	fustis, *a club.*
civis, *a citizen.*	clavis, *a key.*	ignis, *fire.*
navis, *a ship.*	neptis, *a granddaughter.*	supellex, *furniture.*

But *restis*, a rope, has more commonly *reste*.

§ 12. GENITIVE PLUR.—In the genitive plur. have *ium* instead of *um*: 1. Parisyllables in *-es* and *-is;* as, *vulpes, vulpium*, a fox; *collis, collium*, a hill; 2. Monosyllables in *s* and *x* impure; as, *urbs, urbium*, a city; *arx, arcium*, a citadel; 3. The words *imber*, a shower; *linter*, a boat; *venter*, the belly; *caro.-rnis*, flesh; and the monosyllables *mas, maris*, a male; (*faux*) *faucis*, the throat,

as, assis, *the as.*	lis, litis, *a quarrel.*	nix, nivis, *snow.*
os, ossis, *a bone.*	glis, ris, *a dormouse.*	nox, noctis, *night.*

and generally, also, *mus, muris*, a mouse, and *fraus,-dis*, a cheat. *Oor, cordis*, the heart, *sal*, salt, and *vas, vadis*, a surety, probably had *cordium, salium, vadium.—Lar*, a tutelar deity, has more frequently *larum* than *larium*.

NOTE 1.—The following have *um: opes* (from *ops*), wealth; *gryps,-phis*, a griffin; *lynx,-cis, sphynx,-gis, ambages* (pl.), evasions;

strues, *a pile.*	juvenis, *a youth.*	canis, *a dog.*
vates, *a prophet.*	senex, senis, *an old man.*	panis, *a loaf.*

And generally also *apis*, a bee; *volücris*, a bird, and *sedes*, a seat.

NOTE 2.—Polysyllables in *ns* and *rs*, as *cliens, infans, cohors, serpens, sapiens, adolescens*, together with *Quiris, itis*, and *Samnis, itis*, and the plural nouns *penates*, household gods, and *optimates*, the nobles, generally have *ium.—But parentes*, "parents," has more commonly *um ; palus, ūdis*, a swamp, has *um* and *ium*.

§ 13. NEUTERS in *e, al*, and *ar* (Gen. *-āris*), have *i, ia, ium*, that is, they have *i* in the abl. sing.; *ia* in the nom., acc., and voc. plur.; and *ium* in the genitive plural; as, *mare*, the sea, *mari, maria, marium*. Thus, *rete*, a net; *sedīle*, a seat; *tribūnal*, a tribunal; *vectīgal*, revenue, tax; *calcar*, a spur; *exemplar*, a pattern, etc.

FOURTH DECLENSION.

§ 14. The following words of the fourth declension make the dative and ablative plur. in *ubus* instead of *ibus:*

acus, *a needle.*	lacus, *a lake.*	specus, *a cavern.*
arcus, *a bow.*	partus, *a birth.*	tribus, *a tribe.*
artus, *a joint.*	quercus, *an oak.*	pecu, *cattle.*

NOTE.—*Ficus*, a fig (also, a fig-tree), has *ficubus ;* but the form *ficis*, of the second declension, is preferable.—*Portus*, a harbor, has both *ibus* and *ubus.—Veru*, a spit, generally has *verubus*, and *tonitru* (better *tonitrus, ūs*, or *tonitruum,-i*), more commonly *-ibus*.

IRREGULAR AND COMPOUND SUBSTANTIVES.

§ 15. Special attention must be paid to the declension of the following words :

	An ox, a cow. (c.)	Violence. (f)	A house. (f.)	An oath. . (n.)	Commonwealth. (f.)
S. N.	Bos	vis	domus	jusjurandum	respublica
G.	bovis	—	domus *and* domi	jurisjurandi	reipublicæ
D.	bovi	—	domui	jurijurando	reipublicæ
A.	bovem	vim	domum	jusjurandum	rempublicam
V.	bos	—	domus	jusjurandum	respublica
A.	bove	vi	domo	jurejurando	republica
P. N.	boves	vires	domus	jurajuranda	respublicæ
G.	boum	virium	domuum *and* -orum	——	rerumpublicarum
D.	bubus *or* bobus	viribus	domibus	——	rebuspublicis
A.	boves	vires	domus *and* -os	jurajuranda	respublicas
V.	boves	vires	domus	jurajuranda	respublicæ
A.	bubus *or* bobus	viribus	domibus	——	rebuspublicis

☞ *Domus* is partly of the second and partly of the fourth declension. The gen. *domi* is used only in the sense of "at home." *Jupiter* is thus declined : Jupiter, *Jovis, Jovi, Jovem,* Jupiter, *Jove. Sus,* a swine, has in the dat. and abl. plur. *subus* instead of *suibus*

II. RULES OF GENDER.

§ 16.—The Gender of Latin nouns is determined—first by their *signification* , and secondly by their *termination.*

RULES OF GENDER IN REFERENCE TO SIGNIFICATION.

MASCULINE : The names of men and male beings ; of nations, winds, rivers, months, and mountains ; as, *Mars, Cæsar, Persa, Consul ; boreas, auster, aquilo ; Ister, Tiberis, Euphrātes ; Athos, Eryx, Atlas.*

EXCEPTIONS.

1. *Copiæ,* troops; *excubiæ* and *vigiliæ,* sentinels; *custodia,* a guard ; *operæ,* laborers, and *Amāzŏnes,* the Amazons, are FEMININE.—*Auxilia,* auxiliary troops, and *mancipium, servitium,* a slave, are NEUTER.

2. The names of r i v e r s in *a,* as *Allia, Garumna, Matrŏna, Sequăna,* etc., are by modern writers commonly used FEM.; the ancients, in most cases, used them as MASC. —*Styx* and *Lethe* are FEM.

3. The names of m o n t h s are by the best writers used only as adjectives.

4. The names of m o u n t a i n s, when the word *mons* is not added, depend upon their termination. Thus *Ida, Ætna, Œta, Alpes,* are FEMININE ; *Pelion* and *Soraote,* NEUTER.

FEMININE : The names of women and female beings; of countries, islands, towns, trees, and gems; as, *Venus, Dido, Phanium; Ægyptus · Delos, Salāmis; Lacedœmon, Tyrus; cedrus, juniperus.*

EXCEPTIONS.

1. Among the names of countries, *Bosporus, Pontus, Hellespontus,* and *Isthmus* are MASCULINE. Those in *um* and plurals in *a* are NEUTER; as, *Latium, Bactra.*— Among the names of islands, the Egyptian *Delta* and a few in *um* are NEUTER.

2. The names of cities in *i, orum*; as, *Delphi, Veii,* etc., together with *Tunes, -ētis, Hippo, Narbo, Frusino,* and *Sulmo* (sometimes also *Croto, Pessinus, -untis,* and *Selīnus, -untis*), are MASCULINE.

The following are NEUTER: a) Those in *um* and plurals in *a*, as *Tarentum, Sagur-tum, Ilion, Susa, Leuctra, Ecbatăna, Arbēla;* b) Those in *e* and *ur,* as *Reate, Prœneste, Tergeste, Anxur, Tibur;* c) The indeclinable names *Illiturgi, Asty* and some others which are defective, as *Hispal, Gadir.—Argos* is indecl. and NEUTER in the Singular: its plural *Argi, orum,* is regular and MASCULINE.

3. Among the names of trees, and shrubs, *oleaster, pinaster, styrax, amarantus, asparăgus, calamus, dumus, hellebŏrus,* and *intŭbus,* are MASCULINE; *raphanus* and *rubus,* both MASC. and FEM.

4. Among the names of gems, *beryllus, carbunculus, opălus,* and *smaragdus,* are MASCULINE.

COMMON : The names of persons that are common to both sexes; as, *hic* and *hœc adolescens,* a young man or woman.   Thus:

affinis, *a relation.*	heres, *an heir*	par, *a mate.*
artifex, *an artist.*	hostis, *an enemy.*	parens, *a parent.*
auctor, *an author.*	incola, *an inhabitant.*	patruelis, *a cousin.*
augur, *a soothsayer.*	index, *an informer.*	præs, *a surety.*
civis, *a citizen.*	infans, *an infant.*	præses, *a president.*
comes, *a companion.*	interpres, *an interpreter.*	præsul, *a president.*
conjux, *a consort.*	judex, *a judge.*	princeps, *a chief.*
consors, *a partner.*	juvenis, *a youth.*	sacerdos, *a priest.*
conviva, *a guest.*	martyr, *a martyr.*	satelles, *a life-guard.*
custos, *a keeper.*	miles, *a soldier.*	testis, *a witness.*
dux, *a leader.*	municeps, *a burgess.*	vates, *a prophet, a poet.*
exul, *an exile.*	obses, *a hostage.*	vindex, *an avenger.*

☞ Whenever the female sex is not particularly to be specified, these words are regularly considered and treated as of the masculine gender.

The forms *antistes,* a priest, and *hospes* a host, in the sense of "priestess," "host-ess," are less common than the forms *antistita, hospita.*

NEUTER : All indeclinable substantives, as *gummi, pascha, sinăpi*;— the names of letters and all words and expressions, quoted merely as words, as *ultimum* VALE.

RULES OF GENDER IN REFERENCE TO TERMINATION.

FIRST DECLENSION.

✝ § 17.—Words in -*a* of the first declension are *feminine*; as, *barba longa, vita beata.*✝–But the following are masculine :

Adria, the Adriatic Sea ; *etesiæ*, the trade-winds, and all names of men and male beings ; as, *Catilina, Sylla, Persa, Scytha,*

agricola *a farmer.*	nauta, *a sailor,*	perfuga, *a deserter.*
auriga, *a charioteer.*	collega, *colleague,*	poeta, *a poet,* etc.

SECOND DECLENSION.

✝ § 18.—Words in -*us* and -*er* of the second declension are *masculine*; as, *cervus timidus, liber Latinus.*✝–But the following words in -*us* are *feminine* :

Alvus, the belly ; *colus*, a distaff; *ficus*, a fig ; *humus*, the ground ; *vannus*, a sieve ;—Greek words, such as *atomus, methodus, periodus, synodus, paragraphus, dialectus, diphthongus*,—and the names of countries, towns, and trees ; as, *Peloponnesus, Epīrus ; Rhodus, Corinthus ; pinus, populus, sambucus*, etc.

The following in -*us* are NEUTER : *pelagus*, the sea ; *virus*, poison ; and *vulgus*, the crowd. The latter is sometimes masculine, as *hic vulgus.*

THIRD DECLENSION.

MASCULINE are the words ending in *o, or, os, er,* and *es* increasing ; as, *leo magnanimus, pavo superbus, amor sincerus, flos cadūcus, passer contemptus, palmes (palmitis) fecundus, pes (pedis) firmus.*

EXCEPTIONS.

1. In O.—FEM. : Words in -*io* that do not denote corporeal things; as, *actio, lectio, mentio, opinio, regio, religio,* etc., and those in *do* and *go,* as *grando,* hail, *imago,* a picture, etc. ;—but *cardo,* a hinge; *ordo,* order; *ligo,-onis,* a spade; *margo* (also *fem.*), a brink ; *harpago, ōnis,* a hook, and those in -*io* that denote corporeal things, as *titio,* a firebrand ; *pugio,* a dagger, *papilio,* a butterfly, *vespertilio,* a bat, and also *septentrio,* the North, are MASCULINE.

2. In OR.—FEM. : *arbor,* a tree.—NEUT. : *ador,* spelt ; *aequor,* the sea; *cor, ·rdis,* the heart, and *marmor,* marble.

3. In OS.—FEM. : *cos,-tis,* a whetstone, and *dos,-tis,* a dowry.—NEUT. : *os, oris,* the mouth ; *os, ossis,* a bone ; and the Greek words *chaos, epos,* and *melos.*

4. In ER.—FEM. : *linter* (rarely *masc.*), a boat.—NEUT. : *ver,* the spring ; *cadaver,* a corpse ; *iter,* a journey ; *spinther, ēris,* a bracelet ; *tuber,* a hump ; *uber,* a teat, breast, and all the names of plants in *er ;* as, *acer,* a maple ;

cicer, a chick-pea ; *papāver*, a poppy ; *piper*, pepper ; *siler*, a brook-willow ; *siser*, a carrot (pl. *siseres*, m.), and *suber*, the cork-tree.

5. In ES increasing.—FEM.: *merges*, *ĭtis*, a sheaf ; *abies*, *ĕtis*, a fir ; *seges*, *ĕtis*, a crop ; *tegis*, *ĕtis*, a mat ; *merces*, *ēdis*, a reward ; *quies* and *requies*, *ētis*, rest ; the plural *compedes* (-*ium*), fetters ; and generally also *ales*, *ĭtis*, a bird, and *quadrŭpes*, *ĕdis*, a quadruped.—NEUT.: *œs*, *æris*, brass. •

FEMININE are the words ending in *as*, *is*, *aus*, *x*, *s* impure, and parisyllables in *es* ; as, *ætas aurea*, *turris alta*, *laus merita*, *fraus impia*, *nix candida*, *radix amara*, *mors certa*, *hiems frigida*, *vulpes astuta*.

EXCEPTIONS.

1. In AS.—MASC.: *as*, *assis*, the as ; *gigas*, *antis*, a giant ; *adamas*, *antis*, a diamond ; and *elephas*, *antis*, an elephant. *Mas*, *maris*, a male, and *vas*, *vadis*, a surety, are masculine by their signification.—NEUT.: the indeclinable *fas*, *nefas*, and the word *vas*, *vasis*, a vase.

2. In IS.—MASC.: *cinis*, *-eris*, ashes ; *pulvis*, *-eris*, dust ; *cucŭmis*, *-eris*, a cucumber ; *glis*, *-ris*, a dormouse ; *lapis*, *idis*, a stone ; *pollis*, (also *pollen*, n.) *-ĭnis*, fine flour ; *sanguis*, *-ĭnis*, blood, and the following parisyllables :

amnis, *a river.*	fascis, *a bundle.*	panis, *bread.*
axis, *an axletree.*	finis, *an end.*	piscis, *a fish.*
callis, *a foot-path.*	follis, *bellows.*	postis, *a post.*
canalis, *a channel.*	funis, *a rope.*	scrobis, *a pit.*
caulis, *a stalk.*	fustis, *a club.*	torris, *a firebrand.*
collis, *a hill.*	ignis, *fire.*	unguis, *a claw.*
crinis, *the hair.*	mensis, *a month.*	vectis, *a lever.*
ensis, *a sword.*	orbis, *a circle.*	vermis, *a worm,*

together with *molaris* (Abl. *molari* sc. *lapide*), a millstone ; *natalis* (Abl. *natali* sc. *die*), birth-day, and the plural nouns *casses*, meshes ; *sentes*, a thorn-bush ; *annales*, annals, and *pugillares*, writing-tablets.

☞ The words *callis*, *canalis*, *scrobis*, and also *finis* and *cinis* in the singular, are sometimes used as feminines.—*Anguis*, a snake, and *tigris*, *-idis* a tiger, are of either gender.—*Canis*, a dog, is generally masculine ; but in the sense of a dog used in hunting, it is sometimes, and when the female sex is to be denoted, always feminine. ·

3. In X.—MASC.: (*a*) the Greek words *corax*, *ācis*, a raven, and *thorax*, *ācis*, a breastplate ;—(*b*) the majority of words in *ex* ; as

apex, *a point.*	frutex, *a shrub.*	pulex, *a flea.*
codex, *a ledger.*	grex, gis, *a herd.*	ramex, *a hernia.*
cimex, *a bug.*	latex, *any fluid.*	sorex, *a shrew-mouse.*
culex, *a gnat.*	pollex, *the thumb.*	vertex, *top, whirlpool.*

The words *rex*, a king ; *pontifex*, a high-priest ; *carnifex*, a hangman ; *remex*, *-ĭgis*, a rower ; and *vervex*, *ēcis*, a ram, are masculine by their signification.—*Imbrex*, a shingle ; *cortex*, rind ; *obex*, a bolt ; *pumex*, a pumice-stone ; and *silex*, flint-stone, are oftener masculine than feminine ; but *faex*, *-cis*, dregs ; *lex*, *-gis*, a law ; *nex*, *-cis*, death ; (*prex*) *preces*, prayers ; *carex*, *ĭcis*, sheer-grass ; *forfex*, *-ĭcis*, a pair of scissors ; *ilex*, *ĭcis*, a holm-oak ; and *supellex*, *-lectilis*, furniture, are feminine ;—(*c*) the following in *ix* : *calix*, a cup ; *calyx*, the bud of a flower ; *fornix*, a vault ; *phœnix*, *-ĭcis*, the phœnix ; *bombyx*, *-ycis*, the silk-worm (*bombyx*, silk,

2

is fem.); *coccyx,-ygis*, the cuckoo; and commonly *varix*, a swollen **vein**. —*Perdix, -icis*, a partridge, is of either gender.

4. In S impure.—MASC.: *chalybs,-ybis*, steel; *gryps, -yphis*, a griffin; *hydrops, -opis*, dropsy; *torrens*, a torrent; *confluens*, a confluence, with

fons, *a spring.*	dens, *a tooth.*	triens, *a third.*
mons, *a mountain.*	bidens, *a hoe.*	quadrans, *a fourth.*
pons, *a bridge.*	rudens, *a rope.*	sextans, *a sixth.*

Bidens, a sheep two years old, is fem.—*Adeps*, lard, is more commonly masc., and *forceps*, a pair of pincers, more commonly fem.—*Serpens* and *contirens* are generally fem., *bestia* and *terra* being understood.—*Animans*, any living being, is of all genders: but in the sense of "a rational being," it is generally masc., otherwise fem. rather than neuter.

5. In ES.—Commonly MASC.: *palumbes*, a wood-pigeon; *torques* (also *torquis*), a necklace; and *vepres*, a bramble. ✕

✝ NEUTER are the words ending in *a, e, c, l, n, t, ar, ur*, and *us*: as, *œnigma difficile, mare profundum, lac dulce, vectigal injustum, nomen celebre, caput opertum, calcar argenteum, guttur angustum, genus præclarum, corpus mortale.* ᴦ

EXCEPTIONS.

1. In L.—MASC.: *mugil*, a mullet; *sal*, salt; and *sol*, the sun.—*Sal*, in the sing. is sometimes used as a neuter; but in the plural, it is always masc.
2. In N.—MASC.: *lien*, the milt; *splen*, the spleen; *ren*, the kidneys; *lichen*, the ring-worm; *attdgen*, a hazel-hen; *pecten,-inis*, a comb; *delphin, inis*, a dolphin; *agon, önis*, a contest; *canon, önis*, a rule; and *horizon,-ontis*, the horizon;—but *aëdon*, a nightingale; *icon*, an image; and *sindon*, fine linen, are feminine.

   Paean, Titan, Helicon, daemon, Hymen (-ènis), fidicen, tubicen, tibicen, and *flamen*, are masculine by their signification.
3. In AR.—*Par*, "a pair," is neuter; but *par*, "a mate," "consort," is common.
4. In UR.—MASC.: *furfur*, bran; *turtur*, a turtle dove; and *vultur*, a vulture.— *Fur*, a thief, is common.
5. In US.—MASC.: *tripus* and *Oedipus,-ödis.*—FEM.: all polysyllables in -*us*, (gen. -*utis* or -*udis*): as, *salus, virtus, servitus, incus,-ūdis*, an anvil; *palus, -ūdis*, a swamp, together with *tellus,-ūris*, the earth, and *pecus-ūdis*, a single head of cattle (*pecus,-öris*, n., means cattle collectively, "a herd").

   Lepus,-öris, a hare, and *mus, muris*, a mouse, are masculine—*grus*, a crane, and *sus*, a pig, feminine, when the particular sex is not to be specified.

FOURTH DECLENSION.

✕ § 20. Words of the fourth declension end in -*us*, masculine, and in -*u*, neuter; as, *exercitus Romanus, genu distortum.* Thus, ⌐

adventus, *arrival.*	exercitus, *an army.*	passus, *a pace.*
cœtus, *an assembly.*	fluctus, *a wave.*	spiritus, *breath.*
conatus, *an effort.*	fructus, *fruit.*	strepitus, *a noise.*
cruciatus, *torture.*	impetus, *an attack.*	sumptus, *expense.*
currus, *a chariot.*	metus, *fear.*	vultus, *countenance.*
equitatus, *cavalry.*	motus, *a movement.*	gelu, *ice;* genu, *knee.*

But the following in -*us* are feminine :

acus, *a needle.*	idus (pl.), *the Ides.*	porticus, *a portico.*
domus, *a house.*	manus, *a hand.*	quercus, *an oak.*
ficus, *a fig.*	penus, *provisions.*	tribus, *a tribe.*

☞ Besides *penus,-ūs,* there are two other forms of the same signification ; viz. , *penum,-i,* and *penus,-ŏris,* both neuter.—*Specus,* a cavern, is generally masculine ; in poetry, it is often used as a feminine, and occasionally even as a neuter.

Anus, an old woman ; *nurus,* a daughter-in-law ; and *socrus,* a mother-in-law, are feminine by their signification.

FIFTH DECLENSION.

§ 21. Words of the fifth declension end in -*es*, and are feminine ; as, *res præclara.*   Thus,

acies, *battle array.*	pernicies, *ruin.*	durities, *hardness.*
effigies, *an effigy.*	res, *a thing.*	materies, *matter.*
facies, *the face.*	series, *a series.*	mollities, *softness.*
fides, *faith.*	spes, *hope.*	mundities, *neatness.*
glacies, *ice.*	species, *an appearance.*	planities, *a plain.*
ingluvies, *gluttony.*	superficies, *surface.*	segnities, *sloth.*

Exc.—*Dies,* a day, is common in the singular (fem., chiefly when a definite day—"a day fixed upon"—is denoted), but always masculine in the plural.—*Meridies,* midday, is masculine, and is used only in the singular.

III. Some Particulars about Substantives.

§ 22.—Several substantives occur, for the most part, in the plural number only ; as,

cunæ, *a cradle.*	liberi, *children.*	natales, *parentage.*
deliciæ, *delight.*	posteri, *descendants.*	optimates, *the nobles.*
divitiæ, *riches.*	arma, *arms.*	penates, *the penates.*
insidiæ, *snares.*	spolia, *booty.*	preces, *prayers.*
minæ, *threats.*	Alpes (ium), *the Alps.*	proceres, *the chiefs.*
nugæ, *trifles.*	ambages, *evasions.*	sordes, *filth.*
nundinæ, *the market.*	compedes, *fetters.*	mœnia, *city-walls.*
nuptiæ, *a wedding.*	fauces, *the jaws.*	verbera, *lashes.*
tenebræ, *darkness.*	majores, *ancestors.*	viscera, *the bowels,* etc.

§ 23.—Several substantives have in the plural number a meaning different from that of the singular ; as,

ædes, is, *a temple.*	fortuna, *fortune.*	opera, *labor.*
ædes, ium, *a house.*	fortunæ, *wealth.*	operæ, *workmen.*
copia, *plenty.*	gratia, *a favor.*	sal, *salt.*
copiæ, *troops.*	gratiæ, *thanks.*	sales, *witticisms.*
finis, *an end.*	littera, *a letter.*	tabula, *a board.*
fines, *territory.*	litteræ, *an epistle.*	tabulæ, *an account-book.*

§ 24.—Several substantives change in the plural either gender, or declension, or both ; as,

locus, *a place,* pl. i *and* a.	cœlum, *heaven,* pl. i,-orum.
frenum, *a bridle,* pl. i *and* a.	balneum, *a bath,* pl. æ, arum.
carbasus, *flax,* pl. a,-orum.	epulum, *feast, meal,* pl. æ,-arum.
Pergamus, *Troy,* pl. a,-orum.	vas, vasis, *a vessel,* pl. vasa,-orum.
Tartarus, *hell,* pl. a, orum.	Argos (n.), *Argos,* pl. Argi,-orum.

§ 25.—Several substantives are redundant either in termination, gender, or declension ; as,

alveare *and* -ium, *a bee-hive.*	palatum *and* -us (-i), *the palate.*
amygdala *and* -um, *an almond.*	pileum *and* -us (-i), *a cap, hat.*
balteus *and* -um, *a girdle.*	postulatio *and* -atum, *a request.*
cochlear, -are, -arium, *a spoon.*	potio *and* potus, (-ŭs), *a drink.*
conatus (-ûs) *and* -um, *an effort.*	præsepe,-es, *and* -ium, *a manger.*
cubitum *and* -us (-i), *a cubit.*	segmentum *and* -gmen, *a segment.*
elephantus *and* -phas, *an elephant.*	sinapi (n,) *and* sinâpis (f.), *mustard.*
exemplar *and* -are, *a copy.*	tapetum,-ete,-es (-etis), *a carpet.*
galerum *and* -us (-i), *a hat.*	vespera,-er (-i *and* -is), *evening.*

The words *ficus, laurus, pinus,* and *cupressus,* take in the gen. and abl sing., and in the nom. and acc. plural, besides the endings of the second de clension, to which they properly belong, those also of the fourth declension ; as, *G. fici* and *ficûs,* Abl. *fico* and *ficu ;* N. pl. *fici* and *ficûs,* etc.

Ilia, the entrails, has *iliorum* and *iliis* along with *ilium* and *ilibus.—Jugerum,* an acre, in the sing. usually follows the second declension ; in the plural, the third.

§ 26.—Several substantives are defective in case ; some in one, others in more than one.

1.—Of the following words, one case only is in use : DAT., *derisui, despicatui, ostentui,* in connection with *esse, ducere,* or *habere.—*ACC., *incitas, infitias,* and *suppetias,* in the phrases *redactus ad incitas,* reduced to a strait ; *infitias ire,* to deny ; *suppetias ferre,* to bring supplies.—ABL., *noctu,* by night ; *natu,* by birth, in combination with *grandis, magnus, parvus, major, minor,* etc.—*Concessu, indultu, permissu, hortatu, invitatu, mandatu, jussu, injussu, oratu, rogatu,* and the like, in connection with a genitive or a pronoun ; e. g., *mandatu Caesaris,* at Cæsar's command ; *rogatu tuo,* at your request ; *meo arbitratu,* according to my opinion.

2.—Of the following words, two cases only are in use : NOM. and ACC., *grates, munia, jura, rura, thura, mella ; inferiae,* and *inferias,* " sacrifices to the dead ;" and *secus* (n.), in the sense of *sexus,* as *virile secus, muliebre secus.—*NOM. and ABL., *vesper* and *vespere* or *vesperi.—*GEN. and ABL., *repetundarum* and *repetundis,* " extortions."—ACC. aud ABL., *foras* and *foris* (both forms used adverbially), " out of doors ;" e. g., *ire foras, coenare foris ; sordem, sorde,* filth, and *veprem, vepre,* a bramble. (☞ *Sordes* and *vepres* are both complete in the plural.)

3.—Of the following words, three cases are in use : *astus, astu,* and *astus* (acc. pl.), craft. *Lues, luem, lue,* a plague. (Ops) *opis, opem, ope,* help ; the plural *opes,* wealth, power, is complete. *Vicis* (gen.), *vicem, vice,* place or stead ; plur. *vices,* etc., but no genitive occurs.

4.—Of the following words, four cases are in use : *virus, viri, virus* (acc.), *viro,* poison. (Frux) *frugis, frugi, frugem, fruge,* fruit ; pl. *fruges,* complete. (Daps) *dapis, i, em, e,* food, banquet ; pl. *dapes,* complete, but no genitive seems to occur. (Ditio) *ditionis, i, em, e,* dominion. (Internecio) *internecionis, i, em, e,* carnage, utter destruction.

IV. Declension of Greek Words.

FIRST DECLENSION.

§ 27.—Greek words of the first declension end in *e* (fem.) and in *as* and *es* (masc.).—Those that admit of a plural, are declined in that number like Latin nouns. Their declension in the singular is as follows :

N.	epitom-ē ✗	Æne-ās ⟍	Atrid-ēs	Anchis-ēs
G.	epitom-ēs	Æne-æ	Atrid-æ	Anchis-æ
D.	epitom-æ	Æne-æ	Atrid-æ	Anchis-æ
A.	epitom-ēn	Æne-am (ăn)	Atrid-ēn	Anchis-ēn
V.	epitom-ē	Æne-ă	Atrid-ē *and* ă	Anchis-ē
A.	epitom-ē ´	Æne-ă	Atrid-ā *and* ē	Anchis-ē

Notes.—(1.) The acc. of words in *as* is in prose generally *am*, in poetry frequently *an*.—(2.) The voc. and abl. of words in *es*, end both in *e* and *a* :—in the abl., *a* is the regular ending.—(3.) The gen. plur. of patronymics in *es* is often contracted, as *Æneădúm, Dardanīdúm,* for *Æneadarum, Dardanidarum,* from *Æneădes, Dardanīdes.*—(4.) Greek words in *e* and *es* often follow the Latin declension ; thus we find *musica, grammatica, rhetorica, Persa, sophista,* etc., along with, and even in preference to, *musice, grammatice, rhetorice, Perses, sophistes.*

SECOND DECLENSION.

§ 28.—Greek words of the second declension end in *os* (masc. and fem.) and in *on* (neut.).—They are thus declined :

N.	Rhod-ŏs (*or* us)	Ili-on (*or* um)	Ath-ŏs	Orph-eus
G.	Rhod-i	Ili-i	Ath-o	Orph-eï (*or* eos)
D.	Rhod-o	Ili-o	Ath-o	Orph-eo (*or* ei)
A.	Rhod-ŏn (*or* um)	Ili-on (*or* um)	Ath-ŏn (*or* o)	Orph-eum (*or* ea)
V.	Rhod-e	Ili-on (*or* um)	Ath-ŏs	Orph-eu
A.	Rhod-o	Ili-o	Ath-o	Orph-eo

Notes.—(1.) Greek words in *ōs* (*ως*), as *Ceŏs, Cōs, Teŏs, Androgeŏs,* either follow the Greek (Attic) declension, like *Athōs,* or take the Latin forms, as *Androgeus, i, o, um, us* (not *e*), *o. Atho* in the acc. and abl. sing. sometimes follows the third declension, as *Athonem, Athone.*—(2.) Proper names in *eus,* as *Orpheus, Perseus, Theseus,* make the voc. always in *eu.* In the gen., dat., and acc. they follow either the second Latin, or third Greek declension.—(3.) Words in *on* are sometimes contracted in the gen. plur., as *Bucolicōn, Georgicōn,* for *Bucolicorum, Georgicorum.*

THIRD DECLENSION.

	lamp-	her-	poes-	· Teth-	Par-
N.	as	os	is	ys	is
G.	adis (ados)	ŏis	is (eos)	yis (yos)	idis (idos)
D.	adi	ŏi	i	yï (y)	idi [in]
A.	adem (ada)	ŏem (ŏa)	im (in)	ym (yn)	idem (ida), im
V.	as	os	i	y	is (i)
A.	ade	ŏe	i	ye (y)	ide

§ 29.—Note 1. Greek words in *o,* as *echò, Dido, Io, Clio, Clotho, Sappho,* have in the genitive, *ús* (*ος*) ; in all other cases, *o.*—The Latin forms *onis, oni, onem, one,* are but rarely used.

NOTE 2. The neuters *melos, epos, chaos,* and *cetos* (plur. *mele, cete*), are scarcely used in any other case than the nom., accus., and voc.—*Cetos,* a whale, is declined also after the second declension, as *cetos, ceti, ceto, cetos, cetos, ceto*; plur., *cete, cetorum, cetis, cete, cete, cetis.*

NOTE 3. *Argos,* the name of a city, is in the sing. an indeclinable neuter, used only in the nom. and acc.—In the plural it is masculine, and is thus declined: *Argi, orum, is, os, i, is.*

GENITIVE, ACCUSATIVE, AND VOCATIVE.

(Singular.)

§ 30.—GENITIVE SING.—Greek proper names in *es* have in the gen. sing. often *i* instead of *is ;* as, *Socrati, Aristoteli, Ulixi, Achilli, Pericli,* instead of *Socratis, Aristotelis,* etc.—After the time of Cicero, however, the form *is* alone was used.

ACCUSATIVE SING.—1. Greek words whose genitive ends in -*is* (-*os*) impure, as *lampas, rhetor, Hector, Agamemnon, Cyclops, Babylon, Marathon,* etc., and also the three words *Tros,-ois, heros,-ois,* and *Minos,-ois,* make the accus. sing. in *em* and *a.*

The ending *a* is regularly used in *aër, æther,* and *Pan.*

2. Greek words in *is* and *ys* (Gen. *os* pure), as *poesis, basis, thesis, syrtis, Tethys, Halys,* make the accus. sing. both in *im* and *in.*

Greek words in *is, -idis* (Barytons in *ις, ιδος*), as *Paris, Agis, Daphnis, Ibis, Iris, Serāpis, Tigris, Zeuxis,* etc., have in the accus. sing. both *im* (*in*) and *idem* (*ida*),—but more commonly *im.*

Greek words in *is, -idis* (Oxytons in *ις, ιδος*), as *ægis, pyramis, tyrannis, Chalcis, Colchis, Phocis,* etc., have but *idem* (*ida.*)

3. Proper names in *es, -is,* which follow in Greek the first declension (*ης, -ου*), as *Xerxes, Mithridates, Simonides, Cambyses, Æschines, Euphrates,* etc., have in the accus. sing. both *em* and *en.*—This is the case also, though much less frequently, with proper names in *es,* that follow in Greek the third declension, as *Sophocles, Hippocrates,* etc. : acc. *Sophoclem,* more rarely *Sophoclen.*

Thales and *Chremes* (Gen. *is* and *etis*) have *Thalem* or *Thaletem* and *Thalen,* etc.

VOCATIVE SING.—The vocative sing. of Greek words is generally like the nominative.—But proper names in *is, ys, eus,* and *as* (G. *antis*), drop the final *s* of the nominative, as *Pari, Thai, Coty, Orpheu, Theseu, Atla, Calcha.*

Words in *is, -idis,* however, make the vocative just as often like the nominative, as *Paris, Thais, Bacchis.*

Proper names in *es, -is,* sometimes have *e* in the vocative, as *Socrate, Simonide, Damocle, Sophocle,* etc., instead of *Socrates,* etc.

GENITIVE, DATIVE, AND ACCUSATIVE.

(Plural.)

§ 31.—GENITIVE PLUR.—The genitive plural of Greek words is generally the same as that of Latin words; but sometimes, especially in titles of books, the Greek ending *ōn* (*ων*) is retained, as *epigrammatōn, metamorphoseōn.*

DATIVE PLUR.—Greek words in -*ma* have in the dat. and abl. plur. more frequently *is* than *ibus,* as *poëmatis, epigrammatis,* etc., instead of *poematibus,* etc.

ACCUSATIVE PLUR.—Words that have *em* and *a* in the accus. sing., have *es* and *as* in the accus. plur. ; as, *aspidas, heroas, phalangas, Cyclōpas, Æthiopas, Arcadas, Macedoņas,*—and in Cæsar and Tacitus we find even *Allobrogas, Lingonas, Vangionas,* and others, which are not Greek national names at all.

CHAPTER III.

ADJECTIVES.

ADJECTIVES are divided into three classes; namely, (1.) adjectives of *three* endings, (2.) adjectives of *two* endings, and (3.) adjectives of *one* ending.

ADJECTIVES OF THREE ENDINGS.

§ 32.—Adjectives of three endings end in *us, a, um,* and *er, a, um.* They are in the masculine declined like *servus,* in the feminine like *rosa,* and in the neuter like *regnum.*—Those in *er, a, um,* make the vocative like the nominative, and, for the most part, drop *e* before *r.*

Declension of *bonus,* "good," and *piger,* "lazy."

	(m.)	(f.)	(n.)		(m.)	(f.)	(n.)
S. N.	bon-us	bon-a	*bonum*	N.	piger	pigra	*pigrum*
G.	bon-i	bon-æ	bon-i	G.	pigri	pigræ	pigri
D.	bon-o	bon-æ	bon-o	D.	pigro	pigræ	pigro
A.	bon-um	bon-am	*bonum*	A.	pigrum	pigram	*pigrum*
V.	bon-e	bon-a	*bonum*	V.	piger	pigra	*pigrum*
A.	bon-o	bon-a	bon-o	A.	pigro	pigra	pigro
P.N.	bon-i	bon-æ	*bona*	N.	pigri	pigræ	*pigra*
G.	bon-orum	bon-arum	bon-orum	G.	pigrorum	pigrarum	pigrorum
D.	bon-is	bon-is	bon-is	D.	pigris	pigris	pigris
A.	bon-os	bon-as	*bona*	A.	pigros	pigras	*pigra*
V.	bon-i	bon-æ	*bona*	V.	pigri	pigræ	*pigra*
A.	bon-is	bon-is	bon-is	A.	pigris	pigris	pigris

Words for practice.

acerbus, *harsh.*
acidus, *sour.*
acutus, *sharp.*
æmulus, *vying with.*
ægrotus, *sick.*
æquus, *just.*
albus, *white.*
altus, *high.*
amarus, *bitter.*
amœnus, *pleasant.*
amplus, *large.*
angustus, *narrow.*
antiquus, *ancient.*
apricus, *sunny.*
aptus, *fit.*
arctus, *narrow.*
astutus, *cunning.*
austerus, *harsh.*
avarus, *covetous.*
avidus, *greedy.*
barbarus, *savage.*
beatus, *blessed.*
benignus, *kind.*
blandus, *flattering.*

caducus, *fading.*
cæcus, *blind.*
calidus, *warm.*
callidus, *cunning.*
calvus, *bald.*
candidus, *candid.*
carus, *dear.*
castus, *chaste.*
cautus, *cautious.*
cavus, *hollow.*
certus, *certain.*
clarus, *famous.*
claudus, *lame.*
crassus, *thick.*
cunctus, *all.*
curtus, *short.*
curvus, *crooked.*
decorus, *graceful.*
densus, *thick.*
dignus, *worthy.*
disertus, *eloquent.*
diuturnus, *lasting.*
doctus, *learned.*
dubius, *doubtful.*

durus, *hard.*
ebrius, *drunk.*
egenus, *needy.*
egregius, *remarkable.*
exiguus, *small.*
eximius, *excellent.*
externus, *outward.*
facetus, *witty.*
facundus, *eloquent.*
falsus, *false.*
ferus, *savage.*
fessus, *weary.*
festinus, *hastening.*
fidus, *faithful.*
firmus, *firm.*
flavus, *yellow.*
fœdus, *ugly.*
formosus, *fair.*
frivolus, *trifling.*
garrulus, *prattling.*
gratus, *thankful.*
humanus, *human.*
humidus, *moist.*
idoneus, *fit.*

ignarus, *ignorant.*
ignavus, *cowardly.*
improbus, *wicked.*
incautus, *inconsiderate.*
incertus, *uncertain.*
inclytus, *renowned.*
industrius, *diligent.*
infĭdus, *unfaithful.*
invĭdus, *envious.*
invītus, *unwilling.*
jucundus, *pleasant.*
justus, *just.*
lætus, *joyful*
latus, *broad.*
lentus, *slow.*
longinquus, *far off.*
longus, *long.*
lubrĭcus, *slippery.*
lucidus, *bright.*
maturus, *ripe.*
mirus, *wonderful.*

molestus, *troublesome.*
mundus, *neat.*
mutus, *dumb.*
nimius, *too much.*
novus, *new.*
noxius, *hurtful.*
nudus, *bare.*
obscurus, *dark.*
odiosus, *hateful.*
opīmus, *fat, rich.*
pallidus, *pale.*
periculosus, *dangerous.*
perfĭdus, *treacherous.*
planus, *plain.*
plenus, *full.*
præditus, *endowed.*
pravus, *wicked.*
probus, *honest.*
profundus, *deep.*
pudĭcus, *chaste.*
sanus, *sound.*

sevērus, *severe.*
siccus, *dry.*
sobrius, *sober.*
strenuus, *active.*
stultus, *foolish.*
subitus, *sudden.*
superbus, *proud.*
surdus, *deaf.*
tacitus, *silent.*
tantus, *so great.*
tardus, *slow.*
tepidus, *lukewarm.*
tumidus, *swollen.*
turbidus, *muddy.*
tutus, *safe.*
varius, *various.*
verecundus, *bashful.*
venustus, *comely.*
verus, *true.*
vivus, *alive.*
vicīnus, *neighboring.*

æger, *sick.*
ater, *black.*
creber, *frequent.*
impiger, *unwearied.*
integer, *entire.*
macer, *lean.*

pulcher, *fair.*
ruber, *red.*
sacer, *sacred.*
sinister, *left.*
teter, *foul.*
vafer, *crafty.*

asper, *rough.*
lacer, *torn.*
liber, *free.*
miser, *wretched.*
prosper, *prosperous.*
tener, *tender.*

Note.—The adjectives from *æger* to *vafer* drop the *e* before *r* and are declined like *piger.*—*Asper* and the rest, together with the compounds of *fero* and *gero*, as *opifer, signifer, armiger, laniger,* etc., retain the *e* throughout.

Dexter, right, sometimes retains, but oftener rejects the *e* before *r.*—*Satur,* sated, makes *satŭra, satŭrum ; g. satŭri,* etc.

ADJECTIVES OF TWO ENDINGS.

§ 33.—Adjectives of two endings end in *is, e,*—(in *is* for the masc. and fem., in *e* for the neuter)—They all follow the third declension, but have *i, ia, ium,* that is, they make the abl. sing. in *i* ; the nom., acc. and voc. neut. plur. in *ia* ; and the gen. pl. in *ium.*

Declension of *levis,* "light," and *acer.* "sharp."

	(m.)	(f.)	(n.)		(m.)	(f.)	(n.)
S.N.	lev-is	lev-is	*leve*	N.	*acer*	acris	*acre*
G.	lev-is	lev-is	lev-is	G.	acris	acris	acris
D.	lev-i	lev-i	lev-i	D.	acri	acri	acri
A.	lev-em	lev-em	*leve*	A.	acrem	acrem	*acre*
V.	lev-is	lev-is	*leve*	V.	*acer*	acris	*acre*
A.	lev-i	lev-i	le v-i	A.	acri	acri	acri
P.N.	lev-es	lev-es	*levia*	N.	acres	acres	*acria*
G.	lev-ium	lev-ium	lev-ium	G.	acrium	acrium	acrium
D.	lev-ibus	lev-ibus	lev-ibus	D.	acribus	acribus	acribus
A.	lev-es	lev-es	*levia*	A.	acres	acres	*acria*
V.	lev-es	lev-es	*levia*	V.	acres	acres	*acria*
A.	lev-ibus	lev-ibus	lev-ibus	A.	acribus	acribus	acribus

Words for practice.

acclīvis, *ascending.*	grandis, *great.*	pinguis, *fat.*
æqualis, *equal.*	gravis, *heavy.*	placabilis, *placable.*
agilis, *nimble.*	hilaris, *cheerful.*	popularis, *popular.*
agrestis, *rustic.*	humilis, *low.*	proclīvis, *prone.*
amabilis, *lovely.*	ignobilis, *mean.*	qualis, *of what kind.*
brevis, *short.*	illustris, *famous.*	regalis, *kingly.*
civīlis, *civil.*	imbecillis, *weak.*	rudis, *rough, rude.*
cœlestis, *heavenly.*	imberbis, *beardless.*	salutaris, *wholesome.*
comis, *courteous.*	immanis, *huge.*	segnis, *sluggish.*
credibilis, *credible.*	inanis, *void, vain.*	similis, *like.*
crudelis, *cruel.*	incolumis, *safe.*	solemnis, *solemn.*
debilis, *weak.*	inermis, *defenceless.*	stabilis, *steadfast.*
declīvis, *sloping.*	infāmis, *infamous.*	sterilis, *barren.*
deformis, *ugly.*	insignis, *remarkable.*	suavis, *sweet.*
dissimilis, *unlike.*	insomnis, *sleepless.*	sublīmis, *lofty.*
docilis, *docile.*	jugis, *perpetual.*	subtīlis, *subtle.*
dulcis, *sweet.*	lenis, *gentle.*	talis, *such.*
exanimis, *lifeless.*	liberalis, *liberal.*	tenuis, *thin.*
exīlis, *thin, poor.*	mediocris, *middling.*	terribilis, *dreadful.*
facilis, *easy.*	mirabilis, *wonderful.*	tristis, *sad.*
fertilis, *fertile.*	mitis, *meek.*	turpis, *base.*
fidelis, *faithful.*	mobilis, *movable.*	unanimis, *unanimous.*
flebilis, *lamentable.*	mollis, *soft.*	utilis, *useful.*
fortis, *brave.*	mutabilis, *changeable.*	vilis, *worthless.*
fragilis, *brittle.*	nobilis, *noble.*	viridis, *green.*
gracilis, *slender.*	omnis, *all, every.*	vulgaris, *vulgar.*
alacer, *cheerful.*	equester, *equestrian.*	salūber, *wholesome.*
campester, *level.*	paluster, *marshy.*	silvester, *woody.*
celeber, *famous.*	pedester, *on foot.*	terrester, *earthly.*
celer, *swift, quick.*	puter, *rotten, decaying.*	volŭcer, *winged.*

NOTE.—The adjectives in *er*, *is*, *e* (thirteen in number; viz., *acer*, *alacer*, *campester*, etc.), are declined throughout like *levis*, except that in the nom. and voc. sing. they have a distinct form in *er* for the masculine.

Celer retains the *e* before *r*, and has in the gen. plur. *celerum* instead of *celerium.—Salubris, equestris, celebris, silvestris, terrestris*, and *palustris*, are sometimes joined to masculine nouns; as, *annus salubris* for *annus saluber.* Thus, *locus celebris, tumultus silvestris*, etc.

ADJECTIVES OF ONE ENDING.

§ 34. Adjectives of one ending end variously and may be joined to substantives of any gender; as, *felix rex, felix regina, felix regnum.* They are throughout declined like adjectives of two endings, except that the nominative, accusative, and vocative neut. sing. are the same as the nominative masc. The ablative sing. sometimes ends in *e* instead of *i*.

Declension of *felix,* "happy."

	(m.)	(f.)	(n.)
S. N.	felix	felix	*felix*
G.	felic-is	felic-is	felic-is
D.	felic-i	felic-i	felic-i
A.	felic-em	felic-em	*felix*
V.	felix	felix	*felix*
A.	felic-i (e)	felic-i (e)	felic-i (e)
P.N.	felic-es	felic-es	*felicia*
G.	felic-ium	felic-ium	felic-ium
D.	felic-ibus	felic-ibus	felic-ibus
A.	felic-es	felic-es	*felicia*
V.	felic-es	felic-es	*felicia*
A.	felic-ibus	felic-ibus	felic-ibus

Words for practice.

audax, *bold.*
capax, *capacious.*
efficax, *effectual.*
fallax, *deceitful.*
ferax, *fertile.*
loquax, *talkative.*
mendax, *lying.*
mordax, *biting.*
minax, *threatening.*
pertinax, *obstinate.*
pervicax, *stubborn.*
rapax, *rapacious.*
sagax, *sagacious.*
tenax, *tenacious.*
vorax, *devouring.*
simplex, *simple.*
duplex, *double.*

atrox, *cruel.*
ferox, *ferocious.*
præcox, *premature.*
velox, *swift.*
trux, *wild, fierce.*
hebes, ĕtis, *dull.*
sons, *guilty.*
insons, *guiltless.*
expers, *destitute of.*
sollers, *clever.*
concors, *agreeing.*
discors, *at variance.*
excors, *silly.*
constans, *constant.*
elegans, *elegant.*
petulans, *wanton.*
præstans, *excellent.*

amens, *mad.*
clemens, *merciful.*
demens, *senseless.*
eloquens, *eloquent.*
frequens, *frequent.*
impatiens, *impatient.*
impudens, *impudent.*
ingens, *huge.*
insipiens, *foolish.*
innocens, *guiltless.*
negligens, *careless.*
opulens, *wealthy.*
prudens, *prudent.*
recens, *fresh.*
repens, *sudden.*
sapiens, *wise.*
vehemens, *vehement.*

Decline together : *Ager ferax—insula ferax—ingenium ferax. Terror ingens—bellua ingens—bellum ingens. Famulus astutus, piger et mendax—vir prudens, sagax et eruditus—saxum ingens et immobile—tempus praeteritum, praesens et futurum—ingenium praestans et paene divinum,* and the like.

NOTE 1.—The following adjectives of one ending have only *e* in the abl. sing.: (1.) the compounds of *pes, color,* and *corpus;* as, *tripes, quadrupes, discolor, versicolor, bicorpor, tricorpor;* (2.) Participles in *ns,* when used as such, and not as adjectives; (3.) Adjectives in general, when used substantively; as, *artifex,* an artist; *vigil,* a watchman; *Clemens, Pertinax, Fidelis, Vitalis;* and (4.) the adjectives *juvenis,* young; *senex,* old; along with

cælebs, *unmarried.*
compos, ŏtis, *master of.*
deses, ĭdis, *idle.*

pubes (*and* -er), *adult.*
impubes, *beardless.*
princeps, ipis, *chief.*

pauper, *poor.*
sospes, itis, *safe.*
superstes, *surviving.*

NOTE 2.—The following adjectives of one ending have only *um* in the genitive plur.: (1.) the compounds in *-ceps;* as, *anceps, ipitis,* doubtful; *præceps,* headlong;

particeps, ipis, partaking; (2.) those that have only *e* in the ablative; and (3.) the adjectives *artifex,* skilful; *vigil,* watchful; along with

compar, *equal.*	ales, itis, *winged.*	dives, itis, *rich.*
impar, *unable.*	cicur, ŭris, *tame.*	inops, *helpless.*
dispar, *unlike.*	degĕner, *degenerate.*	supplex, *suppliant.*

Note 3.—*Memor,* mindful; *immemor,* forgetful; and *uber,* plentiful, have *i* in the abl. sing. and *um* in the genitive plur.—*Par,* equal, has *pari, paria, parium;* but its compounds have *i* (*e*) *ia, um.*—*Vetus,-eris,* old, has *veteri* (e), *vetera, veterum.*—*Sons,* guilty; *insons,* guiltless; and *locuples,ētis,* rich, have *um* and *ium.*

COMPARISON OF ADJECTIVES.

§ 35. There are three degrees of comparison : the positive, the comparative, and the superlative.

The *positive* degree is that which is expressed by the adjective in its simple form; as, "An elephant is large; a mouse, small; a lion, fierce, active, bold, and strong."

The *comparative* is that form, which indicates that the quality, denoted by the adjective, exists in one object in a higher or lower degree than in another; as, "An elephant is smaller than a whale; a mouse, smaller than a rat."

The *superlative* is that form which indicates that the quality, denoted by the adjective, belongs to an object in a very high (low), or in the highest (lowest) degree; as, "The wolf is very strong; the tiger, still stronger; and the lion, the strongest of all."

The comparative and superlative, in Latin, are formed by adding *-ior* and *-issimus* to the stem. Thus :

POSITIVE.	COMP.	SUPERL.
longus, *long,*	long-ior,	long-issimus.
gravis, *heavy,*	grav-ior,	grav-issimus.
felix, *happy,*	felic-ior,	felic-issimus.

Comparatives end in *ior* for the masc. and fem., and in *ius* for the neuter. They are declined like adjectives of two endings; except that they have *e* (*i*) in the abl. sing., *a* in the nom. acc., and voc. neut. plur., and *um* in the genitive plural.

	SINGULAR.			PLURAL.		
N.	levior	levior	*levius*	leviores	leviores	*leviora*
G.	levioris	levioris	levioris	leviorum	leviorum	leviorum
D.	leviori	leviori	leviori	levioribus	levioribus	levioribus
A.	leviorem	leviorem	*levius*	leviores	leviores	*leviora*
V.	levior	levior	*levius*	leyiores	leviores	*leviora*
A.	leviore (i)	leviore (i)	leviore (i)	levioribus	levioribus	levioribus

Decline together : *Puer verecundus, verecundior, verecundissimus—arbor alta, altior, altissima—aquila rapax, rapacior, rapacissima—vir sapiens, sapientior, sapientissimus—verbum fallax, fallacius, fallacissimum—vox pulchra, pulchrior, pulcherrima—opus difficile, difficilius, difficillimum—poeta bonus, melior, opti-*

mus—res mala, pejor, pessima—nomen magnum, majus, maximum—labor parvus, minor, minimus, and the like.

Exc. 1.—Adjectives in *-er* form the superlative by adding *-rimus* to that ending; as,

| miser, *wretched*, | miser-ior. | miser-rimus. |
| celeber, *famous*, | celebr-ior. | celeber-rimus. |

Exc. 2.—The adjectives *facilis, difficilis, similis, dissimilis, gracilis*, and *humilis* form the superlative by adding *limus* to the stem; as,

| gracilis, *slender*, | gracil-ior. | gracil-limus. |
| humilis, *low*, | humil-ior. | humil-limus. |

Exc. 3.—Adjectives in *-dĭcus, -fĭcus*, and *-vŏlus* (from *dico, facio*, and *volo*), add *entior, entissimus* to the stem; as,

| benevolus, *kind*. | benevol-entior. | benevol-entissimus. |
| maledicus, *abusive*. | maledic-entior. | maledic-entissimus. |

IRREGULAR AND DEFECTIVE COMPARISON.

§ 36.—The following adjectives are wholly irregular in comparison:

bonus, *good*,	melior,	optimus.
malus, *bad*,	pejor,	pessimus.
magnus, *great*,	major,	maximus.
parvus, *small*,	minor,	minimus.
multus, *much*,	plus,	plurimus.

ADJECTIVES WITH A DOUBLE SUPERLATIVE.

exterus, *outward*,	exterior,	extremus (extimus).
inferus, *below*,	inferior,	infimus *and* imus.
superus, *above*,	superior,	suprēmus *and* summus.
posterus, *hind*,	posterior,	postremus (postumus).

NOTE 1.—The comparative of *multus* has in the sing. two forms only; viz., *plus* (nom. and acc. neut.) and *pluris*, more. But the plural *plures* is complete; as, nom. and acc. *plures, plura* (rarely *pluria*), gen. *plurium* (better than *plurum*), dat. and abl. *pluribus.*—*Complures* has in the neut. plur. both *complura* and *compluria*.

Multus and *plurimus* are in poetry often used in the sense of many, as *multa tabula, multa victima, plurima avis*, instead of *multæ tabulæ*, etc.—The English "a great many" and "most" are rendered by *plurimi* or *plerique.*

NOTE 2.—The adj. *exterus, inferus, superus*, and *posterus*, but rarely occur in the singular, and their nom. sing. masc. is not found at all in good prose.—*Dives*, rich, has either *divitior, divitissimus*, or *ditior, ditissimus.*—*Vetus*, old, has *vetustior* for the comp. and *veterrimus* or *vetustissimus* for the superlative.—*Providus*, cautious, and *egenus*, needy, either prefix *magis, maxime* to the positive, or are supplied by *providentior, providentissimus*, and *egentior, egentissimus.*

NOTE 3.—*Nequam*, worthless, and *frugi*, temperate (both indeclinable), have *nequior, nequissimus*, and *frugalior, frugalissimus.*—*Maturus*, ripe, and *imbecillis* (also *imbecillus*), weak, have in the superl. either *maturrimus, imbecillimus*, or *maturissimus, imbecillissimus.*

§ 37.—The following adjectives want the positive:

citerior, citimus, *near, close to.*	prior, primus, *former, first.*
ulterior, ultimus, *farther, last.*	ocior, ocissimus, *swifter, swiftest.*
interior, intimus, *inner, inmost.*	deterior, deterrimus, *worse, worst.*
propior, proximus, *nearer, next.*	potior, potissimus, *better, chief.*

The following adjectives want the terminational comparative:

bellus, bellissimus, *lovely.*	invictus, invictissimus, *invincible.*
diversus, diversissimus, *different.*	meritus, meritissimus, *deserving.*
falsus, falsissimus, *false.*	novus, novissimus, *new, last.*
inclytus, inclytissimus, *famous.*	sacer, sacerrimus, *holy, sacred.*

The following adjectives want the terminational superlative:

alacer, alacrior, *lively.*	proclivis, proclivior, *inclined.*
deses, desidior, *indolent.*	protervus, protervior, *impudent.*
diuturnus, diuturnior, *lasting.*	propinquus, propinquior, *near.*
longinquus, longinquior, *far off.*	terribilis, terribilior, *dreadful*, etc.

NOTE 1.—*Juvenis* and *adolescens*, young, and *senex* (G. *senis*), old, have *junior*, *adolescentior*, and *senior*. Their superlative is supplied by *natu minimus*, the youngest, and *natu maximus*, the oldest.

NOTE 2.—Adjectives compounded with *per* and *præ*, as *præaltus, prædives, perbrevis, peridoneus, perjucundus, permagnus*, ect., admit of no further comparison.—*Præstans* and *præclarus* alone have -*ior, issimus.*

NOTE 3.—Many adjectives do not form the comp. and superl. by -*ior* and -*issimus*, but by prefixing the adverbs *magis*, more, and *maxime*, most, to the positive. Such are:

a) the adjectives in -*us* pure (those in -*quus*, as *æquus, iniquus, antiquus*, etc. excepted); as, *dubius, arduus, industrius, noxius, idoneus, necessarius, perspicuus, strenuus;*.

b) nearly all in *ĭcus, ĭmus, ŭlus, ālis, ĭlis, ŏrus, andus, endus*, and *bundus*, as, *lubricus, modicus, legitimus, credulus, garrulus, sedulus, exitialis, mortalis, principalis, anilis, hostilis, scurrilis, decorus, sonorus, laudandus, expetendus, furibundus, venerabundus;*

c) the adjectives *albus, almus, caducus, calvus, canus, curvus, ferus, furtivus, gnarus, lacer, mutilus, lassus, mediocris, memor, mirus, merus, mutus, navus, nefastus, par, parilis, dispar, properus, trepidus, rudis, trux*, and *vagus.*

NUMERAL ADJECTIVES.

§ 38.—There are four classes of numerals; viz, *Cardinal, Ordinal, Distributive*, and *Adverbial* numerals.

The CARDINALS answer to the question *how many?*—one, two, three ... They are indeclinable from 4 to 100 inclusive: but the first three and the hundreds up to 1000, can be declined.

The ORDINALS denote the *place* any thing holds in a series; as, the first, second, third .... They are all declined like *bonus.*

The DISTRIBUTIVES answer to the question *how many apiece? how many at a time?*—one apiece, or one at a time .... They are all declined like *boni, æ, a*, and make the gen. plur. generally in *um* instead of *orum;* but *singuli* has always *singulorum.*

The ADVERBIALS answer to the question *how many times?*—once, twice, thrice .... They are all indeclinable.

Declension of the first three cardinals: *unus*, one; *duo*, two; and *tres*, three.

N.	unus,	una,	unum	duo,	duæ	duo	tres,	tres,	tria
G.	unius,	} for all genders		duorum,	duarum,	duorum	trium,	} for all genders	
D.	uni			duobus,	duabus,	duobus	tribus,		
A.	unum,	unam,	unum	duos et duo,	duas,	duo	tres,	tres,	tria
A.	uno,	una;	uno	duobus,	duabus,	duobus	tribus,	tribus,	tribus

No.	CARDINAL.	ORDINAL.	DISTRIBUTIVE.	ADVERBIAL.
	one, two.	*first, second.*	*one by one.*	*once, twice.*
1	unus	primus	singuli	semel
2	duo	secundus	bini	bis
3	tres	tertius	terni (trini)	ter
4	quatuor	quartus	quaterni	quater
5	quinque	quintus	quini	quinquies
6	sex	sextus	seni	sexies
7	septem	septimus	septeni	septies
8	octo	octavus	octoni	octies
9	novem	nonus	noveni	novies
10	decem	decimus	deni	decies
11	undecim	undecimus	undeni	undecies
12	duodecim	duodecimus	duodeni	duodecies
13	tredecim	tertius	terni	tredecies
14	quatuordecim	quartus	quaterni	quatuordecies
15	quindecim	quintus } decimus	quini } deni	quindecies
16	sedecim	sextus	seni	sedecies
17	septendecim	septimus	septeni	septiesdecies
18	duodeviginti	duodevicesimus	duodeviceni	duodevicies
19	undeviginti	undevicesimus	undeviceni	undevicies
20	viginti	vicesimus	viceni	vicies
21	viginti unus	vicesimus primus	viceni singuli	vicies semel
22	viginti duo	vicesimus secundus	viceni bini	vices bis
30	triginta	tricesimus	triceni	tricies
40	quadraginta	quadragesimus	quadrageni	quadragies
50	quinquaginta	quinquagesimus	quinquageni	quinquagies
60	sexaginta	sexagesimus	sexageni	sexagies
70	septuaginta	septuagesimus	septuageni	septuagies
80	octoginta	octogesimus	octogeni	octogies
90	nonaginta	nonagesimus	nonageni	nonagies
100	centum	centesimus	centeni	centies
200	ducenti, æ, a	ducentesimus	duceni	ducenties
300	trecenti	trecentesimus	treceni	trecenties
400	quadringenti	quadringentesimus	quadringeni	quadringenties
500	quingenti	quingentesimus	quingeni	quingenties
600	sexcenti	sexcentesimus	sexceni	sexcenties
700	septingenti	septingentesimus	septingeni	septingenties
800	octingenti	octingentesimus	octingeni	octingenties
900	nongenti	nongentesimus	nongeni	nongenties
1000	mille	millesimus	singula millia	millies
2000	duo millia	bis millesimus	bina millia	bis millies
3000	tria millia	ter millesimus	terna millia	ter millies

Note. 1.—*Ambo*, both, is declined like *duo*, and has likewise two forms for the accus., *ambos* and *ambo*.

Note 2.—From 20 to 100, either the less number precedes with *et*, or the larger number precedes without *et;* e. g., 23, *tres et viginti* or *viginti tres; tertius et vicesimus* or *vicesimus tertius.*

Above 100, the large number always precedes, either with or without *et;* but *et* is never put twice; e. g., 322, *trecenti viginti duo* or *trecenti et viginti duo.*

Note 3.—Instead of *sedecim* (also *sexdecim*) and *septendecim*, we may also say *decem et sex, decem et septem;* and instead of *tredecies, quatuordecies, quindecies,* and *sedecies,* the forms *terdecies, quaterdecies, quinquiesdecies, sexiesdecies, octiesdecies, noviesdecies,* are also used.

Note 4.—The two numbers before every ten, viz., 18, 19 ; 28, 29 ; 38, 39, etc., are more commonly expressed by the subtractive forms *duode-* and *unde-;* e. g., 89, *undenonaginta;* 99, *undecentum;* 58, *duodesexaginta.* Such forms, however, as *nonaginta novem, nonaginta octo, septuaginta novem, septuaginta octo,* and the like, are found also.—Thus we may say (18, 19) *decem et octo, decem et novem* along with *duodeviginti, undeviginti;* but the forms *octodecim* and *novendecim* are supported by no authority.

Note 5.—The ordinals 21, 22 ; 31, 32 ; 41, 42, etc., are frequently expressed by *unus et vicesimus, alter et vicesimus; unus et tricesimus, alter et tricesimus,* instead of *primus et vicesimus, secundus et vicesimus.* But we say correctly *vicesimus primus, vicesimus secundus,* etc.

CHAPTER IV.

Pronouns.

Pronouns are divided into the following classes : *personal, demonstrative, relative, interrogative, indefinite, possessive,* and *correlative* pronouns.

I. Personal Pronouns.

§ 39.—There are three personal pronouns : *ego, tu, sui.* They are thus declined :

S. N.	ego, *I*	tu, *thou*	————
G.	mei, *of me*	tui, *of thee*	sui, *of himself*, etc.
D.	mihi, *to me*	tibi, *to thee*	sibi, *to himself*, etc.
A.	me, *me*	te, *thee*	se, *himself*, etc.
A.	me, *with me*	te, *with thee*	se, *with himself*, etc.
P. N.	nos, *we*	vos, *you*	————
G.	nostri (-um), *of us*	vestri (-um), *of you*	sui, *of themselves*
D.	nobis, *to us*	vobis, *to you*	sibi, *to themselves.*
A.	nos, *us*	vos, *you*	se, *themselves*
A.	nobis, *with us*	vobis, *with you*	se, *with themselves*

Note 1.—To express the English emphatic " self," the syllable *met* is (with or without *ipse*) annexed to all the cases of the personal pronouns, the genitives plur. and the nominative sing. of *tu* excepted ; as, *egomet* or *egomet ipse*, I myself; *tibimet* or *tibimet ipsi; nosmet ipsos; vobismet ipsis.*—" Thou thyself," is rendered by *tute,* or *tu ipse,* or *tutemet.*

Note 2.—The accusatives *me, te,* and *se* are sometimes doubled, *meme, tete, sese.*—The vocative of any pronoun, if used at all, is like the nominative.—Respecting the difference between *nostri, vestri,* and *nostrum, vestrum,* see § 137.

II. Demonstrative Pronouns.

§ 40.—The Latin demonstrative pronouns are *hic, hæc, hoc—ille, illa, illud—iste, ista, istud—is, ea, id*, to which may be added the adjunctive *ipse, ipsa, ipsum*, "self." They are thus declined ·

		"*this*"			"*he*" or "*that*"	
S. N.	hic	hæc	hoc	ille	illă	illud
G.	hujus}	*for all genders*		illīus}	*for all genders*	
D.	huic			illi		
A.	hunc	hanc	hoc	illum	illam	illud
A.	hoc	hac	hoc	illo	illă	illo
P. N.	hi	hæ	hæc	illi	illæ	illă
G.	horum	harum	horum	illorum	illarum	illorum
D.	his	his	his	illis	illis	illis
A.	hos	has	hæc	illos	illas	illă
A.	his	his	his	illis	illis	illis

Note 1.—Like *hic* are declined the emphatic *hicce, hæcce, hocce*, and the interrogative *hiccine, hæccine, hoccine*, through all cases, ending in *c* and *s;* as, *hujusce hunccce, hisce, hasce, huiccine.*

Note 2.—Like *ille* is declined the pronoun *iste, istα, istud*, this, that.—This pronoun generally refers to the person spoken to and to the things appertaining to him e. g., *iste liber*, that book of yours ; *negotium istud*, that business of yours. It sometimes implies scorn or contempt: as, *quid iste dicit?* what does that fellow say ? *tuus iste frater*, that fine brother of yours.

Note 8.—Besides *iste, ista, istud* and *ille, illa, illud*, the early Latin writers used also the forms *istic, istæc, istoc* or *istuc* and *illic, illæc, illoc* or *illuc*, but only in the nom. acc., and abl. sing., and in the nom. and acc. neut. plural.—The neut. *istuc* and *istæc* sometimes occur even in Cicero.

The familiar expressions *eccum, eccam? ellum, ellam! eccos, eccas, eccillum, eccillam*, stand for *ecce eum, en illum*, etc.

		"*that*."			"*self*."	
S. N.	is	eă	id	ipse	ipsă	ipsum
G.	ejus}	*for all genders.*		ipsīus}	*for all genders*	
D.	ei			ipsi		
A.	eum	eam	id	ipsum	ipsam	ipsum
A.	eo	eă	eo	ipso	ipsă	ipso
P. N.	ii	eæ	eă	ipsi	ipsæ	ipsă
G.	eorum	earum	eorum	ipsorum	ipsarum	ipsorum
D.	iis	iis	iis	ipsis	ipsis	ipsis
A.	eos	eas	eă	ipsos	ipsas	ipsă
A.	iis	iis	iis	ipsis	ipsis	ipsis

Note 4.—The pronouns *is, ille, iste*, and *ipse*, when used alone without a substantive, are translated by *he, she, it.*

Like *is* is declined the compound *idem, eădem, idem*, "the same;" but in the accusative *eundem* and *eandem* are preferable to *eumdem, eamdem*, and in like manner the genit. plur. *eorundem, earundem* to *eorumdem, earumdem.* The nom. plural *ei* (for *ii*) is rare, and *eidem* (for *iidem*) does not occur at all. Also *eis* and *eisdem* are not so common as *iis* and *iisdem.*

N.	Idem	eădem	Idem		iidem	eædem	eădem
G.	ejusdem				eorundem	earundem	eorundem
D.	eidem	} *for all genders*			iisdem	iisdem	iisdem
A.	eundem	eandem	Idem		eosdem	easdem	eădem
A.	eodem	eădem	eodem		iisdem	iisdem	iisdem

NOTE 5.—The pronoun *ipse*, when joined to another demonstrative pronoun, is equivalent to the English "very;" as, *hoc ipso die,* on this very day ; *eo ipso tempore,* at that very time.

III. RELATIVE AND INTERROGATIVE PRONOUNS.

§ 41.—The Latin relatives are *qui, quæ, quod,* "who, which," and *quicunque,* "whoever." They are called relatives, because they generally relate to some word going before.

The Latin interrogatives are *quis, quid?* who, what ? and its compounds *quisnam, quidnam?* who then, what then? and *ecquis, ecquid?* is there any one (or any thing) who ....? does any one or any thing ....?

The relative *qui* and the interrogative *quis* are thus declined :

		"who, which."			"who, what ?"		
S. N.	qui	quæ	quod		quis *or* qui	quæ	quid *or* quod
G.	cujus				cujus		
D.	cui	} *for all genders.*			cui	} *for all genders*	
A.	quem	quam	quod		quem	quam	quid *or* quod
A.	quo	qua	quo		quo	qua	quo
P. N.	qui	quæ	quæ		qui	quæ	quæ
G.	quorum	quarum	quorum		quorum	quarum	quorum
D.	quibus	quibus	quibus		quibus	quibus	quibus
A.	quos	quas	quæ		quos	quas	quæ
A.	quibus	quibus	quibus		quibus	quibus	quibus

NOTE 1.—Like the relative *qui* is declined the compound *quicunque, quæcunque, quodcunque* (never *quidcunque*), the suffix -*cunque* being simply added to the different cases. Instead of *quibus, queis* is sometimes used.

NOTE 2.—The interrogatives *quis, quisnam,* and *ecquis* are declined like the relative *qui* except that in the nom. sing. they have two forms for the masculine ; *quis, qui;* and in the nom. and accus., two forms for the neuter: *quid, quod.*

The forms *quis* and *quid* are used substantively, that is, they stand either alone without a substantive, or when they are joined to a substantive, the latter is put in the genitive: e. g., *quis est? quis nescit? quisnam vocat? ecquis hoc intelligit? quid est? quid times? quidnam vides? ecquid audis? quis Romanorum? quisnam mortalium? ecquis philosophorum? quid periculi? quid præmii? quidnam sceleris? ecquid commodi?*

The forms *qui* and *quod,* on the contrary, are used adjectively, that is, they are used in connection with a substantive either expressed or understood, and agree with it

accordingly ; e. g., *qui rex ? qui miles ? quinam puer ? ecqui philosophus ? quod periculum ? quod præmium ? quodnam scelus ? ecquod commodum ?*
The interrogative *qui* sometimes stands substantively for *quis*, especially in indirect questions ; e. g., *qui scit ? nescimus qui sis ; non possum oblivisci qui fuerim, non sentire qui sim ;*—and *quis*, vice versa, adjectively for *qui*, as *quis rex ? quis miles ? quis homo ? quis hospes ? quis philosophus ?* but in these expressions the words *rex, miles, homo,* etc., are to be regarded as placed in apposition to the interrogative *quis.*
Ecquis has in the nom. fem. sing. and in the neuter plural both *ecquæ* and *ecqua.*

IV. INDEFINITE PRONOUNS.

§ 42.—The following indefinite pronouns are declined like the relative *qui ;* but in the neut. sing. they have two forms, one in -*quid,* used substantively ;. the other in -*quod,* used adjectively ; as, *aliquid temporis, aliquid præmii,* and *aliquod tempus, aliquod præmium.*

> Quidam, quædam, quoddam *or* quiddam, *a certain one.*
> Quilibet, quælibet, quodlibet *or* quidlibet, *any one you please.*
> Quivis, quævis, quodvis *or* quidvis, *any one you please.*
>
> Quispiam, quæpiam, quidpiam *or* quodpiam, *some one.*
> Aliquis, aliqua, aliquid *or* aliquod, *some one, something.*
> Quisque, quæque, quidque *or* quodque, *every one.*
> Unusquisque, unaquæque, unumquidque *or* -quodque, *each.*

NOTE 1.—*Quidam* usually changes *m* before *d* into *n,* as *quendam, quandam, quorundam,* instead of *quemdam, quamdam,* etc.

NOTE 2.—*Aliquis* has in the nom. fem. sing. and in the nom. and acc. neut. plur. *aliqua.* It is thus declined :

S. N.	aliquis	*aliqua*	aliquid or -quod
G.	alicujus ⎫ *for all genders*		
D.	alicui ⎭		
A.	aliquem	aliquam	aliquid or -quod
A	aliquo	aliqua	aliquo
P. N.	aliqui	aliquæ	*aliqua*
G.	aliquorum	aliquarum	aliquorum
D.	aliquibus	aliquibus	aliquibus
A.	aliquos	aliquas	*aliqua*
A.	aliquibus	aliquibus	aliquibus

Aliquis with its derivatives *aliquo* and *aliquando,* generally loses the prefix *ali,* when *si, nisi, ne, num, quo, quando,* or *quanto* precedes, and then in the fem. sing. and the neut. plur., the form *qua* is used along with *quæ ;* hence we may say *siqua, nequa, numqua,* or *si quæ, ne quæ, num quæ.*

NOTE 3.—*Unusquisque,* each, and *quotusquisque,* how many ! or how few ! occur in the singular only, and have both parts declined. The latter scarcely occurs in the oblique cases ; the former is thus declined :

N. unusquisque	unaquæque	unumquidque *or* -quodque
G. uniuscujusque ⎫ *for all genders*		
D. unicuique ⎭		
A. unumquemque	unamquamque	unumquidque *or* -quodque
A. unoquoque	unaquaque	unoquoque

NOTE 4.—*Quisquam,* any one, and *quisquis,* whosoever, are almost always used substantively, and have, therefore, in the neuter regularly *quidquam* (or *quicquam*) and

quidquid (or *quicquid*).—*Quisquam* has neither fem. nor plur. The double forms *quœquœ, quemquem, quoquo, quibusquibus* (from *quisquis*), are not so frequent as those formed by the suffix *-cunque.*

V. Possessive and Patrial Pronouns.

§ 43.—The possessive pronouns are formed from the genitive of the personal and are declined entirely like adjectives of three endings. They are as follows :

meus,	mea,	meum,	*my* (*Voc. masc.* mi)
tuus,	tua,	tuum,	*thy*
suus,	sua,	suum,	*his, her, its ;* pl. *their*
noster,	nostra,	nostrum,	*our*
vester,	vestra,	vestrum,	*your*

Patrial pronouns are such as have reference to a person's country, family, or party. They are three in number; viz.,

cujas, -ātis, what countryman ? of what family or party ?
nostras, -ātis, our countryman, of our family or party.
vestras, -ātis, your countryman, of your family or party.

The pronouns *cujas, nostras,* and *vestras,* are declined like *felix.* Plur. nom., acc., and voc., *nostrates, nostratia ;* gen., *nostratium ;* dat. and abl., *nostratibus.*

§ 44.—Here belong also the so-called pronominals or pronominal adjectives *alius, alter, uter, neuter, ullus,* and *nullus.* These adjectives, together with *solus* and *totus,* make the genitive sing. in *-ius* and the dative in *i,* for all genders ; as,

solus, *alone,*	G. solīus	D. soli
totus, *whole,*	G. totīus	D. toti
alius, *another,*	G. alīus	D. alii
alter, *the one, the other (of two),* . .	G. alterīus	D. altĕri
uter, *which of the two ?*	G. utrīus	D. utri
neuter, *neither of the two,*	G. neutrīus	D. neutri
ullus, *any one,*	G. ullīus	D. ulli
nullus, *no one,*	G. nullīus	D. nulli

Thus the compounds *uterque,* each of the two, both ; *utervis, uterlibet, utercunque,* whichever of the two.—*Alteruter,* either the one or the other (of two), has in the gen. both *alterutrīus* and *alterīus utrīus ;* dat. *alterutri ;* acc. *alterutrum ;* abl. *alterutro.*

VI. Correlative Pronouns.

§ 45.—Correlative pronouns are such as express a mutual relation to each other and represent this relation by a corresponding form.

talis, *such, of such a kind ;* qualis, *as, of what kind ?*	qualiscunque, *of whatever kind.* talis-qualis, *such as.*
tantus, *such, so great ;* quantus, *as great, how great ?*	quantuscunque, *how great soever.* tantus-quantus, *as great as.*
tot, *so many ;* quot, *as many, how many ?*	quotcunque, *how many soever.* tot-quot, *as many as.*

Decline together: *Hic fortissimus miles ; hæc benigna mater ; illustre illud ac præclarum facinus.—Ego et doctissimus ille vir ; et ego, et tu, et hic, et hæc, et illa.—Tu ipse et hic infelix frater meus ; hæc et quælibet alia causa ; tu solus nec quisquam alius.—Hic magnanimus rex et clemens illa regina ; idem semper vultus eademque frons ; ego idem et non alius ; vir ille innocentissimus idemque doctissimus,* and the like.

CHAPTER V.

THE VERB.

§ 46.—Verbs are divided into two main classes,—*transitive* and *intransitive.*

A *transitive* verb is a verb which takes an object in the accusative, in answer to *whom* or *what,* placed after it ; e. g., I praise (praise *whom?*—) the scholar ; *laudo discipulum.* I write (write *what?*—) a letter ; *scribo epistolam.*

An *intransitive* verb is a verb which takes either no object at all, as *sto,* I stand ; *sedeo,* I sit ; *curro,* I run ; *ambulo,* I walk ;—or, if it takes one, does not take it in the accusative, but in some other case ; as, *obedio,* I obey ; *parco,* I spare ; *faveo,* I favor ; and several other verbs which, though transitive in English, are intransitive in Latin, because they take their object in the dative.

Such verbs, of course, must be learned chiefly by observation and practice, the student in the mean time taking as a general rule, to consider verbs that are transitive in English, as transitive also in Latin.

☞ A verb is *transitive* in English, when the word "somebody" or "something" can be placed after it. Thus, *to praise, to blame, to see, to learn, to hear, to do,* etc., are transitive in English, because we can say, to praise, blame, see, hear, etc., *somebody* or *something.*

VOICES, MOODS, AND TENSES.

§ 47.—Voice is a particular mode of inflecting or conjugating verbs. There are two voices, called the *active* and *passive* voices.

The *active* voice ends in *o ;* the *passive,* in *or.* In the former, the subject is represented as acting ; in the latter, as acted upon ; as, act., *laudo,* I praise ; pass., *laudor,* I am praised.

Transitive verbs have both the active and passive voices. Intransitive verbs have only the active in *o,* and they cannot be used in the passive, except impersonally, that is, only in the 3d singular ; as, *curritur, itur, venitur, veniebatur, ventum est, ambulatum est.*

The moods are four,—the *Indicative,* the *Subjunctive,* the *Imperative,* and the *Infinitive.*

The *Indicative* expresses an action or state as a fact, as something real ; as, " It rains."—" He writes."—" They come ;" or asks a question ; as, " Does it rain ?"— " Does he write ?"—" Are they coming ?"

The *Subjunctive* expresses an action or state not as a fact, but merely as possible, conditional, doubtful, and contingent; as, "It may rain."—"If thou write."—"If they should come."

The *Imperative* is used in commanding, exhorting, or entreating; as, "Depart thou."—"Come and see."—"Forgive me."

The *Infinitive* expresses an action or state indefinitely, without limiting it to number and person; as, "To err is human."—"To lie is base."—"To forgive is divine."

§ 48.—The tenses are six: the *Present, Imperfect, Perfect, Pluperfect, Future,* and *Fut.-Perfect.*

Prs.	scribo, *I write, I am writing, I do write.*
Imp.	scribebam, *I was writing, I wrote, I did write.*
Prf.	scripsi, *I wrote, I have written.*
Plp.	scripseram, *I had written.*
Fut.	scribam, *I shall write.*
F.-pf.	scripsero, *I shall have written.*

The tenses are divided into *principal* and *historical* tenses.

PRINCIPAL TENSES.	HISTORICAL TENSES.
Prs. scribo, *I write.*	Imp. scribebam, *I was writing.*
Prf. scripsi, *I have written.*	Plp. scripseram, *I had written.*
Fut. scribam, *I shall write.*	Prf. scripsi, *I wrote.*

Numbers and persons of verbs are the same as in English.

GERUNDS, SUPINES, PARTICIPLES.

§ 49.—Gerunds and Supines represent the idea of the verb in the form of substantives; Participles, in the form of adjectives.

Gerunds are verbal substantives of the 2d decl., used only in the oblique cases (*Gen., Dat., Acc.,* and *Abl.*) of the singular number.

Supines are verbal substantives of the 4th decl., used in the *Acc.* and *Abl.* singular. The Supine in *um* has an active meaning; the Supine in *u*, commonly a passive one.

Participles are in form adjectives, but express, at the same time, the different relations of the action or state, whether it is still lasting or terminated.

Regular Latin verbs generally have four Participles;—two in the active, and two in the passive.

In the Active:	In the Passive:
1. The Part. Present in *ns.*	1. The Part. Perf. in *us.*
2. The Part. Future in *urus.*	2. The Participle in *dus.*

The Part. Pres. act. in *ns* corresponds to the English Participle in *ing;* as, *laudans,* praising; *scribens,* writing.

The Part. Fut. act. in *urus* expresses an intention or a wish to do something; as, *scripturus,* one who intends (wishes, is about or going) to write.

The Part. Perf. pass. in *us* corresponds to the English Participle in *ed;* as, *laudatus,* praised; *monitus,* advised.

The Participle in *dus,*—commonly, though improperly, called the Participle Future passive,—does not by itself imply the idea of futurity. A reference to future time may, indeed, be implied, but this arises from the connection rather than from the Participle itself. The Participle in *dus* expresses in the nominative, and occasionally also in the remaining cases, *necessity, obligation,* or *propriety.* Thus, *epistola scribenda* means a letter that *must* be written, not one that *will* be written.

☞ Modern Grammarians often call the Partic. in *dus* the *Gerundive,* from its resemblance to the Gerund.

THE CONJUGATIONS.

§ 50.—There are, in Latin, four conjugations, distinguished by the ending of the Present Infinitive active.

1	2	3	4
-are	-ĕre	-ĕre	-ire

The principal parts of a verb are its *Stem, Infinitive, Perfect,* and *Supine.* The stem of a verb is generally obtained by taking off the ending of the Present Infinitive.

	INFINITIVE.	PERFECT.	SUPINE.	
1. amo,	am-are,	amavi,	amatum,	*to love.*
2. moneo,	mon-ēre,	monui,	monitum,	*to advise.*
3. rego,	reg-ĕre,	rexi,	rectum,	*to rule.*
4. audio,	aud-ire,	audivi,	auditum,	*to hear.*

§ 51. THE FORMATION OF THE TENSES.

From the stem are formed—by adding the proper endings

The Present, Imperfect, and Future INDIC. (Act. and Pass.)
The Present and Imperfect SUBJUNCTIVE (Act. and Pass.)
The IMPERATIVE both Act. and Pass.
The GERUNDS and PARTICIPLES in *ns* and *dus.*

From the Perfect are formed—by changing the final *i* into *eram, ero, erim, issem,* and *isse,* respectively:

The Pluperfect and Future-Perfect INDIC. Act.
The Perfect and Pluperfect SUBJUNCTIVE Act.
The Perfect INFINITIVE Active.

From the Supine are formed—by changing *um* into *us* and *urus,* respectively:

The PARTICIPLE Perfect Pass. in *us.*
The PARTICIPLE Future Act. in *urus.*

NOTE.—The Imperfect Subj. may also be formed by adding *m* for the Active, and *r* for the Passive,—to the Infinitive Present Active.

The Imperative Active may be formed from the Infinitive Act. —by dropping the ending -*re* of the Infinitive.

The Participle in *dus* may be formed from the genitive sing. of the Partic. Present Act.—by changing *tis* into *dus.*

☞ In parsing any verbal form, let the pupil state (1.) the person, (2.) the number, (3.) the mood, (4.) the tense, (5.) the voice, (6.) from what verb, (7.) the meaning, and (8.) the agreement; e. g., *regimini* is the second person plur. of the Indic. Present pass. from the verb *rego, regĕre, rexi, rectum,* "to rule," and agrees with. . . .

§ 52.—The verb "ESSE," *to be.*

	INDICATIVE.	SUBJUNCTIVE.
	PRESENT.	
S.	Sum, *I am.*	sim, *I may be.*
	es, *thou art.*	sis, *thou mayest be.*
	est, *he, she, it is.*	sit, *he may be.*
P.	sumus, *we are.*	simus, *we may be.*
	estis, *ye are.*	sitis, *ye may be.*
	sunt, *they are.*	sint, *they may be.*
	IMPERFECT.	
S.	eram, *I was.*	essem, *I might*, etc., *be.*
	eras, *thou wast.*	esses, *thou mightest be.*
	erat, *he, she, it was.*	esset, *he might be.*
P.	eramus, *we were.*	essemus, *we might be.*
	eratis, *ye were.*	essetis, *ye might be.*
	erant, *they were.*	essent, *they might be.*
	PERFECT.	
S.	fui, *I have been.*	fuerim, *I may* } *have been.*
	fuisti, *thou hast been.*	fueris, *thou mayest*
	fuit, *he has been.*	fuerit, *he may*
P.	fuimus, *we have been.*	fuerimus, *we may*
	fuistis, *ye have been.*	fueritis, *ye may*
	fuerunt, *they have been.*	fuerint, *they may*
	PLUPERFECT.	
S.	fueram, *I had been.*	fuissem, *I might*, etc. } *have been.*
	fueras, *thou hadst been.*	fuisses, *thou mightst*
	fuerat, *he had been.*	fuisset, *he might*
P.	fueramus, *we had been.*	fuissemus, *we might*
	fueratis, *ye had been.*	fuissetis, *ye might*
	fuerant, *they had been.*	fuissent, *they might*
	FUTURE.	
S.	ero, *I shall be.*	futur-us, a, um { sim, *I shall be.*
	eris, *thou wilt be.*	sis, *thou wilt be.*
	erit, *he will be.*	sit, *he will be.*
P.	erimus, *we shall be.*	futur-i, æ, a { simus, *we shall be.*
	eritis, *ye will be.*	sitis, *ye will be.*
	erunt, *they will be.*	sint, *they will be.*
	FUT.-PERFECT.	
S.	fuero, *I shall* } *have been.*	supplied by *fuerim* or *fuissem.*
	fueris, *thou wilt*	
	fuerit, *he will*	
P.	fuerimus, *we shall*	
	fueritis, *ye will*	
	fuerint, *they will*	

IMPERATIVE.

S. es, *be thou*   P. este, *be ye*
  esto, *thou shalt be*   estote, *ye shall be*
  esto, *he shall be*   sunto, *they shall be.*

INFINITIVE.

PRS. esse, *to be*
PRF. fuisse, *to have been*
FUT. futurus (a, um) esse, *to be about to be.*

PARTICIPLES.

PRS. and PRF., wanting
FUT. futurus, a, um, *one who is about to be.*

NOTE 1.—The forms *forem, fores, foret,* and *forent,* are sometimes used for *essem, esses, esset,* and *essent;* and *fore* often stands in place of *futurum esse.*

NOTE 2.—The Participle of the Inf. Future has two cases only; viz., the nom. and acc.; as,

S. N. futurus, a, um esse   P. N. futuri, æ, a esse
  A. futurum, am, um esse   A. futuros, as, a esse.

NOTE 8.—Like *sum* are inflected: *absum,* I am away from; *adsum,* I am present; *desum,* I am wanting; *insum,* I am in; *intersum,* I am present at; *obsum,* I am against or in the way; *præsum,* I preside over, am at the head; *prosum,* I benefit, am useful; *subsum,* I am under; *supersum,* I am left, survive.

Prosum, profui, prodesse, inserts *d* in all forms of *sum* that begin with *e*; as,

prosum	pro-d-eram	pro-d-essem	pro-d-ero
pro-d-es	pro-d-eras	pro-d-esses	pro-d-eris
pro-d-est	pro-d-erat	pro-d-esset	pro-d-erit
prosumus	pro-d-eramus	pro-d-essemus	pro-d-erimus
pro-d-estis	pro-d-eratis	pro-d-essetis	pro-d-eritis
prosunt	pro-d-erant	pro-d-essent	pro-d-erunt.

On the verb *sum* and its compounds.

Historia semper *erit* egregia vitæ magistra.—Contentum *esse* suis rebus maximæ *sunt* certissimæque divitiæ.—Juvenes, ut *fuerit* industria vestra, ita etiam præmium vestrum *erit.*—Multi *essent* doctiores, si diligentiores *fuissent.*—Neque timidus *esto* neque audax.—Quis *sim,* mihi notum *est;* quis *futurus sim,* mihi ignotum *est.*—Ego *sum* principium mundi et finis omnium rerum: ego *sum* trinus et unus, et tamen non *sum* Deus.—Beneficiorum per omnem vitam memores *estote.*—Incertum *est* num vita nostra beata *futura sit.*—Qui *prodest* reipublicæ, *prodest* sibi ipsi.—Non *sum* nescius qua mente tu et prius in me *fueris,* et nunc *sis,* et semper *futurus sis.*—Persæ Græcis infesti *erant.*—Demosthenis ætate multi oratores magni et clari *fuerunt,* et antea *fuerant,* nec postea *defuerunt.*—Suæ quisque fortunæ faber *erit.*—Magno Persarum exercitui dux peritus *defuit.*—Incredibile *est* quanta conscientiæ vis *sit.*—Qualis in alios *fueris,* tales ipsi in te *erunt.*—Ut magistratibus leges, ita populo *præsunt* magistratus.—Avaritia fons *est* atque origo multorum malorum.—Urbs Syracusæ maxima et pulcherrima *erat* omnium Græcarum urbium.—Procellæ nautis perniciosæ *sunt.*

§ 53.—Personal Endings

ACTIVE.

I.	II.	III.	IV.	I.	II.	III.	IV.

INDICATIVE. / SUBJUNCTIVE.

PRESENT. / PRESENT.

	I.	II.	III.	IV.	I.	II.	III.	IV.
S.	o	eo	o	io	em	eam	am	iam
	as	es	is	is	es	eas	as	ias
	at	et	it	it	et	eat	at	iat
P.	amus	emus	imus	imus	emus	eamus	amus	iamus
	atis	etis	itis	itis	etis	eatis	atis	iatis
	ant	ent	unt	iunt	ent	eant	ant	iant

IMPERFECT. / IMPERFECT.

	I.	II.	III.	IV.	I.	II.	III.	IV.
S.	abam	ebam	ebam	iebam	arem	ĕrem	ĕrem	īrem
	abas	ebas	ebas	iebas	ares	eres	eres	ires
	abat	ebat	ebat	iebat	aret	eret	eret	iret
P.	abamus	ebamus	ebamus	iebamus	aremus	eremus	eremus	iremus
	abatis	ebatis	ebatis	iebatis	aretis	eretis	eretis	iretis
	abant	ebant	ebant	iebant	arent	erent	erent	irent

FUTURE. / FUTURE.

	I.	II.	III.	IV.
S.	abo	ebo	am	iam
	abis	ebis	es	ies
	abit	ebit	et	iet
P.	abĭmus	ebĭmus	emus	iemus
	abitis	ebitis	etis	ietis
	abunt	ebunt	ent	ient

The Partic. in *urus* with *sim* or *essem.*

PERFECT. PLUPERF. FUT.-PERF. (*for all conjugations.*) / PERFECT. PLUPERF. FUT.-PERF. (*for all conjugations.*)

	PERFECT.	PLUPERF.	FUT.-PERF.	PERFECT.	PLUPERF.	FUT.-PERF.
S.	i	eram	ero	erim	issem	
	isti	eras	eris	eris	isses	
	it	erat	erit	erit	isset	wanting
P.	imus	eramus	erimus	erimus	issemus	
	istis	eratis	eritis	eritis	issetis	
	ĕrunt	erant	erint	erint	issent.	

I.	II.	III.	IV.

IMPERATIVE.

	I.	II.	III.	IV.
S. 2.	a *or* ato	e *or* eto	e *or* ito	i *or* Ito
3.	ato	eto	ito	Ito
P. 2.	ate *or* atote	ete *or* etote	ite *or* itote	ite *or* itote
3.	anto	ento	unto	iunto

INFINITIVE.

	I.	II.	III.	IV.
Prs.	are	ĕre	ĕre	ire
Prf.	isse	isse	isse	isse
Fut.	urus esse	urus esse	urus esse	urus esse

PARTICIPLES.

	I.	II.	III.	IV.
Prs.	ans	ens	ens	iens
Fut.	urus (a, um)	urus (a, um)	urus (a, um)	urus (a, um)

OF THE REGULAR VERBS.

PASSIVE.							
I.	**II.**	**III.**	**IV.**	**I.**	**II.**	**III.**	**IV.**
INDICATIVE.				**SUBJUNCTIVE.**			
PRESENT.				PRESENT.			
or	eor	or	ior	er	ear	ar	iar
aris	ĕris	ĕris	īris	eris	earis	aris	iaris
atur	etur	itur	itur	etur	eatur	atur	iatur
amur	emur	imur	īmur	emur	eamur	amur	iamur
amini	emini	imini	imini	emini	eamini	amini	iamini
antur	entur	untur	iuntur	entur	eantur	antur	iantur
IMPERFECT.				IMPERFECT.			
abar	ebar	ebar	iebar	arer	ĕrer	ĕrer	irer
abaris	ebaris	ebaris	iebaris	areris	ereris	ereris	ireris
abatur	ebatur	ebatur	iebatur	aretur	eretur	eretur	iretur
abamur	ebamur	ebamur	iebamur	aremur	eremur	eremur	iremur
abamini	ebamini	ebamini	iebamini	aremini	eremini	eremini	iremini
abantur	ebantur	ebantur	iebantur	arentur	erentur	erentur	irentur
FUTURE.				FUTURE.			
abor	ebor	ar	iar				
abĕris	eberis	ĕris	ieris				
abĭtur	ebitur	etur	ietur		wanting.		
abimur	ebimur	emur	iemur				
abimini	ebimini	emini	iemini				
abuntur	ebuntur	entur	ientur				

PERFECT.	PLUPERF.	FUT.-PERF.	PERFECT.	PLUPERF.	FUT.-PERF.
(for all conjugations.)			*(for all conjugations.)*		
Partic. in -*us*	Partic. in -*us*	Partic. in -*us*	Partic. in -*us*	Partic. in -*us*	
with	*with*	*with*	*with*	*with*	wanting.
s u m	e r a m	e r o	s i m	e s s e m	
(fui)	(fueram)	(fuero)	(fuerim)	(fuissem)	

I.	II.	III.	IV.
IMPERATIVE.			
S. 2. are *or* ator	ĕre *or* etor	ĕre *or* ītor	ire *or* ītor
3. ator	etor	itor	itor
P. 2. amini	emini	imini	imini
3. antor	entor	untor	iuntor
INFINITIVE.			
PRS. ari	ĕri	i	iri
PRF. us (a, um) esse	us (a, um) esse	us (a, um) esse	us (a, um) esse
FUT. um iri	um iri	um iri	um iri
PARTICIPLES.			
PRF. us	us	us	us
—— andus	endus	endus	iendus

§ 54.—THE FOUR REGULAR CONJUGATIONS.

ACT

I.	II.	III.	IV.

INDICATIVE.

PRESENT.

I love, am loving, do love ; I advise, rule, hear, am advising, etc., do advise, etc.

S. Am-o	Mon-eo	Reg-o	Aud-io
am-as	mon-es	reg-is	aud-is
am-at	mon-et	reg-it	aud-it
P. am-amus	mon-emus	reg-ĭmus	aud-ĭmus
am-atis	mon-etis	reg-itis	aud-itis
am-ant	mon-ent	reg-unt	aud-iunt

IMPERFECT.

I loved, was loving, did love ; I advised, ruled, heard, was advising, did advise.

S. am-abam	mon-ebam	reg-ebam	aud-iebam
am-abas	mon-ebas	reg-ebas	aud-iebas
am-abat	mon-ebat	reg-ebat	aud-iebat
P. am-abamus	mon-ebamus	reg-ebamus	aud-iebamus
am-abatis	mon-ebatis	reg-ebatis	aud-iebatis
am-abant	mon-ebant	reg-ebant	aud-iebant

FUTURE.

I shall love, advise, rule, hear.

S. am-abo	mon-ebo	reg-am	aud-iam
am-abis	mon-ĕbis	reg-es	aud-ies
am-abit	mon-ebit	reg-et	aud-iet
P. am-abĭmus	mon-ebĭmus	reg-emus	aud-iemus
am-abitis	mon-ebitis	reg-etis	aud-ietis
am-abunt	mon-ebunt	reg-ent	aud-ient

PERFECT.

I loved, have loved ; I advised, have advised.

S. amav-i	monu-i	rex-i	audiv-i
amav-isti	monu-isti	rex-isti	audiv-isti
amav-it	monu-it	rex-it	audiv-it
P. amav-imus	monu-imus	rex-imus	audiv-imus
amav-istis	monu-istis	rex-istis	audiv-istis
amav-ērunt	monu-ērunt	rex-ērunt	audiv-ērunt

PLUPERFECT.

I had loved, advised, ruled, heard.

S. amav-eram	monu-eram	rex-eram	audiv-eram
amav-eras	monu-eras	rex-eras	audiv-eras
amav-erat	monu-erat	rex-erat	audiv-erat
P. amav-eramus	monu-eramus	rex-eramus	audiv-eramus
amav-eratis	monu-eratis	rex-eratis	audiv-eratis
amav-erant	monu-erant	rex-erant	audiv-erant

FUT.-PERFECT.

I shall have loved, advised, ruled, heard.

S. amav-ero	monu-ero	rex-ero	audiv-ero
amav-eris	monu-eris	rex-eris	audiv-eris
amav-erit	monu-erit	rex-erit	audiv-erit
P. amav-erimus	monu-erimus	rex-erimus	audiv-erimus
amav-eritis	monu-eritis	rex-eritis	audiv-eritis
amav-erint	monu-erint	rex-erint	audiv-erint

THE FOUR REGULAR CONJUGATIONS.

IVE. .

	I.	II.	III.	IV.

SUBJUNCTIVE.

PRESENT.

I may love, advise, rule, hear.

	I.	II.	III.	IV.
S.	Am-em	Mon-eam	Reg-am	Aud-iam
	am-es	mon-eas	reg-as	aud-ias
	am-et	mon-eat	reg-at	aud-iat
P.	am-emus	mon-eamus	reg-amus	aud-iamus
	am-etis	mon-eatis	reg-atis	aud-iatis
	am-ent	mon-eant	reg-ant	aud-iant

IMPERFECT.

I might (should, would) love, advise, rule, hear.

	I.	II.	III.	IV.
S.	am-arem	mon-erem	reg-erem	aud-irem
	am-ares	mon-eres	reg-eres	aud-ires
	am-aret	mon-eret	reg-eret	aud-iret
P.	am-aremus	mon-eremus	reg-eremus	aud-iremus
	am-aretis	mon-eretis	reg-eretis	aud-iretis
	am-arent	mon-erent	reg-erent	aud-irent

FUTURE.

I shall love, advise, rule, hear.

	I.		II.		III.		IV.	
S.	amatur- us, a, um	sim sis sit	monitur- us, a, um	sim sis sit	rectur- us, a, um	sim sis sit	auditur- us, a, um	sim sis sit
P.	amatur- i, æ, a	simus sitis sint	monitur- i, æ, a	simus sitis sint	rectur- i, æ, a	simus sitis sint	auditur- i, æ, a	simus sitis sint

PERFECT.

I may have loved, advised, ruled, heard.

	I.	II.	III.	IV.
S.	amav-erim	monu-erim	rex-erim	audiv-erim
	amav-eris	monu-eris	rex-eris	audiv-eris
	amav-erit	monu-erit	rex-erit	audiv-erit
P.	amav-erimus	monu-erimus	rex-erimus	audiv-erimus
	amav-eritis	monu-eritis	rex-eritis	audiv-eritis
	amav-erint	monu-erint	rex-erint	audiv-erint

PLUPERFECT.

I might (should, would) have loved, advised, ruled, heard.

	I.	II.	III.	IV.
S.	amav-issem	monu-issem	rex-issem	audiv-issem
	amav-isses	monu-isses	rex-isses	audiv-isses
	amav-isset	monu-isset	rex-isset	audiv-isset
P.	amav-issemus	monu-issemus	rex-issemus	audiv-issemus
	amav-issetis	monu-issetis	rex-issetis	audiv-issetis
	amav-issent	monu-issent	rex-issent	audiv-issent

FUT.-PERFECT.

I shall have loved, advised, ruled, heard.

wanting.

(generally supplied by the Subj. Perf. or Pluperfect.)

(See § 187.)

THE FOUR REGULAR CONJUGATIONS.

ACTIVE.			
I.	II.	III.	IV.

IMPERATIVE.

love thou, thou shalt l. ;   he shall l. ;   love ye, ye shall l., they shall l.

	I.	II.	III.	IV.
S. 2.	am-a	mon-e	reg-e	aud-i
	am-ato	mon-eto	reg-Ito	aud-Ito
2.	am-ato	mon-eto	reg-ito	aud-ito
P. 2.	am-ate	mon-ete	reg-ite	aud-ite
	am-atote	mon-etote	reg-itote	aud-itote
3.	am-anto	mon-ento	reg-unto	aud-iunto

INFINITIVE.

to love, to have loved, to be about to love.

	I.	II.	III.	IV.
Prs.	am-are	mon-ēre	reg-ĕre	aud-ire
Prf.	amav-isse	monu-isse	rex-isse	audiv-isse
Fut.	amaturus esse	moniturus esse	recturus esse	auditurus esse

GERUNDS.

G. of loving or to love ; D. and A. to love; Abl. by loving.

	I.	II.	III.	IV.
Gen.	am-andi	mon-endi	reg-endi	aud-iendi
Dat.	am-ando	mon-endo	reg-endo	aud-iendo
Acc.	am-andum	mon-endum	reg-endum	aud-iendum
Abl.	am-ando	mon-endo	reg-endo	aud-iendo

SUPINES.

1. (in order) to love ; 2. to love or to be loved.

	I.	II.	III.	IV.
1.	amatum	monitum	rectum	auditum
2.	amatu	monitu	rectu	auditu

PARTICIPLES.

Prs. loving, advising . . . . Fut. being about to love, to advise.

	I.	II.	III.	IV.
Prs.	am-ans	mon-ens	reg-ens	aud-iens
Fut.	amat-urus	monit-urus	rect-urus	audit-urus

§ 55.—NOTES ON THE ACTIVE VOICE.

Note 1.—The third person plural of the Indic. Perfect sometimes ends in *ēre* instead of *ērunt ;* as, *fuēre, amavēre, monuēre, rexēre,* etc., instead of *fuerunt, amaverunt, monuērunt, rexērunt,* etc.

Note 2.—Perfects in *avi* of the first, and in *evi* of the second conjugation, as well as the tenses formed from the Perfect, frequently drop *vi* and *ve* before *r* and *s ;* as, *amarunt, amaram, amarint,* for *amavērunt, amaveram, amaverint ;—amasti, amassent, amasse,* for *amavisti, amavissent, amavisse ;—nerunt, deleram, flesti, complessem,* for *neverunt, deleveram, flevisti, complevissem.* Thus, *consuerunt, consuessem,* of the third conjugation, for *consuevērunt, consuevissem.*

NOTE 3.—Perfects in *ivi*, of the third and fourth conjugations, often drop *v* before *e*, and sometimes before *i*; as, *desierunt, audierunt*, for *desivērunt, audiverunt;—quæsieram, definierat*, for *quæsiveram, definiverāt ;—petierim, audiero*, for *petiverim, audivero ;* more rarely *audiit, muniit, petiissem,audiisse*, for *audivit, munivit, petivissem, audivisse.*

When *ivi* is followed by *s*, the whole syllable *vi* may be dropped; as, *petisti, petissem, audisse, abiissem, redisti, subisse*, for *petivisti, petivissem, audivisse*, etc.

NOTE 4.—*Dico, duco, facio*, and *fero*, with their compounds, have *dic, duc, fer, fac*, in the Imperative.

§ 56.—NOTES ON THE PASSIVE VOICE.

NOTE 1.—The second person singular of the Present and Imperfect Subjunctive, as well as of the Imperfect and Future Indicative, often ends in *re* instead of *ris ;* as, *moneare* for *monearis ; monerere* for *monereris ; amabare* for *amabaris ; amabēre* for *amabēris ; regare* for *regaris ; regēre* for *regēris*, etc.

NOTE 2.—To express more emphatically the completion of an action, the following forms are sometimes used :

> amatus fui *for* amatus sum
> amatus fueram *for* amatus eram
> amatus fuerim *for* amatus sim
> amatus fuissem *for* amatus essem
> amatus fuisse *for* amatus esse.

NOTE 3.—The Participles of the Infinitive Perfect pass. and of the Infinitive Future act.,have two cases only : viz., the nominative and accusative both sing. and plural ; as,

Sing. N.	amatus (a, um) esse	*Plur.* N.	amati (æ, a) esse
A.	amatum (am, um) esse.	A.	amatos (as, a) esse.
Sing. N.	amaturus (a, um) esse	*Plur.* N.	amaturi (æ, a) esse
A.	amaturum (am, um) esse.	A.	amaturos (as, a) esse.

NOTE 4.—The Participle in *dus*, in verbs of the third and fourth conjugations, ends sometimes in *undus*, instead of *endus*, especially when *i* precedes ; as, *regundus, faciundus, capiundus*, and regularly *potiundus.*

Verbs in -io

of the third conjugation.

§ 57.—Verbs ending in *-io*, of the third conjug., as *capio, cupio, fodio, fugio, jacio, rapio*, etc., retain the *i* before *am* and *ar ; ebam* and *ebar ; ens, endus*, and *endi*, throughout,—and also before the endings *unt, untur, unto*, and *untor*,—in other words, they retain the *i* in the Present Subj., in the Imperfect Indic., and in the Future Indic., both active and passive ; besides in the participles in *ens* and *dus*, in the Gerunds, and also in the third person plur. of the Present Indic. and of the Imperat. both active and passive ; as,

Pres. Subj.		Fut. Indic.		Impf. Indic.	
ACT.	PASS.	ACT.	PASS.	ACT.	PASS.
cap-i-am	cap-i-ar	cap-i-am	cap-i-ar	cap-i-ebam	cap-i-ebar.
cap-i-as	cap-i-aris	cap-i-es	cap-i-eris	cap-i-ebas	cap-i-ebaris
cap-i-at	cap-i-atur	cap-i-et	cap-i-etur	cap-i-ebat	cap-i-ebatur
etc.		etc.		etc.	
cap-i-unt *and* -untur,		cap-i-unto *and* -untor,		cap-i-ens *and* cap-i-endus.	

§ 58.—THE FOUR REGULAR CONJUGATIONS.

PASS

	I.	II.	III.	IV.

INDICATIVE.

PRESENT.

I am loved, advised, ruled, heard.

	I.	II.	III.	IV.
S.	Am-or	Mon-eor	Reg-or	Aud-ior
	am-aris	mon-eris	reg-ĕris	aud-iris
	am-atur	mon-etur	reg-itur	aud-itur
P.	am-amur	mon-emur	reg-imur	aud-imur
	am-amini	mon-emini	reg-imini	aud-imini
	am-antur	mon-entur	reg-untur	aud-iuntur

IMPERFECT.

I was loved, advised, ruled, heard.

	I.	II.	III.	IV.
S.	am-abar	mon-ebar	reg-ebar	aud-iebar
	am-abaris (re)	mon-ebaris (re)	reg-ebaris (re)	aud-iebaris (re)
	am-abatur	mon-ebatur	reg-ebatur	aud-iebatur
P.	am-abamur	mon-ebamur	reg-ebamur	aud-iebamur
	am-abamini	mon-ebamini	reg-ebamini	aud-iebamini
	am-abantur	mon-ebantur	reg-ebantur	aud-iebantur

FUTURE.

I shall be loved, advised, ruled, heard.

	I.	II.	III.	IV.
S.	am-abor	mon-ebor	reg-ar	aud-iar
	am-aberis (re)	mon-eberis (re)	reg-ĕris (re)	aud-ieris (re)
	am-abitur	mon-ebitur	reg-etur	aud-ietur
P.	am-abimur	mon-ebimur	reg-emur	aud-iemur
	am-abimini	mon-ebimini	reg-emini	aud-iemini
	am-abuntur	mon-ebuntur	reg-entur	aud-ientur

PERFECT.

I have been loved, advised, ruled, heard.

	I.		II.		III.		IV.	
S.	amat-	sum	monit-	sum	rect-	sum	audit-	sum
	us,	es	us,	es	us,	es	us,	es
	a, um	est	a, um	est	a, um	est	a, um	est
P.	amat-	sumus	monit-	sumus	rect-	sumus	audit-	sumus
	i,	estis	i,	estis	i,	estis	i,	estis
	æ, a	sunt	æ, a	sunt	æ, a	sunt	æ, a	sunt

PLUPERFECT.

I had been loved, advised, ruled, heard.

	I.		II.		III.		IV.	
S.	amat-	eram	monit-	eram	rect-	eram	audit-	eram
	us,	eras	us,	eras	us,	eras	us,	eras
	a, um	erat	a, um	erat	a, um	erat	a, um	erat
P.	amat-	eramus	monit-	eramus	rect-	eramus	audit-	eramus
	i,	eratis	i,	eratis	i,	eratis	i,	eratis
	æ, a	erunt	æ, a	erant	æ, a	erant	æ, a	erant

FUT.-PERFECT.

I shall have been loved, advised, ruled, heard.

	I.		II.		III.		IV.	
S.	amat-	ero	monit-	ero	rect-	ero	audit-	ero
	us,	eris	us,	eris	us,	eris	us,	eris
	a, um	erit	a, um	erit	a, um	erit	a, um	erit
P.	amat-	erimus	monit-	erimus	rect-	erimus	audit-	erimus
	i,	eritis	i,	eritis	i,	eritis	i,	eritis
	æ, a	erunt	æ, a	erunt	æ, a	erunt	æ, a	erunt

THE FOUR REGULAR CONJUGATIONS.

IVE.			
I.	**II.**	**III.**	**IV**

SUBJUNCTIVE.

PRESENT.

I may be loved, advised, ruled, heard.

	I.	II.	III.	IV
S.	Am- er	Mon- ear	Reg- ar	Aud- iar
	am- eris (re)	mon- earis (re)	reg- aris (re)	aud- iaris (re)
	am- etur	mon- eatur	reg- atur	aud- iatur
P.	am- emur	mon- eamur	reg- amur	aud- iamur
	am- emini	mon- eamini	reg- amini	aud- iamini
	am- entur	mon- eantur	reg- antur	aud- iantur

IMPERFECT.

I might (should, would) be loved, advised, ruled, heard.

	I.	II.	III.	IV
S.	am- arer	mon- ērer	reg- ĕrer	aud- irer
	am- areris (re)	mon- ereris (re)	reg- ereris (re)	aud- ireris (re)
	am- aretur	mon- eretur	reg- eretur	aud- iretur
P.	am- aremur	mon- eremur	reg- eremur	aud- iremur
	am- aremini	mon- eremini	reg- eremini	aud- iremini
	am- arentur	mon- erentur	reg- erentur	aud- irentur

FUTURE.

I shall be loved, advised, ruled, heard.

Wanting.

(See § 186.)

PERFECT.

I may have been loved, advised, ruled, heard

	I.		II.		III.		IV	
S.	amat-	sim	monit-	sim	rect-	sim	audit-	sim
	us,	sis	us,	sis	us,	sis	us,	sis
	a, um	sit	a, um	sit	a, um	sit	a, um	sit
P.	amat-	simus	monit-	simus	rect-	simus	audit-	simus
	i,	sitis	i,	sitis	i,	sitis	i,	sitis
	æ, a	sint	æ, a	sint	æ, a	sint	æ, a	sint

PLUPERFECT.

I might (should, would) have been loved, advised, ruled, heard.

	I.		II.		III.		IV	
S.	amat-	essem	monit-	essem	rect-	essem	audit-	essem
	us,	esses	us,	esses	us,	esses	us,	esses
	a, um	esset	a, um	esset	a, um	esset	a, um	esset
P.	amat-	essemus	monit-	essemus	rect-	essemus	audit-	essemus
	i,	essetis	i,	essetis	i,	essetis	i,	essetis
	æ, a	essent	æ, a	essent	æ, a	essent	æ, a	essent

FUT.-PERFECT.

I shall have been loved, advised, ruled, heard.

Wanting.

Generally supplied by the Subj. Perf. or Plupf.

(See § 187.)

4

THE FOUR REGULAR CONJUGATIONS.

PASSIVE.			
I.	II.	III.	IV.

IMPERATIVE.

be thou loved, thou shalt be —, he shall be —; be ye loved, they shall be —.

S. 2. am-are	mon-ĕre	reg-ere	aud-ire
am-ator	mon-etor	reg-ĭtor	aud-ĭtor
3. am-ator	mon-etor	reg-itor	aud-itor
P. 2. am-amini	mon-emini	reg-imini	aud-imini
3. am-antor	mon-entor	reg-untor	aud-iuntor

INFINITIVE.

to be loved ; to have been —; to be about to be —.

Prs. am-ari	mon-eri	reg-i	aud-iri
Prf. amatus esse	monitus esse	rectum esse	auditus esse
Fut. amatum iri	monitum iri	rectum iri	auditum iri

PARTICIPLES.

Prf. loved;—one who must be loved.

Prf. ama-tus	monit-us	rect-us	audit-us
— am-andus	mon-endus	reg-endus	aud-iendus

DEPONENT VERBS.

§ 59.—*Deponent* verbs are such as have the passive form, but an active (trans. or intrans.) signification. They are called deponents, from DEPONO, " to lay aside," as having laid aside the active form ; e. g., *hortor* (trans.), I exhort ; *morior* (intrans.), I die.

Deponent verbs are conjugated only in the passive voice ; but they have also the Gerunds, Supines, and Participles of the active. Their signification is throughout active, the Participle in *dus* excepted, which has always a passive meaning.

There are deponent verbs of all conjugations ; the following is an example of a deponent of the first conjugation :

Miror, mirari, miratus sum, I admire.

INDICATIVE.	SUBJUNCTIVE.
Prs. miror, *I admire*	mirer, *I may admire*
Imp. mirabar, *I was admiring*	mirarer, *I might admire*
Fut. mirabor, *I shall admire*	miraturus sim, *I shall admire*
Prf. miratus sum, *I have admired*	miratus sim, *I may have admired*
Plp. miratus eram, *I had admired*	miratus essem, *I might have admired*
F.-pf. miratus ero, *I shall have admired.*	(*supplied by the* Perfect Subj.)

IMPERATIVE.

S. 2. mirare, -ator, *admire thou.*	P. 2. miramini, *admire ye.*
3. mirator, *let him admire.*	3. mirantor, *let them admire.*

INFINITIVE.

Prs. mirari, *to admire*
Prf. miratus esse, *to have admired*
Fut. miraturus esse, *to be about to admire.*

PARTICIPLES.

Prs. mirans, *admiring*	**Prf.** miratus, *having admired*
Fut. miraturus, *about to admire.*	— mirandus, *one that is to be adm.*

GERUNDS.	SUPINES.
mirandi, o, um, o, *of admiring*, etc.	miratum, -u, *to admire, to be admired.*

NOTE.—The following deponents have in the Perf. Participles, besides the active meaning, a passive one also : *adipiscor, comitor, commentor, comminiscor, complector, confiteor, depopulor, detestor, dimetior, emetior, effari, ementior, experior, exsecror, interpretor, meditor, opinor, paciscor, partior, perfungor, periclitor, stipulor, testor, contestor,* and some others which rely on inferior authority, or are found in poetry only.

adeptus, *obtained*	dimensus, *measured*	opinatus, *imagined*
comitatus, *accompanied*	emensus, *traversed*	pactus, *agreed upon*
commentatus, *discussed*	effatus, *pronounced*	partitus, *divided*
commentus, *invented*	ementitus, *forged*	perfunctus, *endured*
complexus, *comprised*	expertus, *tried*	periclitatus, *tried*
confessus, *acknowledged*	exsecratus, *accursed*	stipulatus, *promised*
depopulatus, *devastated*	interpretatus, *interpreted*	testatus, *attested*
detestatus, *detested*	meditatus, *meditated*	contestatus, *contested.*

§ 60.—The four verbs *audeo, fido, gaudeo,* and *soleo,* are called *semi-deponents,* because in the Present, Imperfect, and Future, they have the active form ; in the Perfect, Pluperfect, and Fut.-Perf., the passive ; as,

INDICATIVE.

Pres. gaudeo, *I rejoice.*	*Perf.* gavisus sum, *I have rejoiced.*
Impf. gaudebam, *I was rejoicing.*	*Plpf.* gavisus eram, *I had rejoiced.*
Fut. gaudebo, *I shall rejoice.*	*F. Pf.* gavisus ero, *I shall have rejoiced.*

INFINITIVE.

Pres. gaudēre, *to rejoice.*
Perf. gavisus esse, *to have rejoiced.*
Fut. gavisurus esse, *to be about to rejoice.*

Thus *audeo,* I venture, *ausus sum ; soleo,* I am accustomed, *solitus sum ; fido,* I trust, with its compounds *confido,* I confide, and *diffido,* I distrust, *fisus, confisus,* and *diffisus sum.* (☞ The active Perfect-forms *confidi* and *diffidi* but rarely occur.)

PERIPHRASTIC CONJUGATION.

There are two conjugations called *periphrastic* or by circumlocution,— the one, active ; the other, passive.

§ 61.—The *active periphrastic conjugation* is formed by the combination of the Participle in *rus* with the tenses of *sum.* It usually expresses an intention or a wish to do something ; as, *scripturus sum,* I intend writing or to write,—I am to write,—am about or going to write,—have a mind to write,—think of, or am on the point of writing.

INDICATIVE.		SUBJUNCTIVE.	
Prs. scripturus, a, um	sum / es / est	Prs. scripturus, a, um	sim / sis / sit
scripturi, æ, a	sumus / estis / sunt	scripturi, æ, a	simus / sitis / sint
Imp. scripturus eram		Imp. scripturus essem	
Prf. scripturus fui		Prf. scripturus fuerim	
Plp. scripturus fueram		Plp. scripturus fuissem	
Fut. scripturus ero		Fut. (*like the Present*.)	

INFINITIVE.

Prs. scripturus (a, um) esse, *to intend writing*
Prf. scripturus (a, um) fuisse, *to have intended to write*
Fut. (*the same as the* Infinitive Present.)

The Participle in *urus* with the verb *sum* does not always express an intention to do something, but sometimes it merely denotes futurity, as it is the case in the Future Subj. and Future Infin. active of the four regular conjugations. Thus, *nescio num venturus sit*, may signify both

1. I do not know whether he will come,—and
2. I do not know whether he has a mind to come.

In case 1, mere futurity is denoted, and *venturus sit* is the Future Subj. act. of *venio*. In case 2, the intention of coming is expressed, and *venturus sit* is the Present Subj. of the periphrastic conjugation.

§ 62.—The *passive periphrastic conjugation* is formed by the combination of the Participle in *dus* with the tenses of *sum*. It always expresses necessity, duty, or conveniency; as, *laudandus sum*, I must or should be praised,—I have or am to be praised,—ought, am worthy, deserve to be praised.

INDICATIVE.		SUBJUNCTIVE.	
Prs. laudandus, a, um	sum / es / est	Prs. laudandus, a, um	sim / sis / sit
laudandi, æ, a	sumus / estis / sunt	laudandi, æ, a	simus / sitis / sint
Imp. laudandus eram		Imp. laudandus essem	
Prf. laudandus fui		Prf. laudandus fuerim	
Plp. laudandus fueram		Plp. laudandus fuissem	
Fut. laudandus ero		Fut. (*like the Present*.)	

INFINITIVE.

Prs. laudandus esse, *that one ought to be praised*
Prf. laudandus fuisse, *that one ought to have been praised*
Fut. laudandum fore, *that one will have to be praised.*

To express passively, what is about to be done, the form *in eo est ut* or *futurum est ut*, with the Present or Imperfect Subjunctive passive is used; e. g., "they are about to be dismissed;"

in eo est *or* futurum est ut dimittantur,
in eo erat *or* futurum erat ut dimitterentur,
in eo erit *or* futurum erit ut dimittantur.

LIST

OF PERFECTS AND SUPINES.

NOTE 1.—Forms printed in Italics occur only in composition; as, -*pleo*, expleo, impleo, compleo.

NOTE 2.—A vowel in parenthesis, at the end of a word, shows the change of the stem-vowel in composition; as, habeo (i),—exhibeo, prohibeo; spargo (e),—aspergo conspergo.

NOTE 3.—A letter in parenthesis, in the middle of a word, denotes the existence of two forms, the one, with that letter; the other, without; as, sanc(i)tum, that is, sancitum or sanctum.

§ 63.—FIRST CONJUGATION.

Verbs of the first conjugation have *avi, atum;* as, *amo, amavi, amatum.*—Thus

abundo, *abound.*
accuso, *accuse.*
ædifico, *build.*
æstimo, *value.*
ambulo, *walk.*
animo, *encourage.*
appello, *call.*
apto, *fit, adapt.*
aro, *plough.*
assevĕro, *affirm.*
ausculto, *listen.*
bello, *wage war.*
cælo, *carve.*
canto, *sing.*
castĭgo, *chastise.*
celebro, *celebrate.*
celo, *conceal.*
certo, *strive.*
clamo, *cry.*
cogito, *think.*
compăro, *compare.*
concilio, *reconcile.*
concordo, *agree.*
confūto, *confute.*
considero, *consider.*
cremo, *burn.*
creo, *create.*
crucio, *torment.*
curo, *care.*
damno, *condemn.*
declāro, *declare.*
declĭno, *decline.*
decŏro, *adorn.*
delecto, *delight.*
delibero, *deliberate.*
delibo, *taste.*
delĭro, *rave.*
desidero, *desire.*

destĭno, *destine.*
devŏro, *devour.*
dissipo, *squander.*
dono, *bestow.*
dūro, *harden, last.*
edūco, *bring up.*
ejulo, *lament.*
emendo, *correct.*
equito, *ride.*
erro, *mistake.*
existĭmo, *think.*
explōro, *explore.*
fascĭno, *fascinate.*
fatĭgo, *weary.*
festĭno, *hasten.*
firmo, *strengthen.*
flagito, *demand.*
flagro, *be on fire.*
formĭdo, *dread.*
formo, *form.*
fraudo, *defraud.*
fundo, *found.*
guberno, *govern.*
gusto, *taste.*
habito, *dwell.*
hæsito, *be at a loss.*
honŏro, *honor.*
ignōro, *not know.*
impero, *command.*
impetro, *obtain.*
indāgo, *investigate.*
instauro, *renew.*
instĭgo, *push on.*
intro, *go into.*
investĭgo, *discover.*
invĭto, *invite.*
irrĭgo, *water.*
irrĭto, *provoke.*

itero, *do again.*
jacto, *boast.*
judico, *judge.*
juro, *swear.*
labōro, *labor.*
lacero, *tear.*
latro, *bark.*
laudo, *praise.*
lēgo, *depute.*
lĕvo, *relieve.*
libero, *free.*
lĭgo, *bind.*
litĭgo, *quarrel.*
loco, *place.*
lustro, *traverse.*
macto, *slay.*
maculo, *defile.*
mando, *command.*
māno, *flow.*
memoro, *mention.*
mendĭco, *beg alms.*
migro, *depart.*
ministro, *serve.*
mitĭgo, *soothe.*
monstro, *show.*
multo, *punish.*
mutilo, *maim.*
mūto, *change.*
narro, *relate.*
navigo, *sail.*
nĕgo, *deny.*
no, nato, *swim.*
nomino, *name.*
nŏto, *mark.*
nūdo, *make bare.*
numero, *count.*
nuncupo, *name.*
nuntio, *tell.*

objurgo, *scold.*
obligo, *oblige.*
obsecro, *beseech.*
obtempero, *obey.*
obturo, *stop up.*
onero, *load.*
opto, *wish.*
orbo, *deprive.*
ordino, *order.*
orno, *adorn.*
oro, *beg, pray.*
paco, *pacify.*
paro, *prepare.*
pecco, *sin.*
penetro, *penetrate.*
persevero, *persevere.*
placo, *appease.*
ploro, *bewail.*
porto, *carry.*
postulo, *demand.*
privo, *deprive.*
probo, *approve.*
procrastino, *put off.*
profligo, *overthrow.*
promulgo, *publish.*
propero, *hasten.*
propino, *drink to.*
pugno, *fight.*
pullulo, *sprout out.*
pulso, *beat.*
purgo, *cleanse.*
puto, *think.*

recupero, *regain.*
recuso, *refuse.*
redundo, *overflow.*
regno, *reign.*
reparo, *repair.*
resero, *unlock.*
rogo, *ask.*
sagino, *fatten.*
salto, *dance.*
saluto, *salute.*
sano, *heal.*
satio, *satiate.*
saucio, *wound.*
sedo, *allay.*
separo, *sever.*
servo, *keep.*
sibilo, *hiss.*
sicco, *dry.*
signo, *mark.*
simulo, *pretend.*
sollicito, *stir up.*
somnio, *dream.*
specto, *behold.*
spero, *hope.*
spiro, *breathe.*
spolio, *rob.*
spumo, *foam.*
stillo, *drop.*
stimulo, *incite.*
stipo, *surround.*
strangulo, *strangle.*
sudo, *sweat.*

suffoco, *stifle.*
supero, *overcome.*
suppedito, *afford.*
supplico, *supplicate.*
tardo, *delay.*
taxo, *rate.*
tempero, *temper.*
tento, *try.*
termino, *limit.*
titubo, *waver.*
tolero, *bear.*
trucido, *kill.*
turbo, *disturb.*
ululo, *howl.*
vacillo, *stagger.*
vaco, *be at leisure.*
vapulo, *be beaten.*
vario, *vary.*
vasto, *lay waste.*
velo, *cover.*
verbero, *flog.*
vexo, *tease.*
vibro, *brandish.*
vigilo, *watch.*
vindico, *revenge.*
violo, *violate.*
vitio, *vitiate.*
vito, *avoid.*
vitupero, *blame.*
voco, *call, name.*
volo, *fly.*
vulnero, *wound.*

The following are irregular:

do[1],	dedi,	datum,	*to give.*
sto[2],	steti,	statum,	*to stand.*
crepo[3],	crepui,	crepitum,	*to creak.*
cubo,	cubui,	cubitum,	*to lie down.*
domo,	domui,	domitum,	*to tame.*
sono†,	sonui,	sonitum,	*to sound.*
tono,	tonui,	tonitum,	*to thunder.*
veto,	vetui,	vetitum,	*to forbid.*
seco†,	secui,	sectum,	*to cut.*
mico[4],	micui,	——————	*to glitter.*
juvo†,	juvi,	jutum,	*to help.*
lavo[5],	lavi,	lotum,	*to wash.*
poto[6],	potavi,	potum,	*to drink.*

†) Part. Fut. act., *sonaturus, secaturus, juvaturus.*—[1]) Thus, *circumdo,* surround, *pessundo,* ruin, and *venundo,* sell;—but those compounded with monosyllables have -*didi,* -*ditum,* and follow the third conjugation; as, *abdo, abdidi, abditum,* hide; thus, *addo,* add; *condo,* build; *edo,* publish; *perdo,* lose, ruin; *prodo,* betray; *reddo,* return; *subdo,* subdue; *trado,* deliver over; *vendo,* sell.—*Abscondo,* conceal, has *abscondi* and *abscondidi.*—[2]) Thus, *antesto, circumsto, supersto;* but those compounded with mono-

syllables have *-stiti, -statum ;* as, *consto,* consist of, cost; *exsto,* exist; *insto,* insist; *obsto,* hinder; *resto,* remain. *Prœsto,* surpass, has *prœstiti, prœstatum* and *prœstitum,* but always *prœstaturus.—*²*)* *Discrĕpo,* differ, and *increpo,* scold, have both *ui, itum,* and *avi, atum.* ⁴*) Emĭco,* dart forth, has *ui, atum. Dimico,* fight, is regular.—⁵*)* Supine, also *lautum* and *lavatum.—*⁶*)* Supine, also *potatum.* The Partic. *potus* signifies both " having drunk" and " having been drunk."

☞ *Neco,* kill, is regular; *enĕco,* vex to death, has both *enecui, enectum,* and *enecavi, enecatum ;* but the Part. is usually *enectus.—Plico,* fold, occurs only in poetry and postclassical prose: its compounds *applico, explico,* and *implico,* have *ui, itum,* and *avi, atum.* The forms *ui, atum,* seem to be the more common.—Those derived from adjectives in *-plex,* as *supplico, duplico, multiplico,* are regular and have *avi, atum.*

The Perfect Participles *cœnatus* and *juratus* (from *cœno* and *juro*) have an active signification, " one who has dined, sworn."

§ 64.—SECOND CONJUGATION.

Perfect *-ui,* Supine *-itum.*

caleo, *am hot.*	habeo (i), *have.*	placeo, *please.*
careo, *want.*	jaceo, *lie.*	displiceo, *displease.*
coerceo, *restrain.*	liceo, *am for sale.*	præbeo, *afford.*
debeo, *owe, must.*	mereo, *merit.*	taceo (i), *am silent.*
doleo, *feel pain.*	noceo, *hurt.*	terreo, *terrify.*
exerceo, *exercise.*	pâreo, *obey.*	valeo, *am well.*

Perfect *-ui,*—no Supine.

arceo, *keep off.*	lateo, *lie hid.*	sordeo, *am filthy.*
areo, *am dry.*	madeo, *am wet.*	splendeo, *am bright.*
candeo, *glow.*	niteo, *shine.*	studeo, *am zealous.*
caneo, *am gray.*	oleo, *smell.*	stupeo, *am stunned.*
egeo, *want.*	palleo, *am pale.*	timeo, *fear.*
emineo, *stand forth.*	pateo, *am open.*	torpeo, *am torpid.*
floreo, *flourish.*	rigeo, *am stiff.*	tumeo, *am swollen.*
horreo, *shudder.*	rubeo, *am red.*	vigeo, *am vigorous.*
langueo, *languish.*	sileo, *am silent*	vireo, *am green.*

Without Perf. and Supine.

aveo, *desire.*	hebeo, *am dull.*	polleo, *am strong.*
calleo, *am skilled in.*	immineo, *threaten.*	promineo, *stand forth.*
flaveo, *am yellow.*	liveo, *am livid.*	scateo, *gush forth.*
fœteo, *smell ill.*	mœreo, *mourn.*	squaleo, *am dirty.*

The following are irregular :

doceo,	docui,	doctum,	*to teach.*
misceo¹,	miscui,	mixtum,	*to mix.*
sorbeo,	sorbui,	*-sorptum,*	*to sip* (ab-).
teneo (i),	tenui (i),	*-tentum,*	*to hold* (con-).
torreo,	torrui,	tostum,	*to roast.*
censeo²,	censui,	censum,	*to estimate.*
deleo,	delevi,	deletum,	*to destroy.*
fleo,	flevi,	fletum,	*to weep.*
neo,	nevi,	netum,	*to spin.*
-pleo,	*-plevi,*	*-pletum,*	*to fill* (re-, etc.).

aboleo,	abolevi,	abolĭtum,	*to abolish.*
adoleo,	adolevi,	adultum,	*to grow up.*
exoleo,	exolevi,	exoletum,	*to fade.*
obsoleo,	obsolevi,	obsoletum,	*to grow obsolete.*
caveo,	cavi,	cautum,	*to beware of.*
faveo,	favi,	fautum,	*to favor.*
foveo,	fovi,	fotum,	*to cherish.*
moveo,	movi,	motum,	*to move.*
voveo,	vovi,	votum,	*to vow.*
cieo[3],	civi,	cĭtum,	*to stir up.*
paveo,	pavi,	———	*to dread.*
ferveo,	fervi, -bui,	———	*to glow, boil.*
conniveo,	(connivi),	———	*to connive.*
prandeo[4],	prandi,	pransum,	*to breakfast.*
sedeo (ĭ),	sēdi,	sessum,	*to sit.*
video,	vidi,	visum,	*to see.*
mordeo,	momordi,	morsum,	*to bite.*
pendeo,	pependi,	pensum,	*to hang.*
spondeo,	spopondi,	sponsum,	*to engage.*
tondeo,	totondi,	tonsum,	*to shear.*
ardeo,	arsi,	arsum,	*to burn.*
hæreo,	hæsi,	hæsum,	*to cleave, stick.*
jubeo,	jussi,	jussum,	*to bid.*
maneo,	mansi,	mansum,	*to remain.*
mulceo,	mulsi,	mulsum,	*to stroke.*
mulgeo,	mulsi,	mulsum,	*to milk.*
rīdeo,	risi,	risum,	*to laugh.*
suādeo,	suasi,	suasum,	*to advise.*
tergeo†,	tersi,	tersum,	*to wipe.*
augeo,	auxi,	auctum,	*to increase.*
torqueo,	torsi,	tortum,	*to twist, torture.*
indulgeo,	indulsi,	indultum,	*to indulge.*
algeo,	alsi,	———	*to shiver with cold.*
fulgeo,	fulsi,	———	*to flash, shine.*
turgeo,	tursi,	———	*to swell.*
urgeo,	ursi,	———	*to press, urge.*
frigeo,	(frixi),	———	*to be cold.*
luceo,	luxi,	———	*to shine.*
lugeo,	luxi,	———	*to mourn.*
strideo†,	stridi,	———	*to hiss, creak.*

(comp. no reduplic.) — bracketed beside the *mordeo*–*tondeo* group.

---

* Also *tergo* and *strido*, of the third conjugation.—[1] Sup., also *mistum.*—[2] *Recenseo* review, has *recensum* and *recensĭtum.*—[3] Also *cio, cire, civi, cĭtum*, of the fourth conjugation; hence *accītus*, summoned; and *excītus*, called out; but *excĭtus*, in the sense of " excited."—[4] The Partic. *pransus* has an active signification, " one who has breakfasted."

§ 65.—THIRD CONJUGATION.

1. Verbs in IO, UO, and VO.

capio (ĭ),	cepi,	captum (e),	to take.
facio[1],	feci,	factum,	to do, make.
jacio (ĭ),	jeci,	jactum (e),	to throw.
⎰ —licio,	—lexi,	-lectum,	(ad, per); – but
⎱ elicio,	elicui,	elicitum,	to draw out.
—spicio,	—spexi,	-spectum,	(ad, in, etc.)
fŏdio,	fŏdi,	fossum,	to dig.
fŭgio,	fŭgi,	fugĭtum,	to flee.
cupio,	cupivi,	cupĭtum,	to desire.
rapio (ĭ),	rapui (i),	raptum (e),	to snatch.
pario†,	peperi,	partum,	to bring forth.
⎰ quatio,	———	quassum,	to shake.
⎱ —cutio,	-cussi,	-cussum,	(ex, in, etc.)
sapio (ĭ),	-ui or iví,	———	to be wise.
acuo,	acui,	acūtum,	to sharpen.
arguo,[2]	argui,	argūtum,	to convict of.
exuo,	exui,	exūtum,	to strip off.
induo,	indui,	indutum,	to put on.
imbuo,	imbui,	imbutum,	to imbue.
minuo,	minui,	minutum,	to lessen.
polluo,	pollui,	pollutum,	to defile.
luo†,	lui,	-lutum,	to atone for.
ruo†,	rui,	-rŭtum,	to rush.
spuo,	spui,	spūtum,	to spit (con).
statuo (ĭ),	statui (ĭ),	statutum (ĭ),	to establish.
suo,	sui,	sŭtum,	to sew (con).
tribuo,	tribui,	tributum,	to give, allot to.
solvo,	solvi,	solutum,	to loosen.
volvo,	volvi,	volutum,	to roll.
struo,	struxi,	structum,	to build, pile.
vivo,	vixi,	victum,	to live.
fluo,	fluxi,	———	to flow.
congruo,	congrui,	———	to agree.
ingruo,	ingrui,	———	to rush into.
metuo,	metui,	———	to fear.
-nuo[3],	-nui,	———	(ad, re, in).
pluo,	plui,	———	to rain.
sternuo,	sternui,	———	to sneeze.

2. Verbs in DO and TO.

claudo (u),	clausi (u),	clausum (u),	to shut (in, ex)
divido,	divisi,	divisum,	to divide.
lædo (ĭ),	læsi (ĭ),	læsum (ĭ),	to hurt.
lŭdo,	lusi,	lusum,	to play.
plaudo,[1]	plausi,	plausum,	to clap hands.
rado,	rasi,	rasum,	to shave, scrape.

rŏdo,	rosi,	rosum,	to gnaw (con).
trudo,	trusi,	trusum,	to push, thrust.
vādo,	-vasi,	-vasum,	to go (in, e, per).
cado (ĭ),²	cecĭdi,	casum,	to fall.
cædo (ĭ),	cecīdi,	cæsum (ĭ),	to cut.
pendo,	pependi,	pensum,	to weigh.
tendo³,	tetendi,	tens- or tent-,	to stretch.
tundo⁴,	tutudi,	tunsum,	to beat.
credo,	credidi,	creditum,	to believe.
vendo,	vendidi,	venditum,	to sell.

(the first five bracketed: compounds no reduplic.)

-cendo,	-cendi,	-censum,	(in, ad, sub).
clūdo,	cudi,	-cusum,	to stamp (ex).
ĕdo,	ēdi,	ēsum,	to eat (also comestus).
mando,	mandi,	mansum,	to chew.
scando (e),	scandi (ē),	scansum (e),	to climb (con, de).
defendo,	defendi,	defensum,	to defend.
offendo,	offendi,	offensum,	to offend.
ostendo,	ostendi,	ostensum,	to show.
prehendo,	prehendi,	prehensum,	to seize.
strido⁵,	stridi,	——	to grate.
fundo,	fudi,	fusum,	to pour.

cedo,	cessi,	cessum,	to yield.
findo,	fĭdi,	fissum,	to split.
scindo,	scĭdi,	scissum,	to cut.
frendo,	(frendui),	fres(s)um,	to gnash.
meto,	messui,	messum,	to reap.
mitto,	misi,	missum,	to send.
pando⁶,	pandi,	passum,	to spread.
peto,	petivi,	petitum,	to ask, attack.
rudo,	rudivi,	——	to bray.
sīdo⁷,	sēdi,	sessum,	to sit down.
sisto⁸,	stiti (obs.),	stătum,	to stop (trans.)
sisto,	steti,	statum,	to stop (intr.)
sterto,	stertui,	——	to snore.
verto⁹,	verti,	versum,	to turn.

3. Verbs in BO and PO.

glubo,	(glupsi),	-gluptum,	to peel.
nubo,	nupsi,	nuptum,	to marry.
scribo,	scripsi,	scriptum,	to write.
carpo (e),	carpsi (e),	carptum (e),	to pluck (ex, de).
rĕpo,	repsi,	reptum,	to creep.
scalpo,	scalpsi,	scalptum,	to carve.
sculpo,	sculpsi,	sculptum,	to chisel.
serpo,	serpsi,	serptum,	to creep.
rumpo,	rūpi,	ruptum,	to break, tear.
bibo,	bĭbi,	bibitum,	to drink (e-)
-cumbo,	-cubui,	-cubitum,	(de, in, sub)

strepo,	strepui,	——	to make a noise.
lambo,	lambi,	——	to lick.
scabo,	scabi,	——	to scratch.

4. Verbs in CO, CTO, GO, and QUO.

cingo,	cinxi,	cinctum,	to gird.
-flīgo[1],	-flixi,	-flictum,	(ad, in, con).
jungo,	junxi,	junctum,	to join.
lingo,	linxi,	linctum,	to lick up.
mungo,	-munxi,	-munctum,	to blow the nose (e-).
plango,	planxi,	planctum,	to bewail.
rego (i),	rexi,	rectum,	to rule.
pergo,	perrexi,	perrectum,	to go on.
surgo,	surrexi,	surrectum,	to rise.
sugo,	suxi,	suctum,	to suck.
tĕgo,	texi,	tectum,	to cover.
tingo,	tinxi,	tinctum,	to dip, dye.
-stinguo,	-stinxi,	-stinctum,	(ex, re, dis).
ungo,	unxi,	unctum,	to anoint.
trăho,	traxi,	tractum,	to draw.
vĕho[2],	vexi,	vectum,	to carry.
dīco,	dixi,	dictum,	to say.
duco,	duxi,	ductum,	to lead.
coquo,	coxi,	coctum,	to cook.
fingo,	finxi,	fictum,	to feign.
pingo,	pinxi,	pictum,	to paint.
stringo,	strinxi,	strictum,	to bind tight.
fīgo,	fixi,	fixum,	to fix.
flecto,	flexi,	flexum,	to bend.
necto,	nexui,	nexum,	to bind.
pecto,	pexi,	pexum,	to comb.
plecto[2],	(plexi),	(plexum),	to twist.
plecto,	——	——	to punish.
ango,	anxi,	——	to torment.
ningit,	ninxit,	——	it snows.
parco[4],	peperci,	parsum,	to spare.
pungo[5],	pupugi,	punctum,	to sting.
tango[6],	tetigi,	tactum,	to touch.
pango[7],	pepigi,	pactum,	to bargain.
⎧ pango,	panxi,	panctum,	to drive in.
⎩ -pingo,	-pēgi,	-pactum,	(con, in).
ago[8],	egi,	actum,	to drive, do.
cogo,	coegi,	coactum,	to compel.
dego,	degi,	——	to spend one's time.
frango (i),	fregi,	fractum,	to break.
lego[9],	lēgi,	lectum,	to gather, read.
ico[10],	ici,	ictum,	to strike.
vinco,	vici,	victum,	to conquer.
linquo,	-liqui,	-lictum,	to leave (de, re).

mergo,	mersi,	mersum,	to dip.
spargo (e),	sparsi (e),	sparsum (e),	to scatter (ad, in).
tergo,	tersi,	tersum,	to wipe.
vergo,	————	————	to incline.

5. Verbs in LO, MO, NO, and RO.

como,	compsi,	comptum,	to adorn.
demo,	dempsi,	demptum,	to take away
prŏmo,	prompsi,	promptum,	to bring out.
sūmo,	sumpsi,	sumptum,	to take.
temno,	-tempsi,	-temptum,	to despise (con).
alo,	alui,	al(i)tum,	to nourish.
{ -cello,	-cellui,	————	(ex, ante); – but
{ percello,	perculi,	perculsum,	to strike down.
colo,	colui,	cultum,	to till, worship.
consulo,	consului,	consultum,	to consult.
molo,	molui,	molitum,	to grind.
occulo,	occului,	occultum,	to conceal.
fremo,	fremui,	fremitum,	to growl, rage.
gemo,	gemui,	gemitum,	to groan.
tremo,	tremui,	————	to tremble.
vomo,	vomui,	vomitum,	to vomit.
gigno,	genui,	genitum,	to bring forth.
pono,	posui,	positum,	to place.
cano[1],	cecini,	cantum,	to sing.
curro[2],	cucurri,	cursum,	to run.
fallo[3],	fefelli,	————	to deceive.
pello[4],	pepuli,	pulsum,	to drive.
cerno,	crevi,	-cretum,	to decree (de).
cerno,	————	————	to see.
lino,	levi or livi,	litum,	to anoint (ob).
sino,	sivi,	situm,	to allow (de).
sperno,	sprevi,	spretum,	to despise.
sterno[5],	stravi,	stratum,	to spread out (pro).
sero,	sevi,	satum (i),	to sow (con, in).
sero[6],	-serui,	-sertum,	to join (con, in, de)
tĕro,	trivi,	tritum,	to rub (con).
furo[7]	————	————	to rage
emo (i),	emi,	emptum,	to buy (ex, per).
premo (i),	pressi,	pressum,	to press.
gero,	gessi,	gestum,	to carry.
ūro,	ussi,	ustum,	to burn (con).
verro,	verri,	versum,	to sweep.
quæro (i),	quæsivi (i),	quæsitum (i),	to seek (ex, in).
tollo,	sustuli,	sublatum,	to lift up, kill.
vello[8],	velli,	vulsum,	to pluck out.
psallo,	psalli,	————	to play on the lyre.

6. Verbs in so, sco, and xo.

texo,	texui,	textum,	to weave.
depso,	depsui,	depstum,	to knead.
pinso[1],	pinsui,	pinsum,	to pound.
vīso,	visi,	visum,	to visit (in, re).
{ arcesso or { accerso[2],	arcessivi, accersivi,	arcessītum, accersītum,	} to send for.
capesso,	capessivi,	capessitum,	to seize.
facesso,	facessi,	facessitum,	to cause.
incesso,	incessivi,	———	to attack.
lacesso,	lacessivi,	lacessītum,	to provoke.
cresco,	crevi,	cretum,	to grow.
nosco[3],	novi,	notum,	to become acquainted.
pasco,	pavi,	pastum,	to feed.
quiesco,	quievi,	quietum,	to rest.
scisco,	scivi,	scītum,	to decree.
suesco,	suevi,	suetum,	to be accustomed.
disco[4],	didici,	———	to learn.
posco,	poposci,	———	to demand.
compesco,	compescui,	———	to restrain.
glisco,	———	———	to blaze up.
hisco,	———	———	to gape.
fatisco,	———	———	to crack open.

1.—†) Part. fut. act., *pariturus, luiturus,* and *ruiturus.*—¹) The compounds with prepositions have *-ficio, -ficere, -feci, -fectum;* Imper., *-fice;* and in the passive, *-ficior, -fici, -fectus sum.* But those compounded of *cale-, tepe-, frige-, are-, made-, pate-, labe-, assue-,* and *satis-,* follow throughout in the active, *facio;* and in the passive, *fio* (§ 70).—²) *Arquiturus* is found in Sallust. "Convicted of" is usually expressed by *convictus* from *convincere.*—³) Of *abnuo, abnuiturus* is found.

2.—¹) Thus *applaudo;* but *explodo* has *explosi, explosum.*—²) Of the compounds of *cado,* only *incido, occido,* and *recido,* have the Supine, as *incasum, occasum, recasum.*—³) *Extendo* and *protendo* have in the Supine both *-sum* and *-tum;* the rest have only *-tum.*—⁴) The compounds of *tundo* have *-tudi, -tusum.*—⁵) Also *strideo, ēre.*—⁶) *Expando* has *expansum* and *expassum; dispando,* only *dispansum.*—⁷) The compounds of *sido,* as *assido, consido, insido, resido, subsido,* have *sēdi* (rarely *sīdi*), *sessum.*—⁸) Its compounds are all intransitive and have *-stiti, -stitum,* as *con-, ad-, de-, in-, ex-, ob-, per-, re-, sub-sisto.*—⁹) *Deverto,* turn in; *praeverto,* anticipate; and *reverto,* turn back, are in the Present, Imperfect, and Future, frequently used as deponents; in the past tenses, the active form is more common.

4.—¹) *Profligo,* overthrow, is of the first conjugation and has *-avi, -atum.*—²) *Vehor, vehi, vectus sum,* be carried, e. g., *curru, navi, equo. Invehor* means "to inveigh against."—³) *Plecto,* twist (the primitive of *amplector* and *complector*), scarcely ever occurs. *Plecto,* punish, is commonly used as a passive (*plector*), and has neither Perfect nor Supine.—⁴) The forms *parsi, parcitum,* are less common.—⁵) The compounds have *-punxi, -punctum,* as *compungo, dispungo, interpungo.*—⁶) The compounds of *tango* have no reduplication, as *attingo, attigi, attactum.*—⁷) *Pango,* in the sense of "to bargain," is supplied in the Present by *paciscor.*—⁸) Thus the compounds *abigo, adigo, exigo, redigo, subigo,* and *transigo. Circumago* and *perago* retain the stem-vowel a. *Prodigo,* "squander," has *prodegi* without Supine. *Ambigo,* "doubt," and *satago,* "be busy," want both the Perfect and Supine.—⁹) Thus *eligo, colligo, deligo. Perlego, praelego,* and *relego,* retain the stem-vowel e. *Diligo,* love; *intelligo,* understand; and *negligo*, neglect, have *-exi, -ectum.*—[10]) *Ico* occurs in the past forms only : *ici, iceram, icisse, ictus esse.* Of the Present, the third person sing. only is found, the rest being supplied by *ferio, -ire.*

5.—[1]) *Concino* has *concinui* without Supine. The other compounds, *accino, præcino, succino,* etc., very rarely occur and generally want both the Perf. and Sup.-.—[2]) The compounds sometimes retain, but oftener reject the reduplication.—[3]) *Refello,* refute, has *refelli* without Supine.—[4]) The compounds drop the reduplication, as *repello, repuli, repulsum.*—[5]) Thus *consterno,* bestrew; but *consterno,* "alarm," is of the 1st conj. and has *consternavi, consternatum.*—[6]) *Desero, resero,* and *dissero,* have always *-serui, -sertum.*—[7]) *Furo,* in the past tenses, is supplied by the verb *insanio.*—[8]) *Convello, revello,* and *divello,* have only *-velli;* but *avello* and *evello* have both *-velli* and *-vulsi.*

6.—[1]) Also, *pinsi, pinsitum* and *pistum.*—[2]) The Infin. pass. is sometimes *accersiri* instead of *accersi;* thus *lacessiri* for *lacessi.*—[3]) Thus *ignosco,* pardon. But *agnosco, cognosco,* and *recognosco,* have *-ovi, -itum. Dignosco* and *internosco* have no Supine.— [4]) *Disciturus* is found in Appuleius.

INCEPTIVES.

§ 66.—*Inceptive* or *inchoative* verbs are such as denote a becoming, or beginning of the act or condition expressed by the primitive. They end in *sco* and follow the third conjugation.

There are two kinds of inceptives,—*verbal* and *nominal.*—*Verbal-inceptives* are derived from verbs, by adding the syllable *-co* to the 2d sing. of the Indic. Pres. act.; they generally take the Perf. and Sup. of their primitives.— *Nominal-inceptives* are derived from nouns, and are, for the most part, without Perfect and Supine.

Verbal-Inceptives.

adolesco,	adolevi,	adultum,	to grow up.
coalesco,	coalui,	coalĭtum,	to grow together.
concupisco,	concupivi,	concupĭtum,	to desire strongly.
convalesco,	convalui,	convalĭtum,	to recover health.
exardesco,	exarsi,	exarsum,	to become inflamed.
inveterasco,	inveteravi,	inveteratum,	to grow old.
obdormisco,	obdormivi,	obdormĭtum,	to fall asleep.
obsolesco,	obsolevi,	obsoletum,	to become obsolete.
revivisco.	revixi,	revictum,	to recover life.

albesco,	ui,	to grow white.		ingemisco,	ui,	to groan.
aresco,	ui,	to grow dry.		intumesco,	ui,	to swell up.
canesco,	ui,	to become gray.		irraucesco,	si,	to become hoarse.
contipesco,	ui,	to become still.		languesco,	ui,	to become weak.
contremisco,	ui,	to tremble.		liquesco,	cui,	to melt away.
defervesco,	bui,	to cool down.		madesco,	ui,	to become wet.
delitesco,	ui,	to lie hid.		marcesco,	ui,	to pine away.
effervesco,	bui,	to boil up.		putresco,	ui,	to moulder.
erubesco,	ui,	to blush.		refrigesco,	xi,	to grow cold.
excandesco,	ui,	to take fire.		resipisco,	ui,	to become reasonable.
exhorresco,	ui,	to shudder.		senesco (con-),	ui,	to grow old.
expallesco,	ui,	to turn pale.		tepesco,	ui,	to grow tepid.
extimesco,	ui,	to fear greatly.		obstupesco,	ui,	to become amazed.
illucesco,	xi,	to grow light.		perhorresco,	ui,	to shudder.
incalesco,	ui,	to grow hot.		viresco (re-),	ui,	to become green.

Nominal-Inceptives.

ditesco (dives), *to become rich.*
dulcesco (dulcis), *to become sweet.*
ignesco (ignis), *to take fire.*
ingravesco (gravis), *to increase.*

mitesco (mitis), *to become mild.*
mollesco (mollis), *to grow soft.*
pinguesco (pinguis), *to grow fat.*
repuerasco (puer), *to become childish.*

The following have -ui in the Perfect.

consanesco (sanus), *to be healed.*
evanesco (vanus), *to vanish.*
innotesco (notus), *to become known.*
maturesco (maturus), *to grow ripe.*

obduresco (durus), *to grow hard.*
obmutesco (mutus), *to become dumb.*
obsurdesco (surdus), *to become deaf.*
percrebesco (creber), *to spread* (intr.).

§ 67.—FOURTH CONJUGATION.

Verbs of the fourth conjugation have *ivi, ītum;* as *audio, audivi, audītum.* Thus:

condio, *season.*
custōdio, *watch.*
defīnio, *define.*
dormio, *sleep.*
erūdio, *instruct.*
esūrio, *be hungry.*
expēdio, *extricate.*
finio, *finish.*
gestio, *exult.*

impēdio, *hinder.*
irrētio, *ensnare.*
lenio, *calm.*
mollio, *soften.*
mugio, *bellow.*
munio, *fortify.*
nutrio, *nourish.*
obēdio, *obey.*
polio, *polish.*

punio, *punish.*
redīmio, *crown.*
scio, *know.*
servio, *serve.*
sitio, *thirst.*
sopio, *lull asleep.*
stabīlio, *establish.*
tinnio, *tinkle.*
vestio, *clothe.*

The following are irregular:

fulcio,	fulsi,	fultum,	*to prop.*
haurio,[1]	hausi,	haustum,	*to draw.*
sancio,	sanxi,	sanc(ī)tum,	*to sanction.*
sarcio,	sarsi,	sartum,	*to patch.*
sentio,	sensi,	sensum,	*to feel.*
sepio,	sepsi,	septum,	*to hedge in.*
vincio,	vinxi,	vinctum,	*to bind.*
amicio,	(-xi, -cui),	amictum,	*to clothe.*
aperio,	aperui,	apertum,	*to open.*
operio,	operui,	opertum,	*to cover.*
comperio,	comperi,	compertum,	*to experience.*
reperio,	reperi,	repertum,	*to find.*
salio,[2]	salui,	———	*to spring.*
sepelio,	sepelivi,	sepultum,	*to bury.*
vĕnio,	vēni,	ventum,	*to come.*

[1]) Partic. Fut. *hausurus* and *hausturus.*—[2]) Thus *desilio, exilio, insilio, prosilio.* The Perfect-form *-silui* is far better than the form *-silii. Salio,* in the sense of " to salt," has *salitum* without a Perfect.

§ 68.—Deponent Verbs.

1. Deponents of the first conjugation.

abominor, *abhor.*
adûlor†, *flatter.*
adversor, *oppose.*
æmulor, *rival.*
altercor, *quarrel.*
aquor, *fetch water.*
arbitror†, *think.*
argumentor, *prove.*
aspernor, *despise.*
assentor, *agree, flatter.*
aucŭpor, *catch birds.*
auguror, *foretell.*
auspicor, *forebode.*
auxilior, *help.*
aversor, *dislike.*
calumnior, *slander.*
cavillor, *ridicule.*
comitor, *accompany.*
concionor, *harangue.*
conor, *attempt.*
consilior, *advise.*
conspĭcor, *behold.*
contemplor, *view.*
convicior, *revile.*
criminor†, *accuse.*
cunctor, *delay.*
dedignor, *disdain.*
deprecor, *deprecate.*
despicor, *despise.*
dignor†, *think worthy.*
dominor, *rule.*
epulor, *feast.*
exsecror, *curse.*
fabricor (-o), *form.*
fabulor, *talk.*
famulor, *serve.*
ferior, *keep holiday.*
fluctuor (-o), *fluctuate.*
frumentor, *fetch corn.*
frustror, *disappoint.*
fûror, *steal.*
glorior, *boast.*

grassor, *to rage.*
gratificor, *gratify.*
gratulor, *congratulate.*
heluor, *gormandize.*
hortor, *exhort.*
imaginor, *imagine.*
imitor, *imitate.*
imprecor, *imprecate.*
indignor, *be indignant.*
infitior, *deny.*
insector, *pursue.*
insidior, *plot.*
interprĕtor, *expound.*
jaculor, *dart.*
jocor, *jest.*
lætor, *rejoice.*
lamentor, *lament.*
latrocĭnor, *rob.*
lenocĭnor, *cajole.*
lignor, *fetch wood.*
lucror, *gain.*
luctor, *wrestle.*
machinor, *devise.*
medicor, *heal.*
meditor, *meditate.*
mercor, *purchase.*
mĭnor (con-), *threaten.*
miseror, *pity.*
moderor, *temper.*
morigeror, *comply.*
moror, *delay.*
mutuor, *borrow.*
negotior, *traffic.*
nidulor, *build a nest.*
nugor, *trifle.*
nundĭnor, *trade, buy.*
obtestor, *beseech.*
oderor, *smell out.*
ominor, *forebode.*
opĭnor, *think.*
opitulor, *bring aid.*
otior, *be at leisure.*

pabulor, *forage.*
palor, *straggle.*
patrocĭnor, *patronise.*
percontor, *ask.*
peregrĭnor, *go abroad.*
periclĭtor, *attempt.*
piscor, *fish.*
populor (-o), *lay waste*
prædor, *plunder.*
præstolor, *wait for.*
precor, *pray.*
prœlior, *fight.*
ratiocĭnor, *reason.*
recordor, *remember.*
refrăgor, *oppose.*
remuneror, *reward.*
rixor, *quarrel.*
rusticor, *rusticate.*
sciscitor, *inquire.*
scitor, *ask, inquire.*
scrûtor (per-), *search.*
sector, *follow.*
sōlor (con-), *comfort.*
spatior, *walk about.*
speculor, *spy out.*
stipulor, *stipulate.*
stomaclior, *be indignant.*
suffrăgor, *assent to.*
suspicor, *suspect.*
tergiversor, *shuffle.*
testificor, *attest.*
testor, *bear witness.*
tricor, *play tricks.*
tristor, *be sad.*
tutor, *protect.*
văgor (e-), *wander.*
vaticĭnor, *foretell.*
veneror, *venerate.*
venor, *hunt.*
verecundor, *be shy.*
versor, *dwell, be in.*
vociferor, *vociferate.*

† Adulor, arbitror, criminor, and especially dignor, are used also as passives.

2. Deponents of the second conjugation.

fateor (i),	fassus (e) sum.	*to acknowledge.*
liceor,	licitus sum,	*to bid on goods.*
medeor[1],	———	*to heal.*

mereor,	meritus sum,	to *deserve.*
misereor,	miser(i)tus sum,	to *pity.*
polliceor,	pollicitus sum,	to *promise.*
reor,	ràtus sum,	· to *think.*
tueor,	tuitus sum,	to *protect.*
vereor.	veritus sum,	to *fear.*

3. Deponents of the third conjugation.

adipiscor,	adeptus sum,	to *obtain.*
amplector,	amplexus sum,	to *embrace.*
comminiscor,	commentus sum,	to *devise.*
expergiscor,	experrectus sum,	to *become awake.*
fruor†,	fructus *or* fruitus s.,	to *enjoy.*
fungor,	functus sum,	to *perform.*
gradior (ĕ),	gressus sum,	to *proceed.*
invĕhor,	invectus sum,	to *inveigh against.*
irascor,[2]	—— ——	to *grow angry.*
làbor,	lapsus sum,	to *fall* (e, re).
lŏquor,	locutus sum,	to *speak* (ad, con).
morior†,	mortuus sum, -	to *die.*
nanciscor,	na(n)ctus sum,	to *obtain.*
nascor†,	natus sum,	to *be born.*
nītor,	nisus *or* nixus s.,	to *strive, rely upon.*
obliviscor,	oblitus sum,	to *forget.*
paciscor,	pactus sum,	to *make a bargain.*
pascor,	pastus sum,	to *feed* (intr.).
pătior (ĕ),	passus (e) sum,	to *suffer* (per).
proficiscor,	profectus sum,	to *start, travel.*
queror,	questus sum,	to *complain.*
reminiscor,[3]	———	to *remember.*
ringor,	———	to *grin.*
sĕquor,	secutus sum,	to *follow.*
ulciscor,	ultus sum,	to *revenge.*
ūtor,	usus sum,	to *use* (ab).
vescor[4],	———	to *eat, feed on.*

4. Deponents of the fourth conjugation.

assentior,	assensus sum,	to *assent.*
experior,	expertus sum,	to *try, experience.*
mentior,	mentītus sum,	to *lie.*
metior,	mensus sum,	to *measure.*
opperior,	opper(ī)tus sum,	to *wait for.*
ordior,	orsus sum,	to *begin.*
orior[5],	ortus sum,	to *rise ;* P. oriturus.

---

†) *Fruiturus, moriturus, nasciturus.*—[1]) Perf. supplied from *medicor.*—[2]) Perf. supplied from *succenseo. Iratus sum* means simply " I am angry."—[3]) Perf. supplied from *recordor.*—[4]) Perf. supplied from *edo.*—[5]) The Present Indic. of *orior, oriri,* follows the

third conjugation, as *orior, orēris* (and *orīris*), *orĭtur; orĭmur, orimini, oriuntur.* In the Imperfect Subj. we find both *orĕrer* and *orīrer.* Thus *coorior* and *exorior;* but *adorior* is regular, and follows throughout *audior.*

Exercises on the preceding irregular Perfects and Supines.

Selected chiefly from Kühner.)

1.

Romani multas gentes ac nationes armis *domuerunt.*—Non *dedit* beneficium qui invītus profuit.—Nulla pestīs humano generi pluris *stetit* quam ira.—Dux milites vehementer *increpuit.*—Augustus carmina Virgilii cremari *vetuit.*—Non solum fortuna, sed etiam tua industria te in hoc negotio *adjuvit.*—Tota urbs vocibus civium de victoria ex hostibus reportata exultantium *percrebuit.*—Nisi libidines *resecueris,* frustra beate vivere studebis.—Hostes obsides, quos Cæsar imperaverat, *dederunt.*—Agricolæ frumenta *desecta* in horrea congerunt.—Si fortuna nos *adjuverit,* splendidam ex hoste victoriam reportabimus.—Dubitandum non est quin Hannibal ceteris imperatoribus prudentia multo *præstiterit.* Urbs tota clamore militum *personuit.*

2.

Deus bonis omnibus mundum *implevit.*—Cras in horto *pransuri* sumus.—Velim mihi dicas quis te Grammaticam *docuerit.*—Gaudeo quod semper mihi meisque studiis *favisti.*—Dici nequit quot pericula, quot miserias, milites in itinere *sustinuerint.*—Cicero omnes artes a Minerva *edoctus* est.—Quo magis *indulseris* dolori, eo intolerabilior erit.—Sicario sicam de manibus *extorserunt.*—Dic mihi quare *fleveris.*—*Spopondistine* pro amico? *Spopondi.*—Dux mitibus verbis *excitos* militum animos *permulsit.*—Tu me tot ac tantis *auxisti* beneficiis, quanta nunquam vel sperare *ausus* sum.—Virgilii carmina discipulorum animos mirifice *permulserunt.*—Multa puer *sustinuit,* sudavit et *alsit.*—Quis est cui semper *arriserit* fortuna?—Quomodo in viro latebit scintilla ingenii, quæ iam in puero *eluxit?*—Multi si *tacuissent,* famam sapientiæ *obtinuissent.*

3.

Xerxes, cum Græciam *subacturus* esset, ingentem exercitum *coegit.*—Milites ne infantibus quidem *pepercerunt.*—Ubi victoria *amissa* est, nihil refert quot in prœlio *cæsi* aut in fuga *capti* sint.—Male *parta* male dilabuntur.—Omnia longe .ateque telis, armis, cadaveribus *constrata* erant.—Quare consilium meum *sprevisti?*—Cives belli calamitatibus *confecti* pacem *expoposcerunt.*—Cuique nostrum amor vitæ est *insitus.*—Tria bella atrocissima *gesta* sunt inter Romanos et Carthaginienses.—Alexander tot regum et populorum victor, tandem iræ *succubuit.*—Dediscet animus sero, quod *didicerit* diu.—Vix *credideris* quantopere garrulus iste homo me garriendo enecuerit.—Socratis responso sic judices *exarserunt,* ut capitis hominem innocentissimum condemnarent.—Explorator ad castra hostium *accessit* ibique magnam partem diei *consumpsit.*—Barbari vallo et fossa hiberna *cinxerunt.*

4.

Homines artes innumeras docente natura *repererunt.*—Omnia superiora damna hac una victoria *sarta* sunt.—Regis sepulchro hæc verba inscripta sunt: Probe vixit, improbos *vinxit,* hostes vicit.—*Septum* undique et vestitum vepri-

bus et dumetis indagavi sepulchrum.—Rex rempublicam labefactatam sua
virtute *fulsit.*—Quo quis affluentius voluptates undique *hauserit,* eo gravius
ardentiusque sitiet.—Homines urbes mœnibus *sepserunt.*—Quis est qui nunquam
Dei munificentiam *senserit ?*—Continuis bellis reipublicæ opes *exhaustæ* sunt.—
Vide quibus præsidiis philosophiæ *septus* sim.—Bellum gravissimum Pompeii
adventu sublatum ac *sepultum* est.—Deus oculos, membranis tenuissimis vesti-
vit et *sepsit.*—Sene curiam ingrediente *surrexerunt* omnes capitaque *aperuerunt.*

5.

Venio meum præsidium tibi *polliciturus.*—Si cunctam terram *intuitus* eris, de
providentia divina non dubitabis.—Quicunque culpas suas *fassi* erant, veniam
impetrarunt.—Cicero præclare de republica *meritus* est.—Quis dubitat quin
aliquando *moriturus* sit?—Cives, cum hostibus *pacti,* pace *fruiti* sunt.—Simu-
latque *experrecti* sumus, visa in somnio contemnimus.—Dic mihi quo et quando
frater tuus *profecturus* sit.—Plura ad te scribam cum plus otii *nactus* ero.—
Senectutem ut adipiscantur, omnes optant : eandem accusant *adepti.*—Avida
est periculi virtus, et quo tendat, non quid *passura* sit, cogitat.—Non adeo ini-
qua fortuna *usi* sumus, ut dignitatis nostræ simus *obliti.*—Dum urbem oppugnare
adorīmur, hostes a tergo nos *aggressi* sunt.

6.

Favemus iis qui eādem quibus ipsi *perfuncti* sumus, pericula ingrediuntur.—
Nihil est virtute amabilius, quam cum *adepti* eritis, Deo bonisque hominibus
cari eritis.—Socrates paulo ante mortem cum amicis de immortalitate animi
collocutus esse dicitur.—Cæsar militum virtuti confisus, sine mora hostium exercitum *adortus* est.—Ridiculi sunt qui quod ipsi *experti* non sunt, id docent
ceteros.—*Coorta* sæva tempestate, omnes nautas ingens pavor occupavit.—
Unde *exorsa* est, ibidem terminetur oratio.—Ex decemvirorum injustitia subito
exorta est maxima perturbatio.—Solem *oriturum* cum maxima voluptate spec-
tamus.—Multi multas variasque terras *emensi,* multas sæpe res prodigiosas
ementiti sunt.—Huic sententiæ dubito num multi *assensuri* sint.

IRREGULAR VERBS.

§ 69.—Irregular verbs are such as in some of their tenses or persons
deviate from the ordinary form of regular verbs. They are, besides the
verb *sum,*

Possum (potis sum), potui, posse, *to be able (can).*
Volo, volui, velle, *to wish, to be willing.*
Nolo (— non volo), nolui, nolle, *to be unwilling.*
Malo (— magis volo), malui, malle, *to wish rather.*
Edo, ĕdi. esum, edere, *to eat.*
Eo, ivi, itum, ire, *to go.*
Fero, tuli, latum, ferre, *to carry, bring.*
Fio, factus sum, fieri, *to be made, become, happen.*

§ 70.—IRREGULAR VERBS.

INDICATIVE.

Prs.	Possum	Volo	Nolo	Malo
	potes	vis	non vis	mavis
	potest	vult	non vult	mavult
	possŭmus	volŭmus	nolŭmus	malŭmus
	potestis	vultis	non vultis	mavultis
	possunt	volunt	nolunt	malunt
Imp.	poteram	volebam	nolebam	malebam
Fut.	potero	volam, es	nolam, es	malam, es
Prf.	potui	volui	nolui	malui
Plp.	potueram	volueram	nolueram	malueram
F.-Pf.	potuero	voluero	noluero	maluero

SUBJUNCTIVE.

Prs.	possim	velim	nolim	malim
	possis	velis	nolis	malis
	possit	velit	nolit	malit
	possĭmus	velīmus	nolīmus	malīmus
	possitis	velitis	nolitis	malitis
	possint	velint	nolint	malint
Imp.	possem	vellem	nollem	mallem
Prf.	potuerim	voluerim	noluerim	maluerim
Plp.	potuissem	voluissem	noluissem	maluissem

IMPERATIVE.

Sing.	———	———	noli, ito	———
Plur.	———	———	nolite, unto	———

INFINITIVE.

Prs.	posse	velle	nolle	malle
Prf.	potuisse	voluisse	noluisse	maluisse
Ptc.	potens (adj.)	volens	nolens	———
Ger.	———	volendi, do	nolendi	———

Edo, edi, esum, edere, *to eat.*

The verb *edo* has, besides its own regular forms, several others resembling those forms of the verb *sum,* which begin with *es;* as,

INFINITIVE.

edere *or* esse.

INDICATIVE.	SUBJUNCTIVE.	IMPERATIVE.
edo	ederem *or* essem	ede *or* ēs
edis *or* ēs	ederes *or* esses	edito *or* esto
edit *or* est	ederet *or* essent	edito *or* esto
edimus	ederemus *or* essemus	edite *or* este
editis *or* estis	ederetis *or* essetis	editote *or* estote
edunt	ederent *or* essent	edunto

IRREGULAR VERBS.

INDICATIVE.

PRS.	Eo	Fero	Feror	Fio
	is	fers	ferris	fis
	it	fert	fertur	fit
	imus	ferĭmus	ferĭmur	fimus
	itis	fertis	ferimini	fitis
	eunt	ferunt	feruntur	fiunt

IMP.	ibam	ferebam	ferebar	fiebam
FUT.	ibo	feram, es	ferar, ĕris	fiam, es
PRF.	ivi	tuli	latus sum	factus sum
PLP.	iveram	tuleram	latus eram	factus eram
F.-PF.	ivero	tulero	latus ero	factus ero

SUBJUNCTIVE.

PRS.	eam	feram	ferar	fiam
	eas	feras	feraris	fias
	eat	ferat	feratur	fiat
	eamus	feramus	feramur	fiamus
	eatis	feratis	feramini	fiatis
	eant	ferant	ferantur	fiant

IMP.	irem	ferrem	ferrer	fierem
FUT.	iturus sim	laturus sim	——	——
PRF.	iverim	tulerim	latus sim	factus sim
PLP.	ivissem	tulissem	latus essem	factus essem

IMPERATIVE.

Sing.	i, ito	fer, ferto	ferre, fertor	fi
	ito	ferto	fertor	——
Plur.	ite, itote	ferte, fertote	ferimini	fite
	eunto	ferunto	feruntor	——

INFINITIVE.

PRS.	ire	ferre	ferri	fieri
PRF.	ivisse	tulisse	latus esse	factus esse
FUT.	iturus esse	laturus esse	latum iri	factum iri

PARTICIPLES.

PRS.	iens, euntis	ferens	PRF. latus	PRF. factus
FUT.	iturus	laturus	— ferendus	— faciendus

GER. and SUP.: eundi, etc. ; ferendi, etc. ;—itum, latum, factum, etc.

The following compounds of *fero* require special attention:

aufero,	abstuli,	ablatum,	*to take away.*
effero,	extuli,	elatum,	*to carry forth.*
differo,	distuli,	dilatum,	*to delay.*

☞ *Suffero,* "endure," and *differo* in the sense of "differ," have neither Perfect nor Supine.

NOTE 1.—Of the passive of *edo*, *estur* sometimes occurs instead of *editur*, and *essetur*, instead of *ederetur*.—The compounds *comĕdo* and *exĕdo*, besides their own regular forms, take likewise those of *sum* that begin with *es*; as, *comesse*, *exesse*, for *comedere*, *exedere*; *comest*, *exest*, for *comedit*, *exedit*, etc.

NOTE 2.—The verb *eo*, in the passive, exists only as an impersonal. But some of its compounds acquire a transitive meaning, and may, accordingly, have a personal passive; e. g., *adeor* (from *adeo*, I approach), *adiris*, *aditur*, *adīmur*, *adimini*, *adeuntur*; Subj. *adear*; Impf. *adibar*, *adirer*; Fut. *adibor*, *adiberis*, *adibitur*; Imper. *adire*, *aditor*, *adimini*, *adeuntor*; Part. *adītus*, *adeundus*.

The compounds of *eo* generally drop *v* in the past tenses, as *abii*, *rediisti*, *obiit*, *subierunt*, *redierat*, *periisse*. Before the letter *s*, the whole syllable *vi* may be dropped, as *inisti*, *abissem*, *subisse*, for *inivisti*, *abivissem*, *subivisse*.

NOTE 3.—*Veneo* (venum eo), "I go to sale" or "I am sold" (Perf. *venii*, *venierim*, *venieram*, etc.), wants the Imperative, the Supines, Gerunds, and Participles.

Ambio, "I go about,"—"sue for an office," is a regular verb of the fourth conjugation; hence the forms *ambiunt*, *ambiam*, *ambiebam*, *ambiet*, *ambiens* (*-ientis*), *ambiendum*;—though the forms *ambibam*, *ambibo*, are occasionally found also.

Like *eo* are conjugated *queo*, I can, and *nequeo*, I cannot; but most of their forms, the Present Indic. and Subj. excepted, very seldom occur.

NOTE 4.—*Fio* (the Greek φύω) is used as a passive of *facio*, in the Present, Imperfect, and Future Indic.; in the Present and Imperf. Subj.; in the Imperative, and in the Present Infinitive. Such forms as *facior*, *faciuntur*, *faciatur*, *faceretur*, *faciebantur*, and the like, are, therefore, carefully to be avoided.

DEFECTIVE VERBS.

§ 71.—Defective verbs are such as are used only in some particular tenses, numbers, and persons; as, 1. *odi*, I hate; *memini*, I remember; *novi*, I know; *cœpi*, I begin, and I have begun; 2. *aīo*, I affirm, say yes (opposed to *nego*); *inquam*, I say; *fari* (poet.), to speak; *salve*, *ave*, hail, welcome, good-day; and *vale*, farewell.

1.

	INDICATIVE.			
Prf.	odi	memini	novi	cœpi
Plp.	oderam	memineram	noveram	cœperam
F-Pf.	odero	meminero	novero	cœpero

	SUBJUNCTIVE.			
Prf.	oderim	meminerim	noverim	cœperim
Plp.	odissem	meminissem	novissem	cœpissem
Fut.	osurus sim	——	——	cœpturus sim

	INFINITIVE.			
Prf.	odisse	meminisse	novisse	cœpisse
Fut.	osurus esse	——	——	cœpturus esse

	PARTICIPLES.			
Prf.	osus (obsol.)	——	——	cœptus (pass.)
Fut.	osurus			cœpturus

NOTE 1.—*Odi* and *memini* have in the Perfect the meaning of the Present; in the Pluperfect, the meaning of the Imperfect; and in the Fut.-Perfect, the meaning of the simple Future.

This is the case also with *novi* (the Perfect of *nosco*, " I am acquainted"); as, *novi*, I know ; *noveram*, I knew ; *novero*, I shall know; *novisse*, to know. The Partic. *notus* is used adjectively.—*Novi* generally drops *vi* and *ve* before *r* and *s*, as *nosti*, *norunt*, *noram*, *nosse*, etc., instead of *novisti*, *noverunt*, *noveram*, *novisse*.

NOTE 2.—*Cœpi* means both " I begin" and " I have begun." The Partic. *cœptus* has always a passive meaning, " begun."—With an Infinitive pass., *cœptus sum* is generally used instead of *cœpi ;* as, *Tyrus oppugnari cœpta est*, for *cœpit ; bello premi sunt cœpti*, for *cœperunt ; de republica consuli cœpti sumus*, for *cœpimus.*

NOTE 3.—The Imperative of *odi* and *novi* is supplied by the Subjunctive ; e. g., *ne oderis*, " do not hate ;" *noverint*, " let them know." *Memini* has *memento*, *mementote*, along with the Subjunctive forms *memineris* and *minineritis*, " remember," *me minerit* and *meminerint*, " let him (them) remember."

NOTE 4.—The obsolete *osus* and its compounds *exosus* and *perosus* have an active meaning, " one who hates or has hated ;" hence, *osus sum*, I have hated.

Prs. IND.	Aio,	ais,	ait,	——	——	aiunt.
SUB.	——	aias,	aiat,	——	——	aiant.
Imp. IND.	aiebam,	aiebas,	aiebat,	aiebamus,	aiebatis,	aiebant.

Prs. IND.	Inquam,	inquis,	inquit,	inquīmus,	inquitis,	inquiunt.
SUB.	——	inquias,	inquiat,	——	inquiatis,	inquiant.
Imp. IND.	inquiebat,	*Prf.* inquisti, inquit.		*Fut.* inquies,		inquiet.

| *Prs.* IND. | Fatur, fantur. | *Fut.* fabor, fabitur. | *Imper.* fare. | *Infn.* fari. |
| PARTIC. | (fans) fantis, i, em, e, and fatus. | GER. fandi, fando. | | |

| IMPER. S. | Ave, -eto ; | Salve (salvebis), -eto ; | Vale (valebis), -eto. |
| P. | avete, | salvete, valete. | INF. avere, salvere, valere. |

NOTE 5.—*Inquit* and *ait*, " says he" or " said he," are placed after one or more words of a quotation. The Imperative forms *inque* and *inquito* are found in Terence and Plautus.

NOTE 6.—*Ain' ?* " what ?" " do you really think so ?" is used instead of *aisne*, in the same way as *nostin'* and *viden'* are used instead of *nostine* and *videsne*.

To the defective verbs belong also *quœso*, *quœsumus*, I (we) beseech ; *ausim*, *ausit*, I (he) might venture ; *faxit*, *faxint*, may he (they) grant; e. g., *faxint dii immortales ;* and *apage*, away, begone.

IMPERSONAL VERBS.

§ 72. There are two kinds of impersonal verbs ; viz., Impersonals, strictly speaking—and Impersonals, in a wider sense.

Impersonals strictly speaking are those of which but the third person singular is used, and which do not admit any nominative either of person or thing. Such are the following six :

| piget, *it grieves.* | tædet, *it disgusts.* | pœnitet, *it repents.* |
| pudet, *it shames.* | miseret, *it pities.* | oportet, *it behooves.* |

Impersonals in a wider sense are those which sometimes admit a nominative of a person or thing (at least that of a neuter pronoun) and consequently may also be used in the third person plural,—or which are used as impersonals only in a particular meaning. Of this kind are :

tonat, *it thunders.*		stat, *it is resolved.*
fulminat, *it lightens.*	decet, *it becomes.*	constat, *it is known.*
pluit, *it rains.*	dedecet, *it is unbecoming.*	præstat, *it is better.*
ningit, *it snows.*	libet, *it pleases.*	patet, *it is plain.*
gelat, *it freezes.*	licet, *it is allowed.*	appâret, *it appears.*
grandinat, *it hails.*	liquet, *it is clear.*	refert, *it concerns.*
lucescit, *it dawns.*		interest, *it concerns.*

The verbs *tonat, fulminat,* etc., and a few others that denote the state of the weather, sometimes admit of a personal subject, such as *Deus, Jupiter, cælum.*

The verbs *decet, dedecet,* etc., often admit a nominative of a thing, especially that of a neuter pronoun, and may accordingly be used also in the plural ; as, *modestia pueros decet—parvum parva decent—non omnibus omnia licent.*

The verbs *stat, constat, præstat,* etc., along with *restat,* it remains ; *juvat, delectat,* it delights ; *fallit, fugit, præterit,* it escapes ; *conducit, convenit, expedit,* it suits, is useful ; *accidit, contingit, evenit,* it happens,—and some more, are used as impersonals in that particular meaning only, being otherwise personal verbs. Most of them, likewise, admit a nominative of a thing, and may accordingly be used in the plural ; as, *non multa effugiunt—talia non omnibus contingunt—non omnia expediunt.*

☞ *Contingit* is said of good events ; *accidit,* generally, of bad ones ; and *evenit,* of both good and bad.

§ 73.—Impersonal verbs are inflected through all the moods and tenses, in the following manner :

pudet,	pudebat,	puduit,	puduerat,	pudebit,	pudere.
pudeat,	puderet,	puduerit,	puduisset,	———	puduisse.

Most of them may in some way be inflected, even through the various persons and numbers of each tense and mood, by adding the accusatives *me, te, illum, nos, vos, illos,* or the datives *mihi, tibi, illi, nobis, vobis, illis,*—respectively ; thus :

pudet me, *I am ashamed*	licet mihi, *I am allowed*
pudet te, *thou art ashamed*	licet tibi, *thou art allowed*
pudet eum, *he is ashamed*	licet ei, *he is allowed*
pudet nos, *we are ashamed*	licet nobis, *we are allowed*
pudet vos, *ye are ashamed*	licet vobis, *ye are allowed*
pudet eos, *they are ashamed*	licet eis, *they are allowed.*

NOTE 1.—Impersonal verbs, as such, are generally without Imperatives, Gerunds, Supines, and Participles. Of *licet, libet, pœnitet, piget,* and *pudet,* however, we have *libens, licens, licitus, pœnitens, pœnitendus, pigendus,* and *pudendus.*—The place of the Imperative is supplied by the Subjunctive ; e. g., *pudeat te* or *vos,* " be ashamed."

NOTE 2.—Any intransitive verb, when used passively, becomes impersonal, that is, it admits only of the third person singular. In translating such verbs we generally use such a word as *one, they, people, we ;* e. g., *itur,* they go ; *curritur,* people run ; *ambulatum est satis,* we have walked enough.

Even transitive verbs may be used impersonally in the third person sing. passive ; as, *scribitur,* they write ; *bibitur,* they drink ; *pie creditur,* it is piously believed ; *actum est,* it is over.

§ 74.—LIST OF VERBS

which are entirely or nearly alike, but differ from one another in conjugation, sense, or pronunciation :

appello, 1. *call*	appello, 8. *land*
collĭgo, 1. *tie together*	collĭgo, 8. *collect*
compello, 1. *address*	compello, 8. *force*
consterno, 1. *alarm*	consterno, 8. *bestrew*
delĭgo, 1. *tie, bind*	delĭgo, 8. *choose*
dĭco, 1. *dedicate*	dĭco, 8. *say*
edŭco, 1. *educate*	edŭco, 8. *lead forth*
fundo, 1. *found*	fundo, 8. *pour out*
indĭco, 1. *indicate*	indĭco, 8. *proclaim*
lĕgo, 1. *send*	lĕgo, 8. *read*
mando, 1. *order*	mando, 8. *chew*
prædĭco, 1. *proclaim*	prædĭco, 8. *foretell*
relĕgo, 1. *send away*	relĕgo, 8. *read over*
vŏlo, 1. *fly*	vŏlo, velle, *be willing*
concĭdo, 8. *fall down*	concĭdo, 8. *cut to pieces*
excĭdo, 8. *fall out*	excĭdo, 8. *cut out*
incĭdo, 8. *fall into*	incĭdo, 8. *cut into*
occĭdo, 8. *fall, set*	occĭdo, 8. *kill*
cælo, 1. *carve*	celo, 1. *conceal*
fugo, 1. *put to flight*	fugio, 8. *flee*
măno, 1. *flow*	maneo, 2. *remain*
permăno, 1. *flow through*	permăneo, 2. *remain*
miseror, 1. *pity*	misereor, 2. *pity*
moror, 1. *delay*	morior, 8. *die*
jaceo, 2. *lie down*	jacio, 8. *throw*
pendeo, 2. *hang*	pendo, 3. *weigh*
delĭgo, 8. *choose*	dilĭgo, 8. *love*
findo, 8. *split*	fido, 8. *trust*
fingo, 8. *feign*	fīgo, 8. *fix*
vinco, 8. *conquer*	vincio, 4. *bind*
venio, 4. *come*	veneo, ire, *be sold.*

Veneo, ire, is commonly used in a passive sense—"to be sold;" but its proper meaning is "I go to sale" (*venum eo*).—Of a similar kind are *vapulare,* "to be beaten," from *vapulo,* "I get a flogging;" and *exulare,* "to be banished," from *exulo,* "I am an exile *or* live in exile."

CHAPTER VI.

PARTICLES.

I. ADVERBS.

§ 75.—There are various classes of Adverbs : viz., adverbs of time, of place, of manner etc.

(TIME.)	(PLACE.)	(MANNER.)
aliquando, *once*	hic, *here*	fere, *almost*
cras, *to-morrow*	illic, ibi, *there*	imprīmis, *especially*
heri, *yesterday*	nusquam, *nowhere*	omnino, *altogether*
hodie, *to-day*	quo, *whither*	palam, *openly*
interdum, *sometimes*	ubi, *where*	pariter, *likewise*
jam, *already*	ubicunque, *wherever*	paulatim, *by degrees*
nunquam, *never*	ubīque, *everywhere*	præsertim, *chiefly*
quotidie, *daily*	unde, *whence*	repente, *suddenly*
semper, *always*	undīque, *from all sides*	saltem, *at least.*

§ 76.—Adverbs are either *primitive* or *derivative.*—Derivative adverbs are mostly derived from adjectives, and admit of the degrees of comparison. They are formed in the following manner :

1. Adjectives in *us* (*er*), *a*, *um*, generally add *e* to the stem ; as,

ADJECTIVE.	ADVERB.	COMP.	SUPERL.
longus,	long-e,	longius,	longissime.
liber,	liber-e,	liberius,	liberrime.
pulcher,	pulchr-e,	pulchrius,	pulcherrime.

2. Adjectives of the third declension add *iter* to the stem ; but those ending in *ns* add *er* only ; as,

acer,	acr-iter,	acrius,	acerrime.
felix,	felic-iter,	felicius,	felicissime.
amans,	amant-er,	amantius,	amantissime.

NOTE 1.—The adjectives *durus, firmus, largus,* and *humanus,* add both *e* and *iter* to the stem, as *dure* and *duriter ; firme* and *firmiter,* etc.— *Violentus* and *fraudulentus* have *violenter, fraudulenter ; luculentus* generally has *luculenter.*

NOTE 2.—In several adjectives in *us,* the ablative sing. supplies the place of the adverb ; as, *continuo,* immediately ; *crebro,* frequently ; *falso,* falsely ; *merito,* deservedly ; *necessario,* necessarily ; *perpetuo,* continually ; *raro,* rarely ; *sedulo,* sedulously ; *subito,* suddenly ; *tuto,* safely, etc.

Facilis, impūnis, and *sublimis,* have *facile, impune,* and *sublime ; audax,* bold, has *audacter ;* and *difficilis* has *difficile, difficulter,* and *difficiliter.*

NOTE 3.—The following adverbs deserve particular notice : *bene,* well ; *male,* badly ; *parum,* not enough ; *multum,* much ; *satis,* enough ; *prope,* near ; *diu,* long ; *nuper,* lately ; *secus,* otherwise ; and *sæpe,* often.

POS.	COMP.	SUP.	POS.	COMP.	SUP.
bene	melius	optime	parum	minus	minime
male	pejus	pessime	multum	plus	plurimum
(*more*)	magis	maxime	(*sooner*)	ocius	ocissime
(*worse*)	deterius	determine	(*rather*)	potius	potissimum (e)
satis	satius	———	nuper		nuperrime
prope	propius	proxime	secus	secius	
diu	diutius	diutissime	sæpe	sæpius	sæpissime

II. PREPOSITIONS.

§ 77.—Some prepositions govern the accusative ; others, the ablative ; and a few govern both the accusative and ablative.

PREPOSITIONS GOV. THE ACCUSATIVE.

ad, *to, unto*
apud, *at, by, with*
ante, *before*
adversus, }
adversum, } *against*
cis, }
citra, } *on this side*
circa, }
circum, } *around, about*
circiter, *about*

contra, *against*
erga, *towards*
extra, *beyond, without*
infra, *beneath, below*
intra, *within*
inter, *between, among*
juxta, *next to*
ob, *on account of*
penes, *in the power of*
per, *through, during*

pone, *behind*	secundum, *according to*
post, *after*	supra, *above*
præter, *beside, except*	trans, *on the other side*
prope, *near by*	versus, *towards*
propter, *on account of*	ultra, *beyond*

PREPOSITIONS GOV. THE ABLATIVE

a, ab, abs, *from, by*	e, ex, *out of, from*
absque (obsol.), *without*	præ, *before, owing to*
coram, *in presence of*	pro, *before, for*
cum, *with* .	sine, *without*
de, *down from, concerning*	tenus, *as far as, up to*

PREPOSITIONS GOVERNING BOTH THE ACC. AND ABL.

in, *in, on, into, towards*	super, *above, concerning*
sub, *under, towards*	subter, *under, beneath*

Note 1.—*A* and *e* never stand before a vowel or *h; ab* stands before vowels, and often, also, before consonants; *ex* stands indiscriminately before vowels and consonants. *Abs* is used only in the combination *abs te*, for which, however, *a te* is used also. *Absque* is obsolete.

Note 2.—The preposition *cum* is always annexed to the ablatives *me, te, se, nobis*, and *vobis*, and commonly to *quo, qua, quibus*, and to *qui* when used for *quo;* as, *mecum, tecum, secum, nobiscum*, etc.

Note 3.—The prepositions *ob, post, de, ex, in, cum*, and *inter*, are not unfrequently placed between the substantive and its adjective. *Tenus* and *versus* generally follow their cases. E. g., *quam ob causam, aliquot post menses, certis de causis, magna ex parte, hac in re, magna cum voluptate, medios inter hostes, cœlo tenus, Romam versus.*

Note 4.—Several of the above-mentioned prepositions are sometimes used as adverbs; as, *ante*, before; *post*, afterward; *contra*, on the contrary; *prope*, almost; *circiter*, about.—When used adverbially, they, of course, govern no case.

IN and SUB.

§ 78.—IN takes 1. The ACCUSATIVE with verbs of motion (*whither?*), and when *tendency toward* or *against* is denoted; as, *eamus in hortum, proficiscor in Galliam, pietas in Deum, amor in patriam, odium in Hannibalem, Ciceronis oratio prima in Catilinam*, etc.—2. The ABLATIVE in answer to *where?* when rest in a place is denoted; as, *ambulat in horto, cecidit in prælio, fuistine in schola? hoc in fratre tuo laudo, in flumine Istro pons erat.*

Note 1.—With *esse, haberi, poni, duci*, and *numerari*, IN takes the ablative in the sense of "among"; as, *in bonis civibus* (*in magnis viris, in optimis scriptoribus*) *esse, haberi*, etc., *dolor a multis in maximis malis ducitur.*

Note 2.—IN takes the ablative, also, with verbs of "placing," as *ponere, locare*, and *collocare;* e. g., *pone librum in mensa.*—Thus the verbs *defigere, inserere*, and *inscribere*, are frequently construed with *in* and the ablative; as, *oculos in alicujus vultu defigere, inscribere in basi*, etc.

SUB. takes 1. The ACCUSATIVE with verbs of motion (*whither?*), and when *the time toward* or *about which*, is denoted; e. g., *venire sub oculos, mittere sub jugum, sub imperium redire, sub vesperam, sub idem tempus;*—2. The ABLATIVE in answer to *where?* when rest in a place is denoted; as, *esse sub oculis, sedere sub scamno, esse sub regibus, sub imperio, esse sub dio*, "to be in the open air."

SUPER, in the sense of *over, above*, takes the accusative in answer to *where* and *whither;* as, *avis volat super aquam, avis nidum construit super aquam.*—In the sense of *concerning, about,* it takes the ablative; as, *super hac re* (much better, *hac de re*) *pluribus ad te scribam.*

SUBTER, *under, beneath,* is rarely used, and in prose with the accusative only.

PREPOSITIONS IN COMPOSITION.

§ 79.—Several prepositions when compounded with other words, undergo a change for the sake of euphony. The following ´cases are of most common occurrence:

AD is assimilated before *c, f, g, l, p, r, s* and *t ;* as, *accedo, affero, aggredior, alludo, appono, arrideo, assisto, attingo.*—Before *q,* the *d* generally changes to *c,* as *acquiro, acquiesco.*

PER and INTER remain unchanged, except in the words *pellicio, pejĕro (perjūro),* and *intelligo.*

OB is assimilated before *c, f, g,* and *p ;* as, *occurro, offero, oggannio, oppono.*

TRANS drops the *s* before *s ;* as, *transcribo, transilio, transcendo.*—In *trado, traduco, trajicio,* and *trano,* the *ns* is better omitted, though *transdo, transduco,* etc., are found also.

A stands before *m* and *v ;* as *amitto, averto ; abs,* before *c* and *t,* as *abscondo, abstineo.*—In all other combinations *ab* is used.—In the words *aufero* and *aufugio, ab* is changed into *au* (av).

COM remains unchanged before *b, p,* and *m ;* it is assimilated before *l, n,* and *r,*—and changes to *n* before the remaining consonants; as, *comburo, compono, committo ;*—*colligo, connecto, corripio ;*—*concludo, conduco, confero, conjungo,* etc.—Before *h* and vowels the *m* is dropped, as *cohibeo, cohæreo, coalesco, coerceo.*

EX is assimilated before *f,* as *effero, efficio, effugio, effundo.* In the words *exsequor, exsilium, exsul, exsulo, exspecto, exstinguo,* the *s* is often dropped, as *exequor, exilium, exul,* etc.

IN changes final *n* into *m* before *b, p,* and *m ;* as, *imbibo, impono, immitto.* Before *l* and *r* it is assimilated ; as, *illudo, irruo, irrumpo.*

SUB is assimilated before *c, f, g, p,* and *r ;* as, *succurro, suffero, suggero, suppono, surripio,* though commonly *subrideo.*—Before *sp,* the final *b* is dropped, as *suspiro, suspicio, suspecto.*—In *suscipio, suscito, suspendo, sustineo,* and the perfect *sustuli,* the *b* has been replaced by the letter *s.*

INSEPARABLE PREPOSITIONS.

§ 80.— Inseparable prepositions are such as are found only in composition ; as, *amb, dis, re,* and *se.*

AMB (*ἀμφί*), " around ;" as, *ambigo, ambio, amburo.* In *amplector* and *ampŭto* the *b* is dropped ; before *c, h,* and *q,* and also in the word *anfractus, amb* changes to *an ;* as, *anceps, anhēlo, anquiro.*

DIS, " asunder," drops the final *s* before all consonants, except *c, p, q, t,* and *s* followed by a vowel ; as, *digredior, dilābor, dimitto, diripio, divello ;* but *discedo, dispono, disquiro, disturbo, dissemino, dissuadeo.* Before *s* followed by a consonant, *di* is used, as *disto, dispergo, distinguo.*—Before *j,* both *dis* and *di* are found, as *disjicio, disjungo ;* but *dijudico.*—Before *f* the final *s* is assimilated, as *differo, diffido, diffundo.*

RE (before *h,* and a vowel, *red-*), " back ;" as, *reduco, refero, remitto; redhibeo, redeo, redintegro.*

SE, " apart," " aside ;" as, *seduco, sejungo, sepono.*

III. CONJUNCTIONS.

§ 81.—There are several classes of conjunctions: viz.,

1. *Copulative;* as, *et, ac, atque, que,* and; *nec, neque,* and not, nor; *etiam, quoque,* also; *item,* likewise; *et—et,* both—and; *quum—tum,* both—and especially, not only—but also; *tum—tum,* both—and, as well—as, not only—but also; *tam—quam,* as well—as.

2. *Disjunctive;* as, *aut, sive, seu, vel, ve,* or; *aut—aut, sive—sive, seu—seu, vel—vel,* either—or; *nec—nec, neque—neque* (both very frequent), *neque—nec* (sometimes), *nec—neque* (very rare), neither—nor.

3. *Concessive;* as, *etsi, etiamsi, tametsi, licet, quamvis, quamquam,* although; *quamtumvis, quamlibet,* how much soever; *ut,* granting, although; *quidem,* truly, indeed, certainly.

4. *Adversative;* as, *sed, autem, verum, vero, at, atqui,* but, but in fact; *tamen, attamen, verumtamen,* yet, but yet, nevertheless, however; *enimvero,* yes indeed, to be sure.

5. *Conditional;* as, *si,* if; *si forte,* if perchance; *si modo, modo, dummodo,* if but, if only; *si tamen,* if however; *sin, sin autem, sin vero,* but if, if on the contrary; *nisi,* if not, unless; *dummodo ne, modo ne,* provided that not.

6. *Causal;* as, *nam, namque, enim, etenim,* for; *quod, quia, quoniam, quum,* because; *quando, quandoquidem, siquidem,* since, since indeed; *quippe* (commonly in connection with *qui*), because, since.

7. *Conclusive;* as, *ergo, igitur, itaque, ideo, idcirco, proinde, propterea,* therefore; *unde, quocirca, quare, quapropter, quamobrem,* wherefore.

8. *Final;* as, *ut, uti, quo,* that, in order that; *ne, neve (neu),* in order that not; *quin, quominus,* that not.

9. *Temporal;* as, *quum,* when; *tum,* then; *ubi, ut, ubi primum, ut primum, quum primum, simul ac, simul atque,* as soon as; *antequam, priusquam,* before; *postquam,* after; *dum,* while; *dum, usque dum, quoad, donec,* until; *quamdiu,* as long as.

10. *Comparative;* as, *ut, sicut, velut, ceu,* as, like; *tamquam, quasi, ac si,* as, as if; *ac* and *atque* in the sense of "as" after *æque, pariter, perinde, pro eo, similiter, totidem, aliter, contra, secus.*

§ 82.—NOTE 1. *Ac* never stands before a vowel and *h; atque* stands most commonly before vowels, but before consonants also. *Que* and *ve* are always appended to the following word, as *terra marique, ter quaterve.*

NOTE 2.—*Enim, autem,* and *vero,* never stand at the beginning of a sentence, or of any member of a sentence, but always after the first or second word. They are placed after the second, when one of the first two words is either the verb *sum* or a preposition; as, *incredibile est enim,—ad vos autem pertinet.*

NOTE 3.—*Quidem,* "indeed," "at least," and *quoque,* "also," are always placed after the emphatic word; as, *hoc quidem tempore,—tu quoque contra me es!*

The English "not—even" is expressed by *ne—quidem,* the emphatical word being placed between *ne* and *quidem;* as, *ne patrem quidem veretur.*

§ 83.—INTERJECTIONS are words uttered to express some emotion of the mind. Such are:

Evoe or *evax,* hurrah!—*Euge,* bravo!—*Vae,* woe!—*Hei, heu, eheu, proh,* alas!—*Heus, eho, ehodum,* holla!—*Phui, vah,* away, begone!—*Pax,* hush!—*Infandum,* shame!—*Age* or *agite,* quick!—*Sodes,* pray do!—*Mehercle,* by Hercules! and the like.

§ 84 —GENERAL DIRECTIONS AND CAUTIONS.

(For beginners.)

1. In translating English into Latin, the young student who pays due attention to the directions given in § 1, for the employment of the Latin Cases,
will spare himself much time and trouble, and will soon become familiar
with the structure of Latin sentences. As in every sentence the nomina
tive is the first thing to be sought for, let his first question always be
who or *what* placed before the finite verb, and the word answering to the
question will be the nominative.

In the following sentence all *six* cases occur : " My son, by good works
men secure to themselves the everlasting joys of heaven."—This and like
sentences the pupil ought to parse thus :

Who secure ? men secure.—" Men" is the nominative (*homines*) because it answers
to *who* or *what* placed before the finite verb.

Secure *what ?* the everlasting joys.—" The everlasting joys" is the accusative (*æterna
gaudia*) because it answers to *whom* or *what* placed after a verb transitive.

The joys *of what ?* of heaven.—" Of heaven" is the genitive (*cœli*) because it answers
to the question *of whom* or *what*, asked in connection with a noun.

Secure *to whom ?* to themselves.—" To themselves" is the dative (*sibi*) because the
dative answers to the question *to whom* or *what ?*

By what ? by good works.—" By good works" is the ablative (*bonis operibus*) because the ablative answers to the questions *when ? where ? by (from, with)
whom* or *what ?*

" My son" is the person addressed, and is, therefore, put in the vocative.

The whole sentence, accordingly, runs thus in Latin : *Fili mi, bonis operibus
homines æterna cœli gaudia sibi parant.*

    ☞ It is, of course, not enough merely to see in what case each noun or
adjective has to be put : the pupil must moreover take into consideration
the gender, number, declension, agreement, etc.

2. Every finite verb agrees with its nominative in number and person ; as,
" The boys play."—*Who* play ? " The boys ;" *Pueri ludunt.*

3. Adjectives, adjective pronouns, and participles, agree with their substantives
in gender, number, and case ; as, " A good man ;" *Vir bonus.*—" A kind
mother ;" *Benigna mater.*

4. When an adjective or participle (e. g., *wise, poor, rich,—sent, given, written,*
etc.) is separated from its substantive by some intervening word or words.
ask simply the question : " Who is said to be (or have been) *wise, poor,
rich ?*"—" what is said to be (or have been) *sent, given, written ?*" and then
make these adjectives and participles agree in gender, number, and case,
with the word that answers to the question.

5. Translate *the rich, the poor, the wise, the ignorant,* etc., always by the plural,
unless they refer expressly to a singular noun ; as, " Imitate (thou) the
good, and shun the wicked ;" *Imitare bonos, fuge malos.*—" The rich are
not always happy ;" *Divites non semper felices sunt.*—But, " The good
man is happy ; the wicked, unhappy ;" *Vir bonus felix est, improbus
infelix*

3. When the question *what?* placed before the finite verb, is answered by another verb, put the latter in the Infinitive, and when there is an adjective referring to this Infinitive, put it in the neuter gender; as,

"To lie is disgraceful." *What is?* to lie is. *Mentiri turpe est.*
"To err is human." *What is?* to err is. *Errare humanum est.*

7. When the question *what?* placed after a verb transitive, is answered by another verb, the latter is put in the Infinitive; as,

"He wishes (wishes *what?—*) to know." *Vult scire.*
"He begins (begins *what?—*) to speak." *Incipit loqui.*

8. A noun used to explain a preceding noun or pronoun, and designating the same person or thing, is put, by apposition, in the same case; as, "Cicero the Orator;" *Cicero orator.*—"To Philip, king of Macedonia, father of Alexander the Great;" *Philippo regi Macedoniæ, patri Alexandri Magni.*

9. The relative agrees with its antecedent in gender, number, and person · but the case depends on the construction of its own clause; as, "The letter which I wrote;" *Litteræ quas scripsi.*

10. Verbs signifying "to be," "to exist," as *sum, fio, existo, nascor, maneo,* etc., and passive verbs signifying "to be called," "to be chosen," "to be deemed," take both a subject-nominative, and a predicate-nominative:— the former answering to *who* or *what* placed before the verb; the latter, to *what* placed after the verb; as, "I am called Robert;" *Ego vocor Robertus,* etc.

11. Never put *a* and *e* before a vowel or an *h,* but *ab* and *ex.*

12. Never put *enim, vero, autem,* at the beginning of a sentence, or of any member of a sentence.

13. *Que* and *ve* must always be appended to the next word; as, "Father and mother;" *Pater materque,* not *pater que mater.*—"Three or four times;" *Ter quaterve,* not *ter ve quater.*

14. Never forget the Imperatives: *dic, duc, fer, fac.*

15. Translate "not" before an Imperative always by *ne,* never by *non;* as, "Do not fear;" *Ne time.*—"Be not forward;" *Ne procax esto.*—"Do not hasten;" *Ne festina.*

SYNTAX.

§ 85.—Syntax treats of the due arrangement of words in sentences.

The principal parts of a sentence are the *subject* and *predicate*, or the nominative and the finite verb.

The *finite* verb is that verb which is limited to number and person : it is either in the Indicative, Subjunctive, or Imperative.

The SUBJECT or nominative of a sentence is that which answers to— *who* or *what ?* placed before the finite verb.

The PREDICATE is that which is affirmed of the subject. It is generally a verb, but often a substantive or an adjective combined with the verb *esse*, " to be ; " as,

Cæsar conquered.—God is just.—Sylla was Consul.

In these three sentences, *Cæsar*, *God*, and *Sylla*, are the Subjects ; *conquered*, *is just*, and *was Consul*, the Predicates.

§ 86.—Sentences are of two kinds, *simple* and *compound*.—Compound sentences are either *co-ordinate* or *subordinate*.

CO-ORDINATE sentences are those which are introduced by *copulative*, *disjunctive*, *adversative*, *conclusive*, and *comparative conjunctions* (§ 81). Co-ordinate sentences are independent of each other.

SUBORDINATE sentences or clauses are those which are introduced by *concessive*, *conditional*, *causal*, *final*, and *temporal* conjunctions (§ 81), also relative clauses, indirect questions, and clauses containing the Accusative with the Infinitive.

A sentence with which a subordinate clause is connected, is called, in reference to the latter, the principal or *leading* sentence ; its subject, the principal or *leading* subject ; and its verb, the principal or *leading* verb.

CHAPTER I.

THE FOUR CONCORDS.

I. Of the Finite Verb with its Nominative.

Ego valeo.

§ 87.—Every finite verb agrees with its nominative in number and person ; as, " I am well." *Magister docet, discipuli audiunt. Animalia currunt. Lupi ululant. Ranœ coaxant.* ·

NOTE 1.—The nominative of a sentence is commonly a noun or pronoun ; but any part of speech,—even a whole clause may take the place of the nominative ; as, *Errare humanum est. Et monere et moneri proprium est veræ amicitiæ. Cras istud quando venit ? Incertum est quam longa cujusque vita futura sit.*

NOTE 2.—The nominatives *ego, tu, nos,* and *vos,* are generally omitted : but, when contrast or emphasis is intended, they must be expressed. E. g., *Quid agis, amice ? Si salutaris, resalūta.—Ego aio, tu negas.*[1] *Nos ridemus, vos fletis. Tu hoc fecisti.*

Est and *sunt* are likewise often omitted, especially in proverbial sentences ; as, *Omne rarum carum. Omnia præclara rara. Aurora musis amica. Ubi opes, ibi amici. Ubi bene, ibi patria. Qualis rex, talis grex. Acti labores jucundi. Corruptio optimi pessima. Quot capita, tot sententiæ.*

NOTE 8.—Collective nouns, such as *plebs, pars, turba, multitudo,* etc.—also *uterque, alius—alium, alter—alterum,* and especially *pro se quisque,* " every one for his part," sometimes take a verb in the plural ; as, " Each lays the blame on the other ;" *Alter in alterum causam conferunt. Pars Sabinis eunt subsidio, pars Romanos adoriuntur. Locros omnis multitudo abeunt. Uterque eorum ex castris exercitum educunt. Alius alium, ut proelium incipiant, circumspectant.*

A plural verb is often used, also, when a nominative singular, by means of *cum,* is joined to an ablative plural, especially when the latter is followed by a relative clause ; as, *Demosthenes cum ceteris qui bene de republica mereri existimabantur, in exilium erant expulsi.*

NOTE 4.—When there are two or more nominatives sing., the verb is generally put in the plural ; and when the nominatives are of different persons, the verb agrees with the first person rather than the second, and with the second rather than the third ; as, *Romulus et Remus Romam condiderunt. Si tu et Tullia valetis, ego et suavissimus Cicero valemus. Tu et frater tuus vapulabitis.*

When the nominative denote things, the verb frequently agrees with the

---

[1] I say " yes ;" and you, " no."

nearest : but, if one of the nominatives is plural, the verb is generally put in the plural also.—The agreement with the nearest takes sometimes place even when *persons* are denoted. E. g., *Tempus necessitasque hoc postulat. Beneficentia, liberalitas, justitia, funditus tollitur. Vita, mors, divitiæ, paupertas, omnes homines vehementissime permovent.—Dixit hoc Zosippus et Ismenias, homines nobilissimi. Vos ipsi et Senatus frequens restitit.*

NOTE 5.—When of two nominatives belonging to the same verb, different things are asserted, the verb always agrees with the nearest ; as, *Ego misere, tu feliciter vivis.*—With two nominatives connected by *et—et* or *aut—aut*, the verb is more commonly put in the singular. With *nec—nec*, the singular is likewise preferred, unless one of the nominatives denotes a first or second person. E. g., *Et ego et Cicero meus flagitabit. Nec Cæsar nec Pompeius insidias effugere potuit. Hæc neque ego neque tu fecimus.*

The phrases *Senatus Populusque Romanus* and *unus et alter* regularly take a verb in the singular number ; as, *Senatus Populusque Romanus hoc intelligit. Unus et alter dies intercesserat*

II. OF THE ADJECTIVE WITH ITS SUBSTANTIVE.

Vir bonus.

§ 88.—Adjectives, adjective pronouns, and participles, agree with their substantives in gender, number, and case ; as, " A good man." *Vir sapiens felix est. Boni homines bonis hominibus cari sunt. Amicus certus in re incerta cernitur. Sincera fides jungit veros amicos.*

NOTE 1.—When an adjective relates to a substantive quoted merely as a word, or to an Infinitive, Imperative, adverb, or a whole clause, it is put in the neuter gender ; as, *Rex est monosyllabum, regina polysyllabum. Dulce et decorum est pro patria mori. Turpius est fallere quam falli. Supremum vale dixit. Incertum est quid cras futurum sit.*

Sometimes the adjective does not agree with its substantive, but with another, understood in the former ; as, *Pars in crucem acti, pars bestiis objecti sunt. Capita conjurationis securi percussi sunt. Samnitium cæsi sunt tria millia ducenti. Latium Capuaque agro multati sunt.*

NOTE 2.—An adjective, adjective pronoun, or participle, in the nom. or acc., with the word t h i n g s expressed or understood, is generally put in the neuter plural ; as, " We cannot change the past," i. e., past things ; *Præterita mutare non possumus.*— Thus, *Audi multa, loquere pauca. Supra lunam æterna sunt omnia. Video meliora proboque, deteriora sequor. Permulta parentibus, Deo omnia debemus. Tria vobis propono.*

Instead of the neuter plural, however, the word *res* may be used also, as *Res omnes mutationi sunt obnoxiæ. Res magnæ non viribus, sed consilio geruntur. Res humanæ fragiles caducæque sunt.*

The addition of *res* is even necessary in those cases in which the neuter form does not differ from that of the other genders, as in the genitive, dative, and ablative. Thus e. g., " of many things" must be rendered by *multarum rerum*, not by the neuter *multorum*, because the form *multorum* would leave it doubtful, whether t h i n g s or p e r s o n s are meant.

NOTE 3.—When an adjective or participle belongs to two or more substantives, it is generally put in the plural; as, *Bos, equus et asinus sunt utilissimi. Collis et ager floribus vestiti sunt. Luna et terra globosæ sunt.*

When the substantives are of different genders, see whether they denote persons or things:

a) If they denote p e r s o n s, the adjective is put in the plural of the masculine gender; as, *Jam pridem pater mihi et mater mortui sunt.*

b) If they denote t h i n g s, the adjective either agrees with the nearest or is put in the neuter plural; as, *Error in hac causa atque invidia versata est. Tibi omnium salus, liberi, fama, fortunæ sunt carissimæ.—Perspicua suum consilium conatusque omnibus fecit. Porta murusque de cælo tacta sunt.*

c) If partly p e r s o n s, partly t h i n g s are denoted, the adjective either takes the gender of the person or is, again, put in the neuter plural ; as, *Rex regiaque classis una profecti sunt. Romani regem regnumque Macedoniæ sua futura sciunt.*

With two or more *feminine* substantives, denoting a b s t r a c t ideas, the adjective is sometimes put in the neuter plural ; as, *Ira et avaritia imperio potentiora sunt. Stultitia, temeritas, injustitia, et intemperantia fugienda sunt.*

NOTE 4.—An adjective standing in immediate connection with two substantives, is either repeated with each,—or it is placed immediately before or after the first,—or it follows the last. Accordingly we may say—*meo consilio et auctoritate mea, meo consilio et auctoritate, consilio meo et auctoritate,* and *consilio et auctoritate mea.—Hominis utilitati agri omnes et maria parent. Metellum multifilii et filiæ in rogum imposuerunt.*

When an adjective belongs to two or more substantives j o i n t l y, so that it cannot be applied to them taken separately, it is always put in the plural ; as, *Inter se contraria sunt beneficium et injuria. Grammatice quondam et musice junctæ fuerunt.*

NOTE 5.—When *hic, is, ille, qui* ("this, that, what"), are joined to a following substantive by means of *sum,* or a verb of n a m i n g, s e e m i n g, d e e m i n g, they agree with that substantive in gender, number, and case ; e. g., "That was the very cause of the war ;" *Ea ipsa causa belli fuit. Eas divitias, eam bonam famam magnamque nobilitatem putabunt.[1] Quæ est ista servitus[2] de qua loqueris? Hæc fuga est, non profectio. Idem velle atque idem nolle, ea demum[3] firma amicitia est. Quæ pertinacia quibusdam, eadem aliis constantia videtur.[4]*

When the interrogative " what ?" does not inquire after the quality, but after the very nature or definition of a thing, it must be expressed by *quid ;* as, *Quid est servitus? Quid est Deus? Quid mors ipsa sit, primum videndum est.*

NOTE 6.—When the words " beginning, end"—" top, summit, surface, foot, bottom"—" heart, middle, centre, extremity"—" rest, whole,"—are to be translated by the adjectives *primus, ultimus—summus, imus—intimus, extremus—medius, reliquus, universus,*—in Latin, these adjectives agree in gender and number with the noun following, and are put with it in the case in which the words b e g i n n i n g, e n d, t o p, etc. themselves would be placed if they were to be expressed by substantives ; as, " On the summit of the Alps the snow never melts ;" *In summis Alpibus nix nunquam liquescit. Persuadere conantur mathematici terram in medio mundo* (in the centre of the world) *esse sitam. Mento summam* (the surface of) *aquam attingens, siti enecatur Tantalus. Summus* (the summit of) *mons a T. Labieno tenebatur. Alexandriam reliquamque* (the rest of) *Ægyptum invisere cupio. Antistius abdidit se in intimam* (the very heart of) *Macedoniam. Mediam urbem interfluit amnis. Tantum bellum Pompeius extrema hieme apparavit, ineunte vere suscepit, media æstate confecit.*

---

[1] T h a t they thought riches, t h a t . . . .   [2] W h a t is that slavery . . . .   [3] T h a t is . . . .   [4] W h a t seems to some . . . . t h a t seems to others . . . .

III. Of the Relative with its Antecedent.

Ego qui loquor.

§ 89.—The relative agrees with its antecedent in gender, number, and person ; but the case depends on the construction of its own clause ; as, " I who am speaking."

Arbores serit agricola quarum fructus ipse aspiciet nunquam. O te *ferreum, quem tanta mala non moveant!* Nobis quidem, qui te *amamus, hoc gratissimum erit. Adestote animis, qui adestis corporibus.*

NOTE 1.—When the antecedent is a demonstrative (*hic, is, ille*), the latter is commonly omitted, especially when it is in the same case as the relative ; as, *Contemnuntur merito* (ii), *qui nec sibi nec aliis prosunt. Lauda* (id), *quod laudem meretur. Nobilis est* (is), *quem sua virtus nobilitat.*

NOTE 2.—When the relative refers to a whole clause, it is put in the neuter. In this case, *id quod* or *quæ res,* is sometimes used instead of the simple *quod.* E. g., *Lacedæmonii Agim regem, quod* (or *id quod*) *nunquam antea apud eos acciderat, necaverunt. Multæ civitates a Cyro defecerunt, quæ res multorum bellorum causa fuit.*

NOTE 8.—When the relative refers to two or more antecedents, it agrees with them in gender and number, just as the adjective does with two or more substantives. E. g., *Homerus et Virgilius quorum carmina miramur. Rex et regina qui una profecti sunt. Ego et tu qui scribimus.*

When, however, the antecedents denote *things* and are of different genders, the relative is regularly put in the neuter plural (as, *Otium et divitiæ quæ prima mortales putant*), and it should not be made to agree with the nearest, except when the antecedents express similar ideas, or when the relative is intended to refer to the last only ; e. g., *Eæ fruges atque fructus quos terra gignit ;—decus et gloria quam consecutus es ;—naves et captivi qui ad Chium capti erant.*

NOTE 4.—The antecedent is often taken from its own sentence and put in the relative clause in the same case with the relative. The relative clause is then commonly placed first. E. g.,

> Paulo ante accepi litteras, quas ad me dedisti.
> Paulo ante accepi, quas ad me dedisti litteras.
> *Quas ad me dedisti litteras, paulo ante accepi.*

Ad quas res aptissimi erimus, in iis potissimum elaborabimus, instead of: In iis rebus potissimum elaborabimus, ad quas aptissimi erimus. *Bestiæ in quo loco natæ sunt, ex eo se non commovent.*

A similar transposition sometimes takes place, when the antecedent is a superlative ; e. g., " Of the many most glorious and joyous days which P. Scipio witnessed in the course of his life, this day was the most glorious," *P. Scipioni ex multis diebus, quos in vita celeberrimos lætissimosque vidit, ille dies clarissimus fuit. Themistocles de servis suis quem habuit fidelissimum, ad Xerxem misit.*

Note 5.—The expression " he was the first (the last, the only one) that . . . . .," is commonly contracted, in Latin, into one sentence,—by omitting the relative and the verb *sum* of the preceding clause, and putting the adjectives *primus, ultimus, solus,* etc., with the noun or pronoun to which they refer, in the case in which the relative would otherwise stand. E. g., " This city was the first that Cæsar approached," *Hanc urbem primam Cæsar adiit,* instead of: Hæc urbs fuit prima quam Cæsar adiit. *Unum te*[1] *sapientem et appellant et existimant. Thales Milesius omnium Græcorum primus*[2] *defectionem solis prædixit.*

Note 6.—When the relative, by means of *sum* or a verb of *naming, deeming,* etc. is joined to a substantive of a different gender from that of its antecedent, or when it refers to two antecedents, denoting the same object, but of different genders, it may agree with either. E. g., *Sempiterni illi ignes quas stellas dicimus. Animal hoc sagax quem vocamus hominem. Domicilia conjuncta quas urbes dicimus. Thebæ quod Bœotiæ caput est.—Flumen Rhenus qui (or quod) in Oceanum influit.*

Note 7.—When the relative stands in the nominative or accusative, it is frequently omitted in Latin. The verb of the relative clause is then changed into its corresponding participle, and the latter made to agree in gender, number, and case, with the antecedent. (☞ If the relative stands in the accusative, the relative clause must first be changed into the passive.)—E. g., " Think of death which always threatens thee ;" *Cogita mortem tibi semper imminentem. Nemo cunctam intuens terram de divina providentia dubitabit. Male agentis animus*[3] *numquam est sine metu. Sudanti*[4] *frigida potio perniciosissima est. Felicitas hominis adhuc viventis non minus incerta est ac dubia, quam militis adhuc pugnantis victoria. Compara tibi divitias perpetuo duraturas.*[5] *Adulator aut laudat vituperanda, aut vituperat laudanda.—Beneficiorum a Deo acceptorum*[6] *semper memor esto. Timotheus a patre acceptam gloriam*[7] *multis auxit virtutibus.*

Sometimes, when *sum, esse,* is the verb of the relative clause, both the relative and the verb *sum* are omitted, the predicate-noun or adjective being then made to agree with the antecedent accordingly ; as, " The man that is contented with his lot, is happy ;" *Homo sua sorte contentus, felix est. Multas res nobis incognitas*[8] *posteri scient. Cunem tibi infensum mitigare studes : quidni et hominem ?*

When the relative refers to the person included in a possessive pronoun, the predicate-noun or adjective of the relative clause must be put in the genitive (see § 188); e. g., " Thy speech, who wert once my preceptor, is approved by all ;" *Tua præceptoris quondam mei oratio omnibus probatur.*

Note 8.—The rule for the agreement of the relative with its antecedent, applies also to the following correlatives :

> *idem—qui* (or *ac, atque*), " the same as ;"
> *talis—qualis* (or *ac*), " such—as" (of quality);
> *tantus—quantus,* " such—as," i. e., as great—as (of size).

E. g., " He is the same as (or that) he has ever been ;" *Idem est qui* (or *ac, atque*) *semper fuit. Iidem abeunt qui venerunt. Hoc idem est ac illud. Talis es qualem te*

---

1) You are the only one whom they both . . . . . 2) Thales was the first that foretold . . . . . 3) The mind of him who does ill. 4) To him who is perspiring. 5) that will last for ever. 6) which you have received . . . . Pass., which have been received [by you]. 7) the glory (which) he had inherited from . . . . 8) which are unknown to us.

semper putabam. Xerxes cum tantis copiis Græciam invasit, quantas neque antea neque postea habuit quisquam. Quanta potui celeritate accurri, i. e., *celeritate tanta quanta potui,* " as quick as possible."

IV. Of a Substantive with a Substantive.

Cyrus rex.

§ 90.—A noun used to explain a preceding noun or pronoun and designating the same person or thing, is put, by apposition, in the same case ; as, " Cyrus, the king."

Apud Herodotum, patrem historiæ, sunt innumerabiles fabulæ. Seleucus, rex Syriæ, Berenicen, sororem Ptolemæi, regis Ægypti interfecit. Marcellus Syracusas, urbem pulcherrimam, vi consilioque cepit. Tullia, deliciæ nostræ, salutem tibi plurimam adscribit. Me, præceptorem vestrum, pueri, audite. Hoc tibi juventus Romana¹ indicimus bellum.

Note 1.—When to the common nouns c i t y, i s l a n d, m o n t h, the proper name of a city, island, or month is added, the two substantives are put in the same case, though the sign " of" intervenes ; as, *Insula Cyprus, insulam Cyprum, in insula Cypro. Urbs Roma, urbem Romam. Mensis Maius, mense Maio.*

Note 2.—When *urbs, civitas,* or *oppidum,* is placed in apposition to a plural name of a town, the verb commonly agrees with the substantive in apposition ; as, *Tungri, civitas Galliæ, fontem habet insignem. Volsinii, oppidum Tuscorum opulentissimum, totum concrematum est fulmine.*

Note 3.—When the noun in apposition admits of two forms, one masculine, the other feminine, the masculine form must be used, when the preceding noun is either masculine or neuter ; but the feminine, when the former is feminine. Thus we say: *Usus, magister egregius ; Vinum, curarum expulsor ; Deus, consiliorum meorum adjutor* etc.; but we must say : *Philosophia, magistra morum, virtutis indagatrix expultrixque vitiorum ; Assentatio, vitiorum adjutrix.*

Note 4.—When a name belongs to two or more persons in common, it is used but once, generally in the plural ; as, *Lucius et Spurius Mummii, fratres. Mihi Cneius et Publius Scipiones fortunati videbantur.*—Thus also with other substantives, as *Martia et quarta legiones* and *legio Martia et quarta. Quartam et Martiam legiones mecum futuras putavi.*

---

¹) i. e., *Hoc tibi bellum nos, juventus Romana, indicimus.*

CHAPTER II.

1. The interchange of the Active and Passive constructions.—2. The English conjunction THAT.—3. The Accusative with the Infinitive.—4. Questions and Answers.

I. THE INTERCHANGE OF THE ACTIVE AND PASSIVE CONSTRUCTIONS.

§ 91.—The active construction is made passive, by changing

the Nominative into the Ablative,
the Accusative into the Nominative, and
the active voice into the passive.

☞ In changing the active construction into the passive, and *vice versa*, the mood and tense of the verb remain always the same, but the number and person depend on the new nominative.—When the ablative denotes a p e r s o n or any thing p e r s o n i-f i e d, the preposition *ab* must be prefixed. E. g.,

Act. *Præceptor discipulos monuit ;* Pass. *Discipuli a præceptore moniti sunt.*—Act. *Sol terram collustrat ;* Pass. *Terra sole* (or *a sole*) *collustratur.*

NOTE.—Instead of the ablative (of the Agent) with *ab*, the dative is sometimes used ; e. g., *Difficillimum est facere quod omnibus probetur. Honesta bonis viris, non occulta quæruntur. Cui non sunt auditæ Demosthenis vigiliæ ?*

§ 92.—The passive construction is made active, by changing

the Nominative into the Accusative,
the Ablative into the Nominative, and
the passive voice into the active.

E. g., Pass. *Impii a Deo punientur ;* Act. *Deus impios puniet.*—Pass. *Esto bonus et ab omnibus amaberis ;* Act. *Esto bonus et omnes te amabunt.*

NOTE 1.—The change of the passive construction into the active is necessary, whenever an English passive verb is to be rendered into Latin by a Deponent ; because deponent verbs, though passive in form, are (with very few exceptions) but active in signification and do not, therefore, admit of a passive construction. E. g., "Cicero's cloquence is admired *(miror)* by all ;" Act. " All admire Cicero's eloquence ;" *Ciceronis eloquentiam omnes mirantur,*—not, *Ciceronis eloquentia ab omnibus miratur.*

NOTE 2.—When in changing the active construction into the passive, there appears no nominative, the verb is construed i m p e r s o n a l l y, that is, it is put in the 3d person sing., and the Participle, if the tense is a compound one, in the neuter singular ; e. g., " We have now walked enough ;" *Satis jam (nos) ambulavimus ;* Pass. *Satis jam (a nobis) ambulatum est.*—*Ad Alpes quum pervenissent ;* Pass. *Ad Alpes quum (ab iis) perventum esset.*

II. THE ENGLISH CONJUNCTION "THAT."

§ 93.—The English conjunction THAT is expressed in Latin by *quod, ut,* or *quo ;* and THAT NOT, by *quod non, ut non, ne, quin,* or *quominus.*—Very often THAT is not expressed in Latin at all, and then the construction of the Accusative with the Infinitive takes place.

NOTE 1.—The conjunctions *ut, quo, ne, quin,* and *quominus,* always govern the Subjunctive. *Quod* takes the Indicative, when the speaker or writer states his own opinion,—and the Subjunctive, when the opinion or allegation of some other person is expressed. (Compare § 199, IV.)

NOTE 2.—An Infinitive or a participial noun being often employed in English, where in Latin the Subjunctive with one of the above-mentioned conjunctions is used, the pupil, in translating English sentences into Latin, should always change such Infinitives and participial nouns—by means of "that" or "because"—into subordinate clauses, but so that a principal tense (§ 188) in the leading clause be followed by a principal tense in the subordinate clause ; and an historical tense in the leading clause, by an historical tense in the subordinate clause. E. g.,

(Eng.) I *come* to see you. (Lat.) I *come* that I *may* see you.
(Eng.) I *came* to see you. (Lat.) I *came* that I *might* see you.

Gaudeo quod vales.

§ 94.—**Quod** (" that," " the fact that," " because," or " of [in, for]" with a participial noun) is used :

1.) When the clause which it introduces, contains the explanation of a former statement, or when it is a purely periphrastic nominative, as for example, in the sentence : "The fact that I am at Rome (== my stay at Rome) causes suspicion to many."—Such explanatory and periphrastic clauses generally refer to a preceding demonstrative, such as *hoc, id, illud, in eo, ex eo* (or *inde*), *ex hoc* (or *hinc*), *ideo, idcirco, propterea,* either expressed or understood.

2.) After the expressions *bene (male, jucunde, humaniter ....) facere ; bene (male, commode, percommode) factum est, accidit, evēnit ; prætereo* and *mitto,* in the sense of " to pass over in silence ;" and generally after *adde, adjice,* and *accedit,* "add to this," "to this must be added that," " beside (or, in addition to) this."

3.) After verbs denoting a feeling of joy or pain, as *gaudeo, lætor, delector, juvat me, gratum* or *jucundum mihi est, miror, doleo, angor, sollicitor, succenseo, indignor, ægre (graviter, indigne, moleste) fero,* and also after verbs of praising, censuring, accusing, pardoning, thanking, consoling, congratulating, and complaining. E. g., "I am glad that you are well."

Magnum beneficium est naturæ, quod necesse est mori.[1] *Mihi quidem videntur homines hac re maxime belluis præstare, quod loqui possunt. Quod Romæ sum, multis suspicionem movet. Facis fraterne,*[2] *quod me hortaris. Percommode accidit quod Cæsarem vidi. Non pigritia facio,*[3] *quod non mea manu ad te scribo. Quod abes, gratulor. Adde huc quod litteræ tuæ nullo modo perferri potuerunt. Quod spiratis, quod vocem mittitis, indignantur. Merito reprehenderis, quod non scripsisti.*[4]

NOTE 1.—Verbs expressing an affection or feeling of the mind, as *gaudeo, doleo, miror,* etc., are more frequently construed with the Acc. c. Inf.; as, *Gaudeo tibi jucundas esse meas litteras. Macedönes indigne ferebant Eumenem sibi anteponi. Ego te abfuisse tamdiu a nobis, et dolui quod carui fructu jucundissimo consuetudinis, et lætor quod absens omnia es consecutus.*

NOTE 2.—*Accedit* is sometimes (though rarely) followed by *ut;* as, " Besides being old, he was also blind ;" *Ad hominis senectutem accedebat ut cæcus esset.*
With *excusare,* the thing excused is expressed by *quod;* and the excuse alleged, either by a noun in the accusative or by the Acc. c. Inf. ; e. g., "He pleaded illness as his excuse for not having come yesterday ;" *Quod heri non venerit, morbum excusavit,* or *excusavit se ægrotasse.*

NOTE 3.—The pronouns *hoc, id, illud,* are often used pleonastically with verbs that require *ut* or *ne* after them; as, *Illud te moneo ut in munere tuo sis diligentissimus. Te illud primum rogo, ne quid invitus mea causa facias.*

Cura ut convalescas.

§ 95.—**UT** is used in the following cases :

1.) When an intention ("in order that," or "in order to"—with the Inf.) or a consequence (" so that," *or* "so [such] as to"—with the Inf.) is expressed. In the latter case *ut* is always preceded by such a word as *sic, ita, adeo, tam, tantus, tot, talis, ejusmodi,* or *is* (for *talis*) either expressed or understood ;

2.) After verbs signifying to *make, effect, care, strive, endeavour, re-*

---

[1] The necessity of dying. [2] You act a brother's part in .... [3] It is not from indolence that ...., or the fact that .... does not arise from indolence. [4] for not having written.

solve, *beg, request, advise, persuade, encourage, excite, compel, commision,* and *command* (the verb *jubeo* excepted), because clauses dependent on these verbs generally express an intended effect ;

3.) After the phrases *in eo esse, id (illud) ago, operam do, animum* (or *in animum*) *induco, consilium capio, nihil antiquius habeo* (or *duco*) *quam, consuetudo (mos* or *moris) est, consuetudo (natura) fert, lex est, hoc consilio, hac conditione ;*

4.) After the impersonal expressions : " hence it is," be it that," " it is the case," " it happens," etc., *est, futurum est, esto, fit, accidit, contingit, evenit, usu venit, occurrit, fore* or *futurum esse, restat, superest, reliquum (extremum, prope* or *proximum) est.* E. g., "Take care that you get well."

Edimus ut vivamus, non vivimus ut edamus.   Tanta vis probitatis est ut eam vel in hoste diligamus.   Sol efficit ut omnia floreant.   Enitar ut vincam.   Nihil antiquius habui quam ut te convenirem.   Fieri protest ut fallar.   Restat ut de litterarum utilitate loquar.   Vetus est lex ut idem amici velint.   Equidem in me ipso sœpissime experior[1] ut exalbescam in principiis dicendi et tota mente atque omnibus artubus contremiscam.

NOTE 1.—The verb *cogo*, instead of *ut* with the Subj., sometimes takes the Infinitive after it.—*Studeo*, in the sense of " to wish," almost exclusively takes the Inf. or the Acc. c. Inf.—Even *impero*, " I command," is occasionally construed with the Acc. c. Inf., when the latter is passive. E. g., *Quis te cogit abire ?   Omnibus se gratum videri studet.   Dux urbem diripi imperavit.*

NOTE 2.—Verbs of r e s o l v i n g. as *statuo, constituo, decerno, animum induco, consilium capio,* are generally followed by the Infinitive, when the subordinate and leading clauses have the same subject. Thus we may say both, *Constituerunt naves conscendere* and *ut naves conscenderent,* " They resolved to embark on board their ships." But we can say only, *Constituerunt ut nemo navem conscenderet,* because here the subjects are different.—*Consilium capio,* besides *ut* and the Infinitive, takes also the Genitive of the Gerund.

NOTE 8.—Verbs of a s k i n g, a d v i s i n g, and r e m i n d i n g, and also *decerno.* take sometimes the Subjunctive without *ut ;* as, *Cæsar consolatus Divitiacum rogat finem orandi faciat.   Senatus decrevit darent operam Consules ne quid respublica detrimenti caperet.*—This omission of *ut* regularly takes place after *velim, nolim, malim, vellem, nollem, mallem,* and the Imperative *fac.*

The phrase *in eo esse,* " to be about or on the point of...." is generally construed impersonally ; as, *In eo est ut pontem rescindant ;—in eo fuit ut palam reprehendereris ; —in eo est ut abeamus.*—The personal construction (*in eo sunt ut pontem rescindant—in eo fuisti ut palam reprehendereris—in eo sumus ut abeamus*) is rare and should be avoided.

☞ Verbs of a d v i s i n g, p e r s u a d i n g, e n c o u r a g i n g, i m p e l l i n g, are, by way of exception, sometimes construed with the simple Infinitive, especially in the

---

[1]) equivalent to Sæpissime mihi accidit, *ut.* . . .

poets and later prose writers; e. g., *Reipublicæ dignitas hæc minora relinquere hortatur. Persuasit Dionysio libertatem reddere Syracusanis*, etc.—Such constructions, however, should not be imitated.

Note 4.—*Facio ut* with the Subj. often stands periphrastically for the simple Indicative.—In the sense of "to represent or introduce," *facio* is construed with the Participle or also with the Infinitive passive. E. g., *Invitus quidem feci ut L. Flaminium e Senatu ejicerem*, instead of *invitus ejeci. Xenophon facit (fingit) Socratem disputantem. Isocratem Plato admirabiliter laudari a Socrate facit.*

The Imperative *fac*, in the sense of "suppose;" *efficio*, in the sense of "to prove," "infer;" *persuadeo*, in the sense of "to convince a person of the truth of something;" *decerno*, in the sense of "to judge," and *moneo, admoneo*, in the sense of "to remind a person that a thing is" (without intending that a thing be done), are followed by the Acc. c. Inf.; as, *Fac rem ita se habere. In his libris vult efficere, animos esse immortales. Mihi nunquam persuadebis, animum posse interire. Unum illud te moneo, artem sine assiduitate dicendi non multum juvare. Mea virtute atque diligentia perditorum hominum patefactam esse conjurationem decrevistis.*

Censeo, "to decree," "to think," "to vote for or give one's opinion to the effect that,"—is construed with *ut*, the Acc. c. Inf., and frequently with *esse* and the Participle in *dus*; as, *Plerique censebant ut noctu iter facerent. Quid mihi animi in navigando censes fore? Erant sententiæ quæ castra oppugnanda censerent. Ego vero censeo Carthaginem esse delendam.*

Note 5.—The English "instead of," "far from," or "so far from," is often expressed in Latin by *tantum abest ut—ut;* e. g., "I am so far from blaming him that I rather praise him,"-or "Far from blaming him, I rather praise him;" *Tantum abest ut eum reprehendam ut contra* (or *etiam,*—but not *potius*) *laudem,* or *Laudo eum, tantum abest ut reprehendam.—Tantum abest ut hi voluptates consectentur, ut etiam curas, sollicitudines, vigilias perferant,* or *Tantum abest ut hi voluptates consectentur, etiam curas, sollicitudines, vigilias perferunt.*

If the tense of the English leading verb is past, the formula *tantum abest ut* changes to *tantum aberat* (*abfuit*) *ut;* if future, to *tantum aberit ut;* as, "Instead of being praised, you will be blamed;" *Tantum aberit ut lauderis ut etiam reprehendaris.*

Repetam quo melius intelligas.

§ 96.—**QUO** ("that hereby" [*ut eo*], "in order that so much the") is generally used when an intention or purpose is expressed, and a comparative enters the sentence; as, "I will repeat that you may understand the better."

Medico aliquid dandum est, quo sit studiosior. Legem brevem esse oportet quo facilius ab imperitis teneatur. Obducuntur cortice arbores quo sint a frigore et calore tutiores. Ager aratur et iteratur quo meliores fructus possit et grandiores edere.

Note.—*Non quo* (or *non quod, non eo quod*) means "not as if;" and *non quin* (or *non quo non, non quod non*), "not as if not;" e. g., *Ad te litteras dedi non quo haberem magnopere quod scriberem, sed ut loquerer tecum absens. Non quin confiderem diligentiæ tuæ, sed quia* (or *quod*) etc.

Cave ne cadas.

§ 97.—**NE** ("in order that not," "lest," "in order not to"—with the Infinitive) is used when a negative intention or purpose is expressed: hence, in general, when any thing is forbidden, prevented, or guarded against by way of *begging, entreating, endeavoring, advising, persuading, exciting, commanding.* (☞ Instead of the simple *ne*, Cicero frequently uses *ut ne*.) E. g., "Take care lest you fall."

Gallinæ pennis fovent pullos ne frigore lædantur. Animum advertamus oportet ne callida assentatione capiamur. Fugiendum est illud ne offeramus nos periculis sine causa. Themistocles quærebat angustias ne multitudine circumiretur. Tu cura ut ne scintilla teterrimi belli relinquatur.

Note 1.—*NE* regularly stands with prohibitive Imperatives and also in formulas of swearing and protesting. E. g., *Ne festina. Ne animum desponde. Crabrones ne irrita.—Ne sim salvus* (or *ne vivam*) *si aliter scribo ac sentio.*

Note 2.—When a clause introduced by *ut* or *ne*, is to be continued by another—negative clause, the latter is generally introduced by *neve* or *neu*, more rarely by *neque*. E. g., *Cæsar milites hortatus est, uti suæ pristinæ virtutis memoriam retinerent, neu perturbarentur animo. Thrasybulus legem tulit ne quis ante actarum rerum accusaretur, neve multaretur.*

Note 3.—In clauses expressing an intended effect, the English "that nobody," "that nothing," "that no," "that never," are rendered by *ne quis, ne quid, ne ullus,* and *ne unquam ;*—but in clauses expressing a mere consequence without any previous intention, "that not" is rendered by *ut non ;* "that nobody," by *ut nemo ;* "that nothing," "that no," "that never," by *ut nihil, ut nullus, ut nunquam.* E. g., *Consules edixerunt ne quis urbe excederet. Vide ne quid desit.—Tum forte ægrotabam ut ad nuptias tuas venire non possem. Quis tam contentus vivit ut jam nihil desideret?*

Note 4.—With verbs of fearing "that" must be rendered by *ne,* and "that not," by *ut,*—and the English Future by the Latin Present or Imperfect. Instead of *ut, ne non* is sometimes used.

E. g.,   *Timeo ne eat,* I fear that he will go (i. e., I wish he may not go).
        Timeo ut eat, I fear that he will not go (i. e., I wish he may go).

Vereor ne labores tuos augeam. Pavor ceperat milites ne mortiferum esset Scipionis vulnus.—Avarus semper veretur ut satis habeat. Timeo ut pax firma sit.—Timeo ne non impetrem. Unum vereor ne Senatus Pompeium nolit (— ut velit) dimittere.
When no wish or desire is implied, verbs of fearing are followed by the Infinitive; e. g., *Non timeo dicere. Vereor laudare præsentem.*

Non possum quin exclamem.

§ 98.—**QUIN** ("that not," "but that," or "without" before a participial noun) is used, in general, after negative sentences and such interrogative clauses as expect a negative answer.—In particular, *quin* stands

1.) Instead of *qui non, quæ non, quod non,* after *nemo, nullus, nihil, vix, ægre—est, invenitur, reperitur; quis est? ecquis est? numquis est?*

2.) After *facere non possum* (or simply *non possum*), *fieri non potest; nulla causa* or *nihil causæ est, quid causæ est? nihil (paulum* [not *parum*], *haud multum, haud procul) abest; non, vix, ægre—abstineo* or *me contineo; tenere me* or *temperare mihi non possum,* "I cannot refrain from ;" *nihil prætermitto,* " I leave nothing undone ;" as, " I cannot help crying out," or " I cannot but cry out." ·

3.) In the sense of "that" or "but that," after *non dubito, non est dubium, dubitari non potest, nemo dubitat, quis dubitat?*—and sometimes, instead of the more usual Acc. c. Inf., after *quis ignorat?* and *negari non potest.*

Nunquam accedo quin abs te abeam doctior. Nihil causæ est[1] *quin idem tibi liceat. Nemo est tam bonus quin peccet interdum.*[2] *Dies fere nullus est quin* (or *quo non) ad te scribam. Facere non possum*[3] *quin rideam. Nihil abest*[4] *quin sim miserrimus. Paulum abfuit*[5] *quin caderem. Ego nihil prætermisi*[6] *quin Pompeium a Cæsaris conjunctione avocarem.*

NOTE 1.—*Qui non* and *quin* are used indiscriminately after *nemo est, nullus est, nihil est,* etc. Hence we may say both, *Quis est quin cernat* and *quis est qui non cernat?* " Who is there that does not see ?"—But when after these and other negative expressions, the particle *non* either belongs to some particular word, and not to the leading verb of the sentence, or when it is used emphatically, *qui non* and *ut non* must be used respectively, and not *quin.* E. g., *Non adeo imperitus sum ut nesciam* (not *quin sciam*). *Adhuc neminem cognovi poetam, qui sibi non optimus videretur. Tu non potuisti ullo modo facere ut mihi illam epistolam non mitteres. Fieri non potest ut Deus non sit beatissimus.*

NOTE 2.—*Non dubito* is sometimes construed with the Acc. c. Inf., especially in Nepos and later writers. When followed by a negative, it is equivalent to *credo* or *certus sum ;* as, *Nunc mihi non est dubium, quin legiones venturæ non sint,* " Now I am sure that the legions will not come." *Dubitandum non est, quin nunquam possit utilitas cum honestate contendere,* " We must believe that utility, etc.''
The English " I doubt whether" is expressed by *dubito num, dubito sitne, dubito utrum—an, dubito sitne—an ;* as, " I doubt whether I should give you the same advice ;" *Dubito num idem tibi suadere debeam. Deum esse qui dubitet, haud sane intelligo cur non idem sol sit an nullus sit, dubitare possit.* ·

---

[1] There is no reason. [2] as not to..... [3] I cannot but.... or I cannot help....
[4] Nothing is wanting to make me .... [5] I was near (not far from or within a little of) falling. [6] I did all in my power.

The English "I doubt that" is rendered by *dubito num* with the Subjunctive ; as, "I doubt that this is the case ;" *Dubito num res ita se habeat.*

Dubito and *non dubito*, in the sense of "to hesitate," "to scruple," are followed by the Infinitive ; as, *Non dubito affirmare. Eumenes non dubitavit prælium statim committere.*

NOTE 3.—To render the English "without" before a participial noun—by *quin*, it is necessary that the preceding sentence be negative. If this is not the case, some other construction must be employed, for which see § 221, III. 8.

NOTE 4.—*Quin* is sometimes used adverbially in the sense of "nay," "even,"—and sometimes as a particle of encouragement in the sense of "why not ;" as, *Credibile non est quantum scribam die, quin etiam noctibus. Quin conscendimus equos ?* i. e., *conscendamus equos !*—It also stands with Imperatives in the sense of "well," "pray ;" as, *Quin audi ! Quin dic uno verbo !*

Quid obstat quominus eam ?

§ 99.—**QUOMINUS** ("in order that not," usually "from" with a participial noun) stands after verbs of h i n d r a n c e, as *deterrere, impedire, intercedere, obstare, officere, obsistere, prohibere, recusare, repugnare, per me stat, per me fit, non pugno, nihil moror,* and others of the same meaning ; as, "What prevents me from going ?" Lit. What stands in the way by which I should go the less ?

Lex naturæ prohibet quominus alteri noceamus. Infirma valetudo me tenuit quominus ad vos venirem.[1] Per Trebonium stetit quominus oppido potirentur.[2] Non Isocrati quominus haberetur summus orator, offecit, quod infirmitate vocis, ne in publico diceret, impediebatur.

NOTE.—Verbs of hindrance are sometimes followed by *ne,* and when a negative precedes, even by *quin.—Non impedio, non prohibeo, non interdico,* however, are usually construed with *quominus.*

Impedio, recuso, deterreo, and especially *prohibeo,* are also found with the Infinitive; e. g., *Tuæ me lacrimæ prohibent ne plura dicam. Recusare non possum quin a me dissentiatis.[3] Non recuso mori. Hæc commemorare pudore deterreor.*

III. THE ACCUSATIVE WITH THE INFINITIVE.

§ 100.—The conjunction THAT is frequently left untranslated in Latin, and then the construction of the Accusative with the Infinitive takes place.

The construction of the Acc. c. Inf. consists in leaving out the conjunction THAT, and putting the nominative after THAT into the accusative, and the verb into the Infinitive of the same tense.

---

[1] prevented me from visiting you.   [2] It was owing to, or it was T's fault that. . . .
[3] I cannot object to your dissenting from me.

Patet Deum esse.

§ 101.—The construction of the Accusative with the Infinitive is used

1.) After the verbs *sentiendi* and *declarandi ;*
2.) After *jubeo,* " I bid," and *veto,* " I forbid ;"
3.) After the expressions denoting " it is clear," " it is known," "it is evident," etc.,—*constat, patet, apparet, credibile (apertum, certum, manifestum) est, intelligitur, percipitur, memoriæ proditum est, fama fert, spes est, rumor est, opinio est,* and the like ; as, " It is evident that God exists."

Those verbs are called verbs *sentiendi,* which denote the exercise either of our senses or our intellectual powers ; as, to *see, hear, feel, think, understand, perceive, hope, remember, forget, judge, suspect, believe, imagine, be convinced, know, conclude, consider, reflect*—and the like.

Those verbs are called verbs *declarandi,* which denote the communication of thought by way of speaking, writing, etc. ; as, to *say, relate, write, inform, reveal, betray, report, show, conceal, answer, affirm, deny, announce, promise, pretend, prove, witness, swear, threaten,* and the like.

Democritus dicit innumerabiles esse mundos. Aristoteles docet poetam Orpheum nunquam fuisse. Scribit meas litteras magnum apud te pondus habituras esse. Amicitiæ nostræ memoriam spero sempiternam fore. —Videmus Dei providentia mundum administrari. Existimare debes omnium oculos in te esse conjectos. Patet hominum causa factam esse terram. Spero consilium meum tibi probatum iri.

NOTE 1.—When a verb *sentiendi* or *declarandi* is parenthetically inserted in a sentence, or when the nominative of the subordinate clause is either drawn into the principal clause or introduced before the Infinitive by the sign " for," the proposition ought to be arranged so that the verb *sentiendi* or *declarandi* be placed before " that," and the nominative of the subordinate clause after " that." E. g., " Cæsar, I think, acted well," i. e., " I think that Cæsar acted well." Thus,

Livy relates of *Cato* that he	}	{ Livy relates that *Cato*....
It is right for *you* to obey.		{ It is right that *you* should obey.

NOTE 2.—When a verb *sentiendi* or *declarandi* is followed by a simple Infinitive, resolve the latter into a subordinate clause with " that ;" thus,

You think to understand it.	}	{ You think that you understand it.
He pretended to be sick.		{ He pretended that he was sick.

☞ Translate the English " he," " she," and " they" by *sui, sibi, se,* when they refer to the nominative of the leading clause ; but by *is, ea, id,* when they do not refer to that nominative ; e. g., " Caius thinks that he acted wisely ; but I think (that) he acted unwisely ;" *Caius putat se prudenter egisse, ego vero eum imprudenter egisse existimo.*

Note 3.—After verbs of h o p i n g, p r o m i s i n g, s w e a r i n g, and t h r e a t e n i n g, the English Infinitive Present is generally rendered by the Infinitive Future ; as, "I hope to return soon" (— that I shall soon return) ; *Spero me brevi rediturum esse.* "He promised to come to-morrow" (— that he would come) ; *Promisit se cras venturum esse.*—"Regulus swore to return to Carthage" (— that he would return) ; *Regulus juravit se Carthaginem rediturum.*—"The general threatens to plunder the city" (—that he will plunder) ; *Dux minatur se urbem direpturum (esse).*

☞ The English " would" after a past tense generally denotes futurity.

Instead of the Infinitive Future, both act. and pass., *fore ut* (— *futurum esse ut*) with the Subjunctive Pres. or Imperf. may also be used, and this circumlocution is even necessary, whenever the verb of the subordinate clause wants the Supine. Thus we can say *Mihi persuasum est fore aliquando ut omnis hic mundus deflagret*, as well as *Mihi persuasum est omnem hunc mundum aliquando esse deflagraturum. Exaudita vox est futurum esse ut Roma caperetur*, and *Exaudita vox est Romam captum iri.*—But we can only say : *Video te velle in cœlum migrare et spero fore ut contingat id nobis. Te constantiæ tuæ puto fore ut nunquam pæniteat.*

Note 4.—When in the construction of the Acc. c. Inf. two accusatives come together, and from this circumstance an ambiguity is likely to arise, the subordinate clause must first be made passive ; as,

(Eng.) It is certain that Milo killed Clodius.
(Lat.) It is certain that Clodius was killed by Milo.

Constat Clodium a Milone interfectum esse, not *Milonem Clodium interfecisse*, because from this text we would not know which of the two accusatives is the acc. of the sub ject, and which that of the object ;—in other words, we would not know whether Milo killed Clodius, or Clodius Milo.—Thus, *Quod scribis te a Cæsare quotidie plus diligi* (not *te Cæsarem plus diligere*) *immortaliter gaudeo. Nunquam auditum est crocodilum violatum esse ab Ægyptio* (not *crocodilum Ægyptium violasse*). But where no such ambiguity is to be apprehended, two accusatives may well stand together ; as, *Spero te cum voluptate hunc librum perlecturum esse. Quis non videt Deum omnem hunc mundum sapientissime gubernare ? Spero me brevi vos* (or *matrem meam*) *visurum esse. Legimus Alexandrum captivas esse consolatum.*

Note 5.—A *past* tense after a *present* is always rendered by the Infinitive Perfect ; as, "He says that it pleased him ;" *Dicit sibi placuisse.*
A past tense after another past tense, is rendered—sometimes by the Infinitive Perfect and sometimes by the Infinitive Present. It is rendered by the Inf. Perf., when the notion expressed by the verb after *that*, is prior to the notion expressed by the verb before *that ;* and by the Inf. Present, when the notions expressed by the two verbs are simultaneous, that is, when they exist together. E. g.,

He said that it pleased him ; *dixit sibi placuisse.*
He said that it pleased him ; *dixit sibi placere.*

Here, *sibi placuisse* means that he was pleased previously, that is, some time before his saying it ; and *sibi placere*, that he was pleased at the very time he said it.

Note 6.—The Infinitive form—*urum esse* is used in the following three cases ; 1.) When we wish to express m e r e f u t u r i t y ; as, "I think (that) I shall be able to pay ;" *Puto me solvendo parem futurum esse.*—2.) When an i n t e n t i o n, a w i s h, a b e i n g a b o u t, is to be expressed ; e. g., "He says that he has no mind to do it ;" *Negat se id facturum esse.* "It is rumored that the ambassadors are about to return ;" *Rumor est legatos domum redituros esse.*—3.) In h y p o t h e t i c a l clauses, to denote what under a certain condition, either expressed or understood, would take place ; e. g., " I think he would give, if he had ;" *Puto eum daturum esse si haberet.*

The Infinitive form—*urum fuisse* should never be used to express mere futurity. A state or an action completed in future time, is expressed—actively by *fore ut* with the Subjunctive Perf. or Pluperf., and—passively by *fore* with the Participle Perfect. E. g., " I hope you will have finished the business to-morrow at this time ;" *Spero fore ut cras hoc ipso tempore rem confeceris. Credebam fore ut tunc epistolam scripsisses.* —*Spero cras hoc ipso tempore rem confectam fore,* or *Non dubito quin cras hoc ipso tempore confecta jam res futura sit.*

The Infinitive form—*urum fuisse* is used, however, like the form—*urum esse,* in the following two cases : 1.) When an i n t e n t i o n, a w i s h, a b e i n g a b o u t, is to be expressed ; as, " I know that you had the intention to write ;" *Scio te scripturum fuisse.*—2.) In h y p o t h e t i c a l clauses, to denote what under a certain condition, either expressed or understood, would have taken place ; as, " I think he would have given, if he had had ;" *Credo eum daturum fuisse si habuisset.*—*Stantes plaudebant in re ficta ; quid in vera facturos fuisse arbitramur ? Pollio Asinius Cæsarem suos rescripturum et correcturum commentarios fuisse existimat* (sc. *si diutius vixisset*).

To express passively what under a certain condition would have taken place, the circumlocution with *futurum fuisse ut* and the Subjunctive Imperf. is used ; e. g., " The king did not know that the city would have been surrendered to him, if.... ;" *Rex ignorabat futurum fuisse ut sibi urbs traderetur si unum diem expectasset.*

☞ When the consequence of a hypothetical clause depends on such a verb as *puto, credo, opinor,* it is often advisable (and if the dependent verb wants the Supine, even necessary) to express the consequence or apodŏsis by the Subjunctive ; as, *Cautius, credo, viverent homines, si cogitarent se brevi morituros. Si Romæ nunc esses, valeres, opinor, melius quam vales. Citius, opinor, didicisses, nisi cessator ac negligens fuisses.*

Note 7.—After *memini,* the English Infinitive Perfect is rendered by the Infinitive Present, when the speaker mentions an event which he has witnessed himself and which he wishes to represent as continuing ; e. g., " I recollect Cato to have asserted in conversation with myself and Scipio..... ;" *Memini Catonem mecum et cum Scipione disserere. Memini Pamphilium mihi narrare.*—But when a fact is to be represented as completed, the Infinitive Perfect should be used ; as, *Ego memini summos fuisse in civitate nostra viros.*

After *video* and *audio,* the English Infinitive Present is generally expressed by the Participle Present, to denote the particular state in which we see or hear somebody or something ; e. g., *Audio te canentem,* " I hear you sing or singing." (*Audio te canere* would signify, " I hear [i. e., I am told—hear from others] that you are singing)."—*Socratem Xanthippe eodem semper vultu vidit exeuntem et revertentem. Lacesse iracundum et videbis furentem. Etiam voce dignoscimus amicum quum eum loquentem audimus.*

Note 8.—When in the construction of the Acc. c. Inf. the nominative of the subordinate clause, by means of *qui, qualis, quantus, quot, quam, ut, sicut, ac* or *atque* (" as"), is joined to another nominative, the latter is likewise changed into the accusative. But when either the preceding verb is repeated or the second subordinate clause has a verb of its own, the nominative remains unchanged and the verb agrees with it accordingly ; e. g., *Decet patriam nobis cariorem esse quam nosmetipsos,* or *quam nosmetipsi sumus. Suspicor te iisdem rebus quibus me ipsum permoveri,* or *quibus ego ipse permoveor. Pompeium audio plura bella gessisse quam ceteri legerunt.*

Sometimes, when two subordinate clauses are connected by *potius* or *citius quam,* the construction of the Acc. c. Inf. extends also to the latter ; as, *Dixerunt se in cor-*

pora sua cítius sœvituros quam fidem violaturos esse, instead of the more regular *quam violarent* or *quam ut violarent. Tibi affirmo quidvis me potius perpessurum quam ex hoc loco abiturum,* instead of *quam* (or *quam ut) abeam.*

NOTE 9.—*Video,* in the sense of "to care ;" *censeo,* in the sense of "to advise ;" and the verbs *dico, scribo, nuntio,* and *respondeo,* when implying a command or a wish that something be done or omitted, are construed with *ut* or *ne,* accordingly ; as, *Navem idoneam ut habeas, diligenter vide. Hoc tantum ad te scribo ut valetudinem tuam quam diligentissime cures. Respondit eis Cæsar, ne timerent, ut contra bono animo essent; et enim non amplius veterum injuriarum velle reminisci.*

Jubeo, when used absolutely, that is, without an accusative of the person commanded, takes the Subjunctive with or without *ut ;* as, *Jube mihi multa rescribat. Jubeo ut hoc fiat. Jussit ne longius procederent.*

☞ *Sic, ita, hoc, id, illud,* are often used pleonastically with verbs *sentiendi* and *declarandi,* of course, without influence upon the construction ; as, *Sic habeto (— scito) non te esse mortalem sed corpus hoc. Ita tibi persuadeas, nihil bonum esse nisi honestum. Illud te intelligere volo pergraviter illum esse offensum.*

Cupio te valere, or Cupio ut valeas.

§ 102.—The Accusative with the Infinitive, or *ut* with the Subjunctive is used :

1.) After verbs signifying "to be willing," "to wish," "to permit," (as *volo, nolo, malo, cupio, opto, sino, patior, permitto, concedo, licet ;)*

2.) After the expressions denoting: It follows (*sequitur, efficitur*), it is rare, strange, fair, right, just, convenient, useful, expedient, necessary, true, false, probable, that . . . . . . ; as, "I wish you to be in good health."

Paccm conservari (ut pax conservetur) omnes boni optant.   Quod vis alium silere (ut alius sileat) primus sile.   Non est rectum-minori parêre majorem (ut minori pareat major).   Si hoc verum non est, sequitur esse falsum (ut falsum sit).   Eam rem tibi volo bene et feliciter evenire (ea res ut tibi eveniat).

NOTE 1.—*Necesse est,* "it is necessary that," "must," and *oportet,* "it behooves,' "ought," take either the Acc. c. Inf. or the Subjunctive without *ut ;* as, *A Deo mundum regi (mundus regatur) necesse est.   Legem brevem esse (lex brevis sit) oportet.— Necésse est* sometimes takes the dative of the person ; as, *Mihi necesse est dicere. Nobis necesse est mori.*

NOTE 2.—*Patior* and *sino* are generally followed by the Acc. c. Inf., rarely by *ut. Concedo* and *permitto* may take either the Infinitive or *ut* with the Subjunctive : the latter is the practice of the best prose writers.

NOTE 3.—The verbs *volo, nolo, malo, opto, cupio,* and *studeo* (in the sense of *cupio*), are in Latin constructed with the simple Infinitive when the subject of the latter is the same as the subject of the verbs *volo, nolo, malo,* etc. themselves ; as, *cupio videre, volumus abire, noluit intelligere,* etc.

When the Infinitive is one of those verbs that are construed with two nominatives, such as *esse, fieri, haberi, judicari,* etc., and the subject remains the same, the verbs *volo, nolo, malo,* etc. are construed either with the simple Infinitive, the predicate-noun or adjective being then put in the nominative, or with the Acc. c. Inf., in which case the predicate together with the personal pronoun implied in the leading verb, is put in the accusative. Accordingly we can say *Volo esse clemens* as well as *Volo me esse clementem. Volumus esse benefici* and *beneficos nos esse volumus,* etc. etc. *Omnibus gratus videri studet* and *omnibus gratum se videri studet. Princeps esse mavult quam videri* and *principem se esse mavult quam videri. Volo is esse* (and *eum me esse volo*) *quem tu me esse voluisti.*

When the subjects are not the same, either the Acc. c. Inf., or *ut* with the Subjunctive must be used; as, *Cupio te valere* or *cupio ut valeas.*

NOTE 4.—With *licet,* the person allowed or permitted is generally put in the dative; as, *Per me tibi abire licet. Cur mihi idem facere non liceat? Quid deceat vos, non quantum liceat vobis, spectare debetis.*

When the accompanying infinitive (especially *esse, fieri, vivere, egredi, invehi,* and the like) has a predicate-noun or adjective joined to it, the latter, too, is put in the dative; as, *Tibi quieto esse licet. Mihi negligenti esse non licet. Rogavit ut sibi triumphanti* (" in triumph") *urbem invehi liceret. Patricio Romano tribuno plebis fieri non licuit.*—The same construction is found, also, with *necesse est, datur, lubet,* in connection with *licet;* as, *Non datur omnibus esse opulentis, sed licet omnibus esse bonis. Illis timidis et ignavis licet esse, vobis necesse est fortibus viris esse.*

The Acc. c. Inf. with *licet* is found also, though less frequently, and for the most part only when no definite subject is expressed; e. g., *Syracusanum in insula habitare non licet. Non licet esse negligentem.*—Still more rare is it to find both cases in the same sentence, as *Medios esse non licet poetis. Is erat annus quo per leges ei Consulem fieri liceret.*

☞ *Licet* and *volo* are often construed with the simple Subjunctive; as, *Per me abeas licet. Per me vel stertas licet, non modo quiescas. Quid vis faciam? Visne te Latine interrogem?—Volo ut* intimates a strong emphasis, as *Volo ut taceas, ut respondeas,* etc.

THE NOMINATIVE WITH THE INFINITIVE.

§ 103.—The verbs of "saying" and "thinking," as *dico, trado, fero, puto, credo,* etc., are often, in English, construed impersonally: "it is said," "it is reported," "it is thought,"—or with an indefinite subject-nominative: "they say," "they think," "people say," "people think." Whenever this is the case, the verbs *dico, trado, fero,* etc., are either put in the 3d pers. plur. act. (*dicunt, tradunt, ferunt*) and construed with the Acc. c. Inf., or they are expressed passively and construed with the Nom. c. Inf., that is, the nominative of the subordinate clause is drawn into the principal sentence and made the subject-nominative of the whole proposition. With this nominative, the verbs *dicor, trador, feror,* etc., are then made to agree in number and person, whereas the verb after "that" is put in the Infinitive of its own tense.

Rex esse credor.

§ 104.—The nominative with the Infinitive is used with the passive verbs *dicor, trador, feror, putor, credor, habeor, judicor, existimor, me-*

moror, narror, nuntior, perhibeor, demonstror, negor (jubeor,) vetor ; as,
" They take me for a king," or " They think (that) I am a king."

*Xanthippe morosa admodum fuisse fertur.   Castor et Pollux victoriæ
nuntii fuisse perhibentur.   Luna solis lumine collustrari putatur. In-
sectis medulla inesse negatur.   Jam adesse Cæsaris equites nuntiabantur.
Senatores vetiti sunt ingredi Ægyptum.*

NOTE 1.—The verb *videor*, " I seem," is regularly construed with the Nom. c. Inf.:
as, " It seems (that) I have mistaken," Lat., " I seem to have mistaken ;" *Videor
errasse.—*" It does not seem as if you were (— that you are) dangerously sick," Lat.,
" You do not seem to be d. s. ;" *Non videris periculose ægrotare.*
    With the dative of a person, *videor* corresponds to the English " think," " imagine,"
" fancy ;" as, " You think (— it seems to you that) I have mistaken," Lat., " I seem
to you to have mistaken ;" *Videor tibi errasse.—*" I think (— it seems to me that) you
acted imprudently," Lat., " You seem to me to have acted imprudently ;" *Videris
mihi imprudenter egisse.—Videor mihi videre imminentes reipublicæ tempestates.*

NOTE 2.—When the dependent Infinitive is an impersonal verb, the verbs *dicor,
trador, feror, putor, credor*, etc., are likewise construed impersonally ; as, *Eos igno-
rantiæ suæ pænituisse dicitur.   Omnium vehementer interesse videtur.*

IV. QUESTIONS AND ANSWERS.

§ 105.—There are two kinds of questions : viz., simple and double.

A *simple* question is one that consists of one member only ; as, " Whence do you
come ?"   " Where are they ?"   " Who is it ?"   " How is your cousin ?"
    A *double* question is one that consists of two or more members connected dis-
junctively by *or ;* as, " Is this wine or water ?"   " Am I right or wrong ?"   " Was it
you or James or Henry that did it ?"
    Both simple and double questions are either direct or indirect.
    A question is said to be *direct*, when it asks positively, that is, when it does not
depend on any word or phrase going before ; as, " Where are my books ?"   " Why
do you laugh ?"   " Was it my fault or yours ?"
    A question is said to be *indirect*, when it depends on some word or phrase going
before, such as *ask, doubt, see, consider, know, try, it matters, it makes a difference, it
is uncertain*, and the like ; as, " I should like to know where my books are."   " I
know why you are laughing."   " It matters little whether it was my fault or yours."

In *direct* questions, the INDICATIVE ; in *indirect*, the SUBJUNCTIVE is
used.

(Simple Questions.)

Quid rides ?

§ 106.—Simple questions, both direct and indirect, are introduced
either

a) By interrogative pronouns and adverbs, such as *uter, quis, quis-*
am, ecquis, qualis, quantus, quam, quamdiu, quo, quot, quoties, quomodo,
uando, quorsum, ubi, unde, cur, quare ;—or

b) By the interrogative particles *ne, num, nonne ;* e. g., "Why do
ou laugh ?"

[Direct.] *Unde venis? Estne frater tuus domi? Ecquid audis?* [1]
?ur me excrucio? Nonne canis similis est lupo? Quis vestrum igno-
at? Quamdiu patientia nostra abuteris? Num quid vis? Num
egare audes?

[Indirect.] *Incertum est quid cras futurum sit. Olim quæstio erat*
:um terra rotunda esset. Scire velim numquid necesse sit esse Romœ.
Quæritur umquamne fuerint monocerotes. Non video, cur te excrucies.

NOTE 1.—NE asks simply for information and is generally appended to the verb of the
entence. When annexed to the emphatic word, it usually expects a negative an-
wer. E. g., "Do you hear ?" *Audisne?*—"Have you done this ?" or, "You have
1ot done this. Have you ?" *Tune hoc fecisti ?—In nostrane potestate est quid me-*
ninerimus?

NUM in direct questions expects the answer *no ;* in indirect questions it implies
1either negative nor affirmative.

NONNE always expects the answer *yes ;* as, "Have not you done this ?" or, "You
1ave done this. Haven't you ?" *Nonne tu hoc fecisti ?* or, *Tu hoc fecisti, nonne ?—*
Nonne vir sapiens beatus est ? or, *Vir sapiens beatus est, nonne ?*

NE and NUM, in direct questions, are not translated ; in indirect questions, they
1re translated by *whether.*

Instead of *num* sometimes *numne, numquid,* and *ecquid* are used, the *quid* in this
:ase having no meaning at all ; as, *Deum ipsum numne vidisti ? Numquid vos duas*
habetis patrias ? Ecquid audis ? i. q. *num audis ?*

NOTE 2.—When the interrogative nature of a sentence is clear from the context, the
interrogative particle is often wholly omitted ; but in this case the emphatic word is
placed first ; as, *Tu innocentior Metello ?—Miser ergo Archelaus ?—Potest quidquam esse*
absurdius ?—Tu in forum prodire, tu lumen conspicere, tu in horum conspectum venire
audes ?

NOTE 8.—When a question asks d o u b t i n g l y, that is, when it does not require
an answer for information, but simply expresses some emotion or perplexity of mind,
the Subjunctive must be used, though the question be direct. The English language,
in this case, generally employs the auxiliaries *may, can, will, shall, could, should,* etc. ;
as, "What can I do ?" *Quid faciam ?*—"What am I to say ?" *Quid dixam ?*—"What
could (should) he do ?" *Quid faceret ?—*"What was he to say ?" *Quid diceret ?—*
"What ought I to have done ?" *Quid facerem ?—Quo me vertam ? Quis Deum non*
timeat ?

NOTE 4.—Questions are sometimes put in a direct form with the Indicative, where
the Subjunctive might be expected. This is especially the case a) after the Impera-

---

[1] Do you hear any thing !

tives *dic, dic mihi,* and *vide ;—*b) after *mirum quam, mirum quantum, nimium quantum,* when these expressions are equivalent to *mirabiliter* or *plurimum ;* and c) after *nescio quis, nescio quid, nescio quem, nescio quomodo,* etc., when they stand for *aliqui, aliquid, aliquem, aliquomodo,* etc. ; as, *Dic, quæso, fuistine heri in schola ? Vide quam conversa res est ! Id consilium mirum quantum mihi profuit. Prope me hic nescio qui loquitur.*

NOTE 5.—Questions conveying the idea of s u r p r i s e , s c o r n , s o r r o w , or i n d i g n a t i o n, are frequently expressed by the Acc. c. Inf., where *estne credibile ?*—or by *ut* with the Subjunctive, where *fierine potest ?* may be supplied ; as, *Tene hoc dicere tali prudentia præditum ? Adeone hominem infelicem esse quemquam ut ego sum ?— Egone ut te interpellem ? Te ut ulla res frangat ? Victamne ut quisquam victrici patriæ præferret.*

(Double Questions.)

Par an impar ?

§ 107.—In double questions the first member is introduced by *utrum* or the suffix *ne,* and the second by *an ;—*or the first member has no interrogative particle at all, and the second takes *an* or the suffix *ne ;* e. g., "Odd or even ?"

[Direct.] *Utrum major est sol an minor quam terra ? Casune mundus est effectus an vi divina ? Stellarum numerus par est an impar? Sol mobilis est immobilisne ?*

[Indirect.] *Si sitis, nihil interest utrum aqua sit an vinum ? Unum illud nescio gratulerne tibi an timeam ? Stellarum numerus par sit an impar, nescitur. Multum interest valentes imbecilline simus.*

NOTE 1.—Instead of the simple *utrum* and *an, utrumne* (mostly separated) and *anne* are sometimes used ; as, *Quæritur tria pauca sint anne multa. Videamus utrum ea fortuitane sint an ....*
The English " or," in double questions, must not be translated by *aut* or *vel,* but by *an* or the suffix *ne.—*The English " or not," in direct questions is generally rendered by *annon,* in indirect by *necne.* E. g., *Hoccine facies, annon ? Hiccine est quem quæris, annon ?—Amazones fuerint necne, quæritur. Quæritur sintne dii necne sint.*

NOTE 2.—The particle *an,* in the best Latin writers, and especially in Cicero, the chief model of good Latinity and first authority in matters of Grammar, is never used either in simple direct or simple indirect questions, but only in the latter member of double questions, and always in the sense of " or." It is only with the later writers that the use of *an* in the sense of " whether" originated. Constructions therefore as the following: *An legisti Ciceronem ? An frater tuus domi est ? Quæritur an hoc verum sit ?* etc., should be avoided, and we ought to say rather : *Legistine Ciceronem ? Estne frater tuus domi ? Quæritur num hoc verum sit.*
An (*anne, an vero*), it is true, frequently seems, even in Cicero, to introduce simple interrogative clauses. But in these passages *an* is used exclusively in the sense of "or," ' or perhaps," " or rather," " then," so that a preceding alternative question is always to be supplied by the mind. Such questions, therefore, are simple questions only in

appearance, but double or disjunctive in reality. E. g., *Dicis te crediturum si hilarem me videris. An tu esse me tristem putas?* " Do you, then, believe me to be sad ?" Supply before *an : Nonne hilarem me esse vides?*—Thus, *Invitus te offendi : an putas me delectari lædendis hominibus ?* Supply: *credisne hoc ?*—*Oratorem irasci minime decet. An tibi irasci tum videmur, quum quid in causis acrius et vehementius dicimus ?* Supply : *Nonne ab ira temperare nos vides ?*

When another question precedes, *an* generally introduces the answer to that question and is then equivalent to *nonne* (" not"); e. g., *Quando autem ista vis evanuit ? an postquam homines minus creduli esse cœperunt ?* Supply before *an : utrum alio tempore ?* " Did it not disappear after.... ?"—*Quidnam beneficio provocati facere debemus ? an imitari agros fertiles qui multo plus efferunt quam acceperunt ?* Supply before *an : utrum aliquid aliud ?* " Should we not imitate, etc. ?"

From this rule, however, we must except the use of *an* after *nescio, haud scio,* and other expressions denoting u n c e r t a i n t y, such as *delibero, hæsito, dubito, dubium est, incertum est.* In these combinations, *an* is taken in the sense of " whether not," and as the English " whether not," " whether not perhaps," always inclines towards a modest affirmation, the expressions *nescio an, haud scio an,* etc., may be translated by " probably," " perhaps," " I might almost ....," " I feel inclined to .... ;" as, *Dubito an Hannibalem ceteris omnibus anteponam.*[1] *Timiditatem dico ? nescio an melius ignaviam dicere possim.*[2] *Moriendum certe est, et id incertum an eo ipso die.*[3] *Quæ parare arduum fuit nescio an tueri difficilius sit.*[4] *Haud scio an perficere possis.*[5] *Haud scio an non possis perficere.*[6] *Huic uni contigit quod nescio an nulli* (not *ulli*).[7] *Haud scio an habeat parem neminem* (not *quemquam*).[8] *Hoc haud scio an nunquam* (not *unquam*) *futurum sit.*[9]

But, when more uncertainty is denoted, without any inclination towards either the affirmative or negative, *num* or the suffix *ne* must be used after *nescio, haud scio, dubito,* etc. ; as, *Dubito num idem tibi suadere debeam. Hæc nescio rectene litteris committantur.*

An sometimes occurs in the sense of " or," in sentences which do not seem to be of an interrogative nature. In these instances *incertum est* or *non constat,*" it is uncertain whether .... or," must be supplied ; e. g., *Themistocles, quum ei Simonides an quis alius, artem memoriæ polliceretur, oblivionis, inquit, mallem. Nos hic te ad mensem Januarium expectamus, ex quodam rumore an ex litteris tuis ad alios missis.*

NOTE 8.—From double or disjunctive questions the so-called *parallel* questions must be carefully distinguished. By the latter are meant two or more interrogative members or clauses which are connected by " or," but not disjunctively, that is, not so as to exclude one another, as is the case in double questions.—In parallel questions, the English " or" is either expressed by *aut (ve),* or the interrogative particle *num (ne)* is repeated with every member. E. g., *Voluptas melioremne efficit aut laudabiliorem virum ? Numquid simile Populus Romanus audierat aut viderat ? Quid ergo, solem dicam aut lunam aut cœlum deum ? Quid primum querar ? aut unde potissimum ordiar ? aut quod aut a quibus auxilium petam ? deorumne immortalium ? Populine Romani ? vestramne hoc tempore fidem implorem ?—Quæro a te, num Cornelius legem neglexerit, num Consuli vim attulerit, num armatis hominibus templum tenuerit, num religionem polluerit, ærarium exhauserit, rempublicam compilarit ?*

---

[1] I might almost prefer.... [2] I might perhaps with more right call it cowardice. [3] and perhaps on that very day. [4] it is perhaps still more difficult.... [5] You will probably be able to do it. [6] You will perhaps not be able to do it. [7] what perhaps happened to no one. [8] He has probably not his equal. [9] This probably will never be the case.

Intelligisne ?—Intelligo.

§ 108.—The answers "yes" and "no" are variously expressed in Latin : viz.,

The answer " yes :" a) by *ita, ita plane, ita prorsus, ita est, sic est, sane, sane quidem, etiam, vero, certe, profecto, utique ;*—b) by repeating the emphatical word ; e. g., " Do you understand ?" Yes, or I do.

The answer "no :" a) by *non, minime, minime vero, nequaquam, neutiquam, nullo modo ;*—b) by repeating the emphatical word with *non* placed before it ;—c) by *immo* or *immo vero* with the addition of the contrary.

Hæccine tua domus est? Ita.—Visne tecum eam? Sane et libenter quidem.—Certumne hoc est? Certissimum.—Tunc te hinc abiisse negas? Nego enimvero.—Fierine potest? Potest.—Dasne[1] deorum immortalium numine naturam omnem regi? Do sane.

Non pudet te vanitatis? Minime.—Num tu hæc fecisti? Minime vero.—Estne frater intus? Non est.—Fuistine heri in schola? Non fui.—Visne desinam? Immo perge.—Num Crassus pauper fuit? Immo divitissimus.—Siccine hunc decipis? Immo vero ille me decipit.

CHAPTER III.

SUBSTANTIVES.

Arma Achillis.

§ 109.—Any substantive which answers to the question " whose?" or, " of whom or what ?" asked in connection with another substantive. is put in the genitive ; as, " The arms of Achilles."

Initium sapientiæ est timor Domini. Ordo est anima rerum. Verecundia est maximum ornamentum adolescentiæ. Mirum me tenet desiderium urbis, incredibile meorum atque imprimis tui.

NOTE 1.—The sign of this genitive is generally either the apostrophic "'s" or the preposition "of" placed between two nouns. Not unfrequently, however, other prepositions, also, are used as connectives ; as, Skill i n war, *peritia belli.*—Incitement to

---

[1]) Do you grant ?

virtue, *incitamentum virtutis.*—Access to praise, *aditus laudis.*—Disgust for labor, *tædium laboris.*—Longing for repose, *desiderium otii.*—Escape from danger, *fuga periculi.*—Longing after riches, *cupiditas divitiarum.*—Remedy for pain, *remedium doloris.*—Converse with friends, *consuetudo amicorum,* etc.

NOTE 2.—The genitive dependent upon another substantive, has often a twofold meaning, a *subjective* and an *objective,* according as it denotes that which does something, or that which is the object of the action or feeling spoken of. Thus *amor Dei* may denote either the love of God towards men, and then the genitive is subjective, because it denotes the subject which exercises the act of loving, or it may signify the love of men towards God, and in this case the genitive is objective, because it denotes that which is the object of man's love.—The same can be said of the following combinations : *pietas parentum, cura liberorum, odium Hannibalis, desiderium meorum, horum amicitia, triumphus Gallorum, injuriæ Helvetiorum, judicium Verris, fuga hostium,* etc.

In these and similar expressions the context generally decides whether the genitive is to be taken subjectively or objectively.—In case, however, of any real ambiguity, it is advisable to use a preposition instead of the objective genitive ; e. g., *amor in Deum, pietas erga parentes, cura de liberis, de Verre judicium, amicitia cum his, odium in* or *adversus Hannibalem, triumphus de Gallis,* etc.

NOTE 3.—When to the words *vox, verbum, nomen, cognomen,* the name itself is added, the latter is put in the genitive ; as, *Quid sonat vox voluptatis ?*[1] *Cæsar recepit prænomen imperatoris, cognomen patris patriæ. Ex amore nomen amicitiæ ductum est.*

NOTE 4.—The words *instar,* "like ;" *causa, gratia,* "for the sake of ;" and *nihil,* "nothing" (before a substantive, "no"), are in reality substantives, and as such govern the genitive of the noun following.—*Causa* and *gratia* are generally, and *instar* often, placed after the genitive. E. g., *Plato mihi unus instar est omnium.*[2] *Montium instar maris fluctus exsurgunt. Romani habebant domos instar urbium. Multi utilitatis causa fingunt amicitias. Bestias hominum gratia generatas esse videmus. Justitia nihil expetit præmii. Fortuna nihil habet stabilitatis. Nihil timent qui nihil mali commiserunt. Nihil novi sub sole.*

The English "on my (thy, his, our, etc.) account," "for my (thy, his, our, etc.) sake," is expressed in Latin by *mea (tua, sua, nostra, vestra) causa ;* as, *Deus omnia nostra causa fecit. A te peto, ut id cum tua, tum mea causa facias. Non tam mea quam tua causa doleo te non valere.*

Puer bonæ indolis, or bona indole.

§ 110.—A substantive having an adjective agreeing with it, and expressing a quality or property of a former substantive, is put in the genitive or ablative ; as, " A boy of a good disposition."

Vir præstantis ingenii or *præstanti ingenio. Homo antiqua virtute et fide. Vir claris natalibus.*[3] *Vir insignis prudentiæ. Spelunca infinita altitudine. Tarquinius fratrem habuit Aruntem, mitis ingenii juvenem. Cæsar ad Ariovistum Valerium misit, summa virtute et humanitate adolescentem.*

---

[1] What does the word pleasure mean ? [2] is to me as good as all. [3] of noble birth.

Note 1.—Sometimes both constructions are found in the same sentence; as, *Lentulum nostrum, eximia spe summæque virtutis adolescentem, tibi etiam atque etiam commendo. Neque monere te audeo præstanti prudentia virum, nec confirmare maximi animi hominem.*

Note 2.—When the accompanying adjective is a n u m e r i c a l one, the genitive only can be used; as, "Corn for thirty days;" *Frumentum triginta dierum. Iter unius diei. Exilium decem annorum. Classis ducentarum navium. Fossa quindecim pedum. Colossus centum viginti pedum. Homo trium litterarum.*[1]

Note 3.—When the qualifying noun has no adjective agreeing with it, it cannot be expressed, in Latin, by a substantive, but must be rendered by an adjective; as, "A man of talent," *Vir ingeniosus*, not *vir ingenii*. "A man of learning—of courage—of experience, etc.," *Vir eruditus, vir fortis, vir expertus,*—not *vir eruditionis, fortitudinis, experientiæ.*

Magno timore sum.

§ 111.—A substantive expressing the *situation* or *condition*, in which the subject of the verb is, is put in the ablative; as, " I am in great fear."

Ego sum spe bona. Incredibili sum sollicitudine de tua valetudine. Quanto fuerim dolore, meministi. Apud regem plebemque longe maximo honore Servius Tullius erat. Ut meliore simus loco, ne optandum quidem est.

Note.—The preposition *in* is sometimes added to this ablative; as, *Eram in magna spe. Arx Romæ capitoliumque in ingenti periculo fuit.*—The preposition *in* is even necessary, when the ablative has no adjective agreeing with it, as *esse in spe, in honore, in periculo, in deliciis*, etc.

Natione Gallus.

§ 112.—A substantive *limiting* the meaning of another substantive (verb, or adjective) to some particular part or circumstance, is put in the ablative; as, " A Gaul by birth."

Sunt quidam homines non re,[2] *sed nomine. Agesilaus claudus erat altero pede.*[3] *Centum numero sumus. Erat Persarum exercitus numero amplissimus, firmitate exiguus. Epaminondæ nemo Thebanus par erat eloquentia. Populus Romanus omnes gentes virtute superavit.*

Note 1.—This ablative is called "the ablative of limitation."—It is in English generally expressed by a s t o, i n, w i t h r e g a r d t o, in respect of, according to, and answers the questions " in what?" " as to what?" "in what respect?" etc.; as, *primus ordine; prior tempore; puer ætate;*[4] *pietate filius, consilio parens,*

---

[1] i. e., *Fur.*　　[2] not in reality.　　[3] in one of his feet.　　[4] in years.

vir nobilitate excellens, virtute eximius, eloquentia summus; natu major, natu minor; oculis pedibusque æger; oculis et mente captus,[1] *crine ruber, statura procerus; meo judicio, mea opinione; more* or *consuetudine Græcorum,* etc.

NOTE 2.—Such expressions as *nudus membra, saucius pedes, humeros oleo perfusus, os humerosque deo similis, miles fractus membra labore, redimitus tempora lauro, omnia Mercurio similis vocemque coloremque et crines flavos,* and the like, are Greek imitations, which should not be admitted into prose.

Constat talento.

§ 113.—A substantive denoting the *price* or *value* of a thing, is put in the ablative ; as, " It costs one talent."

Viginti talentis unam orationem Isocrates vendidit. Multo sanguine ea Pœnis victoria stetit. Lis ejus centum talentis æstimata est[2] *Sextante sal et Romæ et per totam Italiam erat.*[3] *Quingentis sestertiorum millibus villam æstimabant. Modius tritici binis sestertiis, ad summum ternis erat. Triginta millibus Cœlius habitat.*[4]

NOTE 1.—When the price of a thing is expressed—not by a substantive, but indefinitely by such adjectives as " much," " more," " little," " less," " as much as," etc., in Latin, the genitives *magni, permagni, maximi,—pluris, plurimi,—parvi, minoris, minimi,—tanti, quanti, quanticunque,* are used (☞ but never *multi* and *majoris*);[5] as, " What does the peck sell for?" *Quanti modius venit ? Asse et pluris.—Mercatores non tantidem vendunt, quanti emerunt. Dimidio minoris vendo quam ceteri. Pluris quam decem millibus emerunt. Quanti Cœlius habitat ? triginta millibus. Rogas me quanti doceam ?*[6] *talento.*

NOTE 2.—With verbs of costing, buying, and selling, the ablatives *magno, permagno, plurimo, parvo, minimo, nimio,* and *nihilo,* are found also ; as, " Wheat sells very dear;" *Permagno triticum venit. Magno patri meo constiti. Non potest parvo res magna constare. Venditori expedit rem venire quam plurimo.*—☞ " To cost nothing," is rendered by *constare gratis* or *nihilo.*

Fame periit.

§ 114.—A substantive denoting the *cause, manner, means,* or *instrument* of an action, is put in the ablative ; as, " He died of hunger."

Metu pallet. Gaudio exultat. Flagrat cupiditate. Ardet iracundiâ.—Sapiens æquo animo moritur. Deos pura et incorrupta mente venerari debemus.—Concordia res parvæ crescunt, discordia maximæ dilabuntur.—Cornibus tauri, apri dentibus, morsu leones, aliæ fuga se, aliæ occultatione tutantur.

---

¹) blind and crazy. ²) was rated at. ³) was worth—was sold for—stood at. ⁴) pays for his lodging. ⁵) Instead of *multi* use *magni,* and instead of *majoris, pluris.* ⁶) what my terms are in teaching.

Note 1.—An i n t e r i o r cause, that is, a cause which proceeds from the subject itself, as l o v e, h a t r e d, a n g e r, p i t y, h o p e, f e a r, etc., is often expressed by the ablative with an additional Perf. Participle ; as, *timore perterritus, terrore abreptus, pudore adductus, necessitate compulsus, amore captus, odio inflammatus, cupiditate incensus, desiderio incitatus, metu coactus, spe ductus, dolore victus, misericordia motus, injuria lacessitus, blanditiis voluptatum delinitus, religione tactus,* etc.—*Timore perterriti[1] Galli consilio destiterunt. Rex Antiochus seu inopia pecuniæ compulsus, seu avaritia sollicitatus templum Jovis aggreditur.*

An e x t e r i o r cause, that is, one which does not proceed from the subject itself, is generally expressed by *ob, propter, causa,* and *gratia,* with their respective cases : as, *Mors propter incertos casus quotidie imminet. Ego te propter humanitatem et modestiam tuam diligo. Plurima facimus amicorum causa. Illa brevitatis gratia prætereo.*

A p r e v e n t i v e cause ("for," "by reason of,"—in negative sentences, and in clauses with *vix*) is generally expressed by *præ* ; as, *Præ gaudio, ubi sim, nescio. Præ lacrimis nec cogitare nec scribere possum. Decretum exaudiri præ strepitu et clamore non potuit. Præ mærore loqui vix possum. Præ gaudio vix compos est animi.*

Note 2.—The ablative of m a n n e r, when not accompanied by an adjective, generally takes the preposition *cum.* Except are the ablatives *dolo, vi, casu, joco, ordine,* and those that denote by themselves m a n n e r, m i n d, c o n d i t i o n, or i n t e n t i o n, as *modo, more, ritu, ratione, animo, consilio, lege, conditione.* We say, therefore, *cum dignitate vivere, cum gravitate loqui, cum voluptate audire, cum cura et diligentia scribere,* and the like ;—but, without *cum : multa casu fiunt, omnes ordine profecti sunt, urbs dolo capta est,* etc.

When accompanied by an adjective, the ablative may stand either with *cum,* or without *cum.* Thus, we find : *Impetus cæli cum admirabili celeritate movetur,* and *Stellæ circulos suos orbesque conficiunt celeritate mirabili.*—The ablative generally stands with *cum,* when the concomitant circumstance is regarded as something merely additional and accidental, e. g., *Semper magno cum metu incipio dicere ; id cum maximo reipublicæ detrimento accidit ; Divitiacus multis cum lacrimis Cæsarem complexus obsecrare cæpit ;*—and without *cum,* when the concomitant circumstance is regarded as an essential characteristic of the action ; e. g., *amicitiam maxima fide colere ; magno impetu urbem expugnare,* etc., or when the ablative is one of those above-mentioned (*modo, more, ritu, ratione,* etc.) ; as, *Sapiens æquo animo moritur ; divino consilio factum est ; hac lege* or *conditione pacem composuit.*

Instead of the ablative of manner, *per* with the accusative is sometimes used ; as, *per vim,* " violently ;" *per insidias,* "insidiously ;" *per summum dedecus,* "most infamously ;" *per summam injuriam,* "most unjustly ;" *per ludum et jocum,* "in sport and jest," or "jestingly."

Note 3.—The m e a n s by which an action is performed, is put in the ablative without preposition. But when the means is a p e r s o n, the accusative with *per* is generally used ; e. g., *Binas tibi per servum litteras misi. Alcibiades cum Pisandro per internuncios colloquitur. Per te* (or *tua opera, tuo beneficio*) *salvi sumus. Dumnorix summam in spem per Helvetios regni obtinendi venit.*

Note 4.—The i n s t r u m e n t with which an action is performed, is likewise put in the ablative without preposition ; as, *Gladio me defendo.*
When the English " with " denotes accompaniment (— "together with"), it must be rendered by *cum* ; as, *Veni mecum. Curiam cum gladio ingreditur. In foro cum pugione comprehensus est. Servi cum armis traditi sunt.*

---

[1] for, through, out of or in consequence of.

The historians, however, when speaking of military movements, frequently omit *cum*, especially with such verbs as *adesse, sequi, venire,* and *proficisci;* e. g., *Cæsar ingenti exercitu (omnibus copiis, trecentis navibus, quarta et quinta legionibus,* etc.) *profectus est.*

NOTE 5.—The material of which a thing is made, is expressed either by an adjective, or by *ex* with the ablative, where the Participle *factus* is commonly added; as, " A stone-wall ;" *murus lapideus* or *ex lapidibus exstructus; vas aureum* or *ex auro factum; statua marmorea* or *ex marmore facta.*

Fossa sex pedes alta.

§ 115.—A substantive denoting the *extent of space,* is put in the accusative ; as, " A ditch six feet deep."

Milites aggerem latum pedes trecentos, altum pedes octoginta exstruxerunt. A portu stadia centum et viginti processimus. Zama quinque dierum iter abest ab Carthagine.[1] *Bidui* (sc. *iter*) *a castris aberam. Ab hac regula mihi non licet transversum, ut aiunt, digitum discedere.*[2] *Helvetiorum fines in longitudinem* (or *longitudine* without *in*) *millia passuum centum quadraginta patent. Negat se unquam a te pedem*[3] *discessisse. Adrumetum abest a Zama circiter millia passuum trecenta.*

NOTE 1.—The accusative of space answers to the questions—how long? how high? how deep? how wide? how broad? how far? how far distant? and is generally joined to such adjectives and verbs as *longus, altus, latus, crassus,—abesse, distare, patēre, eminēre, procedere, discedere.*

NOTE 2.—The question " how far off?" is answered by the accusative or ablative.— When the distance is indicated by the words *spatium* or *intervallum,* the ablative is regularly used. E. g., *Tria millia passuum ab ipsa urbe loco edito castra posuit. Ab exploratoribus certior factus est, Ariovisti copias a nostris millibus passuum quatuor et viginti abesse. Quindecim ferme millium spatio castra ab Tarento posuit.*

When the place from which the distance is estimated, is not mentioned, but understood from the context, the ablative with *a* (sometimes *ad* with an ordinal) is generally used; e. g., " The Belgians encamped within less than two miles," sc. of Cæsar's camp. *Belgæ ab millibus passuum minus duobus* (sc. a castris Cæsaris) *castra posuerunt. Ab sex millibus passuum abfuit,* sc. ab Urbe Roma. *Ad quintum lapidem sepultus est. Ad tertium milliarium consedit.*

Venit hora tertia.

§ 116.—A substantive denoting the *time when* or *at which,* is put in the ablative ; as, " He came at three o'clock."

Mors omnibus horis impendet. Alexander quarto et tricesimo ætatis

---

[1] five days' journey. [2] not one finger's breadth. [3] one step.

*anno Babylone decessit.   Hieme omnia bella jure gentium conquiescunt.
Excurremus mense Septembri, ut Januario revertamur.   Phædrus Augusti temporibus scripsit.*

NOTE 1.—The ablatives *tempore* and *temporibus,* in the sense of " distress," " circumstances,"—*pueritia, adolescentia,* and *senectute,* generally take the preposition *in; us,* "In the present circumstances ;" *In hoc tempore.   In summo et periculosissimo reipublicæ tempore,* or *in difficillimis reipublicæ temporibus.*—Thus we also find *in bello, in initio, in principio :* but *bello,* when combined with an adjective or a genitive, is more commonly used without *in,* as *Bello Mithridatico, bello Latinorum.* ☞ *Tempore* and *in tempore* are frequently used adverbially in the sense of "at the proper time," "in good time."

NOTE 2.—The t i m e   h o w   l o n g   is expressed by the accusative (sometimes with *per,* "during"), more rarely by the ablative.   E. g., *Septem horas dormisse sat est. Quædam bestiolæ unum diem vivunt.   Nestor tertiam ætatem vixit.   Duodequadraginta annos tyrannus Syracusanorum erat Dionysius.   Dies festus Dianæ per triduum agitur. Per annos quatuor et viginti primo Punico bello certatum est cum Pœnis.—Tredecim annis. Alexander regnavit.*
When the time how long has not yet expired, an ordinal numeral in the sing. may be used instead of a cardinal ; but then the English Perfect and Pluperfect must be rendered by the Present and Imperfect respectively.   E. g., " We have already these twenty days been waiting for you ;" *Nos vicesimum. jam diem te expectamus.*—" He has been reigning more than twenty years ;" *Primum et vicesimum jam annum regnat.*

NOTE 3.—The t i m e   i n   o r   w i t h i n   w h i c h   is expressed either by the ablative, or the accusative with *intra ;*—in both cases with cardinals as well as ordinals ; as, *Agamemnon vix decem annis* or *intra decem annos (decimo anno,* or *intra decimum annum) unam urbem cepit.   Saturni stella triginta fere annis cursum suum conficit.* (☞ *His annis viginti, triginta,* etc., means : " within these [or, the last] twenty, thirty .... years").
The question h o w   o f t e n   during a certain time, is answered by the ablative with *in ;* as, *ter in anno, quater in mense, semel in die.*   Thus, *Sol binas in singulis annis conversiones facit.   Si semper haberem, cui litteras darem, vel ternas in hora darem.*
The question f o r   w h a t   t i m e   or for h o w   l o n g ? is answered by the accusative with *in ;* as, *Sempronium ad cœnam invitavit in posterum diem.   Solis defectiones itemque lunæ prædictæ sunt in multos annos.   Auctio constituta est in mensem Januarium. Quanti habitas (doces) in mensem, in annum ?*—The exact time for which some arrangement has been made, is often expressed by the accusative with *ad ;* e. g., *Vide ut adsis ad horam quintam.   Vult me præsto esse ad horam destinatam.   Solvam ad Græcas Calendas,* i. e., *nunquam.*

NOTE 4.—The time h o w   l o n g   b e f o r e   and h o w   l o n g   a f t e r, when calculated from a definite point of past or future time, is expressed by the ablative.   *Ante* and *post* are then used as adverbs, unless there be a noun or pronoun dependent on them in the accusative.   When used adverbially, they are placed either after the ablative, as *tribus annis ante, tribus annis post,* or between the numeral and its substantive, as *tribus ante annis, tribus post annis.*   Thus we say *multo, paulo, aliquanto, biennio, triennio ante* or *post.*   E. g., *Themistocles fecit idem quod viginti annis ante fecerat Coriolanus.   Socrates supremo vitæ die de immortalitate animi multa disseruit, et paucis ante diebus, quum facile potuisset, educi e custodia noluit.   Homerus multis annis ante Romulum fuit. Lælius sermonem de amicitia habuit paucis diebus post mortem Africani.*

Sometimes, when strict accuracy is not intended, it is indifferent whether the ablative or accusative be used; as, *Messanam rediit ibique tribus diebus post* (or *post tre dies, post diem tertium) decessit. Servi iis etiam judicibus qui multis seculis post* (or *post multa sæcula) de te judicabunt.*

When *ante* and *post* are followed by *quam* and a verb, the phrase may be variously expressed; as, " He died three years after his return ;" *Decessit*

tribus annis postquam redierat,	post tres annos quam redierat,
anno tertio postquam redierat,	post annum tertium quam redierat;

or,

[by omitting either *post* or *quam*]

anno tertio quam (quo) redierat ; post annum tertium quo redierat.

Thus we say :

Pridie (postridie) quam redierat, *the day before (after) his return.*
Priore (postero) anno quam obierat, *the year before (after) his death.*

NOTE 5.—The length of time before or after, when calculated from the present moment, is expressed—the former by *abhinc* (the English "ago"), and the latter by *post. Abhinc* generally takes the accusative, though the ablative is found also: it usually precedes, and is joined to cardinals only. E. g., " About 300 years ago ;" *Abhinc annos fere trecentos. Abhinc sex menses* (also, *ante hos sex menses) maledixisti mihi. Post paucos dies* (or without *post, paucis diebus) ad vos veniam.*—☞ *Paucis his diebus* means " a few days ago," and is equivalent to *abhinc paucos dies.*

§ 117.—NOTE 6. The English "old" is expressed either by *natus* with the accusative of the years, or without *natus* by the genitive, when the latter is closely joined to the name of the person ; e. g., " Alexander died at the age of thirty-three years."

Alexander triginta tres annos natus decessit.
Alexander annorum trium et triginta decessit.

We may also say, *Alexander tertio et tricesimo ætatis anno decessit,* and *Alexander tertium et tricesimum ætatis annum agens decessit.*

The English "above" or "under" a certain age, is expressed by *plus (minus)* or *major (minor),* with *natus* and the accusative of the years (in each case with or without *quam),* or by *major (minor)* with either the genitive or ablative; as, " He is above (under) thirty-three years."

Plus (minus) triginta tres annos natus est.
Plus (minus) quam triginta tres annos natus est.
Major (minor) triginta tres annos natus est.
Major (minor) quam triginta tres annos natus est.

Or, *major (minor) triginta trium annorum est, major (minor) quam triginta trium annorum est, major (minor) triginta tribus annis est;*—also, *jam (nondum) triginta tres annos confecit, complevit,* or *tertium et tricesimum ætatis annum jam (nondum) complevit, excessit; egressus est.*

Habitat Romæ.

§ 118.—The names of cities and smaller islands are construed as follows :

1.) The name of the *town where?* is put in the genitive, when the name is of first or second declension ; but in the ablative without a preposition, when the name is either of the third declension, or plural number ; as, " He lives (*where ?*) at Rome."

2.) The name of the *town whither?* is put in the accusative without a preposition after verbs expressing or implying motion, as *eo, curro, contendo, proficiscor, mitto, venio,* etc. ; as, " He arrived at Rome." Lit " He came (*whither ?*) to Rome." *Venit Romam.*

3.) The name of the *town whence?* is put in the ablative without a preposition ; as, " He fled (*whence?*) from Corinth." *Fugit Corintho.*

Cur Plato Tarentum venit et Locros ? Dionysius Syracusas navigabat. Fui Lipsiæ, Parisiis, Londini, Viennæ, Petropoli, Gadibus et Athenis. Legati Carthagine Romam venerunt. Dionysius Platonem Athenis Syracusas arcessivit. Venetiis proficiscar Romam atque inde Neapolim. Dionysius tyrannus Syracusis expulsus Corinthi pueros docebat.

Note 1.—When *urbs, oppidum, caput, locus,* are placed in apposition after the name of a town, they are put in the ablative in answer to " where ?" and "whence ?" and in the accusative in answer to "whither ?"—sometimes with, but oftener without a preposition. E. g., (Where ?—) *Archias Antiochiæ natus est, celebri quondam urbe et copiosa.* Thus we find : *Tusculi, salubri et propinquo loco. Neapoli, in celeberrimo oppido.*—(Whence ?—) *Demaratus Corintho, urbe amplissima, Tarquinios fugit.* Thus, *Tusculo, ex clarissimo oppido.*—(Whither ?—) *Cicero profectus est Athenas, urbem celeberrimam. Demaratus se contulit Tarquinios, in urbem Etruriæ florentissimam.*

When *urbs, oppidum, caput, locus,* are placed before the name of a town, the same construction takes place, but always with a preposition ; as, *Ad urbem Ancyram, ab urbe Roma, ex oppido Thermis, in oppido Athenis, in urbe Antiochia, in urbe Citio.* (☞ *In urbe Antiochiæ, in urbe Citii,* and the like, are not to be imitated.)

When a city name has an adjective agreeing with it, the ablative in answer to " where ?" generally takes the preposition *in,* as *in ipsa Alexandria, tota* (or *in tota*) *Corintho.*—The accusative and ablative in answer to " whither ?" and " whence ?" are used both with and without prepositions ; as, *proficiscar doctas* (or *ad doctas*) *Athenas.*

Note 2.—When a city name is preceded by such a preposition as *near, around, towards, through, before, as far as,* it must be expressed also in Latin ; as, " in the vicinity of Cannæ," *ad Cannas ;* " in the neighborhood of Rome," *prope Romam ;* " through Vienna," *per Viennam.* Thus we say : *circa Neapolim, Brundusium versus, ante Troiam, supra Byzantium, usque* (or *usque ad*) *Numantiam.—Iter per Thebas fecit. Marius ad* (arrived before) *Zamam pervenit. Tres sunt ad* (in the direction to) *Mutinam viæ.*

NOTE 3.—The names of countries and of larger islands, as *Sardinia, Sicilia, Britannia, Creta, Eubœa,* and of all other places, are regularly construed with prepositions, as, (Where?—) *Bella gessit in Asia, in Gallia, in Britannia. Vidi fratrem tuum paulo ante ambulantem in horto.*—(Whither?—) *Legati in Africam trajecerunt. Eamus in hortum. Multitudo incredibilis in Capitolium convenit. Duces in consilium convenerant.[1]*—(Whence?—) *Cotta ex Sicilia in Africam profūgit. Persarum rex Darius ex Asia in Europam exercitum trajecit.*

☞ *Petere,* in the sense of "to repair to," takes the accusative of the place (whither?) without a preposition; as, *petere Romam, petere urbem, petere loca calidiora,* etc.—In like manner does the ablative of place (where?) when accompanied by *totus,* generally stand without a preposition; as, *tota Asia, tota urbe, toto mari, toto orbe terrarum,* etc.—though also *in toto orbe terrarum, in tota provincia.*

These two cases excepted, the use of names of countries without a preposition, is an irregularity not less than the use of names of towns with the prepositions *in, ab,* and *ex.* Such expressions, therefore, as *Africam transiturus, Macedoniam pervenit, Illyricum profectus,—legati ab Ardea Romam venerunt, has litteras a Brundusio dabam,* should be avoided.

Domus. Rus. Humus.

§ 119.—The words *domus, rus,* and *humus,* are construed like the names of towns; namely,

(Where?)	(Whither?)	(Whence?)
domi, at home,	*domum,* home,	*domo,* from home,
ruri (e), in the country,	*rus,* into the country,	*rure (i),* from the country,
humi, on the ground.	*humi,* to or on the ground.	*humo,* from the ground.

Manlius ruri juventutem egit. Nusquam commodius vivitur quam domi. Qui domo venerit, nescit num domum sit rediturus. Quum Tullius rure redierit, mittam eum ad te. Humi repit hedera. Vix oculos attollit humo. Ego rus ibo atque ibi manebo. Darii mater, perlata fama de Alexandri morte, laceratis crinibus, humi corpus abjecit.

NOTE 1.—*Domus,* when accompanied by an adjective, generally takes a preposition; as, *in illa domo, in domo privata, ad illam domum, ex domo paterna;*—but when accompanied by one of the possessives *meus, tuus, suus, noster, vester,* or the adjective *alienus,* the preposition is more commonly omitted, and the question "where?" answered by the genitive; as, *habitat domi suæ, nostræ, alienæ; domos suas abierunt; modo domo sua egressus est.*

With the genitive of the possessor, the question "where?" may be answered either

---

[1] had met in council.

by the genitive or the ablative with *in;* as, *domi Cæsaris* or (more commonly) *in domo Cæsaris; domi ipsius* or *in ipsius domo.*

The genitive *humi* stands not only in answer to "where?", but also in answer to "whither?"; as, *aliquid humi projicere; exanimis procumbit humi bos.*

NOTE 2.—The words *militia* and *bellum,* in connection with *domi,* are likewise put in the genitive in answer to "where?" as, *domi militiæque, domi bellique,* or *belli domique,* "at home and abroad," "in peace and in war."—Without *domi,* we should say *pace et bello inclytus, magnus bello nec minor pace,* "equally great in war and in peace," and the like.

O dii immortales!

§ 120.—The name of the person or thing addressed, is put in the vocative; as, "O immortal gods!"

Vale, mi suavissime et optime frater.   Puer, abige muscas.   Sollicitat me tua, mi Tiro, valetudo.   O dii boni, quid est in hominis vita diu?   O frustra suscepti mei labores!   O spes fallaces!   O cogitationes inanes meæ!

NOTE.—In exclamations of w o n d e r or g r i e f, when no address is made, the name of the person or thing wondered at, is put in the accusative; as, *O tempora, O mores! O me miserum! O præclaram sapientiam! O fallacem hominum spem! O gratas tuas mihi jucundasque litteras!*

CHAPTER IV.

ADJECTIVES.

I. Government of Adjectives.—II. Use of the Comparative.—III. Numeral Adjectives.

I.—GOVERNMENT OF ADJECTIVES.

ADJECTIVES GOVERNING THE GENITIVE.

Avidus laudis.

§ 121.—Adjectives denoting *desire, knowledge, skill, remembrance, participation, power, fulness,* and their contraries, govern the genitive of the thing of which one is desirous, mindful, ignorant, etc.; as, "Desirous of praise."

Conon rei militaris peritissimus fuit.   Vita sine amicis insidiarum et

metus plena est. Mens criminis conscia tranquilla esse non potest.
Bestiæ rationis et orationis sunt expertes.[1] *Semper appetentes gloriæ*
præter ceteras gentes atque avidi laudis fuistis.

Note 1.—To this rule belong the adjectives *cupidus, avarus, avidus, æmulus, studiosus ;—conscius, inscius, nescius, gnarus, ignarus, rudis, peritus, imperitus, memor, immĕmor, incuriosus ;—compos, impos, potens, impotens, particeps, expers ;—plenus, dives, fertilis, inanis, inops, egenus, indigus*, etc.—also verbal adjectives in *ax*, as *rapax, ferax, tenax*, etc.—and many Participles in *ns*, such as *amans, appetens, diligens, efficiens, fugiens, negligens, patiens, tolerans, observans*, etc., when they are used adjectively, that is, when they do not express a merely transient act or condition, but a habitual, permanent quality, as *puer veritatis amans, vir officii sui negligens, miles fugiens laboris*, etc. In this case, they also admit of the degrees of comparison ; as, *Quis famulus amantior est domini quam canis ? Cum navigare poteris, ad nos tui amantissimos veni.*—But when Participles in *ns* are used as such, that is, when they do not denote a permanent quality, but a merely transient, momentary act, they govern the case of their verbs. Accordingly

> *Patiens frigoris* is said of one that is able to endure cold at any time;
> *Patiens frigus*, of him that endures cold in a particular case only.

Note 2.—The adjectives of f u l n e s s may also be construed with the ablative, and with **refertus** this is regularly done; e g., *Epicureis nihil præstabilius fuit quam vita otiosa et plena voluptatibus. Domus Antonii erat aleatoribus referta et plena ebriorum.*
Rudis often takes the ablative with *in.*—*Conscius*, besides the genitive of the thing, usually takes an additional dative of the person ; as, *Nullius culpæ mihi conscius sum.*—To *peritus* and *consultus*, both *jure* and *juris* may be joined ; as, *jureconsultus* and *jurisconsultus*, etc.

Note 3.—The genitive *animi* stands frequently (esp. in late prose) instead of *animo*, with the adjectives *æger, anxius, audax, certus, confidens, confusus, ferox, furens, ingens, suspensus, territus, turbatus*, and several others, and also with verbs denoting anxiety, as *angor animi, discrucior animi.*—*Ego quidem vehementer animi pendeo.*

Quis mortalium ?

§ 122.—*Partitive* adjectives and adjective pronouns govern the genitive of the whole; as, " Who of mortals ?"

Multæ istarum arborum mea manu sunt satæ. Quotusquisque philosophorum[2] *ita moratus est ut ratio postulat ? Alexander seniores militum in patriam remisit. Gallorum omnium fortissimi sunt Belgæ. Sylla centum viginti quatuor suorum amisit.*

Note 1.—Partitives are words which denote a part of the whole, such as *uter, alter, neuter, uterque, utervis, alius, solus, ullus, nullus, quis, quisque, aliquis, quidam, quili-*

---

[1]) are without .... have neither—nor.   [2]) How many ? or, how few !

bet, multi, plures, plurimi, plerique, pauci, nonnulli, quot, quotcunque, quotusquisque, and also comparatives, superlatives, and numerals, when they are intended to denote a part of the whole.

When these adjectives are not used partitively, that is, when they are not intended to denote a part of the whole, they agree, like other adjectives, with their substantives in gender, number, and case; as, "The other Consul," *alter Consul ;*—"many soldiers," *multi milites ;*—" some trees," *nonnullæ arbores ;*—"a most skilful general," *dux peritissimus.*

Note 2.—The partitive genitive is generally known by the sign "of or out of," "from amongst," "among."—In its place, Latin writers frequently use the prepositions *ex, inter,* and sometimes *de ;* as, *unus ex vobis,* instead of *unus vestrum ; unus e multis, doctissimus inter Græcos, primus inter omnes. De tuis innumerabilibus in me officiis erit hoc gratissimum.*

Note 3.—*Uter* and *neuter* are used with reference to two; *quis* and *nullus,* with reference to many; as, *Utra manuum est agilior ? Uter nostrum tandem, Labiene, popularis est ? tune an ego ?—Quis vestrum, milites, ignorat ?*

Note 4.—The English we both, you both, they both, both these or these two, who both, are expressed in Latin, by *uterque nostrum, uterque vestrum, uterque eorum, uterque horum,* and *quorum uterque ;* as, "We were both present;" *Uterque nostrum adfuit* (or also, without *nostrum, uterque adfuimus*).—But, when *uterque* is joined to a noun, they are both put in the same case, even when a pronoun is added, as *uterque dux, uterque exercitus, utrumque regnum, quod utrumque exemplum.*

☞ The plural of *uterque* is in general used only when there are several individuals on each side; as, *Utrique victoriam crudeliter exercebant. Utrique Socratici et Platonici volumus esse.*

Note 5.—When a numeral adjective, such as few, many, more, ten, hundred, etc., is joined, by means of the sign "of," to a personal, demonstrative, or relative pronoun, the latter is put in the same case with the adjective, when not a part only, but the whole party are spoken of; e. g., "There are ten of us: how many are there of you ?" (— " We are ten in all: how many are you all together ?") *Nos decem sumus; quot ipsi estis ?—Trecenti*[1] *conjuravimus. Venio ad tuas epistolas, quas* (of which) *ego sexcentas uno tempore accepi, aliam alia jucundiorem. De vera loquor amicitia, qualis eorum qui*[2] *pauci numerantur, fuit. Veniamus ad vivos qui* (of whom) *duo de consularium numero supersunt.*

Note 6.—When besides the partitive genitive, there occurs another substantive of a different gender from that of the genitive, the adjective may agree in gender with either; as, *Leones ferarum generosissimi sunt. Indus omnium fluminum est maximus.—Animalium terrestrium maximum est elephas. Velocissimum omnium animalium est delphinus.*

---

[1]) Three hundred of us, i. e., We, three hundred in all, have ....   [2]) of whom very few are recorded.

Multum pecuniæ.

§ 123.—The genitive stands also with the following neuters of adjectives and adjective pronouns : *tantum,* so much ; *quantum,* how much ; *aliquantum,* some ; *tantum—quantum,* as much—as ; and their diminutives *tantulum, quantulum, aliquantulum, quantulumcunque ;—multum, plus, plurimum,—minus, minimum,—paulum, paululum, nimium,— quid* with its compounds *aliquid, quidquid, quidpiam, quidquam,—hoc, id, illud, istud, idem,—quod* in the sense of *quantum,* and *quodcunque* in the sense of *quantumcunque ;* as, " Much (of) money."

Quantum voluptatis[1] *affert liberalitas ! Minus habeo virium quam vestrum utervis. Quid non habet vita laboris ? Undique ad inferos tantundem viæ est. Quid causæ, quid rei est ? Exponam quid hominis sit. Quid tu hominis es ? Quod cuique temporis datur, eo debet esse contentus. Hoc ad te litterarum*[2] *dedi. Tibi idem consilii do quod mihimet ipsi. Sicilia hoc mihi oneris negotiique imposuit.*

Note 1.—Of these neuters,—*plus,* and *quid* with its compounds, are regularly construed with the genitive. For *quid* and its compounds, however, see Note 2.

The rest govern the genitive only under condition a) that they be used in a quantitive sense (*much, more, little, less,* etc.); b) that they be either in the nom. or accus. neut. sing. ; and c) that they be independent of any preposition. Otherwise, they agree, like other adjectives, with their nouns in gender, number, and case.—Hence we say : *tantum laboris,* " so much labor ;" but *tantus labor,* " so great a labor ;"— *multum pecuniæ,* " much money ;" but *multa pecunia,* " a large sum of money ;"— *minus periculi,* " less danger ;" but *minus periculum,* " a smaller danger ;" *multum sanguinis effudit,* but *multo sanguine victoria stetit ;—paululum viæ progressus,* but *pro paulula via magna sæpe merces solvenda ;—multum diei processerunt,* but *ad multum noctem*[3] *colloquebantur,* etc.

Note 2.—The genitive construed with the above-mentioned neuters is not always a substantive, but often the neuter of an adjective, as *aliquid boni, quiddam novi, quid pulchri ?* etc. ;—but with adjectives of the 3d declension we can say only *aliquid memorabile, quidquam tale, nihil utile, nihil suave,* and not *aliquid memorabilis, quidquam talis,* etc., except, perhaps, for the sake of correspondence, in connection with neuters of the 2d declension, as *aliquid novi ac memorabilis, aliquid vagi et instabilis,*— though even in this case it is better to say, *aliquid novum ac memorabile, aliquid vagum et instabile.*

With *quid, aliquid, quidquam,* and *nihil,* an adjective of the 2d decl. is sometimes put in the same case, as it were, in apposition, especially where there is any case dependent on such an adjective ; e. g., *Quid honestum dictu prætenditur ? Nihil expectatione vestra dignum dico. Nihil* (quod est) *altum, nihil magnificum, nihil divinum*

---

[1] How much pleasure ..... (*quantam voluptatem* would signify: how great a pleasure !) [2] that much of a letter. [3] until late at night.

suspicere possunt. Qui se ipse norit, sentiet aliquid se habere (quod est) *divinum.* Thus, *Quid aliud ?* " what else ?"—*Quid mirum ?* " What wonder ?"

NOTE 3.—When *tantum* and *id* are followed by their correlatives *quantum* and *quod*, the former are sometimes omitted ; as, *Medico mercedis quantum poscet, promitti jubeto. Navium quod ubique fuerat,*[1] *unum in locum Cæsar coegerat,* instead of *id navium quod. Vastatur agri quod inter urbem ac Fidenas est. Misit Antiocho vini, olei, quod ei visum erat ; etiam tritici, quod satis esset,* instead of *tantum vini quantum,* etc.

NOTE 4.—To this rule belong also the expressions *extremum anni, ultimum incipis. reliquum noctis, summum montis, summa tectorum, cuncta terrarum, angusta viarum. opaca locorum, incerta belli, incerta casuum, extrema agminis, reliqua rerum tuarum, opportuna locorum, prærupta collium, ardua montium,* and the like, which are fre-quently met with in poets and historians,—and also the phrases *id temporis* and *id (hoc, idem) ætatis,* which often occur in the sense of *eo tempore,* " at that time," and *ea ætate,* " at (of) that age ;" e. g., *Purgavit se quod id temporis venisset. Id ætatis jam sumus, ut omnia fortiter ferre debeamus.*

ADJECTIVES GOVERNING THE DATIVE.

Utilis agris.

§ 124.—Adjectives denoting *usefulness, pleasantness, fitness, readiness, equality, similarity, facility, proximity,* and their contraries, govern the dative of the object to which these qualities are directed ; as, " Useful to (or for) the fields."

Cunctis esto benignus, nulli blandus, paucis familiaris, omnibus æquus. Me omnibus in rebus tibi amicissimum fidelissimumque cognosces. Themistocli pauci pares putantur. Nihil est morti tam simile quam somnus. Voluptatibus maximis fastidium finitimum est. Quid est tam commune quam spiritus vivis, terra mortuis, mare fluctuantibus, litus ejectis ?

NOTE 1.—The adjectives *æqualis* (in the sense of " contemporary"), *communis, peculiaris, proprius,* and *superstes,* beside the dative, take also the genitive ; and the adjectives *propior* and *proximus,* beside the dative, also the accusative. E. g., *Viri propria est maxima fortitudo. Proprium est oratoris ornate dicere. Amicorum omnia sunt communia. Aristides fuit æqualis Themistoclis. Utinam te non solum vitæ sed etiam dignitatis superstitem reliquissem! Crassus cum legione septima proximus Oceanum* (or *Oceano*) *hiemabat. Ubii proximi Rhenum incolunt.*

The adjectives *amicus, inimicus, adversarius, intimus, familiaris, cognatus,* and *necessarius* (" a relative"), are not unfrequently used as substantives, and as such construed with the genitive. This is sometimes the case even when they are used as adjectives, but in the superlative degree ; as, *amicissimus* (*familiarissimus, inimicissimus*) *nostrorum hominum.*

---

[1] as many ships as.

NOTE 2.—Adjectives denoting readiness more frequently take the accusative with *ad;* as, *ad omnia* (*ad pugnam, ad omne facinus*) *paratus; piger ad pœnam, ad præmia velox.*

Adjectives denoting a friendly or hostile disposition often take the accusative with *in, erga, adversus;* as, *benevolus erga cives, acerbus in hostes, crudelis in suos, gratus erga me, fidelis et benignus in omnes.*

Adjectives denoting fitness and usefulness generally take the accusative of the thing with *ad,* but always the dative of the person to or for whom a thing is useful or fit; as, *locus ad insidias aptissimus; corporis motus ad naturam accommodati; Pompeius ad omnia summa natus; homo ad nullam rem utilis. Faciam id quod est ad omnium salutem utilius.*

NOTE 3.—*Similis, consimilis,* and *dissimilis,* govern the dative, when an outward resemblance is spoken of; but the genitive, when an inward resemblance,—a resemblance in character and disposition is referred to; e. g., *Canis nonne similis lupo ? P. Crassus dum Cyri et Alexandri similis esse voluit, et L. Crassi et multorum Crassorum inventus est dissimillimus.* But when the word depending on these adjectives, as also on *par* and *dispar,* is a personal pronoun, the genitives *mei, tui, sui, nostri,* and *vestri,* are always used; as, *Cur semper tui dissimiles defendis ? Q. Metellum, cujus paucos pares hæc civitas tulit, cum Pisone non conferam. Nec habet animi natura in se quicquam admixtum dispar sui atque dissimile.*

Diversus and *absonus,* "unlike," generally take the ablative with *ab.*—*Consentaneus* sometimes takes the ablative with *cum.* E. g., *Certa cum illo qui a te totus diversus est. Nec absoni a voce motus erant. Decorum id est quod consentaneum est hominis excellentiæ,* or *cum hominis excellentia.*

Mutual or reciprocal similarity is generally expressed by the accusative with *inter;* as, *inter se similes; inter se diversi; pessima ac diversa inter se mala, luxuria atque avaritia.*

ADJECTIVES GOVERNING THE ABLATIVE.

Laude dignus.

§ 125.—The adjectives *dignus, indignus, alienus—contentus, fretus, præditus—liber, immunis, vacuus—extorris, orbus, viduus*—and others of a similar meaning, govern the ablative; as, "Deserving of praise."

Excellentium hominum virtus imitatione, non invidia digna est. Quotusquisque sorte sua contentus vivit ? Alienum est magno viro, quod alteri præceperit, id ipsum facere non posse. Omni perturbatione animi liber esto. Datames fretus numero copiarum, confligere cupiebat.

NOTE 1.—*Dignus* and *indignus,* in the sense of "becoming" and "unbecoming," are construed with the ablative of the person; as, *Pigritia homine est indigna. Nulla res juvene magis digna est quam virtutis ac litterarum studium.*

Alienus, "unbecoming," "not suited," takes the ablative with or without *ab,* and sometimes also the genitive; e. g., *Hoc a te alienum est. Non alienum putat dignitate sua* or *suæ dignitatis.*—In the sense of "averse," "disaffected," "hostile," it usually takes the ablative (always with *ab*), and occasionally the dative; as, *homo alienus a litteris; habere animum alienum ab aliquo. Id dicit quod illi causæ maxime alienum est.*

Note 2.—The adjectives *liber*, *immunis*, and *vacuus*, take the ablative both with and without *ab* ; as, *liber omni metu*, *liber ab omni molestia* ;—*animus curis vacuus* and *hora nulla a scelere vacua*.

Adjectives signifying " descending from," as *natus*, *genitus*, *satus*, *ortus*, *oriundus*, are usually construed with the ablatives *loco*, *genere*, *stirpe*, *familia*, *patre*, *parentibus*; e. g., *Agathocles patre figulo natus erat*. *Me equestri loco ortum videtis*. *Archias natus est loco nobili*.

Note 8.—To this rule belong also a) the defective adjective *macte* in the phrases *macte virtute esto* and *macti virtute estote*, " hail to your heroism !" or simply *macte virtute*, " good luck to you !" " well done," " bravo ;"—and b) the adjectives *grandis*, *grandior* ; *magnus*, *major*, *maximus* ; *minor*, *minimus*, to which the ablative *natu* is frequently added to denote age. E. g., *Macte virtute diligentiaque esto*. *Macte nova virtute, puer : sic itur ad astra.*—*Id mea minime refert qui sum natu maximus*. *Adolescentis est majores natu vereri.*—We find also *magno natu*, *maximo natu* ; as, *Timotheus, cum esset magno natu, magistratus gerere desiit*. *A Datame Scismas, maximo natu filius, desciit*.

II. Use of the Comparative.

There are two ways of comparing one object with another : 1.) by *quam*, and 2.) without *quam*.

COMPARISON by QUAM.

Virtus est pretiosior quam aurum.

§ 126.—When two objects are compared by *quam*, they are both put in the same case ; as, " Virtue is more valuable than gold."

Europa minor est quam Asia. *Lingua Latina locupletior est quam Græca*. *Carior mihi est patria quam egomet ipse.*—*Certum est Europam minorem esse quam Asiam*. *Ita sentio linguam Latinam locupletiorem esse quam Græcam*. *Decet cariorem nobis esse patriam quam nosmet ipsos*.

Note 1.—When the same noun belongs to each member of the comparison, it is in Latin expressed in the first clause, and omitted in the second. In English we likewise express it in the first member, but replace it by " that" or " those" in the second. These pronouns, however, are not to be translated into Latin. E. g., " The song of the nightingale is sweeter than that of the other birds ;" *Lusciniæ cantus suavior est quam ceterarum avium* (sc. cantus). *Themistoclis nomen illustrius est quam[1] Solonis* (sc. nomen). *Morbi animi periculosiores sunt quam[2] corporis* (sc. morbi).

Note 2.—The English " still" before a comparative is rendered, in the Classical

---

[1] than that of.   [2] than those of.

writers, by *etiam ;* in later prose, by *adhuc;* as, *Tantum et plus etiam mihi debet. Ut in corporibus magnæ dissimilitudines sunt, sic in animis existunt etiam majores.—* Sometimes it is not translated at all ; e. g., *Indignum est a pari vinci, indignius ab inferiore. Acerbum est ab aliquo circumveniri, acerbius a propinquo.*

Note 8.—When an accusative precedes, and the predicate-adjective belonging to it can be resolved into a relative clause, the object after *quam* is either put in the nominative with *est, fuit,* etc., or else it is attracted into the same case, that is, into the accusative, provided the verb of the preceding clause can be supplied after *quam.* E. g., " I do not know a more jovial man than thou art,"—equivalent to : " I do not know a man that is more jovial than thou art."

> Non novi hominem hilariorem quam tu es, or quam te.

Thus, *Tota Sicilia non vidimus pulchriorem urbem quam Syracusas,* or *quam est urbs Syracusæ. Neminem aut majorem aut utiliorem virum Lacedæmon genuit quam Lycurgum,* or *quam Lycurgus fuit. Ego hominem callidiorem vidi neminem quam Phormionem,* or *quam Phormio est.*

When the preceding substantive with its predicate-adjective is not in the accusative, or when the verb before *quam* cannot be supplied after *quam,* no attraction whatsoever takes place and the object after *quam* must be put in the nominative with *quam est, quam fuit,* etc., expressly added to it ; as, *Hæc sunt verba Varronis, quam fuit Clodius, doctioris,* not *quam Clodii. Librum dedi Caio adolescenti, quam tu es, multo digniori,* not *quam tibi. Sempronio viro eruditiore, quam Elpidius est, familiariter utor,* not *quam Elpidio. Paulum tribus annis natu minorem, quam ipse sum, fratrem amisi,* not *quam me ipsum,* because the verb *amisi* could not be supplied with this accusative.

☞ Let the pupil bear in mind that the preceding examples are elliptical, and that the objects compared with each other belong in reality, though not in appearance, to the same verb, and are in the same case. For instance, *Librum dedi Caio adolescenti, quam tu es, multo digniori*—is in its full construction (see § 89, 7) equivalent to : *Librum dedi Caio, qui est adolescens multo dignior quam tu es.* From this text it is easy to see that the objects grammatically compared by *quam,* are not *Caio* and *tu,* but the relative *qui* and *tu,* both of which belong to the same verb *esse,* and are in the same case, namely, in the nominative.

COMPARISON without QUAM.

Virtus pretiosior est auro.

§ 127.—When two objects are compared without *quam,* the latter is put in the ablative ; as, " Virtue is more valuable than gold."

Lux sonitu velocior est. Tullus Hostilius ferocior etiam Romulo fuit. Elephanto belluarum nulla est prudentior. Mihi nemo est amicior nec jucundior nec carior Attico. Nihil est otiosa senectute jucundius. Nec melior vir fuit Africano quisquam nec clarior.

Note 1.—To omit *quam,* it is necessary (a) that the objects compared be either in the nominative or (in the construction of the Acc. c. Inf.) in the accusative ; (b) that they belong to the same verb ; and (c) that they be not both of the first declension singular.—Accordingly *quam* must be expressed in such sentences as: *Multi contentionis quam veritatis sunt cupidiores. Epaminondas saluti civitatis magis quam victoria Thebanorum consuluit. Pompeius plura bella gessit quam ceteri legerunt. Hibernia minor est quam Britannia.*

In the last example the omission of *quam* (sc. *Hibernia Britannia minor est*) would make it doubtful whether H. is smaller than B., or B. smaller than H., because we would not know which of the two is the nominative and which the ablative.—But no such ambiguity is to be apprehended in the construction of the Acc. c. Inf., and we may, therefore, say without *quam: Constat Hiberniam minorem esse Britannia.*

NOTE 2.—The ablative instead of *quam* with the accusative is more frequent in poetry than in prose. Still we meet, even in the best writers, with such instances as, *Sapiens humana omnia inferiora virtute ducit. Cæsar militum suorum vitam sua ipsius salute habuit cariorem. Neminem Lycurgo utiliorem virum Lacedæmon genuit. Num mittas hominem Servilio digniorem? Aut dic aliquid silentio melius, aut tace.*

In prose the ablative more frequently occurs with demonstratives,—and when a comparative is connected with the relative, the ablative is exclusively used; e. g., *Hoc mihi gratius nihil facere potes. Ne offeras te periculis sine causa, quo nihil potest esse stultius.*[1] *Secundum Punicum bellum quo nullum neque majus neque periculosius Romani gessére,*[2] *finitum est anno,* etc. *Senectus adolescentulos doceat, quo quid potest esse præclarius? Miramur Phidiæ simulacra, quibus nihil in eo genere perfectius videmus.*

NOTE 3.—After the comparatives *plus, amplius,* and *minus,* when joined to numerals, *quam* is often omitted without influence upon the construction, that is, without the nominative or accusative being changed into the ablative, though the ablative may be used also; as, *Plus quam quingenti viri, plus quingenti viri,* and *plus quingentis viris. Mille amplius homines quotidie sustentat.*

The comparatives *plus, amplius,* and *minus,* are in this case i n d e c l i n a b l e, and when any of them, joined to a plural, is the subject of the sentence, the verb must be put in the plural also; e. g., " It is already more than six months;" *Jam amplius (quam) sex menses sunt,* not *est. Minus duo millia hominum ex tanto exercitu effugerunt,* not *effugit. Plus pars dimidia ex quinquaginta millibus hominum cæsa sunt.—Plus quingentos colaphos infregit mihi,* not *plures. Pictores antiqui non sunt usi plus (quam) quatuor coloribus,* not *pluribus.* (☞ But we would say correctly: *Plures tibi colaphos infregit quam mihi;* and, *Num nostræ ætatis pictores pluribus utuntur coloribus quam pictores antiqui usi sunt?,* because in each of these sentences, *plus*—not being joined to any numeral—is a declinable adjective and agrees with its substantive accordingly.)

Sometimes, as it has been observed, the ablative is used instead of the nominative or the accusative; as, *Hora amplius moliebantur. Eo die cæsi sunt Romanis minus quingentis. Roscius nunquam plus triduo Romæ fuit.*

Thus with *longius;* as, *Cæsar ab hostium castris non longius mille quingentis passibus (mille quingentos passus,* and *quam mille quingentos passus) aberat.*

NOTE 4.—To the comparative construction belong also the expressions: *opinione major, spe citius, solito tristior, plus æquo,* and the like; as, " He returned sooner than was expected;" *Spe* or *expectatione citius rediit. Dicto citius*[3] *æquora placat.*

---

[1] than which there is nothing more foolish,—or which is the greatest folly that can be imagined. [2] than which the R. did not wage a greater or more dangerous,—the greatest and most dangerous the R. had ever waged. [3] quicker than the word was spoken.

Cæsar opinione celerius[1] venturus esse dicitur.   *Hoc malum latius opinione disseminatum est.*

Quam pro, joined to a comparative, means "in proportion to," or "too e. g., great, wise .... for ;" as, "A battle too severe (unusually severe) for the number of combatants ;" *Prælium atrocius quam pro pugnantium numero editur.*   *Alexander in regia sella consedit multo excelsiore quam pro habitu corporis.[2]*

NOTE 5.—When the comparison is made—not between two objects, but between the qualities of the same object, in Latin either the comparative with *quam*, or the positive with *magis quam*, is used ; as, "A pestilence more alarming than fatal ;" *Pestilentia minacior quam perniciosior (minax magis quam perniciosa) co-orta est. Romani quædam bella fortius quam felicius (magis fortiter quam feliciter) gesserunt. Acrius quam diutius (magis acriter quam diu) pugnatum est.*

NOTE 6.—The words r a t h e r, t o o, s o m e w h a t, before a positive, are commonly rendered by the comparative, unless they be used emphatically ; e. g., "The crop was rather scanty," etc. *Frumentum in Gallia propter siccitates angustius provenerat. Senectus est natura loquacior. Themistocles liberius vivebat.*

Minor uno mense.

§ 128.—The *measure by which* one thing exceeds or falls short of another, is expressed by the ablative ; as, "Younger by one month."

Hibernia dimidio minor est quam Britannia. Romani duobus millibus plures erant quam Sabini. Turres denis pedibus quam murus, altiores sunt. Februarius duobus vel tribus diebus brevior est quam ceteri menses.

NOTE 1.—The measure is often expressed by such ablatives as *multo, tanto, quanto, aliquanto, paulo, paululo, tantulo, altero tanto,[3] multis partibus,[4] hoc, eo,* and *quo ;* as, "So much the better ;" *Eo* or *tanto melius.*—"So much the worse ;" *Eo* or *tanto pejus.*—"A way twice as long ;" *Via altero tanto longior.*
These ablatives are often used also with verbs that contain the idea of a comparison, such as *malle, præstare, superare, excellere, antecedere,* and the like ; e. g., *Satis docui, hominis natura quanto anteiret omnes animantes.*—With *antecedere, excellere,* and *præstare, tantum* and *quantum* are sometimes used even in the best writers. Thus we find *multo* and *multum præstare.*

NOTE 2.—The English "the—the," before two comparatives, is in Latin expressed by *quo—eo,* or *quanto—tanto ;* as, *Procellæ quanto plus habent virium, tanto minus temporis. Homines quo plura habent, eo cupiunt ampliora. Quo quisque est sollertior et ingeniosior,[5] hoc docet iracundius et laboriosius.*
In sentences containing no definite subject and expressing a mere general idea, Latin writers, instead of *quo—eo* with two comparatives, frequently use *ut quisque—ita* with two superlatives. Thus,

> Quo quis est fortior, eo est generosior,—or,
> Ut quisque est fortissimus, ita est generosissimus.

---

[1] sooner than is believed.   [2] far too high for his stature.   [3] twice as much.   [4] by far or many times.   [5] also, *quo quis est sollertior* or *quo sollertior aliquis est.*

Quo quis melius dicit, eo magis dicendi difficultatem timet, or *Ut quisque optime dicit,
ita maxime dicendi difficultatem timet.*—*Ita* before the second superlative is sometimes
omitted ; as, *Ut quisque maxime perspicit, quid in re quaque verissimum sit, is pruden-
tissimus et sapientissimus rite haberi solet.*

Note 8.—When *ut quisque* is combined with *sum, esse,* the two clauses are frequently contracted into one, by omitting *ut—est* in the former and *ita* in the latter
clause, and putting *quisque* with its superlative in the case of the demonstrative,
either expressed or understood. (☞ *Quisque,* then, is always placed immediately
after the superlative.) E. g.,

(Nominative.)

Quo quid est melius, eo rarius est.
Ut quidque est optimum, ita (id) rarissimum est.
Optimum quidque rarissimum est.

(Genitive.)

Quo quis est melior, eo magis vicem ejus dolemus.
Ut quisque est optimus, ita maxime ejus vicem dolemus.
Optimi cujusque vicem maxime dolemus.

(Dative.)

Quo majus beneficium quodque est, eo plus ei debetur.
Ut quodque beneficium est maximum, ita plurimum ei debetur.
Maximo cuique beneficio plurimum debetur.

(Accusative.)

Quo fortior quis est, eo magis fortuna ipsum juvat.
Ut quisque est fortissimus, ita maxime fortuna eum juvat.
Fortissimum quemque fortuna maxime juvat.

(Ablative.)

Quo quisque est sapientior, eo magis ab eo alienum est.
Ut quisque est sapientissimus, ita maxime ab eo alienum est.
A sapientissimo quoque alienissimum est.

Thus, *Sapientissimus quisque æquissimo animo moritur ; stultissimus iniquissimo.
Occultissima quæque pericula difficillime vitantur. Altissima quæque flumina minimo
sono labuntur. Credulitas in optimi cujusque mentem facillime irrepit. Optimo et
justissimo cuique reditus in cælum patet expeditissimus.*
In translating such sentences, we may either use (a) " the—the" with two comparatives, or say (b) "in proportion as—so," or we may render (c) *quisque* by always
and place it between the two superlatives. Thus the sentence: *Optimum quidque
rarissimum est,* may be rendered :

The better a thing is, *the* rarer it is, or
In proportion as a thing is good, *so* is it rare, or
The best things are *always* the rarest.

☞ *Quisque* preceded by the superlative, expresses u n i v e r s a l i t y, and is, in
general, equivalent to *omnes* with the positive; e. g., *Epicureos doctissimus quisque[1]
contemnit. Nonne optimus quisque et gravissimus confitetur se multa ignorare ? Alexander periculosissima quæque aggrediebatur.*

---

[1] All learned men, or the most learned men.

NOTE 4.—To increase the meaning of the superlative, *quam, vel, multo, longe, facile, unus* with or without *omnis, quam possum,* and *quantum possum,* are frequently added ; as, *quam brevissime,* as short as possible ;—*vel minima,* the very least things ;—*pax vel iniquissima,* the most unjust peace in the world ;—*multo* or *longe felicissimus,* by far the happiest ;—*facile doctissimus,* unquestionably the most learned.—*Marcellus equites quanto maximo possent[1] impetu in hostem irrumpere jubet. Quod me rogasti, quam potero maturrime faciam. Quanto maximo potes studio, in rempublicam incumbe. Dolores me cruciant quanti in hominem maximi cadere possunt.[2] Hoc ego uno equite Romano familiarissime utor. Scævolam unum nostræ civitatis præstantissimum audeo dicere. Eloquentiam rem unam esse omnium difficillimam existimo.*

Quam qui maxime, and *nihil* with the comparative, have likewise the force of an increased superlative ; as, *Fratrem tuum ita amo quam qui maxime,* " as much as any one."—*Tam sum amicus reipublicæ quam qui maxime. Tam mitis sum quam qui maxime,* or *quam qui lenissimus.—Tam mihi gratum id erit quam quod maxime,* or *quam quod gratissimum,* " as dear as possible, or as dear as any thing."—*Tanti fit quanti qui maximi* or *plurimi.—Senectus ibi tantum honoratur quam ubi maxime,* " as much as anywhere."—*Tam piger est quam cum maxime,* " as lazy as ever."—*Nihil me infortunatius, nihil fortunatius est Catulo.—Nihil meo fratre lenius, nihil asperius tua sorore mihi visum est.*

III. NUMERAL ADJECTIVES.

CARDINALS.

§ 129.—The plural of *unus* is used only in connection with substantives which have no singular, or which have in the plural a meaning different from that of the singular; e. g., *unæ nuptiæ,* " one wedding ;" *unæ litteræ,* " one letter ;" *una castra,* " one camp."

It also occurs, though rarely, in the sense of " alone," or " the same ;" as, *Uni Ubii legatos miserant. Lacedæmonii septingentos jam annos unis moribus et nunquam mutatis legibus vivunt.*

Mille and Millia.

§ 130.—MILLE is an indeclinable adjective, and may be joined to any case of a substantive; as,

N. mille viri,	mille milites,	mille dies,
G. mille virorum,	mille militum,	mille dierum,
D. mille viris,	mille militibus,	mille diebus,
A. mille viros,	mille milites,	mille dies,
A. mille viris.	mille militibus.	mille diebus.

Sometimes, in the nominative and accusative, *mille* is used substantively and construed with the genitive ; as, *mille passuum, mille jugerum, mille nummum, mille talentum.—Ea civitas mille misit militum. Ante fundum Clodii facile mille hominum versabatur* (or, *mille* being taken collectively, *versabantur*).

---

[1] with the greatest possible impetuosity. [2] as great as can possibly befall a man, or the greatest that can befall a man.

§ 131.—Millia is a neuter substantive of the 3d declension, and is declined like *tria, trium*.. It is generally preceded by cardinals, and always governs the genitive of the persons or things numbered ; e. g., 753000 foot.

N. septingenta quinquaginta tria millia peditum,
G. septingentorum quinquaginta trium millium peditum
D. septingentis quinquaginta tribus millibus peditum,
A. septingenta quinquaginta tria millia peditum,
A. septingentis quinquaginta tribus millibus peditum.

Note.—In place of the cardinals, the distributives are sometimes used with *millia ;* as, *bina millia, quina millia, dena millia, octogena sena millia*, instead of *duo millia, quinque millia*, etc.
. When *millia* is followed by a lower numeral, the persons or things numbered are either put in the genitive and placed immediately before or after *millia ;* e. g., 3641 horse perished ;

equitum tria millia sexcenti unus et quadraginta perierunt,
tria millia equitum sexcenti unus et quadraginta perierunt ;

or they are put in the same case with *millia*, and placed either at the very beginning or after the smaller number ; as,

equites perierunt tria millia sexcenti quadraginta unus,
tria millia sexcenti unus et quadraginta equites perierunt.

How to read numbers.

§ 132.—Numbers exceeding six figures are not read in Latin by millions, as in English, but by *centum. millia* (usually *centena millia*), " hundreds of thousands."

To facilitate the reading of numbers expressive of millions, it is advisable to cut off the five right-hand figures of the given number,—to express then the number arising from the figures to the left by adverbials, with *centena millia* added, and the number arising from the figures cut off towards the right, by cardinals.

☞ Should the whole number contain units and tens of thousands, their respective value is to be inserted between *centena* and *millia*. E. g.,

1,100403 ⎱ Undecies centena millia quadringenti tres.
11|00403 ⎰

60,300022 ⎱ Sexcenties ter centena millia viginti duo.
603|00022 ⎰

300,023000 ⎱ Ter millies centena *viginti tria* millia.
3000|23000 ⎰

41260 72895 ⎱ Quadragies semel millies ducenties sexagies centena *septuaginta*
41260|72895 ⎰ *duo* millia octingenti nonaginta quinque

To acquire facility in the reading of numbers, let the pupil set down any figure whatever (e. g., the figure 5), and then increase this figure by the addition of as many other optional figures as may be desired. These optional figures (e. g., 2, 7, 3, 9, 4, 8) should be added, in succession, one by one,—first to the left, and then to the right ; thus,

5, 25, 725, 3725, 93725, 493725, 8493725;
5, 52, 527, 5273, 52739, 527394, 5273948,

the pupil each time expressing in Latin, the value of the number thus arising from the successive addition of the several figures.

NOTE.—In poetry, the thousands are generally expressed by *mille* with the adverbials ; as, 43000 men.

> N. quadragies ter mille viri,
> G. quadragies ter mille virorum,
> D. quadragies ter mille viris,
> A. quadragies ter mille viros, etc.

ORDINALS.

§ 133.—The ordinals are sometimes used where in English the cardinals are employed. This is particularly the case, when such questions are asked, as " what year ?"—" what page ?"—" what o'clock ?"—E. g., " The year 1867 after Christ," *Annus post Christum natum millesimus octingentesimus sexagesimus septimus.*—" In the year 245 of Rome," *Anno ab Urbe condita ducentesimo quadragesimo quinto,*—" Page five (sixty-two, hundred and one)," *Pagina quinta (sexagesima secunda, centesima prima).*—" It will soon be one (three, five, eléven) o'clock," *Mox erit hora prima, tertia, quinta, undecima.*—" He arrived at half past one," *Advenit hora prima cum dimidio ;* " at a quarter past three," *quadrante post tertiam,* or *tertia cum quadrante ;* " at a quarter to five," *hora quarta cum tribus quadrantibus.*

DISTRIBUTIVES.

§ 134.—The distributive numerals are used :
(a) In answer to " how many each time ?"—" how many a piece ?"—as, *Lex oratori ternas horas assignavit. Scipio et Hannibal cum singulis* (each with an . . . . .) *interpretibus congressi sunt. Digiti articulos habent ternos, pollex binos. Romæ per quinos dies senatores imperaverunt. Agri Veientani septena jugera plebi* (to each plebeian) *dividebantur.*—When *singuli* is expressly added, a cardinal may be used instead of a distributive ; as, *Romæ per quinque dies singuli senatores imperaverunt.*

(b) In connection with adverbials, in the multiplication of numbers ; as, " Do you know how many twice two make ?" *Didicistine bis bina quot sint ? Quot sunt sexies septena ? Quinquies duodena fiunt sexaginta. Lunæ curriculum quater septenis diebus conficitur.*

(c) Instead of cardinals (in answer to the question " how many ?") with such plural substantives as have either no singular at all, as *nuptiæ, codicilli,*—or, if the singular occurs, have in the plural a signification different from that of the singular, as *litteræ, castra, ædes* But here it must be observed that instead of *singuli* and *terni* commonly *uni* and *trini* are used, *singuli* and *terni* retaining their own distributive signification: hence we say, *uni, bini, trini codicilli; unæ, binæ, trinæ nuptiæ.*

☞ Words like *litteræ, castra, ædes,* that have in the plural a signification different from that of the singular, take in the signification of the plural the distributives; but in that of the singular, the cardinals; as,

unum castrum means one fort,	*una castra* means one camp,
duo castra " two forts,	*bina castra* " two camps,
tria castra " three forts.	*trina castra* " three camps,

una ædes means one temple,	*unæ ædes* means one house,
duæ ædes · " two temples,	*binæ ædes* " two houses,
tres ædes " three temples.	*trinæ ædes* " three houses.

Una (for *singula*) *castra ex binis facta esse videbantur. Unas* (for *singulas*) *binas, ternas, quinas,* etc., *a te accepi litteras. Vox " do" duabus litteris constat.*

Fractional expressions.

§ 135.—Fractions are generally expressed in Latin, as in English; as, ⅓, *dimidium* or *dimidia pars;* $^1/_3$, *tertia pars;* $^1/_5$, *quinta pars;* $\frac{2}{7}$, *duæ septimæ,* i. e. *partes;* $\frac{13}{29}$, *tredecim undetricesimæ;* $\frac{41}{100}$, *una et quadraginta centesimæ,* etc.

When the denominator exceeds the numerator only by one, as $\frac{2}{3}$, $\frac{4}{5}$, $\frac{7}{8}$, $\frac{11}{12}$, etc., the fractions are expressed by *duæ, quatuor, septem, undecim partes,* the denominator being understood. Thus,

$\frac{3}{4}$, is read: *tres* sc. *partes,* i. e., three parts out of four;

$\frac{10}{11}$, is read: *decem* sc. *partes,* i. e., ten parts out of eleven, etc.

CHAPTER V.

P R O N O U N S.

I. PERSONAL AND POSSESSIVE PRONOUNS.

Cura mea—cura mei.

§ 136.—The genitives of the personal pronouns *mei, tui, sui, nostri,* and *vestri,* must not be confounded with the possessives *meus, tuus, suus, noster,* and *vester.* The latter are generally used subjectively; the former, objectively; that is, the possessive pronouns generally denote the person that does or possesses something; the genitives *mei, tui, sui, nostri*, and *vestri*, on the contrary, denote the object, to which an action or a state of feeling is directed. Thus, e. g.,

cura nostra means our care, i. e., the care which we have of others;
cura nostri " the care of us, i. e., the care which others have of us.

amor vester means your love, i. e., the love which you bear to others;
amor vestri " the love of you, i. e., the love which others bear to you.

Memoriam nostri pie inviolateque servate. Nicias vehementer tua sui memoria delectatur. Lysander magnum reliquit sui famam. Peto a te ne me putes oblivione tui rarius ad te scribere quam solebam. Aviam tuam scito desiderio tui mortuam esse. Amore tui fratrem tuum odisse desinam.

Note.—Sometimes, however, the genitive of a personal pronoun takes the place of a possessive, and still oftener does a possessive (especially when joined to *injuria*) stand in place of the genitive of a personal pronoun. E. g., *Neque cuiquam mortalium injuriæ suæ* (for *sui*) *parvæ videntur. Non sua* (for *sui*) *solum ratio habenda est, sed etiam aliorum. Tua* (for *tui*) *hæc est imago,—tam consimilis est quam potest.*

Nostri, vestri,—Nostrum, vestrum.

§ 137.—The genitives *nostri* and *vestri* must be distinguished from the genitives *nostrûm* and *vestrûm*. The forms *nostrûm* and *vestrûm* are used 1.) in connection with partitives (§ 122,1), in the sense of "among or from among us *or* you;" as, "Who among you is ignorant?" *Quis vestrûm ignorat?* and 2.) in connection with the genitive *omnium*; as, "our country is the common parent of us all;" *Patria communis est omnium nostrûm parens.*—In all other combinations the forms *nostri* and *vestri* ought to be used.

Domus utriusque nostrûm ædificatur strenue. Nolo singulos vestrûm excitare.—Voluntati vestrûm omnium parui. Ad illa venio quæ ad omnium nostrûm vitam salutemque pertinent.—Habetis ducem memorem vestri, oblitum sui. Quando te nostri et reipublicæ miserebit?

Note 1.—With *omnium*, the possessives are sometimes used instead of the genitives *nostrûm* and *vestrûm;* as, *Cogor vestram omnium vicem consulere. Nolite, si in nostro omnium fletu nullam lacrimam aspexistis Milonis, hoc ei minus parcere.*—Thus we may say *nostra omnium refert*, or *nostrum omnium refert; vestra omnium interest, or vestrum omnium interest.*

NOTE 2.—We must also distinguish the expressions *pars nostri* and *pars vestri* from *pars nostrum* and *pars vestrum*. The expressions *pars nostrūm*, *pars vestrūm*, signify some of our or your aggregate number (" some among us or among you"), while *pars nostri*, *pars vestri*, mean a part or portion of our or your individual being or nature. E. g., " The more noble part of us is the soul ;" *Nostri pars melior animus est.—Pars tui melior immortalis est. Pars nostri* (i. e., *nostri* " esse") *est sanguis. Cui proposita sit conservatio sui, necesse est huic partes quoque sui caras esse carioresque quo perfectiores sint.*

Mea unius opera.

§ 138.—As the possessives *meus, tuus, suus, noster, vester*, supply the place of the genitives of the personal pronouns : *mei, tui, sui, nostri*, and *vestri*, any word in apposition to the person implied in a possessive pronoun, is put in the genitive. Genitives of this kind are especially *unius, solius* (" alone"), and *ipsius, ipsorum, ipsarum* (" own"). E. g., " Through my care alone," i. e., " Through the care of me alone."

Juravi rempublicam mea unius opera esse salvam. Vestra ipsorum mater advēnit. Meum solius peccatum corrigi non potest. Tuus ipsius frater expectatur. Mea ipsius (or *nostra ipsorum*) *maxime interest.*[1]*—Tua præceptoris quondam mei*[2] *oratio omnibus probatur. Tuum viri gravissimi atque eruditissimi judicium*[3] *plurimi et feci semper et faciam. Vim tuam præsentis exercitusque tui*[4] *experiri noluerunt. Aves fœtus suos libero cœlo suæque ipsorum fiduciæ permittunt. Nonne ei meas præsentis preces profuturas fuisse putas, cui nomen meum absentis honori fuit ?*

NOTE.—When *ipse* stands in apposition to a possessive pronoun in a reflective clause, it usually takes the case of the subject; as, " I am afraid of my own shadow ;" *Meam ipse umbram timeo. Tuam ipse umbram times ; suam ipse umbram timet ; nostram ipsi umbram timemus ; vestram ipsi umbram timetis.— Vestra ipsi virtute*[5] *hanc fraudem vitastis. Nec hostes modo timebant, sed suosmet ipsi cives.*
Sometimes, however, the genitive is found, where the case of the subject should be used; as, *Suamet ipsorum culpa duces victi sunt*, instead of *ipsi. Suismet ipsorum viribus tantam molem belli tolerare non possunt*, instead of *ipsi.*

II. DEMONSTRATIVE PRONOUNS.

Hic—ille.

§ 139.—When *hic* and *ille* refer to persons or things mentioned before, *hic* generally relates to the nearer, and *ille* to the more remote.

---

[1]) It is my (our) own greatest concern.   [2]) Your speech, once my preceptor, or who were once my p.   [3]) Thy judgment, a most grave and learned man, or who art so grave and learned a man.   [4]) Your force, who were on the spot, and that of your army.   [5]) Through your own resolution.

——*Hic*, then, answers to the English "this" or "the latter ;" and *ille*, to "that" or "the former."—This order, however, is not always observed. *Idem et docenti et discenti debet esse propositum ; ut ille prodesse velit, hic proficere. Corydon et Thyrsis ducebant greges: hic oves, ille capellas.—Melior tutiorque est certa pax, quam sperata victoria : hæc* (**pax**) *in tua, illa* (victoria) *in deorum manu est.* .

Cato ille Utioensis.

§ 140.—*Ille* when referring to some well-known or celebrated person, is commonly rendered into English by "the famous," "the well-known ;" as, "That famous Cato of Utica." Thus, *Antipater ille Sidonius. Xenophon, Socraticus ille.—Aristides a Themistocle collabefactus testula illa exilio decem annorum multatus est.*

NOTE—*Ille* is often in partial concessions placed pleonastically before *quidem— sed*, "indeed—but," or "it is true—but ;" e. g., *Res geris magnas illas quidem, sed plenas laboris. Morositas habet aliquid excusationis, non illius quidem justæ, sed quæ probari posse videatur. Multa scripta sunt inconsiderate ab optimis illis quidem viris, sed non satis eruditis.*

Vincula et ea sempiterna.

§ 141.—*Is* in connection with *et, que, atque*, is equivalent to the English "and that," "and that too ;" as, "Imprisonment, and that too perpetual." *Multa prætereo eaque præclara. A te bis litteras et eas quidem perbrèves accepi. Equidem expectabam tuas litteras idque cum multis. Crassum cognovi optimis studiis deditum, idque a puero. Unam rem explicabo eamque maximam. Erant in Torquato plurimæ litteræ, nec ea vulgares.*

NOTE.—*Idem* and *et ipse.—Idem* is used in the sense of "also," "likewise," "at the same time," when different things are predicated of the same subject. *Et ipse* frequently occurs in Livy, Curtius, and later writers, in the sense of "also," when the same thing is predicated of different subjects. E. g., "A speech sublime and at the same time humorous," *Oratio grandis eademque faceta. Libera quam eandem Proserpinam vocant.—Quos amamus, eosdem felices esse cupimus. Cicero orator fuit idemque philosophus. Fuere quidam qui iidem ornate ac graviter* ("at once ...... and ...."), *iidem versute et subtiliter dicerent.— Vespasiano Titus filius successit, qui et ipse Vespasianus est dictus. Darius cum vinci suos videret, mori voluit et ipse. Idem qui, idem ac*, and *idem atque*, are rendered into English by "the same as ;" e. g., "He is the same as he has ever been ;" *Idem est qui semper fuit. Peripatetici quondam iidem erant qui Academici.*

Me ipse consolor.—Me ipsum consolor.

§ 142.—*Ipse*, when joined to a personal pronoun, is either put in the case of the subject, when the subject is contrasted with other sub-jects, or in the case of the object (i. e., of the personal pronoun), when the object is contrasted with other objects; as, *Me ipse consŏlor*, " I (and not another) console myself;"—but *Me ipsum consŏlor*, " I console (*whom?*) myself (and not another)."

De me ipse loquor. Ego me ipse vitupero. Ipse tibi noces. Pro se ipse dixit. Multi sibi ipsi mortem consciscunt.—Ego me ipsum vitupero. Tibi ipsi noces. Pro se ipso dixit. Pompeium omnibus, Lentulum mihi ipsi antepono.

NOTE.—When *ipse* stands in the nominative, it may be placed before or after the pronoun ; as, *Me ipse* or *ipse me consolor :* but, when it is in any of the oblique cases, it is regularly placed after the pronoun ; as, *Se ipsos* (not *ipsos se*) *omnes natura diligunt. Tibi ipsi* (not *ipsi tibi*) *noces.*

Ipse, when joined to a demonstrative, or to words expressing time or number, is equivalent to the English " just," " exactly," " very ;" as, *Demosthenes ejus ipsius artis, cui studebat, primam litteram non poterat dicere. Illo ipso die advenit. Athenis decem ipsos dies fui. Crassus erat triennio ipso minor quam Antonius. Ipsis Nonis Februariis accidit.*

III. REFLEXIVE PRONOUNS.

(In simple sentences.)

Pauci se norunt.

§ 143.—The personal pronouns h i m, h e r, t h e m, are rendered by *sui, sibi, se*, when they refer to the nominative in the sentence (in English we use, in this case, generally the forms h i m s e l f, h e r s e l f, and t h e m s e l v e s) ;—but by *is, ea, id*, when they do not refer to that nom-inative. E. g., " Few persons know themselves."

Cæsar civitatem liberam sibi servire coegit. Omnes sibi cari sunt eque ipsos naturâ diligunt.—Quid eis respondeam, nescio. Quam bonus est Deus! eum semper cole et ama.

NOTE.—When h i m, h e r, t h e m, refer to a noun in the possessive case, they are translated by *suus* in agreement with the noun that governs the said possessive, and the possessive itself is put in the case which the pronoun would otherwise stand; e. g., " Hannibal's fellow-citizens expelled him from his country ;" *Hannibalem sui cives*

patria ejecerunt.—"That man's ambition will ruin him ;" *Sua hominem perdet ambitio.*
—"Often the faults of the teacher fall back on his own head (— on himself);" *Sæpe
sua in magistrum vitia redeunt.*—"Every one's manners make his fortune (— to him);"
Sui cuique mores fingunt fortunam.

Eum officii sui monui.

§ 144.—The possessive pronouns h i s, h e r, t h e i r, are rendered by
suus, sua, suum, when they refer to the nominative or to any other
word of the sentence,—by *ejus, eorum,* and *earum,* when they refer to no
word of the sentence ; e. g., "I reminded him of his duty."

*Alexander moriens annulum suum dederat Perdiccæ. Plurimi homines
sua vitia ignorant. Suum Cæsari gladium restitui. Sua illis nocebit
inertia. Sua eum commendat pietas. Constat cunctis nationibus suas
esse leges.—Ejus eloquentiam omnes admirantur. De eorum reditu
faciam te certiorem. M. Fabio familiarissime utor ; ejus negotium sic
velim suscipias, ut si esset res mea.*

NOTE.—The pronouns h i s, h e r, t h e i r, before the second of two substantives
connected by *et*, are rendered by *ejus, eorum, earum ;* but when the substantives are
connected by *cum*, they are rendered by *suus ;* e. g., "Plato and his scholars," *Plato
et discipuli ejus,* or *Plato cum discipulis suis. Duces eorumque milites a rege defecerunt,*
or *duces cum suis militibus a rege defecerunt.*

(In compound sentences.)

Promisit se venturum.

§ 145.—When in a subordinate clause (§ 86) the personal pronouns
h i m, h e r, t h e m (that he, that she, that they), and the possessives
h i s, h e r, t h e i r, refer to the nominative of the leading clause, the former
are rendered by *sui, sibi, se,* and the latter by *suus, sua, suum ;*—but
when they do not refer to that nominative, h i m, h e r, t h e m, etc. are
rendered by *is, ea, id,* and h i s, h e r, t h e i r, by *ejus, eorum, earum,*
respectively ; as, "He promised to come" (§ 101, 3).

*Sperat plerumque adolescens se diu victurum. Syracusani rogabant ut
sibi ignosceretur. Macedŏnes putabant regem suum vinci non posse.
Per Themistoclem rex certior factus est, adversarios suos in fuga esse.—
Quando putas eum profecturum esse ? Equidem eorum causam justissi-
mam esse arbitror.*

NOTE 1.—To render the pronouns h i m, h e r, t h e m, etc., by *sui* and *suus*, it is not
enough that they merely refer to the nominative of the leading clause; it is, more-

over, necessary that the subordinate clause express the thoughts or words of the leading subject,—which is generally the case in clauses dependent upon, or containing the Acc. c. Inf., and in those, also, introduced by interrogatives, or by *ut* (*ne*) intentional; as, *Roscius postulat ut hunc sibi ex animo scrupulum evellatis. Syracusani orabant ut sibi ignosceretur, quod pro beneficiis sibi tributis gratias nondum egissent. Orator sagaciter investigat quid sui cives cogitent, sentiant, opinentur, expectent.*

When the subordinate clause does not express the sentiment of the leading subject, but is stated by the writer merely as a remark of his own or of some other person, the demonstrative *is* must be used; e. g., *Epaminondas fuit etiam disertus ut* (*ut* consecutive) *nemo Thebanus ei par esset eloquentia. Diogenes contemnebat divitias quod eum felicem reddere non poterant.*[1] *Verres Milesios navem poposcit quæ præsidii causa eum*[2] *Myndum prosequeretur. Gortynii templum magna cura custodiunt, non tam a ceteris quam ab Hannibale ne quid ille inscientibus his tolleret secumque duceret.*

☞ When the Acc. c. Inf. does not immediately depend on the verb to whose subject the pronoun his, her, or their, refers, the demonstrative may be used as well as the reflexive; e. g., *Siculi me sæpe pollicitum esse dicebant commodis eorum* (or *suis*) *me non defuturum esse.*

Note 2.—It is not necessary that the principal subject be always in the nominative: it is often sufficient that it can be conceived as such; as, *A Cæsare invitor* (= *Cæsar me invitat*) *sibi ut sim legatus. Magna Antonium spes tenet* (= *Antonius sperat*) *rerum se potiturum. In suspicionem ei venit* (= *suspicatus est*) *aliquid in epistola de se scriptum esse.*

Note 3.—When the subordinate clause has a nominative of its own, and an ambiguity is likely to arise whether the reflexive *sui* or *suus* refers to the nominative of the principal clause or to that of the subordinate, the reference to the former must be expressed by *ipse*, and the reference to the latter by *sui* or *suus*; e. g., " Narbazanes and Bessus besought Artobazus to plead their cause;" *Narbazanes et Bessus Artobazum orabant, ut causam ipsorum tueretur. Jugurtha legatos ad consulem misit qui ipsi liberisque vitam peterent. Cæsar milites suos incusavit, cur de sua* (militum) *virtute aut de ipsius* (Cæsaris) *diligentia desperarent.*

When it is evident from the context that reference is made to the nominative of the principal clause, and no ambiguity, therefore, is to be apprehended, the reflexives *sui* and *suus* are generally used, though grammatically they refer to the nominative of their own clause; e. g., *Cicero Quintum fratrem rogavit ut ad se veniret. Cicero effecerat ut Q. Curius consilia Catilinæ sibi proderet. Ariovistus respondit, non se Gallis, sed Gallos sibi* (for *ipsi*) *bellum intulisse. Themistocles necessitate coactus domino navis, qui sit, aperit, multa pollicens, si se* (for *ipsum*) *conservasset. Patres conscripti legatos in Bithyniam miserunt qui ab rege peterent, ne inimicissimum suum* (ipsorum) *secum haberet sibique* (ipsisque) *traderet.*

IV. Relative and Indefinite Pronouns.

§ 146.—The relative *qui* is frequently used instead of a personal or denominative with *et, vero, enim, igitur;* e. g., " Philosophy teaches

---

[1]) *Quod eum non poterant*, expresses the sentiment of the writer; *quod eum non possent*, would express the sentiment of some other person,—and *quod se non possent*, the sentiment of Diogenes himself (Compare § 199, IV.). [2]) *quæ se* would express the sentiment and intention of Verres himself.

that the world moves ; *and* if *this* is true, we also necessarily move ;"
Philosophia docet mundum moveri, quod (et hoc) *si verum est, nos quoque moveamur necesse est.*—Thus,

Habes me tibi amicissimum, quem (me vero) *si irritaveris, habebis
inimicissimum. Nihil pretiosius est animi tranquillitate ; qua* (hac
enim) *qui caret, eum nec regiæ opes quidquam juvant. Multas ad res
perutiles Xenophontis libri sunt ; quos* (eos igitur) *legite, quæso, studiose.*

§ 147.—When in English such a clause as *they say, it is said, as—
says,* etc., is inserted parenthetically in a relative sentence, the verb of
that clause becomes, in Latin, the leading verb of the relative sentence
and ꞌis construed with the Acc. c. Inf., that is, the nominative of the
relative sentence is put in the accusative, and its finite verb in the Infinitive. E. g., "Socrates, whom, they say, Apollo himself had declared to
be the wisest of mankind, lived at Athens ;" *Socrates quem dicunt ab
Apolline ipso sapientissimum fuisse judicatum, Athenis vixit.* Thus,

*Gratiam habeo Simonidi illi quem primum ferunt artem memoriæ
protulisse.*[1] *Crassus quem Lucilius semel tantum risisse refert,*[2] *Ciceroni
fere æqualis fuit. Apollonius, cum mercede doceret, eos quos judicabat
non posse oratores evadere, dimisit.*[3]

§ 148.—When in a clause that is connected with, or inserted in, a
relative sentence, there occurs a demonstrative which refers to the preceding relative, in Latin the demonstrative is generally left untranslated,
and the relative put in the case in which the demonstrative would otherwise be placed. E. g., "There are persons who, unless you flatter them,
will be disgusted." *Sunt quidam quibus nisi blandiaris, tædio afficiantur.*
Thus,

Historia res præclgrissime gestas tradit quas quum legimus,[4] *imitandi
cupiditate incendimur. Sunt permulta quæ orator nisi a natura haberet,*[5]
*non multum a magistro adjuvaretur. In hortos me M. Flacci contuli
cui quum publicatio bonorum, exilium, mors proponeretur,*[6] *hæc perpeti
maluit, quam custodiam mei capitis dimittere.*

§ 149.—*Qui* in connection with *sum* and a substantive either in the
nominative or ablative, is often used in explanatory clauses instead of
pro, in the sense of "according to," or "in accordance with." E. g.,

---

[1] who, they say, was the first that taught. [2] who, as Lucilius tells us, never
laughed but once. [3] who in his judgment, or as he judged, were unable. [4] by
which, when we read them. [5] in which an orator, had he them not by nature, would
be little aided. [6] who, when he was threatened with....

"You, being so courteous (or, with your usual courtesy), will take in good part to be advised ;" *Tu pro tua humanitate (quæ tua est humanitas,* or *qua tu es humanitate) æquo animo te moneri patieris.*—Thus,

Spero quæ tua prudentia et temperantia est, te jam bene valere. Qua es prudentia, nihil te fugiet, si meas litteras diligenter legeris. Tu pro tua prudentia (quæ tua est prudentia, or *qua tu es prudentia[1]) quid optimum factu sit videbis.*

Note.—*Quod* often serves merely the purpose of transition, especially when followed by *si, nisi, utinam.* It may then be rendered by n a y, n o w, a n d, or i f t h e n. E. g., *Quod si mundum efficere potest concursus atomorum, cur porticum, cur templum, cur domum, cur urbem non potest?*—*Quod nisi domi civium suorum invidia debilitatus esset, Romanos videretur superare potuisse.*

Quid is sometimes taken in the sense of "why;" as, *Quid venisti? Quid ego taceam! Quid plura? Quid plura disputo ?*

Quisque, Aliquis, Quisquam, Quotusquisque.

§ 150.—1. *Quisque* is always placed immediately (a) after the reflexive pronouns *sui* and *suus,* except in relative clauses where its position is close to the relative ; (b) after superlatives, when universality is expressed ; and (c) after ordinal numerals. E. g., *Trahit sua quemque voluptas. Suum cuique carum est.*—*Maxime decet quod est cujusque maxime suum.[2]*—*Optimus quisque fatetur. Altissima quæque flumina.*—*Vix decimus quisque.[3]*—*Tertio quoque anno.[4]*—*Primo quoque tempore.[5]*

2. *Aliquis* generally loses the prefix *ali* after *si, nisi, ne, quo, quando, quanto:* but when it stands in an antithetical relation to something else, or when it is used emphatically, the prefix *ali* is retained ; e. g., *Timebat Pompeius omnia ne aliquid vos timeretis. Si aliquid de summa gravitate Pompeius, multum de cupiditate Cæsar remisisset. Si aliquid* ("when really something") *dandum est voluptati, senectus modicis conviviis potest delectari.*

3. *Quisquam* and *ullus* "any" (the former substantively, the latter adjectively), are used in negative sentences only, and in such questions as imply a negative,—also after *vix* and *sine,* and in comparative clauses. E. g., *Beatior sum quam quisquam vestrum. Num quisquam est æque miser? Nemo quidquam tale conatur. Vix quemquam invenies qui nesciat. Vix ullum auctorem legit. Sine ullo maleficio iter per provinciam fecerunt.*

When *sine* is preceded by *non, aliquis* is to be used in place of *ullus ;* as, *sine ulla spe ;* but, *non sine aliqua spe,* "not without some hope."

4. *Quotusquisque* designates a small number and may be expressed either by " how many?" in form of a question, or by " how few!" in form of an exclamation ; e. g., *Quotusquisque mortalium sorte sua contentus vivit?*

---

[1] you, being so prudent (who are so prudent, such is your prudence, prudent as you are, or with your usual prudence). [2] which is most peculiarly a man's own. [3] scarcely one in ten, or scarcely every tenth. [4] every three years, or every third year. [5] as soon as possible.

Alius and Alter.

§ 151.—*Alter—alter* or *unus—alter,* " the one—the other," is used of two only ; *alius—alius* or *unus—alius,* " one—another," of more than two.—*Alii* (or *quidam, nonnulli*)—*alii* means " some—others ;" *aliud—aliud,* " one thing— another ;" *alias—alias,* " at one time—at another," or " now—now ;" *aliter— aliter,* " in one way- in another," or " so—otherwise ;" E. g., " The one says yes ; the other, no."

Unus (alter) ait, negat alter. Alii ludunt, cantant alii. Divitias alii præponunt, bonam alii valetudinem, alii potentiam, alii honores, multi etiam voluptates. Aliud est iracundum esse, aliud iratum. Aliter cum tyranno vivitur, aliter cum amico. Alias bellum inferunt, alias illatum defendunt. Aliud loquitur, aliud sentit.[1] *Aliter mihi videtur, aliter tibi.*[2]

§ 152.—*Alius,* when joined to a case of its own, or to one of its derivatives (*alias, alibi, alio, aliter, aliunde*), forms an abridged proposition, for which in English often two sentences with " the one—the other," etc. are used ; e. g., " One likes this, and another that," or " different persons like different things."

Aliud aliis placet. Alias aliud iisdem de rebus judicamus.[3] *Aliis alibi placet.*[4] *Aliis aliunde est periculum.*[5] *Aliter cum aliis loquitur.*[6] *Alius alio mittitur.*[7] *Alius alia de causa* (of two, *alter altera de causa*) *venit.*

NOTE 1.—*Alius atque alius* or *alius aliusque* means " now this, now that," i. e. " different ;" e. g., *Res inchoata sæpe aliis atque aliis de causis differtur. Milites trans flumen aliis atque aliis locis trajiciebant.*

NOTE 2.—In phrases such as " One hand washes the other"—" One wedge drives another"—" One fear overcomes another," etc., the English " other" is not translated by *alius* or *alter,* but by the repetition of the word with which it is contrasted. The words expressing contrasted ideas are then placed by the side of each other ; as, *Manus manum lavat. Cuneus cuneum trudit. Timorem timor vincit. Nulla virtus virtuti contraria est. Cives civibus parcere æquum est. Ex domo in domum migrant. Hominem homini similiorem non vidi.*

This juxtaposition is also to be observed in such expressions as *alius alio fortior, aliud alio melius, alium alio nequiorem.—Alius alio plus habet virium. Aliud ex alio malum nascitur. Me quotidie aliud ex alio impedit.*

NOTE 3.—The English reciprocal " each other," " one another," is expressed in Latin by *alter alteri* or *alterum,* and *alius alii* or *alium ;* e. g., *Alter in alterum causam conferunt. Milvo est bellum cum corvo : ergo alter alterius ova frangit* or *frangunt.*

---

[1] or *aliud loquitur ac* (*atque, quam*) *sentit,* he speaks otherwise than he thinks.
[2] or *aliter mihi videtur ac tibi,* I think differently from you. [3] At different times we think differently on the same subject, or at one time we think so, at another otherwise. [4] Some like to be here, and others elsewhere, or different persons like to be in different places. [5] Different persons are threatened from different quarters. [6] To one he speaks in this way, to another in another, or to different persons he speaks in a different way. [7] One is sent hither, another thither, etc.

Alter alteri subvenit. Nec quidquam secretum alter ab altero habet.—Alius alium increpabant. Alius alii subsidium fert or *ferunt.*

Instead of *alter alterum* and *alius alium*, we may say also *inter se, inter nos, inter vos;* as, *Inter nos percontamur. Dionysius et Dion inter se (— alter alterum) timebant. Aristides et Themistocles obtrectarunt inter se. Furtim inter se aspiciunt.*[1] *Demosthenes et Isocrates inter se discrepant. Complecti inter se lacrimantes milites cœperunt.*—Thus, *inter se diligunt, amant, timent,* etc. (☞ *se mutuo* or *se invicem,* in such phrases, is *Post-classical.*)

THE INDEFINITE PRONOUN "ONE."

§ 153.—The indefinite pronoun *one* is variously expressed in Latin, viz.,

(a) By the Passive; as, "One lives well everywhere," *Ubique bene vivitur.—* "When one deviates from justice, all things become uncertain," *Omnia fiunt incerta, quum a jure discessum est.*

(b) By the 1 pers. plur. Active, when the speaker includes himself under the unknown subject; as, "What one wishes, one gladly believes," *Quæ volumus, libenter credimus.* "There is scarcely one night in which one does not dream," *Nulla fere est nox, qua non somniamus.*

(c) By the 2d sing. Indic. or Subj., according as a definite or an indefinite person is addressed; as, "When one yields to sloth, in vain are the gods implored," *Ubi socordiæ te atque ignaviæ dederis, nequidquam deos implorabis. Non decet ea docere velle, quæ nunquam didiceris. Deum non vides, tamen ut Deum ex operibus agnoscis.*[2]

(d) Sometimes, though rarely, by the Present Partic.; as, "When one is at sea, things that stand, seem to move," *Navigantibus moveri videntur ea quæ stant.*

---

[1] They look stealthily at one another.   [2] One does not see God, yet he may be recognized as God by ....

CHAPTER VI.

THE VERB.

1. Government of Verbs 2. Tenses of Verbs.—3. Moods of Verbs.—4. Gerunds. Supines. Participles.

I. GOVERNMENT OF VERBS.

VERBS WITH TWO NOMINATIVES.

Ego vocor Robertus.

§ 154.—Verbs of " being," " becoming," and " seeing," as *sum*, I am ; *exsisto*, I exist ; *fio*, *evado*, I become ; *màneo*, I remain ; *nascor*, I am born ; *videor*, I seem ; *appareo*, I appear, etc., and passive verbs signifying

"to be named or called," as *dicor*, *nominor*, *vocor*, *appellor*, *nuncupor*, *salūtor* ;

"to be made or chosen," as *creor*, *deligor*, *designor*, *renuntior*, *declāror*, *constituor* ;

" to be deemed or reckoned," as *ducor*, *credor*, *habeor*, *judicor*, *existimor*, *numeror*, *putor*, *agnoscor*, *demonstror*, *deprehendor*, take two nominatives, a subject- and a predicate-nominative : the former answering to the question *who* or *what* placed b e f o r e the verb, and the latter to the question *what* placed a f t e r the verb ; as, " I am called Robert."

Nemo . repente fit pessimus. Multa somnia vera evadunt. Nemo nascitur dives. Scythæ perpetuo invicti manserunt.—Numa rex creatus est. Clodius tribunus plebis est designatus.—Scytharum gens antiquissima semper habita est. Hæc consideremus quæ faciunt ii qui habentur boni.

NOTE 1.—Verbs that are construed with two nominatives, generally agree with the subject-nominative, as *Allobroges sunt genus agreste*, etc.—But, when the predicate is a noun and stands near the verb, the verb not unfrequently agrees with the predicate-nominative ; as, *Hic honos ignominia putanda est. Non omnis error stultitia dicenda est. Paupertas mihi onus visum est miserum et grave. Gens universa Veneti appellati sunt. Universus hic mundus una civitas communis deorum atque hominum existimanda est.*

NOTE 2.—When the predicate-nominative admits of two forms, one masculine, the other feminine, the masculine form must be used when the subject-nominative is either masculine or neuter; but the feminine, when the former is feminine; as, *Eventus* (or *tempus*) *est optimus stultorum magister. Historia est magistra vitæ, nuncia* (not *nuncius*) *vetustatis. Licentia est corruptrix* (not *corruptor*) *morum. Bona conscientia est perpetua* (not *perpetuus*) *comes recte factorum.* (Compare § 90, 3.)

NOTE 3.—The predicate-nominative of an adjective is often used in Latin, where in English an adverb, or a noun with a preposition is used. This is especially the case with the verbs *vivo, morior, eo, sto, venio, sedeo, jaceo, dormio,* and other intransitive verbs, when we wish to express the state or condition of the subject during an action. E. g., " I live most miserably, or in the greatest misery ;" *Vivo miserrimus. Dormiunt securi. Sapiens nil facit invitus. Nemo fere saltat sobrius. Justus moritur securus. Intrepidus ad me venit. Salvi in Ægyptum pervenerunt. Socrates venenum lætus ac lubens hausit.*

NOTE 4.—In the construction of the Acc. c. Inf. both the subject- and the predicate-nominative are changed into the accusative; as, (Brutus exstitit vindex Romanæ libertatis), *Constat Brutum exstitisse vindicem Romanæ libertatis.*

NOTE 5.—The verb *habeor,* instead of the predicate-nominative, sometimes takes the ablative with *pro* or *loco* (*in numero*) with the genitive; as, *Audacia pro muro habetur. Prodigii loco clades habita est. Helvetii in hostium numero habentur.*

VERBS GOVERNING THE GENITIVE.

Memini vivorum.

§ 155.—1. Verbs of *remembering* and *forgetting,* as *memini, reminiscor, recordor,* and *obliviscor,* govern the genitive of the person or thing which one remembers or forgets; as, " I remember the living."

Pueri meminerint verecundiæ. Semper hujus diei et loci meminero. Dulce est meminisse laborum actorum. Jubes me bona cogitare, oblivisci malorum. Hannibal adhortatus est milites ut reminiscerentur pristinæ virtutis suæ neve mulierum liberûmque obliviscerentur. Homo nefarius cum dolore flagitiorum suorum aliquando recordabitur.

NOTE 1.—When the object remembered or forgotten is a *thing,* it is often put in the accusative (especially with *recordor*), and when it is expressed by the neuter of an

NOTE 2.—*Memini,* in the sense of " to remember a person as a contemporary, as one who has lived in our time,"—always takes the acc. of the person. In the sense of " to mention" (*mentionem facere*), it sometimes takes the genitive, but more commonly the ablative with *de.* E. g., *Cinnam memini, vidi Sullam. Utinam, Antoni, avum tuum meminisses! Antipater ille Sidonius quem tu probe meministi.— De homine importunissimo ne meminisse quidem volo. Meministi ipse de exulibus.* ☞ The ablative of the person with *de* is found also with *recordor*, as *Petimus ut de suis liberis recordentur.*

NOTE 3.—The verbs of r e m i n d i n g (*moneo, admoneo, commoneo, commonefacio*) are construed *aliquem alicujus rei* or *de aliqua re,* that is, the person *whom* one reminds, is put in the accusative, and the thing *of which,* either in the genitive or in the ablative with *de ;* as, *Grammaticos officii sui commonemus. Ille te veteris amicitiæ commonefacit. Oro ut Terentiam de testamento moneatis.*—If the thing is expressed by the neuter of an adjective or adjective pronoun, it is put in the accusative ; as, *Hoc unum te moneo. Illud me præclare admones.*—☞ *Monere* with the genitive of the thing is Post-Augustan.

NOTE 4.—With *venit mihi in mentem,* the thing that occurs to one's mind, is commonly put in the genitive, and sometimes in the nominative ; as, *Venit mihi Platonis in mentem. Non dubito quin in metu tuorum tibi scelerum veniat in mentem* (or *tua tibi scelera in mentem veniant). Multa mihi in mentem veniunt. Quid tibi in mentem venit ?*

Facio te magni.

§ 156.—2. Verbs of *valuing* and *esteeming,* as *æstimo, duco, facio, pendo, habeo, puto, taxo,* and *esse* in the sense of " to be worth," " to be estimated," govern the genitive of value, when indefinitely expressed by an adjective ; but, when expressed by a substantive, the ablative is used. E. g., " I esteem thee highly."

Divitiæ a sapienti viro minimi putantur.[1] *Hephæstionem Alexander plurimi fecerat. Si prata et hortulos tanti æstimamus, quanti est æstimanda virtus? Quanti quisque amicos facit, tanti fit ab amicis. Mea mihi conscientia pluris est quam omnium sermo. Tanti est exercitus, quanti imperator.*[2] *Quanti est sapere !*[3]

NOTE 1.—The genitives of value are : *magni, permagni, maximi,—pluris, plurimi,— parvi, minoris, minimi,—tanti, quanti, tantidem, quantivis, quantilibet, quanticunque,* and *nihili ;* but never *multi* and *majoris,* in place of which *magni* and *pluris* are used respectively.—These genitives are variously rendered in English ; for example, *magni,* much, greatly, highly, at a high rate, of great importance ; *parvi,* little, at a low rate, of little importance, etc.

To this class belong also the genitives *assis, flocci, nauci, pili, teruncii,* and *pensi,* generally with a negative. They are used to denote that a thing is worth nothing, and are equivalent to the English expressions : " not to be worth a cent, a farthing, a pin," etc.—" not to care or give a cent, a farthing, a pin, a straw, a hair, a bulrush, for a thing."

---

1) are held very low. 2) The value of an army depends on that of the general. *) What a fine thing it is....

NOTE 2.—The phrase *tanti est*, means " it is worth while,"—or contemptuously with
a fillip : "it is worth so much"! or "I care so much for it;" as, *Video quanta tempestas
invidiæ nobis impendeat : sed est mihi tanti,—dummodo ista privata sit calamitas.*

NOTE 3.—Instead of *aliquid nihili facere*, we find also *aliquid pro nihilo habere,
ducere, putare ;* as, *Philosophi ea quæ plerique vehementer expetunt, pro nihilo ducunt.*—
With *æstimo* the ablatives *magno, permagno, nihilo,* and *nonnihilo,* sometimes occur,
as *Istam gloriosam virtutem non magno æstimo.*

Arguit me furti.

§ 157.—3. Verbs of *accusing, convicting, condemning,* and *acquitting,*
together with *arcesso, cito, defero,* and *postulo,* in the sense of " to summon before the court," " to prosecute," govern the genitive of the crime
of which one is accused, acquitted, etc.—This genitive depends on the
ablative *crimine,* or *nomine* ("pretext," "on account"), which is generally understood, and sometimes expressed. E. g., "He charges me
with theft."

*Athenienses Socratem impietatis insimulabant. Miltiades proditionis
est accusatus. Te convinco non solum inhumanitatis, sed etiam amentiæ.
Nicomēdes furti damnatus est. Ducem proditionis absolvunt. Scaurus
pecuniæ a Jugurtha acceptæ arcessebatur.—Nomine sceleris conjurationis-
que damnati sunt multi. Alcibiades postulabat ne absens invidiæ crimine
accusaretur. Si iniquus es in me judex, condemnabo ego eodem te
crimine.*

NOTE 1.—The verbs of a c c u s i n g and c o n d e m n i n g, instead of the genitive,
sometimes take the ablative with *de ;* as, *Non committam posthac ut me de epistolarum
negligentia accusare possis. Pilius de repetundis M. Servilium postulavit.*—Thus we
say *deferre nomen alicujus* (☞ *deferre aliquem* is Post-Augustan) *de ambitu, de
parricidio, de veneficiis,* etc.—With *accuso* and *convinco* we find even the ablative with
in, as *Primum me tibi excuso in eo ipso, in quo te accuso.*

NOTE 2.—The p u n i s h m e n t to which a person is condemned, is commonly expressed by the genitive, more rarely by the ablative or the accusative with *ad* or *in :*
thus, *damnare aliquem mortis, multæ, pecuniæ, tripli, quadrupli,* etc., or *morte, multâ,
pecuniâ, triplo, quadruplo,*—*damnare ad bestias, ad metalla, ad* (in) *opus publicum, in
expensas.*[1] E. g., *Nympho condemnatur : quanti? fortasse quæritis ;—frumenti ejus
omnis quod in areis esset.—Frusinates tertia parte agri damnati sunt.— Vitia hominum
atque fraudes damnis, ignominiis, vinculis, verberibus, exiliis, morte multantur*
(☞ The verb *multare* is always construed with the ablative.)
When the punishment consists in a definite sum, the ablative is invariably used ;
e. g., *Sex millibus æris damnatus est.*—Capital punishment is expressed both by *capitis*
and *capite,* as *Multi capitis* or *capite damnati sunt.*—The phrase *voti* or *votorum
damnari* means " to be adjudged to the fulfilment of a vow," hence " to obtain what
one wishes."

---

[1]) to pay the expenses.

NOTE 8.—The verbs of acquitting (esp. *libero*), instead of the genitive of the crime or punishment, take also the ablative; as, *Ego me, etsi peccato absolvo, supplicio non libero.* Thus, *absolvere aliquem regni suspicione, supplicio; liberare aliquem culpa, suspicione crudelitatis,* etc.

NOTE 4.—When the verbs of accusing are not taken in a judicial sense, but merely in the sense of " to find fault with," or "to blame one for something," they are usually construed with the accusative of the fault and the genitive of the person; e. g., *Samnites incusabant injurias Romanorum. Tribuni plebis nunc fraudem, nunc negligentiam Consulum accusabant. Pharnabazus in epistola Lysandri avaritiam verfidiamque accusavit.*

Est boni regis.

§ 158.—4. The genitive stands with the verb *sum*, 1.) when in the predicate a substantive is omitted that has been previously expressed; 2.) when in the predicate such a word as *homo, vir, animal,* is omitted; 3.) when *sum* is taken in the sense of " it is a person's business, office, lot, or property," where *indicium, negotium, proprium,* or *officium* is understood ; as, " It is the part of a good king."

Captivorum numerus fuit (numerus) *mille quingentorum.*[1] *Persarum classis fuit* (classis) *ducentarum navium.—Est* (homo) *sui juris.*[2] *Hannibal tum* (puer) *novem annorum erat.—Superstitio est* (indicium) *imbecilli animi. Hoc non est* (negotium) *mearum virium.*[3] *Suadere principi quod oportet,* (res or negotium) *multi laboris*[4] *est. Cujusvis hominis est errare. Fortis et constantis animi est non perturbari in adversis. Hæc studia omnium temporum sunt atque locorum.*[5] *Illud vestræ dignitatis erat.*[6] *Non est meæ virtutis.*[7] *Est adolescentis majores natu vereri.—Periculose emitur quod multorum est.*[8] *Totus Pompeii sum.*[9] *Præter Capitolium omnia hostium erant.*[10]

NOTE 1.—The predicate-genitive with *sum* is variously expressed in English ; as, *it shows, it betrays, it proves ;—it suits, it fits, it becomes ;—it requires, it demands, it is for,* e. g. *the rich,* etc. ;—*it is peculiar to, it is incumbent on, it belongs* or *pertains to ;—any one may, any one is liable to, it is not every one who ;—should, must, ought, use, be want,* etc.—These and similar phrases, when rendered by *sum, esse,* the young student should always reduce to this simple formula :

---

[1] consisted of or amounted to. [2] is at his own disposal—his own master. [3] is beyond my strength. [4] is a difficult task. [5] are suitable for. [6] your dignity required that. [7] it is not consistent with my character. [8] what belongs to many. [9] I am all Pompey's—belong wholly, or am wholly devoted, to Pompey. [10] all was in the power of.

" .... is (*a sign, the part, lot, duty, property*) of....;" as,

(Eng.) Superstition betrays a weak mind.
(Lat.) Superstition is (*a mark*) of a weak mind.

(Eng.) Every man may err, or is liable to err.
(Lat.) To err is (*the lot*) of every one.

(Eng.) A king is bound to protect his subjects.
(Lat.) To protect his subjects is (*the duty*) of a king.

NOTE 2.—When the predicate-genitive expresses a quality and has an adjective agreeing with it, the ablative is frequently used instead of the genitive (§ 110); as, " Socrates was (a man) of a very mild temper ;" *Socrates erat mitissimi ingenii* or *mitissimo ingenio. In omnibus rebus Cato singulari fuit prudentia et industria. Bono semper animo esto. Agesilaus fuit statura humili et corpore exiguo*

NOTE 3.—When the person whose part or duty any thing is, is expressed by a personal pronoun ("it is incumbent on me, on us, on you,"—" you should," "you ought"), instead of the genitives of the personal pronouns: *mei, tui, sui, nostri, vestri,* the neuters of the possessives: *meum, tuum, suum, nostrum,* and *vestrum* (sc. *negotium* or *officium*) are used; as, " It is for us to commence ;" *Nostrum est incipere. Tuum est videre quid agatur. Feci quod meum erat, tu modo fac quod tuum est. Si cujusquam, certe tuum est nihil præter virtutem in bonis ducere. Meum esse puto quid sentiam ostendere.*

In like manner, when *sum* is taken in the sense of " to belong to," "to be the property of," the possessives are used, and made to agree with the subject-nominative in gender, number, and case; e. g., " This book belongs to me ;" *Hic liber meus est. Hæc vestis tua est. Si nos defenditis, vestri ; si deseritis, Samnitium erimus.*—" I am totally devoted to you—am all yours ;" *Totus tuus sum.*

NOTE 4.—Instead of *stulti est, regis est, Romanorum est, cujusvis hominis est,* etc., we may say with equal propriety *stultum est, regium est, Romanum est, humanum est,* etc. ; e. g., *Et facere et pati fortia Romanum est.*—But with adjectives of one ending the genitive only ought to be used, as *sapientis est, insipientis est,* etc.

Sometimes, when the predicate-genitive expresses a quality, the nominative may be used as well as the genitive. Thus we can say, *Frustra niti extremæ dementiæ* or *extrema dementia est. Sic agere summæ levitatis* or *summa levitas est. Nego hoc moris esse Græcorum* or *hunc morem esse Græcorum.*

NOTE 5.—The predicate-genitive stands also with *puto, habeo, existimo,* and *fieri* in the sense of " to come to belong to."—*Facio* with the genitive *ditionis* means " to subdue," " to bring under one's dominion," and is equivalent to: *in ditionem* or *potestatem redigere.*—E. g., *Tempori cedere semper sapientis est habitum. Multi superstitionem imbecilli animi putart. Quæ Macedonum erant, populi Romani facta sunt. Tota Asia populi Romani facta est. Hannibal Italiam suæ ditionis fecit. Scipio omnem oram usque ad Ibērum flumen Romanæ ditionis fecit.*

Tædet me vitæ.

§ 159.—5. The impersonal verbs *pœnitet, piget, pudet, tædet,* and *miseret,* govern the accusative of the person *in whom* the feeling of shame, grief, etc., exists, and the genitive of the thing *which* causes the feeling ; as, " I am weary of life."

> *Pœnitet (me)*, I repent of, Perf. *pœnituit*, Fut. *pœnitebit.*
> *Piget (me)*, I am vexed at, I regret, Perf. *piguit* or *pigitum est.*
> *Pudet (me)*, I am ashamed of, Perf. *puduit* or *puditum est.*
> *Tœdet (me)*, I am tired of, Perf. *pertœsum est*, rarely *tœduit.*
> *Miseret (me)*, I pity, Perf. *miser(i)tum est*, rarely *miseruit.*

Me tui miseret. Pudet me tui hominis vanissimi. Miseret te aliorum, tui nec miseret nec pudet. Nunquam Atticum suscepti negotii pertœsum est. Me civitatis morum piget tœdetque. Malo me fortunœ pœniteat, quam victoriœ pudeat. Ignavum pœnitebit aliquando ignaviœ suœ. Sunt homines quos infamiœ suœ neque pudeat neque tœdeat.

NOTE 1.—When the thing which causes the feeling, is expressed—not by a substantive, but by a verb or the neuter of a pronoun, the former is either put in the Inf. or rendered by a clause with *quod ;* the latter is put in the accusative; as, " I am sorry for having done this ;" *Pœnitet me hoc fecisse. Piget me plura dicere. Non me tam diu vixisse pœnitet. Pœnitet me quod te offendi. Sapientis est proprium nihil quod pœnitere possit, facere.*

NOTE 2.—*Pudet* takes also the genitive (generally without an accusative of the person) in the sense of " to feel ashamed for, or in the sight of ;" e. g., " It is scandalous in the sight of gods and men ;" *Pudet deorum hominumque. Pudet hujus legionis, pudet optimi exercitus. Nonne te hujus templi, non urbis, non vitœ, non lucis pudet ?*—The Participle *pertœsus* often takes the accusative of the thing, instead of the genitive, as *Pertœsus ignaviam suam.*

NOTE 3.—Here are to be noticed the two verbs *misereor* 2. and *miseresco* 3., " I pity." They are both construed personally, that is, the person who pities, is put in the nominative, and with this nominative the verbs themselves agree in number and person ;—but the object which causes the feeling, is put in the genitive ; as, *Boni homines etiam pecoris miserentur. Arcadii, quœso, miserescite regis.*

Miseror 1. and *commiseror* 1., " I pity," are transitive and accordingly take the accusative of the object ; as, *Agesilaus commiseratus est fortunam Grœciœ.*

Interest omnium.

§ 160.—6. The impersonal verbs *interest* and *refert*, " it concerns—matters—is of consequence or importance to," govern the genitive of the person whose interest or concern any thing is ; as, " It concerns all."

Hoc multarum civitatum in Grœcia interfuit. Interest reipublicœ juventutem probe institui. Theodori nihil interest, humine an sublime putrescat.[1]

---

[1]) whether he rot on the ground or on high.

Civium refert legibus obtemperare. Ostendam quantum salutis communis intersit duos consules in republica esse.

NOTE 1.—When the person whom any thing concerns, is expressed in English by a personal pronoun, in Latin the possessive forms *mea, tua, sua, nostra,* and *vestra,* are used; as, *Interest mea ut te videam. Tua quod nihil refert, percontari desinas. Cæsar dicere solebat, non tam sua quam reipublicæ interesse ut salvus esset.*

NOTE 2.—How much or how little one is concerned, is expressed either (a) by the genitives *tanti, quanti, quanticunque; magni, permagni, maximi; pluris, plurimi, parvi, minoris, minimi* (but never *multi* and *majoris*);—or (b) by the neuters *tantum, quantum, aliquantum; multum, plus, plurimum, permultum, infinitum, mirum quantum; minus, minimum; nihil, quid, quiddam;*—or (c) by the adverbs *tantopere, magnopere, magis, maxime, vehementer, tam, quam, minime.* E. g., *Illud mea magni* (or *multum, magnopere*) *interest ut in officio tuo sis diligentissimus. Quantopere* (or *quanti, quantum*) *intersit opprimi Dolabellam, profecto intelligis. Maxime* (or *maximi, plurimum*) *refert, quemadmodum quæque res audiatur. Non tam interest quo animo scribatur epistola, quam quo accipiatur.*

NOTE 3.—The thing which concerns, is expressed in Latin, either (a) by the simple Infinitive or the Acc. c. Inf.; (b) by a subordinate clause with *ut, ne,* or an interrogative; or (c) by a neuter pronoun, such as *hoc, id, illud, quod.*—In English, the thing is commonly expressed by a substantive; as,

(Eng.) The price of corn is of great importance to us.
(Lat.) It concerns us much what corn sells for.

(Eng.) Thy health and diligence concern me much.
(Lat.) It much concerns me that thou be healthy and diligent.

(Eng.) Of what consequence is to you the fall of Troy?
(Lat.) What does it matter you that Troy has fallen?

Magni omnium interest leges servari—ut leges serventur—ne leges perfringantur—utrum leges serventur necne. Multum nostra interest quanti frumentum veneat. Quid tua refert Troiam eversam esse? Multum mea interest ut sis sanus et diligens, or *te sanum esse et diligentem. Vehementer mea interest quid boni homines de me judicent.*

NOTE 4.—When *ipse, unus, solus,* or a noun, is added in apposition to the possessives *mea, tua, sua, nostra, vestra,* it must be put in the genitive (§ 138), unless the noun be added as a vocative of address. E. g., "It is my (our, your) own interest;" *Mea ipsius (nostra, vestra ipsorum) interest.—*"It concerns thee alone;" *Tua unius* or *solius interest. Mea præceptoris vestri plurimum interest. Nullius magis quam tua, mi Tiro, interesse puta.*

NOTE 5.—The object in regard to which or for which a thing is of importance, is expressed by the accusative with *ad;* as, *Equidem ad nostram laudem non multum video interesse. Magni ad honorem nostrum interest quam primum ad urbem me venire.*

NOTE 6.—*Refert,* in the best Latin writers, is but rarely used with a genitive of the person. It oftener occurs with the possessives *mea, tua, sua,* etc.; and most commonly without a genitive or possessive at all. E. g., *Quid mea refert? Illud permagni referre arbitror. Meminero, sed quid meminisse id refert?*

VERBS GOVERNING THE DATIVE.

Do vestem pauperi.

§ 161.—1. The dative may stand with any verb in answer to the question *to whom* or *what?* or, *for whom* or *what?* that is, for whose advantage or disadvantage? as, "I give a garment to a poor man."

Narras fabulam surdo. Pueri, ne socordiæ vos atque ignaviæ tradite. Non scholæ, sed vitæ discimus. Tibi seris, tibi metis. Avarus aliis divitias parat, non sibi. Non solum nobis divites esse volumus, sed liberis, propinquis, amicis, maximeque reipublicæ.

NOTE.—As the preposition "to" is often omitted in English, especially after verbs of *giving, sending, showing, telling, promising,* etc., beginners should carefully distinguish between the o b j e c t given, sent, promised, etc., and the p e r s o n t o w h o m it is given, sent, promised, etc. The former is put in the accusative answering to the question *whom* or *what*; the latter, in the dative answering to the question *to whom* or *what?*. E. g., "Give (to) me this picture;" *Da mihi hanc imaginem.*—"Show (to) your father that letter;" *Ostende patri hanc epistolam.*—"I sent (to) your brother a large sum of money;" *Fratri tuo magnam pecuniæ summam misi.*—"Tell (to) us some news;" *Dic nobis aliquid novi.*

Sunt mihi libri.

§ 162.—2. The verb *sum* in the sense of "to have," takes the dative of the p e r s o n who has, and the nominative of the t h i n g which he has.—The verb *sum;* of course, is to agree with the nominative of the thing, in number and person. E. g., "I have books."

Est homini cum Deo similitudo. Non semper idem color est floribus. Suus cuique mos est.[1] *Nulla potest esse voluptati cum honestate conjunctio. Sunt nauticis corpora dura, agricolis manus tritæ; agilia sunt membra cursoribus.—Videmus non semper eundem esse colorem floribus.*

NOTE.—We must here notice the phrase *est mihi nomen,* "my name is," or "I am called," where the name itself is added either in the dative or nominative, very rarely in the genitive. E. g., *Est mihi nomen Alexandro* or *Alexander.* -*Quodnam est tibi nomen? Marcello* or *Marcellus.—Erat inter illos juvenis cui cognomen postea Coriolano fuit. Consules leges, quibus tabulis duodecim est nomen, in publico proposuerunt. Damaratus duos filios habuit : nomina his Lucumo et Aruns fuere.*
Like *est mihi nomen* is construed the passive phrase *nomen mihi datum (inditum.*

---

[1]) Every one has his own way.

impositum, or *factum*) *est ;* as, *Puero ab inopia Egerio* (or *Egerius*) *nomen inditum est.*
Flumini a celeritate Tigri (or *Tigris*) *nomen est inditum.*—In the active construction,
the proper name stands either in the dative or accusative; as, *Desipiunt omnes qui
tibi nomen insano posuere. Puero Ascanium parentes dixēre nomen. Amphyctiun
civitati nomen Athenas* or *Athenis dedit.*—When the name is an adjective taken substantively rather than a real proper name, the genitive is used also; e. g., *Metello
cognomen Numidici inditum fuit. Mithridati res gestæ Magni cognomen dederunt.*

Est tibi honori.

§ 163.—3. The verb *sum*, in the sense of *to serve for, to cause, to
give, to bring, to afford*, etc., usually takes two datives,—one of the
persons to whom any thing serves for, brings, or affords ; and the
other of the thing which it serves for brings, or affords ; as, " It
does you honor," or " It redounds to your honor."

*Eloquentia principibus maximo ornamento est. Mare est exitio
nautis.*[1] *Curate ut et vobis honori et amicis utilitati et reipublicæ emo-
lumento esse possitis.*[2] *Hoc in tempore nulla civitas Atheniensibus
auxilio fuit. Patri non minori fuit adjumento in periculis quam solatio
in laboribus.*

NOTE 1.—The dative of the thing is variously expressed in English : (a) by the
nominative with the verb " to be ;" (b) by the objective depending upon such a verb
as to serve for, to cause, procure, occasion, bring, give, afford ; and (c)
by an adjective. E. g., *Est solatio*,it affords consolation, it is a (source of) consolation, it is consoling.—*Est voluptati,* It is a pleasure, it gives or affords pleasure, it is
pleasant.

Instead of *Hoc solatio, argumento, documento est,* we may also say *Hoc solatium,
argumentum, documentum est.*

NOTE 2.—A double dative—one of the person to whom, and the other of the
end or purpose for which—stands often also

(a) With *do, duco, tribuo, habeo, verto,* and *fio,* in the sense of " to impute *for* or
as," " to reckon or regard as ;" e. g., *vitio vertere,* to charge as a crime against ;
ludibrio habere, to make a laughing-stock of.... ; *laudi ducere,* to reckon as a
recommendation ; *ignaviæ tribuere,* to attribute as cowardice ; *gloriæ ducere,* to
regard as a source of glory. — *Paupertas probro haberi* or *fieri cœpit. Quis erit qui
hoc tibi vitio vertat? Vitio mihi dant quod mortem hominis necessarii graviter fero.
Id sibi gloriæ duxit.*[3] *Ampla domus sæpe fit dedecori domino, si in ea est solitudo.*

(b) With *do, mitto, venio, proficiscor, accipio, relinquo,* when the purpose of giving,
sending, coming, etc., is expressed in Latin by a substantive; as, " I shall come
to aid you," or " I shall come to your assistance."—*Veniam tibi auxilio. Pausanias
Atticis auxilio venit. Cæsar quinque cohortes castris præsidio* (also *ad præsidium*) *reliquit.*[4] *Virtus sola neque dono datur neque accipitur.*[5]

---

[1] brings ruin upon.   [2] become an honor to yourselves, a benefit to your friends,
and an advantage to....   [3] He thought it glorious for himself.   [4] as a garrison, or
for the protection of the camp.   [5] is neither bestowed as a present.

Note 3.—To this rule are to be referred, also, the phrases *est mihi curæ*, "I care, or am anxious about," and *est mihi cordi*, "I have at heart," "it is dear to me." E. g., "Every one minds his own gratification;". *Curæ est sua cuique voluptas. Est adhuc curæ hominibus fides et officium. Amicos Attico curæ esse cognitum est. Id mihi non minori curæ est quam tibi.*[1] *Hoc mihi magnopere cordi est.*

☞ With *curæ* the adjectives *magnæ, majori, maximæ*, etc.,—with *cordi* the adverbs *magnopere, magis, maxime*, etc., are commonly used.

Studeo Grammaticæ.

§ 164.—4. The dative stands with many intransitive verbs signifying to *please, favor, help, profit, trust*, and their contraries,—to *command, obey, serve, resist, approach, threaten*, and *be angry with*. The principal verbs of this kind are: *placeo, displiceo, arrideo, assentior, assentor, blandior, lenocinor, gratificor, palpor,—faveo, studeo, ignosco, indulgeo, suffrāgor, invideo, insidior, convicior, insulto,—auxilior, opitulor, patrocinor, subvenio, succurro, medeor, incommodo, obtrecto,—prosum, obsum, noceo, officio,—credo, fido, confido, diffido,—impero, mando, præcipio,—obedio, pareo, obsequor, obtempero, morigeror, cedo, dicto audiens sum,—servio, inservio, ministro, famulor, ancillor,—adversor, refrāgor, obsto, renitor, repugno, resisto,—propinquo, appropinquo, occurro, obvius sum* or *fio, obviam eo (fio, venio),—minor, comminor, impendeo, immineo,—succenseo, irascor.* To these must be added *nubo, parco, benedico, maledico, suadeo, persuadeo, dissuadeo, supplico, satisfacio, respondeo*, and the impersonals *libet, licet, liquet, conducit, convenit, expedit, accidit, evenit*, and *contingit.* E. g., "I study Grammar."

adminiculor, 1. *to help.*
adversor, 1. *to oppose.*
ancillor, 1. *to serve.*
appropinquo, 1. *to approach.*
arrideo, 2. *to please.*
assentior, 4. *to agree with.*
assentor, 1. *to flatter.*
auxilior, 1. *to help.*
benedico, 3. *to praise.*
blandior, 4. *to flatter.*
cedo, 3. *to yield.*
comminor, 1. *to threaten.*
confido; 3. *to confide in.*
convicior, 1. *to revile.*
credo, 3. *to trust.*
dicto audiens sum, *to obey.*
diffIdo, 3. *to distrust.*
displiceo, 2. *to displease.*

dissuadeo, 2. *to dissuade.*
famulor, 1. *to serve.*
faveo, 2. *to favor.*
fido, 3. *to trust.*
gratificor, 1. *to gratify.*
ignosco, 3. *to pardon.*
immineo, 2. *to threaten.*
impendeo, 2. *to threaten.*
impero, 1. *to command.*
incommodo, 1. *to molest.*
indulgeo, 2. *to indulge.*
inservio, 4. *to serve.*
insidior, 1. *to lay snares.*
insulto, 1. *to insult.*
invideo, 2. *to envy.*
irascor, 3. *to be angry.*
lenocinor, 1. *to wheedle.*
maledico, 3. *to abuse.*

mando, 1. *to command.*
medeor, 2. *to heal.*
ministro, 1. *to serve.*
minor, 1. *to threaten.*
morigeror, 1. *to gratify.*
noceo, 2. *to hurt.*
nubo, 3. *to marry.*
obedio, 4. *to obey.*
obsequor, 3. *to comply with.*
obsto, 1. *to oppose.*
obsum, *to be against.*
obtempero, 1. *to obey.*
obtrecto, 1. *to disparage.*
obviam eo, *to go to meet.*
obiam venio, *to meet.*
obvius sum, *to meet.*
occurro, 3. *to meet.*
officio, 3. *to hinder.*

---

[1] It is a subject of no less anxiety to me.

opitulor, 1. *to help.*	propinquo, 1. *to approach.*	servio, 4. *to serve.*
palpor, 1. *to wheedle.*	prosum, *to profit.*	studeo, 2. *to apply one's self*
parco, 3. *to spare.*	refrăgor, 1. *to oppose.*	suadeo, 2. *to advise.*
pareo, 2. *to obey.*	renitor, 3. *to resist.*	subvenio, 4. *to aid.*
patrocinor, 1. *to defend.*	repugno, 1. *to oppose.*	succenseo, 2. *to be angry with*
persuadeo, 2. *to persuade.*	resisto, 3. *to resist.*	succurro, 3. *to succor.*
placeo, 2. *to please.*	respondeo, 2. *tŏ answer.*	suffrăgor, 1. *to support.*
præcipio, 3. *to command.*	satisfacio, 3. *to satisfy.*	supplico, 1. *to entreat.*

Mors nulli hominum parcit.   Vir probus nemini invidet.   Mali boni
obtrectare solent.   Festinationi meæ brevitatique litterarum ignosce.   Vir
bonus non incommodat alteri.   Cæsari pro te libentissime supplicabo.[1]
Quis mihi jure succenseat?   Non crimini patrocinamur, sed homini.
Homines plurimum hominibus et prosunt et obsunt.[2]   Dies[3] stultis quo-
que mederi solet.   Voluptas sensibus blanditur.   Hoc rectene an per-
peram fecerim, nondum mihi plane liquet.

NOTE 1.—In the passive construction, the preceding intransitive verbs become impersonal, that is, they are put in the third person singular, retaining the dative which they govern in the active. To this the young student should pay particular attention, as most of them are transitive in English and accordingly admit of a personal passive; as,

Parcitur mihi, *I am spared,*	Favetur mihi, *I am favored,*
parcitur tibi, *thou art spared,*	favetur tibi, *thou art favored,*
parcitur illi, *he is spared,*	favetur illi, *he is favored,*
parcitur nobis, *we are spared,*	favetur nobis, *we are favored,*
parcitur vobis, *ye are spared,*	favetur vobis, *ye are favored,*
parcitur illis, *they are spared.*	favetur illis, *they are favored.*

Thus, "I am molested," *mihi incommodatur,* not *ego incommodor.*—"You are envied," *vobis invidetur,* not *vos invidemini.*—"Thou art obeyed," *tibi obtemperatur,* not *tu obtemperaris.*—"They were abused with impunity," *illis impune maledictum est,* not *illi impune maledicti sunt.*—"I have been persuaded," *i. e.,* "I am convinced," *mihi persuasum est,* not *ego persuasus sum.*

NOTE 2.—The verbs *credo, mando, impero, præcipio, minor, suadeo,* and *respondeo,* besides the dative of the person, take sometimes an accusative of the thing; as, "I am threatened (*minor,* § 92.) with death," *Mortem mihi minantur.*—"He spoke in favor of peace," *Suasit pacem* sc. *civibus.*—"Cæsar demanded arms and hostages from the states," *Cæsar arma et obsides civitatibus imperavit.*

As the accusative of the thing, in the passive construction, becomes the nominative, these verbs may admit of a personal passive and accordingly be used in the plural, if the nominative be plural; e. g., "Matters about which advice is asked, are replied to with very little risk;" *Quæ consuluntur, minimo periculo respondentur.* *Tota Italia delectus habentur, arma imperantur. Æduatici quæ (sibi) imperarentur, facere dixerunt.*

---

[1] entreat in thy behalf.   [2] profit and hurt one another.   [3] Time.

NOTE 3.—When two verbs connected by *et*, of which one governs the dative, the other the accusative, affect in common the same object, the noun is expressed with the first verb, and represented with the other by the appropriate case of the demonstrate *is* or *ille;* as, "The desires of the soul must obey and follow reason ;" *Animi appetitus rationi pareant eamque sequantur necesse est.*

NOTE 4.—With *persuadeo*, the thing of which one persuades himself or another, is commonly expressed by a clause,—sometimes by the accusative of an adjective or adjective pronoun in the neuter gender, as *hoc, id, illud, unum, utrumque, multa*, etc.,—and sometimes by the ablative with *de*, as *persuadere alicui de paupertate, de animi immortalitate*, etc.

The English "to envy some one for something" is rendered in Latin either by the dative of the person with the accusative of the thing, as "I envy no man's honor," *Nulli honorem invideo ; invident nobis optimam magistram, naturam*,—or, what is more common, the thing is expressed by the dative and the person by the genitive or a possessive pronoun. E. g., *Nullius invideo honori. Horum laudi invident. Non ego invideo tuis commodis.*

NOTE 5.—*Insulto* is generally construed with the dative, very rarely with the accusative.—*Benedico* takes the dative in the sense of "to praise ;" the accusative, in the sense of "to bless." The former but seldom occurs, the latter is found only in ecclesiastical writers.—*Nubo*, "to marry," (properly) "to veil," is said of the bride.; *ducere in matrimonium* or simply *ducere*, of the bridegroom.

☞ The verbs *jubeo, juvo, lœdo*, and *offendo*, are transitive, and accordingly govern the accusative.

Annue cœptis.

§ 165.—5. The dative stands with many verbs compounded with *ad, ante, con, de, in, inter, ob, post, prœ, sub*, and *super*, provided the signification of these prepositions be not lost in composition ; as, "Favor our undertakings."

Of these verbs some are transitive ; others, intransitive.

The following are transitive:

addo, 3. *to add.*	confero, *to compare with.*	inūro, 3. *to brand.*
affero, *to bring.*	conjungo, 3. *to join.*	objicio, 3. *to object to*
affīgo, 3. *to fasten to.*	defero, *to confer upon.*	offundo, 3. *to pour before.*
adjicio, 3. *to add.*	derŏgo, 1. *to derogate.*	oppono, 3. *to oppose.*
adjungo, 3. *to join.*	detraho, 8. *to take off.*	posthabeo, 2. *to esteem inferior.*
adhibeo, 2. *to employ.*	eripio, 3. *to snatch away.*	postpono, 3. *to esteem less.*
admoveo, 2. *to lead to.*	immisceo, 2. *to mingle with.*	præfero, *to prefer.*
allīgo, 1. *to bind.*	incīdo, 3. *to cut into.*	præficio, 8. *to place over.*
applico, 1. *to apply.*	infero, *to bring upon.*	præpono, 3. *to prefer.*
antepono, 3. *to prefer.*	injicio, 3. *to throw into.*	subjicio, 3. *to subject.*
comparo, 1. *to compare.*	insoro, 3. *to insert.*	suppono, 3. *to place under.*

The following are intransitive:

accedo, 3. *to approach.*	immŏror, 1. *to linger over.*	præmineo, 2. *to excel.*
adhæreo, 2. *to stick to.*	indormio, 4. *to sleep over.*	præsideo, 2. *to preside.*
adjăceo, 2. *to lie near.*	inhæreo, 2. *to stick to.*	prævaleo, 2. *to prevail.*
allûdo, 3. *to allude to.*	inhio, 1. *to long for.*	succumbo, 3. *to succomb.*
annue, 3. *to grant.*	innascor, 3. *to grow up in.*	supersto, 1. *to stand upon.*
assideo, 2. *to sit near.*	insisto, 3. *to insist on.*	supervenio, 4. *to come upon.*
assurgo, 3. *to rise up to.*	interjaceo, 2. *to lie between.*	supervivo, 3. *to survive.*
cohæreo, 2. *to cohere.*	intervenio, 4. *to come between.*	præsum, *to preside.*
congruo, 3. *to accord with.*	obrēpo, 3. *to steal upon.*	intersum, *to be present at.*
consentio, 4. *to agree.*	obstrĕpo, 3. *to annoy.*	subsum, *to be beneath.*
illacrimo, 1. *to cry over.*	obversor, 1. *to be before.*	supersum, *to be remaining*

Senectus nobis obrēpit. Leonidas securis Persis supervēnit. Nasus quasi murus oculis interjectus esse[1] videtur. Thebanorum genti plus inest[2] virium quam ingenii. Hannibal præfuit[3] equitatui. Aristides pugnæ navali interfuit. Plures cecidissent, ni nox prœlio intervenisset.[4] An vero quisquam paruit, quisquam in curiam venienti assurrexit?

NOTE 1.—Verbs compounded with *ad*, *con*, and *in*, sometimes repeat these prepositions with their respective cases. E. g., *Confer nostram longissimam ætatem cum æternitate. Navis adhæret ad scopulum. Dux signa in hostes inferri[5] jussit. In omnium animis Dei notitiam impressit ipsa natura. Timotheus ad bellicam laudem doctrinæ gloriam adjecit. Cunctus senatus ad Cæsarem supplex accessit.*

NOTE 2.—*Adjaceo* takes sometimes the accusative, but without a preposition; as, *Timotheus socios omnes eas gentes adjunxit quæ mare illud adjacent.*—The accusative without a preposition is found also with *accedo*, as *Hannibal cum quinque navibus Africam accessit.*
Applico is generally construed *se ad aliquid*, e. g., *ad virtutem, ad philosophiam,* etc.; very rarely *se alicui rei.*—*Communico*, in the Classical prose, is construed *aliquid cum aliquo*, occasionally *aliquid inter se, inter nos,* etc.; in late prose only *alicui aliquid.*
Obambulo and *obequito* take the dative, when the meaning is "to walk, ride in front of or towards;" and the accusative, when the meaning is "to walk, ride through or over."
Obrēpo and *obversor*, instead of the dative, sometimes take the accusative with a preposition; as, *obrepere in animum, obversari ante oculos.*

Cui or quem præstolaris?

§ 166.—6. The following verbs take either the dative or the accusative: *antecedo, antecello, anteeo, antesto, procedo, prœcello, prœeo, præ-*

---

[1]) interposed as a wall between....   [2]) possesses more....   [3]) commanded.   [4]) had not interrupted.   [5]) to attack the enemy. Lit., to bear or carry the standards against....

*curro, præsto, præverto; allatro, ausculto, illudo; adůlor, æmulor,
medicor,* and *præstolor;* as, "For whom are you waiting?"

adůlor, 1. *to flatter.*	ausculto, 1. *to listen to.*	præsto, 1. *to excel.*
æmulor, 1. *to vie with.*	illudo, 3. *to ridicule.*	præstolor, 1. *to wait for.*
allatro, 1. *to bark at.*	medicor, 1. *to heal.*	præverto, 3. *to avoid.*

*Certis rebus certa signa præcurrunt. Ut homo iners hominem dili-
gentem præcurrat, fieri non potest.—Quis horum talium virorum digni-
tati illudat? Carneades oratorum præcepta illudere solebat.—Tibi ad
forum Aurelium præstolabantur armati. Quem præstolare, Parmeno,
hic ante ostium?*

NOTE.—The verbs compounded with *præ* and *ante,* when taken in the sense of "to
excell," together with *adůlor, æmulor,* and *allatro,* are more commonly construed with
the accusative.—*Antecedo, præsto,* and *antecello,* however, are used by Cicero with the
dative only.

Hanc tibi imaginem, or Hac te imagine dono.

§ 167.—7. The verbs *aspergo, inspergo, circumdo, dono, impertio*
(and *-ior*), *induo, exuo,* and *intercludo,* are construed both *alicui rem*
and *aliquem re,* that is, they take either the dative of the person with
the accusative of the thing, or the accusative of the person with the
ablative of the thing; as, "I present you this picture."

Hosti commeatum (or *hostem commeatu*) *intercluserat.*[1] *Carnem sale*
(or *carni salem*) *aspergimus. Archiam poetam Tarentini civitate dona-
runt. Orationi aspergantur sales.*

NOTE 1.—*Interdicere,* "to forbid," or "debar from," is generally construed *alicui
re,* and sometimes also, *alicui rem.* E. g., *Ariovistus omni Gallia interdixit Romanis.
Male rem gerentibus bonis paternis interdici solet. Plancum sic contemnit tamquam si
illi aqua et igni interdictum sit.*

NOTE 2.—Such expressions as *galeam indutus, chlamydem lacerto circumdatus, ferrum cinctus,* and the like, are Greek imitations, met with in poetry.

Consulo tibi—Consulo te.

§ 168.—8. The following verbs take at one time the dative; at
another, another case, but in a different signification:

---

[1] intercepted or cut off.—We also find *intercludere aliquem ab aliqua re,* e. g., *aliquem ab exercitu.*

Æquare aliquid alicui rei or *cum aliqua re*, e. g., *Hannibali Philippum*, to equalize, to compare with,—*urbem solo*, to level or to raze to the ground; *aliquem* or *aliquid*, e. g., *majores, majorum, gloriam, cursum equorum*, to equal, attain to; *aliquem aliqua re*, e. g., *majores gloriâ, equitem cursu*, to keep up with, come up to.

Cavere alicui, to provide for, watch over; *aliquem* or *ab aliquo*, to avoid, beware of, guard against; absol., or with *sibi*, to be on one's guard.

Consulere alicui, to take care of, provide for one's interests; *aliquem aliquid* or *de aliqua re*, to consult, ask one's advice; *æqui boni* or *æqui bonique consulere (facere)*, and *boni consulere*, to take in good part.

Convenire aliquem, to visit some one; *convenit mihi*, etc., it suits me; *convenit alicui cum aliquo* or *inter aliquos*, e. g., *mihi tecum*, or *inter nos convenit*, we agree; *convenit inter omnes*, all agree.

Cupere alicui, to favor, wish well to; *aliquid*, to wish something.

Deficere alicui (very rare), *to fail, be wanting;*—usually *deficere aliquem*, as *me vox, vires deficiunt*, or absol., *vox, tempus, memoria deficit; sol, luna deficit*, is eclipsed; *ab aliquo* to forsake, fall off from, revolt against, e. g., *a Romanis, a virtute; ab aliquo ad aliquem*, to desert to; *deficere animo*, to be disheartened, lose courage.

Imponere alicui, to cheat, to impose upon; *alicui aliquid*, to lay something upon some one.

Incumbere rei, to lean upon; *ad* or *in rem*, e. g. *in rempublicam, ad litteras*, to apply or devote one's self to.

Manet mihi, it remains for me; *manet me* it awaits me, as *mors sua quemque manet; manere in sententia*, to adhere to.

Moderari rei, to check, restrain; *rem*, to manage, regulate, govern.

Petere alicui aliquid, to beg something for another; *aliquid ab aliquo*, to ask some one for something, or something of some one; *aliquem*, to attack, aim at; *locum*, e. g., *Romam, urbem, castra*, to go to.

Prospicere (providere) alicui, to take care of, provide for; *aliquid*, to foresee.

Quærere alicui aliquid, e. g., *sibi laudem*, to seek to gain; *aliquem* or *aliquid*, to seek, look for; *ex (ab, de) aliquo aliquid*, to question some one about something, e. g., *ex me quæsitum est*, I was asked; *de aliqua re*, to inquire into juridically.

Recipere aliqu'd, to receive something; *alicui*, to warrant, promise; *aliquem domo, tectis*, to entertain; *in se*, to pledge one's word; *se, animum a (ex) pavore*, to recover from, collect one's self; *se*, or *se in locum*, e. g., *domum*, to retreat, return.

Referre alicui aliquid, to bring or carry back; *gratiam*, to return thanks; *se Romam*, return to; *pedem*, to retreat; *rem* or *de re ad senatum*, to lay before.

Temperare rei, to check, restrain; *sibi ab aliqua re*, to abstain from; *rem*, to manage, regulate; *alicui*, e. g., *hostibus*, to refrain from severity towards, to spare.

Timere (*metuere*) *rei* or *de re, alicui* or *de aliquo,* to fear for something or for some one; *tibi* or *tua causa,* I am alarmed on thy account; *aliquem* or *aliquid,* to fear some one or something; *aliquid ab aliquo,* to fear something from some one.

Vacare rei, to devote one's self to; *re* or *a re,* to be free from, to be without.

NOTE.—The following verbs take, in the same signification, sometimes the dative, and sometimes another case, with or without a preposition:

Acquiescere rei, re, and *in re,* to find pleasure in something.

Adscribere aliquem civitati and *in civitatem,* to receive some one as a citizen.

Assuescere, insuescere rei and (more commonly) *re,* rarely *ad aliquid,* to accustom one's self to.

Attendere aliquem or *aliquid,* more rarely *alicui rei;* also *attendere animum ad aliquid,* to listen to.

Desperare rem, e. g., *rempublicam,* to give up; *de re* or *alicui rei,* e. g., *sibi, fortunis suis,* to despair of.

Excellere alicui (rarely *aliquem*) and *inter omnes,* to excel.

Mittere, scribere alicui and *ad aliquem,* to send, write (to) some one.

Occumbere morte and (more commonly) *mortem,* to fall, to die.

Supersedere alicui rei and (more commonly) *aliqua re,* to omit, desist from.

Quid mihi Celsus agit?

§ 169.—9. The datives *mihi, tibi, sibi, nobis,* and *vobis,* are often used, where the English language has no equivalent expression. They are for the most part redundant, and serve merely for the purpose of indicating familiarity and liveliness of feeling; as, "What is my friend Celsus doing?"

Quid ait tandem nobis Sannio? Hic mihi quisquam misericordiam nominet![1] *Epistolam cum a te avide expectarem, ecce tibi nuncius, pueros venisse Roma. An ille mihi liber,*[2] *cui mulier imperat? Quid hoc sibi vult?*[3] *Quid hæc sibi dona volunt?*[4]

VERBS GOVERNING THE ACCUSATIVE.

Ama Deum.

§ 170.—1. The accusative stands with all transitive verbs in answer to the question *whom* or *what?* placed after the verb; as, "Love (love *whom?*—) God."

---

[1] Let here any one talk to me of mercy. [2] Or can I think him free....? [3] What does this mean? [4] What is the meaning of....?

*Oleum et operam perdidi, surdo cecini, lapidem coxi. Obsequium
amicos, veritas odium parit. Maximum ornamentum amicitiæ tollit, qui
ex ea tollit verecundiam. Fragile corpus animus sempiternus movet.
Hæc studia adolescentiam alunt, senectutem oblectant, secundas res
ornant, adversis perfugium ac solatium præbent.*

NOTE 1.—Transitive verbs compounded with *trans*, take two accusatives; one
depending on the verb, the other upon the preposition. In the passive construction,
the former becomes the nominative, the latter remains unchanged.—E. g., "Agesilaus
led his forces across the Hellespont;" *Agesilaus copias Hellespontum trajecit. Ubii
orabant ut Cæsar exercitum Rhenum transportaret.—Ab Agesilao copiæ Hellespontum
trajectæ sunt. Belgæ Rhenum traducti sunt.* Thus, *Scipio cum classe Pyrenæos montes
circumvectus est.*

NOTE 2.—Many verbs, which are properly intransitive, are often used as transitives, and accordingly take an accusative, especially that of a neuter adjective or
adjective pronoun. E. g., *Hoc gaudeo* or *lætor*, I rejoice at this ; *illud tibi assentior*, I
agree with you in this point; *non possum idem gloriari*, I cannot make the same
boast; *illud non dubito*, I do not doubt that; *omnes hoc unum student*, all are anxious
about this one thing; *idem (multa alia) peccasti*, you have made the same blunder.—
Olere vinum, to smell of wine; *redolere antiquitatem*, to savor of antiquity; *vox sonat
hominem*, the voice sounds like that of a man; *anhelare scelus, crudelitatem*, to be
panting for, to breathe out; *gemere, lugere, lacrimare casum*, to grieve at, or mourn
over; *fastidire preces, mores alicujus*, to be disgusted with; *festinare mortem*, to
accelerate; *horrere tenebras, crimen ingrati animi*, to shudder, be horrified at;—
*indignari vicem suam, erubescere fratres, currere stadium, navigare mare, tertiam vivere
ætatem*, etc.

NOTE 3.—Several intransitive verbs implying motion, become transitive, when
compounded with prepositions governing the accusative, especially with *circum, per,
præter, trans*, and *super*, and accordingly take an accusative ; as, *transnatare flumen ;
circumvenire hostem ; adire regem, provinciam ; subire jugum ; obire mortem ; inire
fædus, prælium.—Ea fama forum et urbem pervasit. Nos undique fata circumstant.
Tanais Europam et Asiam medius interfluit.*

NOTE 4.—Some intransitive verbs take an accusative of kindred signification, but
mostly in connection with an adjective or adjective pronoun ; as, *pugnam pugnare
acerrimam ; somnium mirum somniare ; servire servitutem turpissimam ; jusjurandum
jurare verissimum ; vitam vivere miserrimam ; suum gaudium gaudere ; hanc pugnam
pugnare ; hæc vota vovere*, etc.

NOTE 5.—Here should also be noticed the verb *appellere*, "to land" (properly "to
drive towards"). This verb is in the classical prose thus construed: *Apellimus* or *navem
appellimus*, "we land." Pass., *Apellimur* or *nave appellimur* e. g. *ad Africam*, ad
Italiam, ad Delum, ad Syracusas (more rarely *in Africam*, etc.). We find also *Navis
appellitur* and *ventus (nauta) navem appellit.*—Later writers sometimes use *appellere*
instead of *appelli* with the simple accusative ; as, *Puteolos nave appulit. Triremis
terram appulit. Alexandrina navis Dertosam appulit.*

Urbem Romam vocat.

§ 171.—2. Verbs that take in the Passive two nominatives (§ 154), take in the Active two accusatives, one of the object, the other of the predicate,—the former answering to the question *whom* or *what*, the latter to the question *what* placed after the verb; as, "He called the city Rome."—Such verbs are those signifying

> "to call or name," as *dico, nomino, voco, appello, nuncupo, saluto ;*
>
> "to choose or make," as *creo, deligo, designo, renuntio, declaro, constituo, facio, reddo ;*
>
> "to deem or reckon," as *duco, credo, habeo, judico, arbitror, existimo, numero, puto, agnosco, reperio, invenio.*

Omnes perturbationes animi morbos philosophi appellant. Ciceronem universus populus Consulem declaravit. Socrates totius mundi se incolam et civem arbitrabatur.[1] *Senatus Antonium hostem judicavit.*[2] *Vehementer errant qui corporis voluptatem summum bonum existimant. Cupiditas et avaritia homines cæcos reddit.*

NOTE 1.—The verbs *habere, ducere,* and *putare,* are sometimes followed by *pro* with the ablative, or by *loco, (in) numero* with the genitive ; as, *Quid stultius quam incerta pro certis habere ? Pollionem vetustissimorum familiarium loco habuit.*—Thus *aliquid pro nihilo putare, aliquem in hostium numero habere,* etc.

NOTE 2.—To this rule also belong (a) the verbs *habeo, accipio, sumo, adjungo, do, tribuo, addo,* and *accio,* in the sense of "to have," "to summon," "to take or give some one as .... ;" (b) the expressions *se præstare, se præbere,* to prove or show one's self as ; and (c) the phrase *certiorem aliquem facere de aliqua re* or *alicujus rei,* "to inform some one of...."—E. g., "I shall accompany you ;" *Me tibi comitem adjungam. Tiberius Druso Sejanum dedit adjutorem. Philippus Aristotelem Alexandro filio doctorem accivit.—Bene de me meritis gratum me præbeo. Antistius se præstitit acerrimum propugnatorem libertatis. Tu me de tuis rebus velim quam familiarissime certiorem facias. Faciam te consilii nostri certiorem.*

Doceo pueros Grammaticam.

§ 172.—3. The verbs *doceo* and *edoceo,* I teach ; *dedoceo,* I unteach ; *celo,* I conceal from ; and those signifying to e n t r e a t, d e m a n d, and i n q u i r e, as *oro, rogo, precor ; posco, reposco, flagito ; interrogo,* and *per-*

---

[1] Socrates thought (thought *whom ?*—) himself (thought himself *what ?*—) an inhabitant, etc. [2] The Senate declared (declared *whom ?*—) Antony (declared him *what ?*—) an enemy.

contor, take two accusatives, one of the person, the other of the thing; as, " I teach the boys Grammar."

Ciceronem Minerva omnes artes edocuit. Non te celavi sermonem Ampii. Verres parentes pretium pro sepultura liberorum poscebat. Legati Ennenses ad Verrem adeunt eumque simulacrum Cereris reposcunt.—Me primum sententiam rogavit. Pusionem quendam Socrates apud Platonem interrogat quædam geometrica.

NOTE 1.—When these verbs are made passive, the acc. of the **person** becomes the nominative, but the accusative of the **thing** is retained; as, *Latinæ legiones militiam Romanam edoctæ sunt. Id ego diu celabar. Primus sententiam rogatus sum. Segetes alimentaque debita dives poscebatur humus.*

NOTE 2.—With *celare* and the verbs of **entertaining, demanding,** and **inquiring,** the accusative of the thing is most common, when it is expressed by the neuter of an adjective or adjective pronoun. E. g., " What do you ask me for?" *Quid me rogas?—Hoc te vehementer rogo. Nihil aliud vos oro atque obsecro. His (or ad hæc) quæ te interrogo responde. Hæc te celare nolui.*

NOTE 3.—The verbs of **demanding,** instead of the accusative of the person, frequently take the ablative with *ab*. In the passive construction the accusative of the thing is then changed into the nominative.—E. g., *Quid studia, quid artes a te flagitent, tuvidebis. A me annona flagitabatur. Nunc a te illud primum rogabo, ne quid invitus mea causa facias. Quæ deprecatus sum a diis immortalibus ut ea res mihi Populoque Romano bene atque feliciter eveniret, eadem precor ab iisdem diis immortalibus, ut vestræ mentes atque sententiæ cum Populi Romani voluntate suffragiisque consentiant.*

The ablative of the person with *ab* stands regularly with *peto, exigo,* and *postulo*; as, *Athenienses auxilium a Lacedæmoniis petierunt. Quo facilius id a te exigam, quod (a te) peto, nihil tibi a me postulanti recusabo.*

NOTE 4.—The verbs of **inquiring,** instead of the accusative of the thing, often take the ablative with *de*. This is not rarely the case, also, with *celo,* especially in the Passive.—E. g., *Visne ego te vicissim iisdem de rebus Latine interrogem? Ego illum de suo regno, ille me de nostra republica percontatus est.—De insidiis celare te nolui. Maximis de rebus a fratre celatus sum. Non est profecto de illo veneno celata mater.*

The verbs *quæro* and *sciscitor,* and occasionally also *percontor,* are construed *aliquid ex (ab, de) aliquo*; as, " Atticus was asked his opinion;" *Sententiam ex Attico sciscitabantur* (§ 92). *Dion a medicis quæsivit quomodo se haberet Dionysius. Quæsivit de Zenone quid futurum esset. Non quæro abs te quare patrem Sex. Roscius occiderit.*

NOTE 5.—*Doceo,* in the sense of " to inform," takes the ablative of the thing with *de*; as, *Sulla de his rebus docetur. De itinere hostium senatum edocet.*

In the phrases *aliquem docere fidibus, tibiis, armis,* supply *canere* and *uti* respectively; as, *Docebantur (or discebant) fidibus antiqui,* i. e., *fidibus canere.*

Musica me juvat.

§ 173.—4. The impersonals *decet,* it becomes; *dedecet,* it does not become; *juvat, delectat,* it pleases, delights; *fugit, fallit, præterit,* it escapes (§ 72), take the accusative of the person whom any thing becomes, delights, escapes,—and the nominative of the thing which becomes, delights, or escapes ; as, "I delight in music," or "Music delights me."

Modestia pueros decet, garrulitas dedecet. Parvum parva decent. Candida pax homines, trux decet ira feras. Multum ista me sapientiæ fama delectat. Hominem amentem hoc fugit. Quis est quem nulla res fugiat?

NOTE 1.—The nominative of the thing is often a verb in the Infinitive, an Acc. c. Inf., or a clause with the Subjunctive; as, *Oratorem irasci minime decet. Decet verecundum esse adolescentem. Te hilari animo esse me valde juvat. De Cæsare fugerat me* (I had forgotten) *ad te scribere. Non me præterit* (I know well) *Gallos fama belli præstare. Quid optimum sit, neminem fugit* (every one knows). *Illud alterum quam sit difficile non te fugit, nec vero Cæsarem fefellit.*

NOTE 2.—The phrase *latet me* (rarely *mihi*), "it is concealed from, or unknown to me," is found only in poetry and in Post-Augustan prose writers; as, *Hæc res Hannibalem non diu latuit.*

The verbs *spectare, attinere,* and *pertinere,* in the sense of "it regards, concerns, belongs to," take the accusative with *ad ;* as, *Non est dubium ad quem suspicio maleficii pertineat. Quoniam de eo genere beneficiorum dictum est, quæ ad singulos spectant, deinceps de iis quæ ad universos, quæque ad rempublicam pertinent, disputandum est.*

VERBS GOVERNING THE ABLATIVE.

Mihi libris opus est, or Mihi libri opus sunt.

§ 174.—1. *Opus est,* "there is need," governs the dative of the person who needs, and the ablative or nominative of the thing which is needed; as, "I need books."

Auctoritate tua nobis opus est. Quantum argenti opus est tibi? Corpori cibo et potione opus est. Exempla permulta nobis opus sunt. Non opus est tibi amico, de cujus benevolentia dubites. Ubi rerum testimonia adsunt, quid opus est verbis? Atticus quæ amicis suis opus fuerant, omnia ex sua re familiari dedit.

NOTE 1.—Whenever the thing n e e d e d is put in the ablative, *opus est* is construed impersonally ; but when it is put in the nominative, the verb *sum* is to agree with it accordingly; as, *Mihi libris opus est* or *mihi libri opus sunt. Quid tibi divitiis opus est,* or *quid tibi divitiæ opus sunt? Dux* or *duce adolescentibus opus est.*

The nominative of the thing is most frequently used with the neuters of adjectives and adjective pronouns.

NOTE 2.—When the thing needed is expressed by a verb, either the Infinitive or the Acc. c. Inf., or *ut* with the Subj., or the Supine in *u,* or the ablative of the Perf.

Part. may be used. E. g., *Nihil opus est pluribus verbis commemorare. Nunc opus est te animo valere, ut corpore possis. Nunc tibi opus est ægrum ut simules. Quoad scitu opus est. Opus fuit Hirtio convento.*[1] *Facto, non consulto, in tali periculo opus est.*

Abundat divitiis.

§ 175.—2. The verbs of *abounding*, *wanting*, and *depriving*, such as *abundo, redundo, affluo, scateo ; careo, egeo, indigeo ; orbo, privo, spolio, nudo, fraudo,* etc. govern the ablative of the thing, in which one abounds, which one wants, of which one is deprived ; as, "He abounds in riches."

Antiochia quondam eruditissimis hominibus affluebat. Quid consilii afferre potest, qui ipse eget consilio? Quam paucis, qua parvis rebus eget natura! Miserum est carere consuetudine amicorum. Respublica multis claris viris est orbata. Democritus oculis se privasse dicitur. Arbores nudantur foliis. Grave est spoliari fortunis. Milites mercede fraudati sunt.

NOTE 1.—*Egeo* is sometimes, and *indigeo* often, construed with the genitive ; as, *Gravitas morbi facit ut medicinæ egeamus. Deus nullius rei indiget.*—Also with *compleo* and *impleo* the genitive is sometimes found instead of the ablative.—E. g., *Convivium vicinorum quotidie compleo ;—carcer jam mercatorum completus,—ollam denariorum implere.*

NOTE 2.—*Pluit*, "it rains," is frequently construed with such ablatives as *lapidibus, lapide, lacte, carne, terra, sanguine ;* e. g., *Nuntiatum regi patribusque est, in monte Albano lapidibus pluisse.*—But the accusative is found also ; as, *Sanguinem pluisse Senatui nuntiatum est.*

Hoc me libera metu.

§ 176.—3. The verbs of *freeing* and *removing; keeping off, preventing,* and *desisting,* as *laxo, libero, solvo, expedio ; moveo, amoveo, demoveo, pello, depello, expello, deturbo, dejicio, ejicio ; arceo, absterreo, deterreo, prohibeo, abstineo, decedo, desisto,* etc.—govern the ablative of the thing from which one is freed, removed, or prevented,—either with or without the prepositions *ab, ex, de :* but when separation from a person is expressed, the preposition *ab* is regularly used. E. g., "Free me from this fear."

Te a quartana liberatum gaudeo. Timoleon Dionysium tota Sicilia depulit. Amicitia nullo loco excluditur. Hannibal ex Africa decedere coactus est. Helvetii suis sedibus pulsi sunt. Hostem aditu arcent.

---

[1] to visit, or to speak to.

Tu, Jupiter, hunc a tuis aris, a vita fortunisque civium arcebis. Faba Pythagorœi abstinuerunt. Egredere ex urbe, Catilina, libera rempublicam metu.

NOTE 1.—*Levare, exonerare,* and *exsolvere,* "to free," and *supersedēre,* "to abstain from," "to omit," take the ablative without preposition; as, *Leva me hoc onere. Cæsar prœlio supersedere statuit.*

Abdicare, "to resign," takes either the accusative alone, or the ablative with the accusative of a personal pronoun; as, *Magistratum (dictaturam,* etc.) *abdicavit,* or *Magistratu (dictatura,* etc.) *se abdicavit. Abdico prœturam,* or *me prœturá.*

NOTE 2.—The verbs signifying "to differ" and "to distinguish," as *discerno, secerno, distinguo, differo, discrepo, dissentio, dissideo, disto, abhorreo,* and also *alieno* and *abalieno,* are generally construed with *ab; as, Ab ea opinione Pompeius valde abhorruit.*
The verbs of differing are construed, also, with the dative, though more rarely in prose than in poetry, as *Ipsi sibi singuli discrepabant.*—With *dissentio, dissideo, discrepo,* and especially *discordo,* the ablative with *cum* is also found.

NOTE 3.—The verbs *egredi* and *excedere,* in the sense of "to transgress," are construed with the accusative, as *excedere modum, fines,* etc.

Fungor officio.

§ 177.—4. The ablative stands with the deponent verbs *utor, fruor, fungor* (and their compounds); *potior, dignor, vescor; lætor, glorior, nitor;* as, "I discharge my duty."

utor, 3. *to use,*	potior, 4. *to get, obtain,*	lætor, 1. *to rejoice at,*
fruor, 3. *to enjoy,*	dignor, 1. *to deem worthy,*	glorior, 1. *to boast of,*
fungor, 3. *to discharge,*	vescor, 3. *to eat, feed on,*	nitor, 3. *to rely upon.*

Quousque tandem, Catilina, abutēre patientia nostra? Hannibal multis variisque perfunctus laboribus anno acquievit septuagesimo. Semiramis regno Assyriorum potita est. Numidœ lacte et ferina carne vescebantur. Nulla re tam lœtari soleo quàm meorum officiorum conscientia. Tuo consilio et auctoritate nitor.

NOTE 1.—*Utor* is often used in the sense of "to have," especially when the ablative is accompanied by a noun or an adjective; as, "See what an equitable man you will have (find) in me;" *Hic vide quam me sis usurus æquo. Libertas non in eo est ut justo utamur domino, sed ut nullo. Alexander Aristotele usus est prœceptore.*
Potior is sometimes construed with the genitive, especially the genitive *rerum,* when it means "to obtain supreme power." E. g., *Dion totius ejus partis Siciliœ potitus est, quœ sub Dionysii potestate fuerat. Nemini in opinionem veniebat, Antonium rerum potiturum.*
Dignor is used both actively and passively, as *dignari aliquem honore* and

11

ab aliquo honore, " to deem, or to be deemed worthy of honor."—Cicero uses it mostly in a passive sense.

Glorior and *lætor* are sometimes construed with *de,* or the accusative of a neuter pronoun (§ 170, 2); as, *Lætor de tuo triumpho. Quis de vita misera potest gloriari? Equidem idem gloriari posse vellem. Utrumque lætor.—Gloriari,* " to glory in," takes the ablative with *in,* as *In virtute recte gloriamur.*

Nitor takes sometimes the ablative with *in;* as, *In vita Pompeii nitebatur salus civitatis.*—In the sense of " to strive after," it takes the accusative with *in* or *ad;* as, *Nitimur in vetitum semper cupimusque negata. Optimi cujusque animus maxime ad immortalitatem gloriæ nititur.*

NOTE 2.—To these deponents may also be added the verb *metior,* " to measure, judge, estimate by ....;" as, *Annum solis reditu metimur. Homines quæstu ac voluptate omnia metiuntur (— judicant, ponderant).*

Fame laboro.

§ 178.—5. The ablative stands with the verbs *gaudeo, doleo—valeo, laboro—fido, confido—sto, consto—vivo, floreo,* and *afficio;* as, " I suffer from hunger."

Juvenis gaudet equis.[1] *Duobus vitiis diversis, avaritiâ et luxuriâ, civitas laborat. Britanni lacte et carne vivunt.*[2] *Pericles florebat omni genere virtutis. Conditionibus stare oportet. Plurimum inter eos Bellovaci et virtute et auctoritate et hominum numero valent.*[3] *Delicto dolere, correctione gaudere*[4] *nos oportet.*

Dolere, " to grieve for ;" as, *laude aliena, injuriis civitatis, clade accepta.*—We also find *dolere de (ex) aliqua re.*—In the sense of " to lament," " to deplore," it takes the accusative, as *dolere vicem, casum, injurias, mortem alicujus.*—When used in the sense of " to pain," we say: *dens, caput, pes (mihi) dolet ; dentes, oculi, latera dolent,* " I have the tooth-ache," etc.

Valere, " to be strong," " to have influence," " to prevail ;" as, *corpore, pedibus, stomacho,—gratia, opibus, armis, auctoritate.*

Laborare, " to suffer from," " to labor under ;" as, *morbo, crudelitate domestica, odio apud hostes* (to be hated), *contemptu inter socios,*—and frequently *ex aliqua re,* as *ex pedibus, ex intestinis, ex renibus, ex ære alieno,*[5] *ex invidia,*—also, *a re frumentaria,* " to be in difficulty about supplies."

Fidere and *confidere,* " to trust, confide in," as *alicujus prudentia et consilio, corporis firmitate, natura loci,* and the like.—They are also construed with the dative, especially the dative of the thing, more rarely that of the person.—*Diffido* a l w a y s takes the dative.

Stare, " to adhere or stand to," " to keep," " to persist in," as *promissis,*

---

[1] delights in. [2] live upon. [3] are foremost in. [4] to rejoice at. [5] to be deep in debt.

fœdere, jurejurando, judicio suo, opinione or *decreto alicujus ;* also, *in fide.—
Stat mihi sententia* means "I am determined."

Constare, "to consist of;" as, *tota oratio longioribus membris, brevioribus peri-
odis constat ;*—but it more commonly takes the ablative with *ex,* as *homo ex
animo constat et corpore.*

Florere, "to be eminent, renowned, distinguished ;" as, *rerum gestarum
gloriâ, lepōre dicendi, ingenii laude, justitiæ famâ, nobilitate discipulorum.—
Florere gratiâ* means " to be liked."

Afficere, "to affect some one with something," is construed *aliquem aliqua
re ;"* as, *afficere aliquem laude,* to praise some one; *honore,* to honor; *gaudio,*
to gladden; *beneficio,* to benefit; *voluptate,* to delight; *præmio,* to reward;
pœna, to punish; *injuria,* to injure; *ignominia,* to disgrace; *dolore,* to grieve;
exilio, to banish; *cruciatibus,* to torment; *morte,* to kill; *sepultura,* to bury ;—
and passively, *affici morbo,* to fall sick; *voluptate, lætitia,* to be delighted; *laude,*
to be praised; *admiratione,* to be admired, etc.

E. g., *Studium tuum curaque de salute mea nova me voluptate affecit. Quid
absurdius quam res deformes divino honore afficere ?—Gravi oculorum morbo
Hannibal affectus est, Admiratione afficiuntur ii qui antecunt ceteros virtute.*

II. Tenses of Verbs.

§ 179.—The tenses are divided into *principal* and *historical* tenses.

Principal:	Historical:
PRES. ago, *I do,*	IMPF. agebam, *I was doing,*
PERF. egi, *I have done,*	PERF. egi, *I did,*
FUT. agam, *I shall do.*	PLUP. egeram, *I had done.*

PRESENT AND IMPERFECT.

§ 180.—The PRESENT represents an action as going on at the time
present to the speaker; as, "I am writing," *Scribo.—Omne animal se
ipsum diligit. Ægyptum Nilus irrigat. Plato aliter hac de re judicat*
(i. e., in his works).

NOTE 1.—With *jam diu, jam pridem, jam dudum,* an action that has been going on
for some time and is still going on, is often expressed by the Present, where in
English the Perfect is used; as, " During so many years I have already been waging
war ;" *Tot jam annos bella gero. Annum jam audis Cratippum. Cupio equidem et jam
pridem cupio* (and I have long been desiring) *Alexandriam reliquamque Ægyptum
visere.*

NOTE 2.—In animated narrative, the Present is often used instead of the Perfect, to
represent a past action or event as present. It is then called the historical
Present. E. g., *Pisidas resistentes Datames invadit, primo impetu pellit, fugientes
persequitur, multos interficit, castra hostium capit. Cæsar Dumnorigem ad se vocat,*

fratrem adhibet; quæ in eo reprehendat, ostendit; quæ ipse intelligat, quæ civitas queratur, proponit; monet ut in reliquum tempus omnes suspiciones vitet; præterita se condonare dicit, etc.

§ 181.—The IMPERFECT represents a past action or event as continuing and contemporary with some other past action (or time), either expressed or to be supplied by the mind. E. g., "Whilst thou wast playing, I was writing;" *Dum tu ludebas, ego scribebam. Quum scribebam in expectatione erant omnia. Principio rerum imperium penes reges erat.*[1]

NOTE 1.—The Imperfect is used, also, to express r e p e a t e d and c u s t o m a r y actions; as, *Anseres Romæ publice alebantur in Capitolio. Socrates dicebat* or *dicere solebat.*[2] *Pausanias apparatu regio utebatur, epulabatur luxuriose, superbe respondebat, et crudeliter imperabat. Verres simul atque in oppidum quodpiam venerat, immittebantur homines, qui investigabant et perscrutabantur omnia.*

NOTE 2.—The Imperfect is invariably used, where in English the compound tense "I was reading," "he was playing," "they were singing," etc., is employed; e. g., "I was accidentally going along the via sacra," *Ibam forte viâ sacrâ.*—Sometimes it denotes merely the beginning of an action,—an action intended or attempted, but not carried into full effect. It is then almost equivalent to the past of the active periphrastic conjugation. E. g., "Porsena attempted to frighten him;" *Porsena eum terrebat. Num dubitas id me imperante facere quod jam tua sponte faciebas* (or *facturus eras)? Piso abire se et cedere urbe testabatur et simul curiam relinquebat* (i. e., *relinquere tentabat*).

NOTE 3.—In the epistolary style, the Imperfect is frequently employed instead of the Present, when the writer speaks of actions and events which, though present at the time he writes, are past at the moment the letter is received. He, therefore, in writing, uses the same terms he would employ if he were to arrive himself in place of the letter. E. g., "This is already the 7th day that we are detained in Corfu;" *Jam septimum diem Corcyræ tenebamur.*—"I write you this at midnight;" *Hæc ad te scribebam media nocte. Habes totum reipublicæ statum, qui quidem tum erat cum has litteras dabam. Summa cura expectabam adventum Menandri, quem ad te miseram. Nihil habebam quod scriberem : neque enim novi quidquam audieram et ad tuas omnes rescripseram pridie.*

☞ In translating such passages, the Latin Imperfect must be rendered by the English Present, and the Latin Pluperfect by the English Perfect.

"To-day," in the epistolary style, is often expressed by *eo ipso die cum hæc scribebam;*—"yesterday," by *pridie ejus diei quo hæc scribebam;*—and "to-morrow," by *postridie ejus diei qui erat tum futurus cum hæc scribebam.*

PERFECT AND PLUPERFECT.

§ 182.—The PERFECT Indicative is used both as a principal and an historical tense.

---

[1] The time referred to is implied in *principio.*   [2] the Perfect *solitus est* would represent the habit as a merely historical fact.

As a principal tense, the Perfect Ind. corresponds to the English Perfect with "have," and represents an action or event as just completed at the present time, or existing to the present in its results. E. g., "He is gone, he has left, he has escaped, he has rushed out;" *Abiit, excessit, evasit, erupit.*

As an historical tense, the Perfect Ind. corresponds to the Past English forms *I came, I saw, I wrote, I went,* etc., and represents a past action or event absolutely, without reference either to the present time, or to another past action; as, *Hannibal Hispaniam bello subegit. Alexander Babylone decessit.*

Note 1.—The historical Perfect goes sometimes with the Imperfect: the former denoting a merely historical fact; the latter, a continuing, customary, or repeated action; as, "Hortensius used to speak better than he wrote;" *Hortensius dicebat melius quam scripsit. Ædui se in oppida receperunt murisque se tenebant. In Græcia musici floruerunt discebantque* (used to learn) *id omnes. Ita enim censebat, itaque disseruit* (on a particular occasion).

Note 2.—The conjunctions *ubi, ut, ut primum, simul ac, postquam,* and *posteaquam,* usually go with the Perfect, when two actions are spoken of as following each other in immediate succession. In English, the Pluperfect is then commonly used. E. g., *Hannibal ubi Carthaginem rediit, Prætor est factus. Hostium exercitus postquam intrasse Romanos vidit saltum, repente cum clamore incautus invadit.*—But, when a considerable or definite space of time intervenes, or when actions of repeated occurrence are spoken of, the Pluperfect must be used; as, *Hannibal anno tertio postquam domo profugerat, in Africam venit. Alcibiades simul ac se remiserat, intemperans reperiebatur.*

Note 3.—The Latin Perfect sometimes implies the meaning of *curo* or *jubeo,* "to order," or "to have;" as, *Manlius securi filium percussit* (for *percuti jussit* or *percutiendum curavit,* "he had him put to death"). *Verres ad palum alligavit piratas* ("he had them tied to ...."). *Cimon complures pauperes mortuos suo sumptu extulit* (= *efferri jussit* or *efferendos curavit*).

Note 4.—The Perfect (or Imperfect) Indic., both simple and periphrastic, is sometimes used in hypothetical sentences, instead of the Plupf. Subj. (§ 189, 3), to denote what would have happened, had not some obstacle intervened; as, *Deleri totus exercitus potuit* (= *potuisset*), *si fugientes persecuti victores essent. Vincebat* (= *vicisset*) *paucitas militum, ni Veiens exercitus in verticem collis evasisset. Hannibal nisi fugæ speciem abeundo timuisset, Galliam repetiturus fuit* or *erat* (= *repetiisset*).

§ 183.—The PLUPERFECT represents a past action as completed before another past action; as, *Pausanias eodem loco sepultus est, ubi vitam posuerat. Quum in Lyciam venissemus, naves onerarias dominis restituimus.*

FUTURE AND FUT.-PERFECT.

§ 184.—The FUTURE represents an action or event as future in relation to the present time of the speaker; as, *Dicam si potero Latine.*

Rursus quum procul abesse nos credes, videbis in tuis castris. Si mik probabis ea quæ dices, libenter assentiar.[1]

NOTE.—The English Present after *if, when, as long as*, or a relative,—is generally translated by the Future, when the leading clause contains a future tense, an Imperative, or a Subjunctive used *imperatively*. E. g., " I shall do it, if I can :" *Faciam si potero.*—" I shall be as you wish me to be ;" *Ut voles me esse, ita ero.*—*Naturam n sequemur ducem, nunquam aberrabimus. Qui adipisci veram gloriam volet, fungatur (— fungitor) justitiæ officiis. Dum erimus in terris* (as long as we are on earth) *perfecta felicitate non fruemur.*

§ 185.—The FUTURE-PERFECT represents a future action or event as completed *at* or *before* the time of some other future action or event; as, " When I (shall have) come thither, I shall explain the matter to you ;" *Quum istuc venero, rem tibi exponam. Cum cœnavero, proficiscar. Quid si te rogavero, nonne respondebis?*

NOTE 1.—As the English Present is sometimes translated by the Future, so is the English Present (Perfect or Future) translated by the Fut.-Perfect, when the action expressed by the verb of the subordinate clause is completed before the action relating to it takes place; as, " When I come to Rome, I will write to you what I shall observe ;" *Romam cum venero, quæ perspexero, scribam ad te. Ut sementem feceris* (as you sow), *ita metes. A me quum paullum otii nacti erimus, uberiores litteras expectato. Ut primum librum confecero* (as soon as I have finished) *ad vos veniam.*—Thus we say : *si potuero, si volueris, si placuerit, si otium habuero,* etc.

But, when a future event depends on some *present* circumstance or resolution, the Present is used after *si,* though in connection with a future tense ; e. g., *Si vincimus, omnia nobis tuta patebunt. Perficietur bellum si non urgemus obsessos.*—Thus, *Fac si vis ; defende si potes,* and the like.

NOTE 2.—The Future-Perfect is often used, in leading clauses, to denote the rapidity with which a future action will be completed, and to express with emphasis what otherwise would be expressed by the simple Future. E. g., " If you abandon me, I am lost ;" *Si me deseris, periero. Tu invita senes, ego accivero pueros. Si pergis, abiero. Quæ fuerit causa, mox videro. Recte secusne, alias viderimus. Non imprudenter feceris, si hoc a me celaris. Qui Antonium oppresserit, bellum confecerit. Tolle hanc conditionem* (— si hanc conditionem tollis), *luctum sustuleris.*[2]

§ 186.—The FUTURE SUBJUNCTIVE, both in the Active and Passive Voices, has no form of its own.

In the *Active* Voice, the FUTURE SUBJ. is generally supplied by the Participle in *rus* with *sim* or *essem*, according as a principal or an historical tense precedes.

---

[1] The actions spoken of (*probabis, dices, assentiar*) are contemplated as contemporary in future time, and, therefore, expressed by the simple Future. [2] Do away with this condition, and you will have at once done away with our grief.

In the *Passive* Voice (and, if the verb wants the Supine, also in the *Active*) the FUTURE SUBJ. must be expressed by the circumlocution *futurum sit (esset)* with the Pres. or Impf. Subj.; as,

> Non dubito quin frater tuus brevi rediturus sit;
> Non dubitabam quin frater tuus brevi rediturus esset.
>
> Non dubito quin futurum sit ut ab omnibus lauderis;
> Non dubitabam quin futurum esset ut ab omnibus laudareris.
>
> Non dubito quin futurum sit tu diligentius discas;
> Non dubitabam quin futurum esset ut diligentius disceres.

NOTE 1.—The Future Subj. Pass. should never be expressed by the Participle in *dus* with *sim (essem)*; because the Participle in *dus* combined with *sum, esse*, always conveys the idea of necessity, duty, or propriety,—never that of m e r e f u t u r i t y.

NOTE 2.—As the circumlocution *futurum sit (esset)* with the Present or Imperfect Subj. is of very rare occurrence in the Classical writers, and as the idea of futurity admits of so great a variety of expression, it is always advisable to arrange the sentence in such a manner as to avoid that circumlocution.

Thus, for example, instead of saying: *Non dubito quin futurum sit ut diligentius discas*, we may say:

> Haud dubie diligentius in posterum disces,
> Spero fore ut in posterum diligentius discas,
> Spero te in posterum fore diligentiorem,
> Non dubito quin diligentior posthac futurus sis,
> Spero te diligentiorem operam litteris daturum esse,
> Spero fore ut diligentius in litterarum studia incumbas, etc.

In like manner, instead of saying: *Non dubitabam quin futurum esset ut ab omnibus laudareris*, we may say:

> Minime dubitabam quin omnium laudem assecuturus esses,
> Persuasum mihi erat fore ut ab omnibus laudareris,
> Haud dubium mihi erat quin in ore omnium futurus esses,
> Certum habebam te ab omnibus laudatum iri,
> Nihil dubitabam quin omnes te laudaturi essent,
> Probe sciebam fore ut ab omnibus laude afficereris, etc.

§ 187.—The FUTURE-PERFECT SUBJ. has, like the simple Future Subj., no form of its own.

The Fut.-Perfect Subjunctive, both Active and Passive, is generally supplied by the Perfect and Pluperfect Subjunctive, especially when a future tense occurs in the same sentence.—When no future occurs, it is supplied either by the simple Perfect or Pluperf. Subj., or (more rarely) by the circumlocution *futurum sit (esset) ut* with the Perf. or Pluperf. Subj.—E. g., *Liscus ait* (aiebat) *se non dubitare quin si Helvetios superarint* (superassent) *Romani, Ædui* sint (essent) *libertatem erep-turi.* Thus,

Act.: *Oraculum canit* (cecinit) *eum qui nodum Gordii solverit* (solvisset) *tota Asia regnaturum esse.*

Pass.: *Oraculum canit* (cecinit) *eum a quo nodus Gordii solutus sit* (esset) *tota Asia regnaturum esse.*

Non dubito quin perendie hac ipsa hora frater tuus redierit.
Non dubitabam quin postridie ea ipsa hora frater tuus rediisset.

or,

Fore arbitror ut perendie hac ipsa hora frater tuus redierit.
Fore arbitrabar ut postridie ea ipsa hora frater tuus rediisset.

(More rarely)

Non dubito quin futurum sit ut cras hac ipsa hora frater redierit.
Non dubitabam quin futurum esset ut postridie ea ipsa h. rediisset.

☞ When the subordinate clause expresses what one would have done, or what would have been done, if some obstacle had not intervened, the Fut.-Perf. Subj. Active is supplied by the Participle in *-rus* with *fuerim,* and the Fut.-Perf. Subj. Passive by the Participle in *-us,* with *essem.*—E. g.,

Pollio Asinius non dubitat quin Cæsar, si diutius vixisset, suos rescripturus et correc-turus commentarios fuerit ; or, by the Acc. c. Inf.: *Pollio Asinius Cæsarem existimat suos rescripturum et correcturum commentarios fuisse, si diutius vixisset.*

Non dubito quin si Saguntinis impigre Romani tulissent opem, totum in Hispaniam bellum aversum esset ; or, by the Acc. c. Inf.: *Si Saguntinis impigre Romani tulissent opem, futurum fuisse arbitror, ut totum in Hispaniam bellum averteretur.*

Of the Sequence of Tenses.

§ 188.—General rule : A principal tense must be followed by a principal tense, and an historical tense must be followed by an historical tense.

Principal tenses :

Pres. I ask	wh. he	is doing,	Quæro	quid	agat,
Perf. I have asked		has done,	Quæsivi		egerit,
Fut. I shall ask		will do.	Quæram		acturus sit.

Historical tenses :

Impf. I was asking	wh. he	did, was doing,	Quærebam	quid	ageret,
Perf. I asked		had done,	Quæsivi		egisset,
Plup. I had asked		would do.	Quæsiveram		acturus esset.

NOTE 1.—The historical Present is followed by the Imperf. and Plupf. as well as by the Present and Perfect; as, *Cæsar legatos mittit qui nuntiarent* (or *nuntient*). *Verres eos certiores facit quid opus esset* (or *sit*). *Argilius Pausaniæ aperit quid ex litteris comperisset* (or *compererit*).

NOTE 2.—The *ut* consecutive after an historical tense, is often (especially in Nepos) followed by the Perfect Subj., instead of the Imperfect; as, *Adeo excellebat Aristides abstinentia ut unus post hominum memoriam cognomine Justus sit appellatus. Factum est ut plus quam collegæ Miltiades valuerit. Xerxes adeo angusto mari conflixit ut ejus multitudo navium explicari non potuerit.*

NOTE 3.—When a subordinate clause expresses a general truth—or a result which extends to the present time of the speaker, its verb is put in the Present (or Perfect), whatever may be the tense of the preceding verb. E. g., *Trajanus rempublicam ita administravit ut omnibus principibus merito preferatur.*[1] *Ardebat Hortensius cupiditate dicendi sic ut in nullo unquam flagrantius studium viderim. Atticus fecit ut vere dictum videatur: Sui cuique mores fingunt fortunam. Antiocho pacem petenti ad priores conditiones nihil additum, Africano prædicante neque Romanis si vincantur animos minui, neque si vincant,*[2] *secundis rebus insolescere.*

NOTE 4.—The Imperfect Subjunctive is sometimes used where we might expect the Present. This is the case (a) after the English Perfect with "have," when the action expressed by the Perfect can be conceived in its progress and duration; as, "I have for a long time doubted (conceived in its duration, — I was doubting) if it would not be better;" *Diu dubitavi an melius esset. Quoniam quæ subsidia haberes et habere posses, exposui, nunc de magnitudine petitionis dicam;* (b) after Perfect Infinitives that depend on a preceding present or future tense, and are equivalent to the Perfect Indic. with "have;" as, "I think to have said enough (— that I have said enough) why this war is necessary ...;" *Satis mihi multa verba fecisse videor quare esset hoc bellum genere ipso necessarium, magnitudine periculosum. Præclare mihi videris posuisse ante oculos quid dicere oporteret eum qui orator esset futurus.*—The Present Subj., in such instances, would indeed not be incorrect; but it would be contrary to the usage of the best writers.

III. MOODS OF VERBS.

INDICATIVE.

§ 189.—The INDICATIVE represents an action or state as something real and certain,—as a fact; e. g., *Deus est æternus. Virtus est summum bonum.*

---

[1]) The Present *preferatur* means that Trajan was preferred to all other rulers up to the time of the writer, whereas the Imperfect would mean that he was preferred only to his contemporaries. [2]) Here the Imperfects *vincerentur* and *vincerent* would not be wrong, but the Presents *vincantur* and *vincant* more clearly show that equanimity was one of the leading features of the Roman character, not only on the present occasion, but at all times and under all circumstances.

The Indicative is sometimes used in Latin, where in English the potential mood is employed. This is the case :

1. With the expressions *par, fas, æquum, justum, consentaneum, longum, immensum, infinitum, satius, æquius, melius, utilius,* etc, *est* or *erat,*—when we wish to express that something would be (or have been) just, reasonable, easy, difficult, etc. The Imperfect of the English Potential is then generally rendered by the Present Indicative, and the English Pluperfect by the Imperfect or Perfect Indicative. E. g., "It would lead too far....;" *Longum est enumerare omnia prœlia.*—"There would be no end....;" *Infinitum est ad omnia respondere.*—"How easy would it have been for me....;" *Quam facile mihi erat, orbis imperium occupare Romanis militibus. Longe utilius fuit angustias aditus valido occupare prœsidio. Erat infinitum bene de me merios omnes numerare.*

2. With the verbs *possum, licet, convenit, oportet, debeo,* and *necesse est,* when it is intimated that something *might, could,* or *should* have taken place. The Imperfect Indic. of these verbs is used when we wish to express that something ought to have been done and that the time for doing it is not yet passed,—that it may still be done: the Perfect Ind., when we wish to express, that something should have been done, but that the time for doing it is already passed. E. g., "You ought to have been put to death long ago ;" *Ad mortem te duci jam pridem oportebat. Contumeliis eum onerasti, quem patris loco colere debebas. Deleri totus exercitus potuit, si fugientes persecuti victores essent. Volumnia debuit in te officiosior esse, et id ipsum, quod fecit, potuit facere diligentius. Aut non suscipi bellum oportuit, aut geri pro dignitate Populi Romani.*—Thus in the Periphrastic conjugation : *Quodsi Cn. Pompeius privatus esset hoc tempore, tamen erat mittendus.[1] Qui si hoc tempore non diem suum obiisset, paucis post annis tamen ei moriendum fuit.*

3. In the conclusion of hypothetical sentences when we wish to express what would have happened, had not some obstacle intervened. E. g., *Perieram* (— periissem), *nisi accurrisses. Labebar* (— lapsus essem) *longius, nisi me retinuisses. Mazœus si transeuntibus flumen Macedonibus supervenisset, haud dubie oppressurus fuit* (— oppressisset) *incompositos. Populus Romanus, Cæsare et Pompeio trucidatis, in statum pristinæ libertatis redierat, nisi aut Pompeius liberos, aut Cæsar hæredem reliquisset.*

4. After relative pronouns and adverbs that are either doubled or have the suffix *-cunque,* as *quisquis, quotquot, utut, ubiubi, quicunque, qualiscunque, quantuscunque, utcunque,* and also after *sive—sive.* E. g., *Quidquid id est* ('whatever it may be') *timeo Danaos et dona ferentes. Sapiens ubicunque est* ('wherever he may be') *beatus est. Totum hoc leve est qualecunque est. Utcunque sese res habet, tua est culpa. Sive tacebis sive loquēre, mihi perinde est. Sive verum id est sive falsum* ('be it true or false'), *mihi quidem ita nuntiatum est.*—☞ In these and similar instances, however, later writers frequently use the Indicative.

---

[1] he would have been the person to be sent,

5. After the adverbs *prope* and *pœne*, when we wish to express that an event was on the point of taking place; as, "I had almost forgotten.... ;". *Prope oblitus sum quod maxime scribendum erat. Brutum non minus amo quam tu : pœne dixi, quam te. Pons Sublicius iter pœne hostibus dedit, ni unus vir fuisset.*

Note.—The Present Indic. of *possum* stands frequently for *possem* ; as, *Possum persequi multa, sed ea ipsa quœ dixi, sentio fuisse longiora. Possum sexcenta decreta proferre.*—But also : *Plurima quidem proferre possemus, sed modus adhibendus est.*

SUBJUNCTIVE.

§ 190.—The Subjunctive represents a state or action—not as a fact, but as a mere conception of the mind, as something possible, conditional, or doubtful.¹ The English language commonly expresses the nature of the Latin Subjunctive by the auxiliaries *may, can, shall, might, could, should,* and *would.*—Thus, when I say, *Frater tuus, etsi doctissimus sit* ('though he may be'), *multa tamen se nescire fatebitur,*—I represent your brother's being learned, not as a fact, but as a mere possibility : but, when I say, *Frater tuus, etsi doctissimus est* ('though he is'), *multa tamen se nescire fatetur* his being learned is represented as a fact—as a reality.

Note.—When the English *may, can, might, could,* etc., are not used as auxiliaries, but as principal verbs, they must be translated by *licet, possum, volo, debeo,* or *oportet,* respectively. E. g., "You may go," *Tibi abire licet.*—"I might have gone," *Mihi abire licuit.*—"He could not have come sooner," *Non potuit citius venire.*— "You ought to have done that," *Te oportuit hoc facere.*—"It could not have been done better," *Melius fieri non potuit.*

The English Perfect Inf. after the forms *might, could,* and *ought,* is generally translated by the Present Infin., unless an action is to be represented as completed at or before some specified time ; as, "At that time it ought to have been already done," *Tum jam factum esse (te id fecisse) oportuit.*

SUBJUNCTIVE IN INDEPENDENT SENTENCES.

Peream si mentior.

§ 191.—The Subjunctive (especially the Subj. Present) is used in independent sentences, to express a modest assertion, a wish, a supposition, a concession, a deliberative question, an exhortation, an assurance or protest ; as, "May I perish, if I lie."

Nemo sapiens illud tibi concedat.¹ Feras putem² quibus ex raptu alimenta sunt, meliores quo iracundiores ; sed patientiam laudaverim

---

¹) No wise man probably will concede. ²) I feel inclined to think—but I confess, I admire.

boum et equorum.—Valeant cives mei, valeant, sint incolumes, sint flo-
rentes, sint beati, stet hæc urbs præclara.—Sed dicat[1] nunc aliquis.
Roges[2] me quid sit Deus.—Dixerit Epicurus.[3]   Sit scelestus, sit fur; at
est bonus imperator.—Quis non timeat omnia providentem et animadver-
tentem Deum?   Valerius quotidie cantabat: erat enim scenicus; quid
faceret[4] aliud?—Imitemur nostros Brutos, Camillos, Curios, Fabri-
cios; amemus patriam, pareamus senatui, consulamus bonis.

Note 1.—A modest assertion, or a deliberative question, is often expressed by the
Subj. Perfect rather than the Present; as, "Who would grant you this?" "Who
would doubt?" "By your leave I would say," etc., *Quis tibi hoc concesserit? Quis
dubitaverit? Pace or venia tua dixerim. Haud facile concesserim, dixerim, crediderim.
Forsitan aliquis dixerit. Crediderit forte quispiam. Hoc sine ulla dubitatione confir-
maverim. Voluptati qui se dederit, vix eum virum dixerim. Libenter his accesserim[1]
qui* .... etc.

Note 2.—The English indefinite expressions "One (or, you) might have said,
seen, thought," are generally rendered by the Imperfect Subj. *diceres, videres, putares,*
etc.; as, *Hostes lætos modo, modo pavidos animadverteres. Pedites mæsti, credens
victos, in castra redeunt. Confecto prœlio, tum vero cerneres, quanta audacia fuisset in
exercitu Catilinæ.*

Note 3.—A wish conceived as possible—which, we know, can or will be realized, is
expressed by the Subj. Pres. or Perf.: but a wish conceived as impossible—which,
we know, cannot or will not be realized, by the Subj. Imperf. or Pluperf.; e. g.,

(Of things represented as possible.)

Utinam veniat!   *Would that he may come!*
Utinam venerit!   *Would that he may have come!*

(Of things represented as impossible.)

Utinam veniret!   *Would to God he might come!*
Utinam venisset!   *Would to God he had come!*

*Nolim id factum esse.[6]   Nollem id factum esse.[7]   Quam velim mihi ignoscat!   Quam
vellem mihi ignosceret!   Utinam hoc verum sit!   Utinam hoc verum esset!   Utinam
saluti nostræ consulere possimus!   Vellem adesse posset Panætius!   Utinam, Patres
Conscripti, Calendis Sextilibus adesse potuissem!*

§ 192.—In forms of **protestation** and **swearing**, the formula *ita* (*sic*)
with the Subjunctive ("as true as") is followed by *ut* with the Indicative,

---

[1]) I suppose some one now to say.   [2]) Supposing you ask me.   [3]) Granting that E.
could have said.   [4]) what could (should) he have done else?   [5]) I feel inclined to
accede readily.   [6]) I could wish it not to have happened (— I hope it has not happened).   [7]) I could wish it had not happened.

when a simple assertion is made,—with the Subjunctive, when a wish is expressed. E. g., "As true as I live, I shudder...." *Ita vivam ut toto corpore perhorresco.* "As true as I wish to be happy, there is nothing...." *Ita sim felix, ut nihil est præclarius virtute.*—"As true as I wish that God may help me, so truly do I wish you...." *Ita me Deus adjuvet* (or *ita deos mihi velim propitios*) *ut diutissime vivas.* "As true as I wish to see all my desires accomplished, I should like...." *Tecum esse, ita mihi omnia quæ opto contingant, ut vehementer velim.*

Sometimes *ita* with the Subjunctive is thrown in parenthetically without *ut ;* as, *Sæpe, ita me dii juvent, te auctorem consiliorum meorum desidero. Sollicitat, ita vivam, me tua, mi Tiro, valetudo.*

☞ A negative protest is a l w a y s,—a negative wish or concession g e n e r a l l y, expressed by *ne ;* as, *Ne sim salvus* (*ne vivam*), *si aliter scribo ac sentio. Utinam ne* (more rarely *non*) *tibi in mentem venisset. Ne æquaveritis Hannibali Philippum, Pyrrho certe æquabitis.*[1]

SUBJUNCTIVE AFTER PARTICLES.

Tacet quasi nesciat.

§ 193.—The Subjunctive is used after the particles *O si* (poet.), *utinam,* would that ! *ut,* even if, although ; *ne,* although not ; *quasi, tamquam, velut, ac si, velut si, tamquam si, perinde* (*æque, non secus*) *ac si,* as if ; *licet,* although ; *quamlibet, quantumvis,* how much soever ; *modo, dummodo,* if but, provided that ; *modo ne, dummodo ne, dumne,* provided that not ; and after *nedum,* much less, still less, when followed by a verb. E. g., "He is silent, as if he were ignorant."

Ut desint vires, tamen est laudanda voluntas. Ne sit summum malum dolor, malum certe est. Quod turpe est, id quantumvis occultetur, tamen honestum nullo modo fieri potest. Quid ego his testibus utor, quasi res dubia aut obscura sit ? Multi omnia recta et honesta negligunt, dummodo potentiam consequantur. Vix cum aspicit, nedum amet.

QUAMQUAM AND QUAMVIS.

§ 194.—*Quamquam,* "although," "however much," is in the Classical prose regularly construed with the Indicative,—and *quamvis,* "although," "however much," with the Subjunctive.

Poets and later prose writers, however, construe *quamquam* generally with the Subjunctive, and *quamvis* with the Indicative.—*Quamquam* with the Subj. occurs even in some passages of Cicero.

Quamvis, when taken adverbially, in the sense of "howsoever," has no influence upon the mood of the verb ; as, "I shall be content with ever so small a corner of Italy," *Quamvis parvis Italiæ latebris contentus ero.*

Etsi, tametsi, and *etiamsi,* "although," take the Indic. when an action or a state is represented as a reality, as a fact,—and the Subj., when it is represented as merely possible.

---

[1] Granting that you cannot consider Ph. equal to H., yet you will surely....

ANTEQUAM AND PRIUSQUAM.

§ 195.—1. With *antequam* and *priusquam* the Present Indic. is used, when an action or event is represented as certain and near at hand; the Present Subj., when an event is represented not as a fact, but merely as one that may possibly occur—hence its special use in general, indefinite sentences in which it is stated, what usually happens or should happen, before a certain event takes place. E. g., *Priusquam de ceteris respondeo, de amicitia pauca dicam. Dabo operam ut istuc veniam antequam plane ex animo tuo effluo. Si quemquam nactus eris qui perferat litteras, des antequam discedimus.—Priusquam incipias, consulto opus est. Tempestas minatur* ('usually threatens') *antequam surgat; crepant ædificia, antequam corruant. In omnibus negotiis, priusquam aggrediare, adhibenda est præparatio diligens.*

☞ It must be remembered, however, that the Present Subj. is not unfrequently used even where things are represented as certain and near at hand; as, *De quo priusquam scribamus* (instead of *scribimus*), *hæc præcipienda videntur. Antequam de republica dicam* (instead of *dico*), *exponam breviter consilium profectionis meæ.*

2. In simple narration, *antequam* and *priusquam* are construed either with the Indic. Perfect, or the Subj. Imperf. and Pluperf.;—with the Indic. Perfect, when mere priority of one action or event before another is expressed (in this case *ante* and *prius* are commonly used emphatically), and with the Subj. Imperf. and Pluperf., when between the preceding and subsequent actions there is some closer connection than that of mere priority, when, for instance, one action is declared to be necessary or proper to precede the other, or when a purpose or design is implied. E. g., *Hæc omnia ante facta sunt quam Verres Italiam attigit.*[1] *Non prius inde discessit quam totam insulam devicit.*[2]—*Dies obrepsit hostibus priusquam aggerem extruxissent. Ducentis annis antequam Romam caperent, in Italiam Galli transcenderunt.*—In the following passage of Nepos the Subjunctive seems to be exceptionable: *Hæc pugna facta est prius quam Aristides pœna liberaretur.*

☞ Here must also be mentioned the use of the Subjunctive with or without *ut*, after *antequam, priusquam, citius quam,* and *potius quam,* in the sense of "sooner than," or "rather than," with the Infinitive; as, *Cur non in prœlio cecidisti potius quam* (or *quam ut*) *in potestatem inimici venires?*

DUM, DONEC, QUOAD.

§ 196.—1. *Dum, donec,* and *quoad,* in the sense of "as long as," are commonly construed with the Indicative (*donec,* in this sense, is found only in poetry and late prose); as, *Cato quoad vixit, virtutum laude crevit. Lacedæmoniorum gens fortis fuit dum Lycurgi leges vigebant. Donec eris felix multos numerabis amicos.*

---

[1]) [2]) If, in these two sentences, 'Verres's coming to Italy' and 'the conquest of the island' were to be represented as events that had been intended, the Subjunctive would be necessary—*priusquam attingeret* or *attigisset* and *priusquam devicisset.*

2. *Dum, donec,* and *quoad,* in the sense of " until," take either the Indicative or Subjunctive :—the Indic. (mostly the Perf. Ind.), when an action or event is represented as a fact, and when they merely mark the time up to which the action or state denoted by the principal verb is to be continued, no purpose or design whatsoever being implied; the Subj. (mostly the Pres., Impf., and Plupf.), when an event is conceived as merely possible, or when an intention or purpose is implied. E. g., *Milo adfuit quoad Senatus dismissus est. Epaminondas ferrum in corpore retinuit quoad renuntiatum est vicisse Bœotios* (had the arrival of the victorious tidings been intended, the Subj. *renuntiaretur* or *renuntiatum esset,* would have been used).—*Pulsabam dum ostium aperiretur* (the opening of the door being intended). *Iratis subtrahendi sunt ii, in quos impetum conantur facere, dum se ipsi colligant* (the intention being implied that they may recover themselves).

NOTE.—*Donec,* in the sense of " until," frequently occurs in Livy and the poets, but very rarely in Cicero and Cæsar.—Tacitus uses it with the Subjunctive, even where a simple fact is expressed.
Dum, in the sense of " until," takes in Cicero generally, in Cæsar exclusively, the Subjunctive.—In the sense of "whilst" it is usually construed with the Indic. Present, even when the principal verb is a past tense. E. g., *Dum hæc geruntur, Cæsari nuntiatum est. Dum ea Romani parant, jam Saguntum oppugnabatur;*—but the Imperfect and Perfect are found also; as, *Dum hæc in Apulia gerebantur, Samnites urbem non tenuerunt. Quæ divina res dum conficiebatur, quæsivit a me pater,* etc.

QUUM.

§ 197.—*Quum* either denotes the c a u s e, or expresses the t i m e of an action. In the former case it is called *quum causale ;* in the latter, *quum temporale.*

1. *Quum causale,* " since," " as," and when taken in the sense of *quamvis,* " though," " although," " whereas," always takes the Subjunctive ; as, *Quæ cum ita sint, quid est quod timeas? Quum Athenas tamquam ad mercaturam bonarum artium sis profectus, inanem redire turpissimum est. Phocion fuit perpetuo pauper, quum ditissimus esse posset.*

2. *Quum temporale,* "when," generally takes the Subjunctive Impf. and Pluperf., and the Indicative of the remaining tenses ; as, *Antigonus quum adversus Seleucum pugnaret, in prælio occisus est. Alexander cum interemisset Clitum, vix a se manus abstinuit.—Qui non propulsat injuriam a suis quum potest, injuste facit. Jam ver appetebat,*[1] *quum Hannibal ex hibernis movit. Ager quum multos annos quievit,*[2] *uberiores efferre fructus solet. Sapiens non ejulabit, quum doloribus torquebitur.*

NOTE 1.—*Quum temporale* takes the Indic. Impf. and Pluperf. in the following cases : (a) the Indic. Imperf., when simultaneous actions or events are expressed, the English "when" being then equivalent to *while.* In this case, *interim* or *interea* is usually added to *quum.* E. g., *Cædebatur virgis in medio foro Messanæ civis*

---

[1] The spring was drawing on.   [2] when it has lain fallow.

Romanus quum interim nulla vox istius miseri inter dolorem crepitumque plagarum audiebatur nisi hæc: Civis Romanus sum;—(b) the Indic. Pluperf., when actions of repeated occurrence are spoken of. E. g., *Verres quum* (whenever) *ad aliquod oppidum venerat, lectica usque in cubiculum deferebatur. Quum ver esse cœperat, dabat se labori atque itineribus;*—(c) the Indic. both Imperf. and Pluperf., whenever *quum* describes time in a very marked manner, being then equivalent to *tum quum* or *eo tempore quum.* E. g., *Nuper quum te jam adventare arbitrabamur, repente abs te in mensem Quintilium rejecti sumus. Credo tum quum Sicilia florebat opibus et copiis, magna artificia fuisse in ea insula.*

Note 2.—*Quum* sometimes takes both the Indic. and Subj. in the same sentence, when in one clause it simply marks the time, while in another the passage assumes the character of an historical narrative. E. g., *An tum eratis consules quum cunctus ordo reclamabat, quum .... cupere vos diceretis,* etc.

Note 3.—*Quum* takes the Indicative, also, when it stands for *ex eo tempore quo,* "since;" as, *Multi anni sunt quum Fabius diligitur a me propter summam humanitatem et observantiam. Fere triennium est quum virtuti nuntium remisisti.*

When *quum* stands for *quod,* after *gaudeo, gratulor,* etc. it takes the same mood which *quod* would take itself; as, "I congratulate you on your influence with Dolabella," *Gratulor quum tantum vales apud Dolabellam. Gratias tibi ago quum tantum litteræ meæ apud te potuerunt. Præclare facis quum horum virorum memoriam tenes* (in retaining the recollection of ....).

SUBJUNCTIVE IN CONDITIONAL SENTENCES.

§ 198.—There are four kinds of hypothetical, or conditional, sentences:

Si hoc dicis, erras.

1. Where both the condition and conclusion are considered as facts, and hence as certain. In this kind of conditional sentences the Indicative is used in both clauses. E. g., " If you say this, you err."

Si hoc dixisti, errasti. Si hoc dices, errabis. Stomachabatur senex, si quid asperius dixeram. Si turbidas res sapienter ferebas (as you really did), *tranquilliora læte feres. Nisi quid me etesiæ morabuntur* (as, I hope, will not be the case) *celeriter vos videbo.*

Note.—Instead of the Indicative, the Imperative, or the Subjunctive taken imperatively, may stand in the conclusion; e. g., *Si abire volunt, abeant. Si dormis, expergiscere; si stas, ingredere; si ingrederis, curre; si curris, advola.*

Si hoc diceres, errares.

2. Where it is affirmed that something would take, or would have taken place under a certain condition,—but did not, because the condition was not fulfilled. In this kind of conditional sentences, the Subj. Impf. or Pluperf. stands in both clauses. E. g., " If you said this, you would err."

Sic hoc dixisses, errasses. Si tu hic esses, aliter sentires. Plura scriberem, si possem. Si tacuisses, philosophus mansisses. Si cavere sibi potuisset, viveret. Si ita naturâ paratum esset ut ea dormientes agerent, quæ somniarent, alligandi omnes essent qui cubitum irent. _

NOTE.—The best writers sometimes use in conditional sentences the Imperfect where the Pluperfect should be employed; as, *Mortuis tam religiosa jura majores nostri tribuerunt, quod non fecissent profecto, si nihil ad eos pertinere arbitrarentur,* instead of *arbitrati essent. Num tu igitur eum, si tum esses, temerarium civem aut crudelem putares?* instead of *fuisses* and *putasses.*

Si hoc dicas, errabis.

3. Where the condition is represented as a mere supposition, the realization of which, however, is regarded as possible, and even expected. The clause with *si* (*nisi*) takes then the Subj. Present or Perfect; the conclusion, being represented as certain, the Indicative (commonly Future) or the Imperative. E. g., " If you say this (as may be the case), you will err."

Si quid habeam, dabo. Si abire velint (as possibly they may wish), *abeant. Sapiens non dubitat, si ita melius sit, de vita migrare.*

Si hoc dicas, erres.

4. Where both the condition and the conclusion are represented as a mere supposition, without determining whether the thing supposed be real or not real, possible or impossible. In this case the Subj. Pres. or Perf. stands in both clauses. E. g., " If you should say this, you would err."

Tu si hic sis, aliter sentias.[1] *Tu si hic fueris, aliter senseris. Si tantum eum prudentem dicam, minus quam debeam, prædicem. Si roges me,*[2] *quid aut quale sit Deus, nihil fortasse respondeam. Si gladium quis*[3] *apud te sana mente deposuerit, repetat insaniens : reddere peccatum sit, officium non reddere.*

NOTE.—In animated or oratorical style, sometimes even the impossible is represented as possible, and accordingly expressed by the Subj. Present; as, *Hæc si patria tecum, Catilina, loquatur, nonne impetrare debeat, etiamsi vim adhibere non possit? Si existat hodie ab inferis Lycurgus, gaudeat.*

---

[1]) If you were here (supposing, for a moment, you were here), you would think differently. [2]) If you were now to ask me. [3]) Supposing some one ....

Dignus est qui diligatur.

§ 199.—The Subjunctive is used in relative sentences in the following cases :   .   ᴵ

I. When the relative stands for *ut* with a personal or demonstrative pronoun, as *ut ego, ut tu, ut ille*, through all the cases, genders, and numbers; or for *ut* with a possessive pronoun, as *cujus* for *ut meus, ut tuus ;* *quorum* for *ut noster, ut vester.* E. g., "He is worthy to be loved," Lat., He is worthy who (= that he) should be loved. The relative has this force:

> (a) After the adj. *dignus, indignus, aptus*, and *idoneus;*
> (b) After *tam, tantus, talis, is* or *ille* (for *talis*), *ejusmodi ;*
> (c) When it follows a comparative with *quam;*
> (d) When it introduces a purpose or design.

Voluptas non est digna ad quam (ut ad eam) *sapiens respiciat.*[1] *Digni sunt parentes quorum* (ut eorum) *jussa prompte et alacriter exequamur. Vir probus dignus est cui* (ut ei) *fidem habeamus. Nonne hoc indignissimum est, vos idoneos habitos, per quorum* (ut per vestras) *sententias et jusjurandum id assequantur, quod antea ipsi scelere et ferro assequi consueverunt? Ea est Romana gens quæ* (ut ea) *victa quiescere nesciat. Non ii sumus quibus* (ut nobis) *nihil verum esse videatur. Natura homini rationem dedit qua* (ut ea) *regerentur animi appetitus. Populus Romanus tribunos plebis creavit per quos* (ut per eos) *contra senatum et consules tutus esse posset.*

Noᴛᴇ 1.—After the expressions *non ego is sum qui, non tu is es qui*, etc., the person of the verb following is determined—not by the pronoun *is*, but by the preceding subject-nominatives *ego, tu*, etc. ; as, *Non ego is sum qui tot ac tantis reipublicæ malis non movear. Tu non is es qui re nulla nisi jure civili delecteris* (but we would say : *quem res nulla nisi jus civile delectet*). *Noli oblivisci te eum esse qui aliis consueris præcipere.*

Noᴛᴇ 2.—The demonstratives *is, ille, talis, ejusmodi*, are not always expressed, but must often be supplied before *qui* with the Subjunctive; as, *Dic aliquid quod* (= aliquid tale ut id) *ad rem pertineat. En miles quem* (= talis ut eum) *nulla pericula terreant. Multi vulnerati etiam quos vires sanguisque desererent, ut intra vallum hostium caderent, nitebantur. Nihil agis, nihil moliris, nihil cogitas quod* (= nihil tale ut id) *ego non modo non audiam, sed etiam videam planeque sentiam. Quam longe videtur a carcere atque a vinculis abesse debere qui seipsum jam dignum custodia judicaverit?*

This is generally the case, also, after *unus* and *solus ;* as, *Solus es Cæsar in quo* (= tu solus talis es ut in te) *nitatur civitatis salus. Voluptas est sola quæ nos alliciat suapte natura.*

---

[1] that a wise man should care for it.

NOTE 3.—Special attention must be paid to those clauses that are introduced by *qui* after a comparative with *quam* following. In English, such sentences are commonly expressed in quite a different manner, as can easily be seen from the following examples: "The loss of honor and faith is too great to be estimated," *Famæ et fidei damna majora sunt quam quæ* (— ut ea) *æstimari possint.*—"The Greeks felled trees too large and too branchy for the soldier to carry along with his armor," *Græci et majores et magis ramosus arbores cædebant quam quas* (— ut eas) *ferre cum armis miles posset.*

To translate such sentences into Latin, change the English positive with "too" into the comparative with *than who, than whose, than whom, than which*—accordingly, and the Infinitive into the potential mood with *can, may, might, could.*—When the Infinitive is preceded by "for" with an objective case, omit the sign "for" and make the objective the nominative to the following verb. Thus,

(Eng.) Your benefits are too great to be repaid.
(Lat.) Your benefits are greater than which can be repaid.

(Eng.) The burden is too heavy for the boy to carry.
(Lat.) The burden is heavier than which the boy can carry.

(Eng.) I am too great for fortune to do me harm.
(Lat.) I am greater than to whom fortune can do harm.

Beneficia tua majora sunt quam quæ (ut ea) *referri possint. Onus gravius est quam quod* (ut id) *puer portare possit. Major sum quam cui* (ut mihi) *fortuna nocere possit. Uvæ pendent altius quam quas* (ut eas) *vulpes attingat* or *possit attingere.*

NOTE 4.—Not only relative pronouns, but also relative adverbs require the Subj., when they stand for *ut* with a demonstrative, as *quo* for *ut eo, unde* for *ut inde, ubi* for *ut ibi.* E. g., *Nihil tam alte natura constituit quo* (— ut eo) *virtus non possit eniti. Artaxerxes Lampsacum urbem Themistocli donarat, unde* (— ut inde) *vinum sumeret.*

NOTE 5.—Here is to be noticed, also, the use of the Subjunctive in restrictive clauses, that is, in clauses which limit in some way a preceding general statement. E. g., *Antonius omnium oratorum, quos viderim* ('at least of those I was able to see'), *longe eloquentissimus fuit. Refertæ sunt Catonis orationes, quas quidem* ('those at least which') *aut invenerim aut legerim, et verbis et rebus illustribus. Aristides unus, quod quidem audierimus, cognomine Justus est appellatus.*

Thus: *Quod sciam,* "as far as I know;" *quod intelligam,* "as far as I understand;" *quod salva fide possim,* "as far as I can with good conscience;" *quod sine molestia tua fiat,* "as far as can be done without inconveniencing you." But limitations with *quantum* generally take the Indicative, as *quantum scio, quantum memini, quantum intelligo, quantum in me est,* etc.,—unless the Subjunctive be necessary for some other reason.

Me cæcum qui hæc ante non viderim!

II. When the relative stands for *quum ego, quum tu, quum ille,* etc., that is, when the relative introduces the ground or reason of what is going before; as, "O blind man that I am for not having seen this before." (Why blind?—because I have not seen ....).

O fortunate adolescens qui (quum tu) *tuæ virtutis Homerum præconem inveneris. O magna vis veritatis, quæ facile se ipsa defendat. Caninius fuit mirifica vigilantia[1] qui* (quum is) *suo toto consulatu somnum non viderit. Quid ego te invitem a quo* (quum a te) *jam sciam esse præmissos qui tibi præstolarentur?*

NOTE 1.—*Qui*, when introducing a cause or reason, is often strengthened by the addition of *quippe, utpote,* or *ut;* as, *Mihi quidem tribunorum plebis potestas pestifera videtur, quippe quæ* (quum ea) *in seditione et ad seditionem nata sit. Convivia cum patre non inibat, quippe qui ne in oppidum quidem nisi perraro veniret.*

NOTE 2.—The relative *qui* stands sometimes for *quamvis (si, dummodo) ego, tu,* etc., and then, too, requires the Subjunctive. E. g., *Multi etiamnunc credunt Chaldæis quorum* (quamvis eorum) *prædicta quotidie eventis refellantur. Ego qui* (quamvis ego) *sero Græcas litteras attigissem, tamen complures dies Athenis commoratus sum. An mihi quidquam potest esse molestum, quod* (si id *or* dummodo id) *tibi gratum sit ?*

NOTE 3.—When *qui* is used in its pure, relative sense, without implying any accessory idea of purpose, cause, reason, concession, supposition, or condition, it takes the Indicative. Hence we may say: *Nihil in malis duco quod* (nothing which) *est a Deo constitutum,* as well as *Nihil in malis duco quod* (provided it be) *sit a Deo constitutum. Quid a me petis qui* (of me who) *nihil habeo,* and *Quid a me petis qui* (since I) *nihil habeam ? Nihil bonum est quod* (nothing which) *hominem non facit meliorem,* and *Nihil bonum est quod* (if it does not) *hominem non faciat meliorem.*

Sunt qui dicant.

III. After the general and indefinite expressions *sunt, non desunt, reperiuntur, existunt, exoriuntur ;—quis est? quid est? ecquis* or *numquis est? an quisquam est? quotusquisque est? quot sunt?—nego esse quemquam, nec est, nec ullus est ; nemo, nullus, nihil est, vix est, vix ullus est, vix decimus quisque est.* After these expressions such a word as *is, talis, ejusmodi,* must be supplied before the relative, the *qui* being equivalent to *ut* with a demonstrative. E. g., "There are some (or, there are persons) who say."

Sunt qui vel mundi opificem sapientissimum reprehendere audeant.

---

[1]) To understand this and several other passages from Cicero, a short historical remark may not be unnecessary.—The Consul C. Fab. Maximus had died on the very day when his term of office was to end. This was a few hours after midnight, the last day of December, ab U. C. 709.—Cæsar, professing to be a scrupulous observer of ancient customs, immediately appointed Caninius to be Consul for the deceased till the next regular election, i. e., till six o'clock in the evening of the same day. Cicero, fond of a joke, made this ephemeral Magistracy the subject of many a pointed remark. "Quick, quick," said he to his friends, "let us lose no time, but make haste to pay our compliments to our new Consul, for fear he may already be gone out of office, before we arrive at his house."—This gives the key to the example quoted.

Nihil est quod tam miseros faciat quam impietas et scelus. Quis est qui non oderit libidinosam et protervam adolescentiam ? Quotusquisque est cui sapientia omnibus omnium divitiis præponenda videatur ? Nemo est orator qui se Demosthenis similem (or *qui Demosthenis similis*) *esse nolit.*

Note 1.—When two future events are described as simultaneous, the relative *qui*, after the foregoing indefinite expressions, is construed with the Subj. Present. E. g., "There will always be some who will say," *Semper erunt qui dicant. Venient legiones quæ neque me inultum neque te impunitum patiantur. Quamdiu quisquam erit qui te defendere audeat, vives.*

Note 2.—When the nominative to *sunt*, "there are," is distinct and definite, *qui* takes the Indicative; as, *Sunt bestiæ quædam in quibus inest aliquid simile virtutis, ut in leonibus, ut in canibus, ut in equis.*

But, when the nominative is general and indefinite, as *quidam, nonnulli, pauci, multi, plures*, etc., both the Indic. and Subj. are used ;—the former, when we wish simply to state a fact, as *Sunt quidam e nostris qui hoc negant* (equivalent to the simple statement: *Quidam e nostris hoc negant*) ; the latter, when we wish at the same time to intimate a certain qualification of the subject, as *Sunt quidam e nostris* (i. e., *tales, ejusmodi, tam stulti*, etc.) *qui negent.*

When *sunt* has no nominative expressed at all, the Subjunctive with *qui* is so common in the Classical prose that the Indicative must be regarded as an exception.

Note 3.—We must here notice, also, the phrases *est* (*non est, nihil est, quid est*) *quod, cur,* or *quare*, and *non habeo* (*nihil habeo, quid habes*) *quod,* "there is reason," "there is no reason," "what reason is there ?" followed by the Infinitive. E. g., "Thou hast reason to rejoice," *Est quod gaudeas* (— est aliquid propter quod, — est aliquid tale ut propter id).—"We have no reason to fear," *Nihil est quod timeamus.*—"I have no reason to be ashamed," *Non est quod me pudeat.—Quid est quod* (or *cur*) *festines ? Nihil habeo quod incusem senectutem. Quid habes quod me reprehendas ?*

From the phrase *Non habeo quod*, "I have no reason ....," we must distinguish the phrase *Non habeo quid*, which is an indirect question ; as, "I do not know what to say," *Non habeo quid dicam. Non habebat quid responderet. De pueris quid agam, non habeo.*

Socrates accusatus est quod corrumperet juventutem.

IV. When the relative clause expresses the sentiment or words— not of the speaker or writer, but of some other person either spoken of in the sentence or to be supplied from the context. By "a relative clause" is here meant any clause introduced by a relative pronoun, adverb, or conjunction, such as *qui, quo, qua, quod, quoniam*, etc.— E. g., "Socrates was accused of corrupting the youth."

') because (as it was alleged by his accusers, the Athenians) he corrupted the youth.

Diogenes contemnebat divitias quod se felicem reddere non possent.[1] *Noctu ambulabat in publico Themistocles quod somnum capere non posset.*[2] *Noricis adversus Romanos dabant animos Alpes et nives, quo bellum non posset accedere.*[3] *Aristides nonne ob eam causam expulsus est patriâ quod præter modum justus esset?*[4] *Deum invocabant cujus ad solemne venissent.*[5] *Gyges æneum equum animadvertit cujus in lateribus fores essent.*[6] *Multa sæpe dicit de laude et gloria, quæ sola sit*[7] *digna tot laborum merces. Pætus omnes libros quos frater suus reliquisset,*[8] *mihi donavit.*

NOTE 1.—In the preceding and similar sentences, the Indicative (in the subordinate clauses) would not be incorrect; but it would mean that the writer was convinced of the truth of his assertion, which conviction the Subjunctive does not imply.

NOTE 2.—*Quod* and *quia*, when joined to a negative (*non quod, non eo quod, non ideo quod*), regularly take the Subjunctive, because the clause introduced by *non quod, non quia*, etc., does not state the true reason; as, *Pugiles in jactandis cæstibus ingemiscunt non quod doleant, sed quia profundenda voce omne corpus intenditur. Majores nostri in dominum de servo quæri noluerunt, non quia non posset verum inveniri, sed quia videbatur indignum esse.* (☞ Observe the real reason introduced by *sed quod, sed quia*, with the Indicative.

NOTE 3.—Sometimes the speaker or writer states his own sentiment in such a manner as though it were the sentiment of another person, and accordingly expresses it by the Subjunctive; e. g., *Cæsar graviter Æduos incusat quod tam necessario tempore ab iis non sublevetur. Cæsar quotidie Æduos frumentum quod publice essent polliciti, flagitabat.*

NOTE 4.—The expressions "because he thought," "because he said," are frequently rendered by the Subjunctive (*quod crederet, quod putaret, quod diceret*), where we might expect the Indicative, and where,—not the verbs *credo, puto, dico*, but the Infinitive dependent on these verbs, ought to be expressed by the Subjunctive; e. g., *Quum exisset de castris, rediit paulo post, quod se oblitum nescio quid diceret*, instead of *quod nescio quid oblitus esset.*

---

[1] because (as he [Diogenes] said) they could not ..... ☞ If the writer of this sentence were to allege the substance of the relative clause as his own opinion, he would have said *quod eum felicem reddere non poterant*, and the Indicative would render him responsible for the truth of his allegation. If the relative clause were to express the sentiment neither of Diogenes, nor of the writer, but of some other person, the text would run thus: *quod eum felicem reddere non possent.* Comp. § 145, 1. [2] because (as it was alleged by Themistocles himself, or by some other person) he could not sleep. [3] whether (as they [the Norici] thought) war could not.... [4] because (as the Athenians pretended) he was.... [5] to whose solemnity (as it was alleged by themselves) they had come, — *cujus ad solemne se venisse dixerunt.* [6] in each side of which there was a door (as he [Gyges] observed, or pretended to have observed). [7] which (according to him, or as he asserts) is the only reward.... — *quam solam dicit esse dignam mercedem*, etc. [8] which as he said, his brother.... — *quos fratrem suum sibi reliquisse dicebat.*

Quacunque incederent, impugnabantur.

V. When in a narrative, after relative pronouns and adverbs, actions of repeated occurrence are spoken of. The verb of the leading sentence is then usually the Imperfect Indic., whereas that of the relative clause is the Imperf. or Pluperf. Subj.—E. g., "In whatever direction they marched, they were attacked."

Quemcunque lictor jussu consulis prehendisset, tribunus mitti (i. e., iberari) *jubebat. Si quis rem malitiosius gessisset, dedecus existimabant. Socrates quam se cunque in partem dedisset, omnium facile fuit princeps. Semper habiti sunt* (habebantur) *fortissimi, qui summam imperii potirentur. Hortensius quæ secum commentatus esset, ea sine scripto verbis iisdem reddebat quibus cogitasset. Scævola simul atque luceret, faciebat omnibus sui conveniendi potestatem.*

NOTE.—In such propositions, however, the Indicative is not less frequently used in the subordinate clause than the Subjunctive, and the Indicative would be even necessary, if a distinct, particular case were spoken of.

SUBJUNCTIVE IN INTERMEDIATE CLAUSES.

☞ By intermediate clauses are meant those subordinate clauses which are connected with, or inserted in, other dependent propositions.

Rex imperat ut quæ bello opus sint parentur.

§ 200.—The Subjunctive is used in intermediate clauses, when they express the thoughts or words of the person spoken of, and form an integral part either of the statement implied in the Acc. c. Inf., or of the purpose, request, or command, expressed by the subjunctive clause; as, "The king orders that those things that are necessary for war, be prepared."

Aristoteles ait bestiolas quasdam nasci quæ unum diem vivant. Temere multi credunt eum qui orationem bonorum imitetur, etiam facta imitaturum. Socrates dicere solebat omnes in eo quod scirent, satis esse eloquentes.—Pietas erga Deum postulat ut nihil ab eo expetatur quod sit inhonestum atque injustum. Omnis virtus facit ut eos diligamus quibus ipsa inesse videatur.

NOTE 1.—When such intermediate clauses do not express the thoughts or words of the person spoken of, nor form an integral part either of the statement implied in the Acc. c. Inf., or of the purpose, request, or command, expressed by the subjunctive clause, they must be regarded as merely explanatory remarks of the speaker or writer, and as such be expressed by the Indicative.

For the sake of explanation let us take the following sentences:

(a) *Dixit mihi in somnis Scipio, omnem terram quam incolamus, parvam quandam insulam esse mari circumfusam.*—In this example the words spoken by Scipio, were: *Omnis terra quam incolitis parva quœdam insula est mari circumfusa.* The relative clause *quam incolitis,* forming a part of this statement, is therefore expressed by the Subjunctive. Had Scipio simply said : *Terra parva quœdam insula est mari circumfusa,* then the relative clause, being not included in this statement, would, as a merely explanatory remark of the narrator, be expressed by the Indicative, and the whole proposition would run thus: *Dixit mihi in somnis Scipio, terram quam incolimus, parvam quandam insulam esse mari circumfusam.*

(b) *Hannibal Scipionem prœstantem virum esse credebat quod adversus se dux electus esset.*—Here the subordinate clause *quod adversus se dux electus esset,* forms an integral part of Hannibal's thought (which was: *Scipio vir prœstans est quod adversus me dux est electus*), and is, therefore, expressed by the Subjunctive. Had Hannibal's thought been simply : *Scipio vir prœstans est,* the subordinate clause, being a merely explanatory remark of the writer, would have been expressed by the Indicative: *quod adversus eum dux electus erat.*

(c) *Sempronius rogat ut Virgilii opera, quœ nuper a patre dono accepi, sibi quamprimum transmittam.*—In this proposition the Indicative *accepi* shows that the relative clause is but an explanatory remark of the writer, and not a part of Sempronius's request, which was simply this : *Mitte mihi quamprimum Virgilii opera.*—Had the request been : *Mitte mihi quamprimum Virgilii opera quœ nuper a patre dono accepisti,* the relative clause, forming an integral part of this request, would then have been expressed by the Subjunctive: *quœ nuper acceperim.*

NOTE 2.—When the inserted clause is a mere circumlocution (as, *ii qui audiunt* for *auditores; ii qui prœsunt* for *magistratus, duces,* or *prœfecti; ii qui judicant* for *judices; ii qui post nos futuri sunt* for *posteri; ea quœ Hannibal gesserat* for *Hannibalis res gestœ; ea quœ sciunt homines* for *res cognitœ; ea quœ ignorant* for *res incognitœ,* etc.). it commonly matters little whether such a clause be considered as a part of the sentence to which it belongs, or as a merely explanatory remark of the writer or speaker. We are, therefore, at liberty to use either the Indicative or the Subjunctive. E. g., *Tune putas eos qui oratorem audiunt* (or *audiant*) *ita semper effici, ut orator velit ? Sic habitote magistratibus iisque qui prœsint* (or *prœsunt*) *rempublicam contineri. Eloquendi vis efficit ut ea quœ ignorant* (or *ignorent*) *homines, discere et ea quœ sciunt* (or *sciant*) *alios docere possint.*

SUBJUNCTIVE IN GENERAL SENTENCES.

Tamdiu discendum est quamdiu vivas.

§ 201.—The Subjunctive (especially the 2d pers. sing.) is used in general sentences in which no definite subject is spoken of. The English language, in this case, frequently uses the indefinite pronoun " one" (French, *on ;* German, *man*). E. g., " One must learn, as long as he is alive."

Non decet ea vituperare quœ non intelligas. Stultum est ea docere velle quœ nunquam didiceris. Nulla est excusatio peccati si amici causa peccaveris. Memoria minuitur nisi eam exerceas aut si sis natura tardior. Stultum est timere quod vitare non possis

IMPERATIVE.

Vale, amice!

§ 202.—The IMPERATIVE has two forms : the present (*scribe, scribite*) and the future (*scribito, scribitote, scribunto*).—Thus,

Valetudinem tuam cura diligenter. Si quid in te peccavi, ignosce.— Quum valetudini tuæ consulueris, tum consulito navigationi. Servus meus liber esto. Judices ne præmium capiunto neve[1] danto. Regio imperio duo sunto iique Consules appellantor.

NOTE 1.—The future form is chiefly used by rulers and lawgivers,—in contracts and wills, and, in general, when a command or request is expressed with reference to future time.

NOTE 2.—*Scio* and *memini, habeo* in the sense of "to know," and *sum* in the concessive phrase "be it so," admit of the future form only; as *scito, scitote ; memento, mementote ; sic habeto* or *habetote ; esto* or *verum esto.* E. g., *Dolabella tuo nihil mihi scito esse jucundius. Sic habeto non te esse mortalem, sed corpus hoc.*

NOTE 3.—The English imperative form "let us," as a request or advice, is rendered in Latin by the 1st pers. plur. of the Pres. Subj. ; as, " Let us rise," *Surgamus.* —*Imitemur nostros Camillos, Fabricios ; amemus patriam, pareamus Senatui. Meminerimus nos esse mortales.*

When "let" is equivalent to " allow or permit," it is expressed by *sino, patior,* or *permitto,* with either the Subj., or the Acc. c. Inf. ; e. g., "Let us go," *Sinite abeamus,* or *Sinite nos ubire.*—" Let him write," *Sine scribat.*—" Let me come to you," *Sine ad te veniam,* or *Sine me (patiaris me, permitte mihi) ad te venire.*

§ 203.—The Imperative is either affirmative or negative, according as something is commanded or forbidden.

1. Instead of the **affirmative** Imperative we may use :

(a) The Subj. Present ; as, " Let him come." *Veniat.*—" Let them go," *Abeant.*— " Let your attitude, gait, etc., be decorous," *Status, incessus, vultus, oculi, teneant decorum.*

(b) *Cura, fac, velim,* with the Subjunctive (see § 95. NOTE 3.) ; as, " Keep up good spirits and good hope," *Magnum fac animum habeas et bonam spem. Cura ut quam primum venias. Valetudinem tuam velim cures diligentissime. Nolim me jocari putes.*

(c) The Indicative Future : as, *Si quid acciderit novi, facies ut sciam. Tu et ad omnia rescribes et quando te expectem, facies me certiorem.*

2. Instead of the **negative**, or prohibitive, Imperative we may use :

(a) The Subjunctive with *ne* ; as, *Puer telum ne habeat. Quod dubitas, ne feceris. Ne cui hoc dixeris. Ne dubitaris mittere.* (☞ The 2d pers. sing. of the Subj. Perfect, in the sense of the Present, is quite common.)

---

[1]) With the Imperative render " not" by *ne*,—and " nor," by *neve* (not *neque*).

(b) *Cave* and *fac ne* with the Subjunctive; as, *Cave hoc facias. Cave dixeris. Cave existimes me abjecisse curam reipublicæ. Fac ne quid aliud cures nisi ut convalescas.*

(c) *Noli* with the Infinitive; as, *Noli putare. Noli agere confuse. Nolite timere.*

(d) The Indicative Future with *non ;* as, *Tu non cessabis,*for *ne cessa.*

INFINITIVE.

§ 204.—The INFINITIVE is used either subjectively or objectively :— subjectively, when it stands as the nominative to the verb, as *Errare humanum est ; parcere victis honestum est ;*—objectively, when it stands as the accusative to the verb, as *Sequi signa, ordines servare didicerunt; ferre laborem consuetudo docet.*

NOTE 1.—The Infinitive is used objectively, especially after such verbs as *volo, nolo, malo, cupio, opto, studeo ; propono, decerno, statuo, constituo ; possum, queo, nequeo; soleo, assuesco, consuesco ; conor, nitor, tento, contendo ; festino, maturo, propero ; audeo, debeo ; cœpi, incipio, pergo, persevēro, desino, cesso ; cogo, doceo, disco, scio, nescio, memini, obliviscor,* and others which do not express a complete idea by themselves.

NOTE 2.—When the Infinitive of *sum* or of one of those verbs that are construed with two nominatives (§ 154), is accompanied by a predicate-noun or adjective, the latter is put either in the nominative or accusative.

(a) The predicate noun or adjective is put in the nominative, when the Infinitive is used objectively, that is, when the Infinitive is the accusative to the verb. E. g., *Didici esse prudens. Malo bonus esse quam dives. Audeamus esse boni et sapientes. Desine tandem mihi molestus esse. Perge esse bonus et diligens. Græcia eloquentiæ princeps esse voluit.*

(b) The predicate noun or adjective is put in the accusative, when the Infinitive is used subjectively, that is, when the Infinitive is the nominative to the verb. E. g., *Non cuivis datum est esse prudentem. Præstat bonum esse quam divitem. Memorem esse acceptorum beneficiorum, grati animi est. Contentum esse suis rebus, maximæ sunt certissimæque divitiæ.*

NOTE 3.—With an Infinitive pass., the forms *cœptus sum* and *desitus sum* are generally used instead of *cœpi* and *desii* (§ 71, 2); but the active forms are found also.— E. g., *Vasa fictilia, serpentibus repleta, in naves conjici cœpta sunt. Contemni cœpti erant a finitimis populis.— Veteres orationes a plerisque legi sunt desitæ. Hic est Papirius, qui primus Papirius est vocari desitus. Desitum est videri quidquam in socios iniquum, cum extitisset in cives tanta crudelitas.*

NOTE 4.—In animated narrative and in descriptions the Infinitive Present is often used instead of the Indic. Perfect or Imperf., to represent past events as going on before our eyes. .This is what is called the historical Infinitive. E. g., "The man began to hesitate, to look away, to color ;" *Hærere homo, aversari, rubere. Hic judex ridere, stomachari patronus. Postquam in ædes irruperunt, diversi regem quærere, dormientes alios, alios occursantes interficere, scrutari loca abdita, clausa effringere, strepitu et tumultu omnia miscere.*—And the Poet :

Nos pavidi trepidare metu crinemque flagrantem
Excutere et sanctos restinguere fontibus ignem.

§ 205.—Narration is either *direct* or *indirect.*

Direct Narration is the way of stating the words of another precisely
.s they were uttered ; e. g., He said : "I will come."

Indirect Narration is the way of stating the words of another indi-
·ectly, that is, dependent on a verb *sentiendi* or *declarandi ;* e. g., " He
.aid that he would come."

> (Dir.) He said : " I can scarcely believe what you tell me."
> (Ind.) He said that he could scarcely believe what I told him.

Dicit se venturum si possit.

§ 206.—In indirect Narration,

(a) Principal sentences are expressed by the Acc. c. Infinitive ;
(b) Subordinate clauses are expressed by the Subjunctive. E. g.,

> (Dir.) Veniam si possum (*or* potero).
> (Ind.) Dicit se venturum si possit.
>
> (Dir.) Placet mihi quod facis.
> (Ind.) Dixit placere sibi quod facerem, *or* faciam (Note 5, b).
>
> (Dir.) Dabo tibi si vis.
> (Ind.) Dixit se mihi daturum si vellem, *or* velim (Note 5, b).

Note 1.—Clauses introduced by *nam, enim, igitur, ideo, propterea, quippe, videlicet.
sed, verum, autem, quidem,* and relative clauses in which the relative is equivalent to
et with a demonstrative, are regarded as principal sentences and accordingly expressed by the Acc. c. Inf. E. g., *Themistocles apud Lacedæmonios liberrime professus
est, Athenienses suo consilio Deos patrios muris sepsisse ; nam illorum urbem ut pro-
pugnaculum oppositam esse barbaris, avud quam* (et apud eam) *jam bis classes regias
fecisse naufragium.*

Note 2.—Questions of the 1st and 3d persons, which in direct Narration are
expressed by the Indicative, are in indirect Narration generally expressed by the Acc.
c. Inf. ; but questions addressed to the 2d person, and also Imperatives and requests,
are expressed by the Subjunctive. E. g.,

(Dir.) [Words of the populace.] *Quid vivimus ? quid in parte civium censemur, si
quod duorum hominum virtute partum est, id obtinere universi non possunt ?*
(Ind.) *Plebs fremit, quid se vivere ? quid in parte civium censeri, si quod duorum
hominum virtute partum sit, id universi obtinere non possint ?*

(Dir.) [Words of the general.] *Omnia perdita sunt. Nonne hostem videtis undique
irruentem ? quid spei vobis reliquum est, aut quid ego auxilii ferre possum ? Ipsi vobis
consulite, fuga salutem petite.*
(Ind.) *Hæc fere militibus dux : omnia esse perdita—nonne hostem viderent undi-*

que irruentem ? quid ipsis spei reliquum esse, aut quid se auxilii ferre posse ? ipsi sibi consulerent, fuga salutem peterent.

Questions of the 1st and 3d persons, which in direct Narration are expressed by the Subjunctive, in indirect Narration either retain the same mood, or are rendered by the Acc. c. Inf. ; E. g.,

(Dir.) What (said he) shall I do? *Quid faciam ?*

(Ind.) *Quid* (inquit) *faceret ?* or *quid se facturum ?*

(Dir.) Who (said he) will persuade himself? *Quis sibi persuadeat ?*

(Ind.) *Quis sibi persuaderet?* or *quem sibi persuasurum ?*

Note 3.—The verb, or participle on which the Infinitive or Subjunctive depends, is often omitted in indirect Narration; as, *Legatos ad Cæsarem mittunt* (dicentes), *sese paratos esse portas aperire. Procumbunt Gallis ad pedes Bituriges* (obsecrantes), *ne pulcherrimam prope totius Galliæ urbem suis manibus succendere cogerentur.*

Note 4.—When a subordinate clause does not make part of the words or thoughts of the person spoken of, but is thrown in as an explanatory remark of the writer himself, the Indicative is used (Compare § 200, 1).—E. g., *Themistocles certiorem regem fecit, id agi ut pons quem ille in Hellesponto fecerat, dissolveretur. Disseruit Cæsar non quidem ea sibi ignara quæ de Silano vulgabantur, sed non ex rumore statuendum.*

Note 5.—In indirect Narration, the Present and Perfect Subj. are often used, where the general rule would require the Imperfect and Pluperfect. This is the case:

(a) When the clause expresses a g e n e r a l t r u t h, i. e., when that which is said, holds good at all times and in all places; as,

(Dir.) *Pauci eo quod habent, contenti sunt.*

(Ind.) *Zeno dicebat paucos eo quod habeant, contentos esse.*

(Dir.) *Invitus feci quod quereris : nemo enim vult eum offendere a quo beneficia accepit.*
(Ind) *Affirmabat se invitum fecisse quod quereret. Neminem adeo insipientem esse ut eum offendere velit a quo beneficia acceperit.*

(b) After the Present and Future Infin., when they depend on a past tense, and after the Perfect Infin., whatever be then the tense of the leading verb, provided the Present and Perfect stand in direct Narration.—Cæsar, in case (b), generally uses the Present and Perfect Subj.; Cicero and Livy, on the contrary, use the Imperfect and Pluperfect. E. g.,

(Direct.)

Intelligo ⎫   ⎧ agat.
Intellexi ⎬ quid ⎨ egerit.
Intelligam ⎭   ⎩ acturus sit.

(Indirect.)

Dicebat ⎫ se intelligere, *or*
Dixit ⎬ se intellecturum
Dixerat ⎭   ⎫ quid ageret *or* agat.
                                                      ⎬ quid egisset *or* egerit.
After any ⎫   ⎭ quid acturus esset *or* sit.
tense ⎬ se intellexisse
of Dico ⎭

THE PARTICIPLE IN -DUS.

§ 207.—The Participle in *dus*, or as it is often called, the Gerundive, is a verbal adjective of three endings, expressing in the nominative (and, in the construction of the Acc..c. Inf., in the accusative also) *necessity*, *duty*, or *conveniency ;* as, *liber legendus*, a book worth reading—a book to be read—a book which must be, or ought to be read.

In the remaining cases, the Participle in *dus* often seems to change its meaning, but it only appears to do so; as,

Consilium epistolæ scribendæ, an intention of writing a letter (= an intention with respect to a letter to-be-written).

Idoneus ferendis oneribus, fit for carrying burdens (= fit for burdens to-be-carried).

Vinculum ad connectendas amicitias, a bond for forming friendships (= a bond for friendships to-be-formed).

NOTE.—The Participle in *dus* does not convey by itself the idea of futurity, but simply denotes *necessity*. Thus, e. g., *epistola scribenda* means a letter that *must* be written, and not one that *will* be written.—A reference to future time may indeed be implied, but this arises from the connection rather than from the Participle itself, as in the following sentences: *Missus erat ad naves comparandas. Avi capta magis capior*[1] *quam capiendâ. Ego censeo Carthaginem esse delendam*, etc.

§ 208.—The Participle in *dus* is expressed in English by such words and phrases, as *must, ought, should, to be bound, to be obliged, it is necessary, it is* e. g. *to be done,*[2] *it has to be done*, etc. When these and similar expressions remain untranslated in Latin, their value must be given by the Participle in *dus*. Thus, the sentence : " It is necessary for all to practise virtue," can be rendered

Omnes virtutem colere debent,
Omnes virtutem colant oportet,
Virtus ab omnibus colatur necesse est,

or, by omitting *debeo, oportet, necesse est*, and changing the verb *colo* into the Participle in *dus* with *sum :*

Virtus omnibus colenda est.

NOTE.—In the use of the Participle in *dus* let the pupil attend to the following directions :

(1.) Change the verb connected with must, ought, or any other word implying necessity, into the Participle in *dus* with *sum ;*

---

[1] A bird in the hand is worth two in the bush. [2] When *it is* followed by the Inf. pass., is equivalent to *it may* or *it can*, do not render it by the Partic. in *dus*, but translate it by *possum*; e. g., " This passage is to be found in the first book" — this passage may or can be found, etc.

(2.) See whether this verb be transitive or intransitive (§ 46), and if transitive, whether its object be expressed or not;

(3.) See whether the **Agent** be expressed, that is, the *person by whom* any thing is to be done,—who has to do, or is bound to do any thing.

☞ To find the object and the Agent, simply ask these two questions:

    1. **W h a t** must be e. g. loved, praised, given, sent, etc. ?
    2. **W h o** must love, praise, give, send, etc. ?

The answer to the first question is the *object ;* that to the second, the *Agent.*

Deus amandus est.

§ 209.—When the verb is **transitive** and its object expressed, the object is put in the nominative **and** the Participle in *dus* with *sum*, made to agree with it accordingly; as, "God deserves to be loved," or "God is to be loved."

Summa pietati laus tribuenda est.　Quæritur sitne præponenda divitiis gloria?　Suo quæque tempore facienda sunt.—Senes venerandos esse quis neget?　Tibi persuadeas velim virtutem vel in hoste esse laudandam. Omnem memoriam discordiarum oblivione sempiterna delendam esse censeo.

NOTE.—When the object of a verb transitive is a whole clause, or when no object is expressed at all, the Participle in *dus* with *sum* is construed impersonally. E. g., "It will always be necessary to learn," *Semper discendum erit.　Modo legendum est, modo scribendum.—Confitendum est omne animal esse mortale.　Videndum est non modo quid quisque loquatur, sed etiam quid quisque sentiat.*

Promissis standum est.

§ 210.—When the verb is **intransitive**, the Participle in *dus* with *sum*, is construed impersonally, and when any case depends on the verb, it must be retained in Latin, whatever be the case employed in English; as, "Promises must be kept," or "It is necessary to keep one's promises."

Moriendum certe erit.　Quæris ex me, quemadmodum sit cum amicis vivendum.　Si in alterutro peccandum est, malo videri nimis timidus quam parum prudens.—Non est obliviscendum reipublicæ.　Hosti victo parcendum est.　Audiendi non sunt qui graviter irascendum (esse) inimicis putant.　Tempore et occasione utendum est.

NOTE 1.—The impersonal construction sometimes occurs even with transitive verbs, but only in ante- and post-classical writers; e. g., *Æternas pœnas in morte timendum est ; mihi hac nocte agendum est vigilias*, etc., instead of *Æternæ in morte pœnæ timendæ sunt ; mihi hac nocte agendæ sunt vigiliæ.*—Whoever aspires to purity of language, should carefully avoid this unclassical form; nor should any one allege in his favor the two isolated passages in which even Cicero employs it, once with the verb *ingredior:* *Via quam* (according to others, *qua*) *nobis quoque ingrediendum est,*— and another time, in some fragment, with the verb *obliviscor:* *Obliviscendum nobis putatis matrum in liberos scelera?*—In Cicero, such forms of expression are exceptions that must be r e s p e c t e d, but not imitated.

NOTE 2.—The verbs *utor, fruor, fungor,* and *potior,* though they govern the ablative, are often in the Participle in *dus* construed like transitive verbs; as, *Non paranda nobis solum, sed etiam fruenda est sapientia. Omnia bona ei utenda ac possidenda tradiderat.*

Etiam senibus discendum est.

§ 211.—The *Agent* is put in the dative, and when there is already another dative, in the ablative with *ab;* as, "Even old men have to learn."

Sua cuique sors ferenda est. Tria videnda sunt oratori, quid dicat, quo quidque loco, et quomodo. Quis est qui nesciat sibi quandoque moriendum esse? Juveni parandum, seni utendum est.—Aguntur bona multorum civium, quibus est a vobis consulendum. Non tibi a me, sed a te mihi ratio reddenda est.

NOTE 1.—The datives *mihi, tibi, nobis,* and *vobis,* are commonly left out in Latin, (a) when no particular person is meant, but people in general; (b) when "we" and "you" are joined to verbs that govern the dative, and (c) when the person meant can easily be supplied from the context. E. g., "Sooner or later we shall have to die," *Serius ocius moriendum erit. Non cuivis homini credendum est. Discendum* (tibi) *est ut possis docere. Edendum* (nobis) *est, ut possimus vivere.*

NOTE 2.—With the verbs *do, trado, tribuo; concedo, permitto; accipio, suscipio; mitto, appono, relinquo,* and others of a similar meaning, the purpose for which any thing is given, sent, received, etc., is expressed p a s s i v e l y by the Partic. in *dus,* which is to agree in gender, number, and case, with the object given, sent, received. E. g., "I send you this book to read," *Mitto tibi hunc librum legendum. Demus nos philosophiæ excolendos. Rex Harpago Cyrum infantem occidendum tradidit. Lentulus totam Italiam vastandam diripiendamque Catilinæ attribuit. Datames urbes tuendas* (the defence of) *suis tradidit. Diomedon Epaminondam pecunia corrumpendum* (undertook to bribe) *suscepit. Hæc porcis comedenda relinquimus. Natura mulieri domestica negotia curanda* (intrusted the care of) *tradidit.*

This use of the Participle in *dus* often, also, occurs with *loco,* "to give something in contract," i. e., to contract for having a thing done; *conduco,* "to contract for doing a thing, and *curo,* in the sense of "to cause or order a thing to be done," or "to have it done." E. g., *Redemptor columnam Jovis faciendam conduxerat.*[1] *Mummius maximorum artificum tabulas ac statuas in Italiam portandas locavit.*[2] *Conon muros a Lysandro dirutos reficiendos curavit.*

---

[1] The contractor had undertaken to erect.... [2] contracted for having ...... brought to Italy, or gave the transportation of .... in contract, or contracted for the freight of .... to Italy.

GERUNDS.

§ 212.—The GERUND is nothing else than the neuter of the Participle in *dus.*—Gerunds govern the case of their verbs, but are used only in the oblique cases, that is, in the Gen., Dat., Acc., and Abl. singular.

GENERAL REMARK.—When any Gerund is followed by an object-accusative, the object is generally put in the case of the Gerund; the Gerund itself is changed into the Participle in *dus,* and the latter made to agree with the object in gender, number, and case.

Ars scribendi.

§ 213. The GENITIVE of the Gerund is used: (a) after certain substantives, such as *ars, causa, consilium, consuetudo, cupiditas, facultas, libido, metus, modus, occasio, potestas, ratio, scientia, spes, studium, timor, vis, voluntas,* etc., when the question *what,* asked in connection with any of these substantives is answered by a verb; as, "The art (*what* art?—) of writing;"—(b) after those adjectives which govern a genitive, as *avidus, cupidus, studiosus, certus, ignarus, nescius, peritus, imperitus,* etc., when they belong to a verb, as "Desirous (*of what?*—) of learning," *cupidus discendi;* "Skilled (*in what?*—) in swimming," *peritus natandi;* and (c) after *causa* and *gratia,* "for the sake of."

Sapientia est ars bene vivendi. Optime peccatum evitat qui occasiones fugit peccandi. Titus Augustus equitandi peritissimus fuit. Avari homines non solum libidine augendi cruciantur, sed etiam metu amittendi. Quidam canes venandi gratia comparantur.

With an object-accusative.—*Quis ignorat Gallos usque ad hanc diem retinere illam immanem ac barbaram consuetudinem hominum immolandorum* (immolandi homines)? *Timotheus civitatis regendae* (regendi civitatem) *peritissimus fuit.*

NOTE 1.—The change of the Gerund into the Partic. in *dus* is not allowed, (a) when the object-accusative is the neuter of an adjective or adjective pronoun, such as *hoc, id, illud, ea, vera, multa,* etc. Accordingly we ought to say: *Cupiditas haec vel illa videndi; ars vera et falsa dijudicandi,* and the like; and not, *Cupiditas horum videndorum; ars verorum et falsorum dijudicandorum,* because from these constructions we would not know whether things or persons are meant; (b) when the object-accusative does not depend on the Gerund, but on a preposition understood; as, *Cupidus sum proficiscendi Romam,* not *Romae proficiscendae;* (c) when the too frequent repetition of the same termination would produce an uncouth, monotonous sound, as in the following sentence: *Romanos splendidorum et magnificorum majorum templorum ac deorum simulacrorum sanctissimorum videndorum desiderium tenebat.* How much better hus : *Romanos splendida et magnifica majorum templa ac deorum simulacra sanctissima nidendi desiderium tenebat.*

NOTE 2.—When the accompanying object-accusative is one of the personal pro-nouns *me, te, se, nos,* or *vos,* the pronoun is generally put in the case of the Gerund *(mei, tui, sui, nostri, vestri*), but the Gerund itself is left unchanged, though the pronoun be plural or of the feminine gender. E. g., *Legati sui purgandi causa vene-runt. Vestri salutandi et confirmandi gratia adveni.*

NOTE 3.—*Tempus est,* "there is a time for," "to have leisure for," is followed by the genitive of the Gerund ; as, "There is a time for speaking and a time for being silent," *Est tempus loquendi et tempus tacendi. Certe tibi tempus est paululum hic com-morandi.*—But when *tempus est* is equivalent to *tempestivum est,* " it is now high time to," the Infinitive should be used. E. g., *Expergiscere, Marcelle, tempus est surgere. Tempus est hujus libri finem facere. Tempus est jam majora conari.*

NOTE 4.—Such forms as *exemplorum eligendi potestas,* Cic. ; *agrorum condonandi facultas,* Cic. ; *eorum adipiscendi causa,* Cic. ; *licentia diripiendi pomorum,* Suet. ; *rejiciendi amplius quam trium judicum potestas,* Cic., and the like, though found in the best writers, are irregularities which are difficult to be accounted for, and which should not be imitated in good prose.

In like manner, expressions such as *cantare peritus, cupidus attingere, cedere nescius, avidus committere pugnam,* etc., being purely poetical, ought to be avoided in prose.

Utilis arando.

§ 214.—The DATIVE of the Gerund is used : (a) after adjectives denoting fitness and usefulness, as *par, impar, noxius, aptus,* idoneus, *utilis, inutilis,* etc., e. g., " Good for ploughing ;"—(b) after certain verbs and expressions denoting a purpose or design, such as *studere, operam dare, intentum esse, tempus insumere* or *impendere, sufficere, praeesse, satis esse,* and *esse* in the sense of " to be able," " to serve or."

Charta emporetica inutilis est scribendo. Magius solvendo non erat. Non omnis debitor est solvendo. Aqua nitrosa utilis est bibendo. Rubens ferrum non est habile tundendo.

With an object-accusative.—*Sunt nonnulli acuendis puerorum ingeniis* (acuendo ingenia) *non inutiles lusus. Consul placandis diis*[1] (placando deos) *dat operam. Non sum oneri ferendo* (ferendo onus). *Omnem laborem meum hominum periculis sublevandis* (sublevando pericula) *impertiam. Romana juventus revocandis in urbem regibus* (revocando reges) *studebat.*

NOTE 1.—*Utilis, inutilis, aptus, idoneus, sufficere,* and *satis esse,* instead of the dative of the Gerund, often take the accusative with *ad ;* as, *Bene sentire recteque facere*

---

[1] is engaged in appeasing the gods.

satis est ad bene beateque vivendum. *Palpebræ aptissimæ sunt ad claudendas pupillas* d *ad aperiendas.*

Note 2.—*Esse*, in the sense of "to serve for," "to tend to," is sometimes construed with the genitive of the Gerund; as, *Regium imperium initio conservandæ libertatis atque augendæ reipublicæ fuerat. Hæc prodendi imperii Romani, tradendæ Hannibali victoriæ sunt.*

Inter . cœnandum.

§ 215.—The Accusative of the Gerund is used only with prepo.· tions, especially *ad* and *inter;* as, "While dining," or "during dinner."

Non solum ad discendum propensi sumus, verum etiam ad docendum. Ut ad cursum equus, ad arandum bos, sic ad intelligendum et agendum homo natus est. Mores puerorum se inter ludendum simplicius detegunt.

With an object-accusative.—*Homo multa habet instrumenta ad adipiscendam sapientiam* (ad adipiscendum sapientiam). *Ferrum ad colendos agros* (ad colendum agros) *necessarium est. Ad connectendas amicitias* (ad connectendum amicitias) *tenacissimum vinculum est morum similitudo.*

Note 1.—With verbs denoting a purpose, later writers frequently use the dative of the Gerund, where in the Classical period the accusative with *ad*, or a clause with *ut* would have been employed; as, *Multi canes propellendis hominum ac ferarum injuriis comparantur. Tiberius firmandæ valetudini in Campaniam concessit.*

Note 2.—The phrase *interest inter*, "there is a difference between," is followed by the Infinitive, when the difference exists between two actions; as, *Multum interest inter legere et intelligere. Philosophus Pyrrho dixit nihil interesse inter optime valere et gravissime ægrotare.*

Errando discimus.

§ 216.—The Ablative of the Gerund is used (a) without a preposition, as an ablative of the instrument; and (b) with the prepositions *a, de, ex,* and *in,* when the questions *from what* and *in what* are answered by a verb. E. g., "By erring we learn."

Fabius a cunctando Cunctator est appellatus. Providentia ex providendo est appellata. Adhibenda est in jocando moderatio. Nihil agendo homines male agere discunt. Aristotelem non deterruit a scribendo amplitudo Platonis. Ego vapulando, ille verberando usque ambo defessi sumus.

With an object-accusative.—*Omnis loquendi elegantia augetur legendis oratoribus et poetis* (legendo oratores et poetas). *In voluptate spernenda* (in spernendo voluptatem) *virtus vel maxime cernitur. Multi in equis parandis* (in parando equos) *adhibent curam, in amicis deligendis* (in deligendo amicos) *negligentes sunt.*

Note.—The change of the ablative of the Gerund into the Partic. in *dus*, always takes place when the ablative depends on a preposition, and nearly always, when the Gerund is used as an ablative of the instrument.

☞ Though the verbs *utor, fruor, fungor,* and *potior,* govern the ablative, yet in the gerundial construction they are often considered and treated as transitives; as, *Qui aliquid tribuit voluptati, diligenter ei tenendus est ejus fruendæ* (for *ea fruendi*) *modus.*—Thus, *spes urbis potiundæ; fiducia regni Persarum potiundi; oculus probe affectus ad suum munus fungendum; expetuntur divitiæ ad perfruendas voluptates,* etc.

SUPINES.

✓

§ 217.—The Supines are, in form, nothing else than cases of verbal substantives of the fourth declension.

There are two Supines, one in *um,* the other in *u :* the former has an active—the latter, generally a passive signification.

The Supine in *um,* moreover, governs the case of its verb, that is, it takes the same case as the verb, from which it is formed.

Eo ambulatum.

¶ § 218.—The Supine in *um* stands with verbs denoting or implying motion, such as *ire, proficisci, contendere, venire, mittere, trajicere,* etc.,—and expresses the purpose or end of the motion; as, "I go to walk."

Themistocles Argos habitatum concessit. Lacedæmonii Agesilaum bellatum miserunt in Asiam. Totius fere Galliæ legati ad Cæsarem gratulatum convenerunt. Cœlius, cum cœnatus cubitum cum duobus adolescentibus filiis isset, inventus est mane jugulatus. Hannibal patriam defensum ex Italia Carthaginem revocatus est. Philippus, cum spectatum ludos iret, juxta theatrum occisus est.

Note 1.—Verbs of hastening, as *festinare, properare, maturare,* though they express motion, are generally construed with the Infinitive; as, *Scipio oppugnare urbem festinavit. Quin huc ad vos venire propero? Exercitum flumen transducere maturavit.*

Note 2.—When the purpose of going, coming, sending, etc., is passive, instead of the Supine in *um,* either the Participle in *dus,* or a passive clause with *ut* must be used. E. g., "Youth is sent to school to be instructed;" *Juventus in scholam mittitur erudienda,* or *ut erudiatur. Multi Romanorum filios suos Athenas miserunt erudiendos,* or *ut erudirentur.*

Note 3.—The verb *eo* with the Supine is, in general, equivalent to *velle* with the Infinitive, and corresponds to the English "I intend—wish—am about—am going to." Sometimes, especially in dependent clauses, it is used as a circumlocution, instead of a simple verb.—E. g., *Cur te is perditum? Fuere cives qui se remque vublicam perditum irent. Qui paucis sceleratis parcunt, bonos omnes perditum eunt,* i. q., *perdunt. Obtestatus est filium ne pertinacia sua gentem universam perditum iret,* i. q., *perderet.*

NOTE 4.—It must be remembered that the Supine in *um* is of comparatively rare occurrence, and that the best Latin writers, in its place, generally employ one of the following constructions: (a) *ut* or *qui* with the Subj. Pres. or Imperf.; (b) the genitive of the Gerund with *causa* or *gratia ;* (c) the accusative of the Gerund with *ad ;* or lastly (d) the Participle in *urus,* which is to agree in gender, number, and case, with the person that has to perform the action denoted by the Latin subordinate verb. E. g., " The Veientes sent ambassadors to Rome to sue for peace ;" *Veientes oratores pacem petitum Romam miserunt,* or

> (a) *ut* or *qui pacem peterent,*
> (b) *pacem petendi* (pacis petendæ) *causa* or *gratia,*
> (c) *ad petendum pacem* (ad pacem petendam),
> (d) *pacem petituros.*

¶ **Mirabile visu.**

§ 219.—The Supine in *u* stands (a) with the substantives *fas, nefas,* and *opus ;* (b) with the adjectives *facilis, difficilis, gratus, jucundus, injucundus ; suavis, dulcis, acerbus ; mollis, durus ; turpis, honestus ; dignus, indignus ; utilis, memorabilis, mirabilis, incredibilis,*—when the question "in what respect ?" asked in connection with any of these adjectives is answered by a verb; as, " A thing wonderful (*in what respect ?*—) to behold, or to be beheld."

Videtis nefas esse dictu miseram fuisse Fabii senectutem. Quod optimum factu videbitur, facies. De apibus multa narrantur notatu dignissima. Uva primo est peracerba gustatu, deinde maturata dulcescit. Difficile dictu est quantopere conciliet animos hominum comitas affabilitasque sermonis.

NOTE.—The Supine in *u,* like that in *um,* is of rare occurrence. Those actually in use are principally the following: *auditu, cognitu, dictu, factu, intellectu, inventu, memoratu, visu.*

Instead of the Supine in *u* after *facilis, difficilis,* and *jucundus,* Latin writers prefer the following constructions :

(a) The Infinitive ; as, *Facile est justam causam defendere. Non facile est invenire* (aliquem), *qui quod sciat ipse, non tradat alteri.*

(b) The Passive,—the adjectives *facilis, difficilis,* etc., being then changed into adverbs ; as, *Justa causa facile defenditur. Ea sunt animadvertenda peccata maxime, quæ difficillime præcaventur.*

(c) The Gerund with *ad ;* as, *Justa causa facilis est ad defendendum. Eo cibo utendum est qui sit facillimus ad concoquendum. Orator verbis ad audiendum jucundis utatur.*

(d) A verbal substantive ; as, *Justæ causæ facilis est defensio. Virtutum ac vitiorum facilis est distinctio. Natura Dei difficiles explicatus habet.*

(e) Sometimes the Participle Present ; as, *Justa causa defendenti facillima est. Decemviri colloquentibus difficiles erant,* i. e., erant aditu difficiles.

THE CONSTRUCTION OF PARTICIPLES.

§ 220.—Participles, like Gerunds and Supines, govern the case of their verbs ; as, *scribens epistolam, parcens hosti, furti accusatus, regem aditurus, liberalitate utens.*

To make use of the Participial construction, it is necessary that there be in English two sentences or clauses,—a principal and a subordinate.

Subordinate clauses (see § 86) are either complete or abridged ;—*complete*, when the conjunction is expressed ; *abridged*, when it is not expressed. E. g.,

> (Complete.) When shame is lost, all virtue is lost.
> (Abridged.) Shame being lost, all virtue is lost.

§ 221.—The rules to be observed in the construction of Participles, are as follow :

I. See whether in the principal sentence there be a pronoun referring to some substantive in the subordinate clause. If so, put the pronoun in the place of the substantive and the substantive in the place of the pronoun. Thus,

> While Cato was dining, it was announced to him.
> It was announced to Cato, while he was dining.

> After Cæsar had defeated the Gauls, he pursued them.
> Cæsar pursued the Gauls, after he had defeated them.

> When the enemy had taken the city, they pillaged it.
> The enemy pillaged the city, after they had taken it.

Note 1.—When the Participial construction is to take place in a sentence containing a verbal noun, the latter must first be changed into a subordinate clause, either complete or abridged ; as,

> During the reign (*regno*) of Augustus, Christ was born.
> Augustus reigning, or while Augustus was reigning, etc.

> At the approach (*appropinquo*) of spring, the swallows return.
> Spring approaching, or when spring approaches, etc.

> After the fall (*capio*) of Troy, Æneas came into Italy.
> Troy being taken, or after Troy had been taken, etc.

Note 2.—When two clauses are connected by "and," the former usually is made the subordinate, by changing its verb into the present or the past Participle, according as the actions or events expressed by the two clauses are simultaneous or not ; as,

> Alexander took the cup *and* said to the physician.
> Alexander taking the cup, said to the physician.

Ambassadors came *and* sued for peace.
Ambassadors came suing for peace.

The wolf seized the lamb *and* tore it into pieces.
The wolf having seized the lamb, tore it into pieces.

II. Leave out the conjunction, and change the verb of the subordinate clause into its corresponding Participle.

(1.) To the Present and Imperfect Act. (and also to the simple Future Act., when there is another Future tense in the principal clause), the Participle Present in *ns* corresponds.

(2.) To the Perfect, Pluperfect, and Fut.-Perfect Active, and to any tense of the Passive, the Participle Perfect in *us* corresponds. E. g.,

When spring comes (*appropinquans*), the swallows return.
His strength failing (*deficiens*), he fell on the ground.

While Augustus was reigning (*regnans*), Christ was born.
If you will do this (*faciens*), you shall be safe.

When you have lost (*perditus*) heaven, you have lost all.
Having crossed (*trajectus*) the river, we attacked the enemy.

When thou art rebuked (*reprehensus*), do not reply.
Henry blushed, when he was praised (*laudatus*).

Shame being lost (*sublatus*), all virtue is lost.
Troy having been destroyed (*eversus*), Æneas came to Italy.

Note 1.—Instead of the Participle Present, the Participle Perfect is not unfrequently used when the verb is deponent; as,

Forgetting (*oblitus*) me, think of you and your children.
Fearing (*veritus*) Alexander's wrath, Darius sued for peace.

Note 2.—When the subordinate clause contains the Perfect, Pluperfect, or Fut.-Perfect Active, the clause must first be changed into the Passive, unless the verb be deponent, in which case the English active clause is left unchanged. E. g.,

Having crossed (*trajicio*) the river, we attacked the enemy.
The river having been crossed (*trajectus*), we attacked, etc.

Scipio burnt the city, after he had plundered it (*diripio*).
Scipio burnt the city, after it had been plundered (*direptus*).

Having crossed (*transgressus*) the river, we encamped.
Cæsar having addressed (*allocutus*) his army, ordered, etc.

☞ The Perfect Participle of certain deponents (see § 59, note) has besides the active signification also a passive. This Perf. Participle, however, should never be used in a passive sense in the construction of the ablative absolute. Forms like *partito exercitu, partita classe, partitis copiis, depopulatis agris*, etc., in which the Participles *par-*

titus and *depopulatus* are used in a passive sense, must be looked upon as exceptions not to be imitated.

NOTE 3.—When the subordinate clause expresses a wi s h or a being about to do something, its verb is changed into the Participle in *urus ;*—but when it is intimated that a thing is to be done, into the Participle in *dus ;* as,

When the storks are to migrate (*migraturus*), they all assemble.
The camel lies down, when it is to be laden (*onerandus*).

III. See whether the nominative of the subordinate clause refer to some word in the principal, or not.

(a) When it does, the nominative of the subordinate clause (in this case always a pronoun) is left untranslated in Latin, and the Participle made to agree in gender, number, and case, with the word in the principal sentence, to which the nominative of the subordinate clause refers. Thus,

Whilst he read, I fixed my eyes upon his countenance.
Oculos in vultum legentis intendi.

I met your brother, as he was going home.
Fratri tuo domum redeunti obviam factus sum.

When I think of this, it appears wonderful to me.
Cogitanti mihi hac de re mirum videtur.

Having crossed the river, we fortified the camp.
Amnem transgressi castra munivimus.

(b) When the nominative of the subordinate clause does not refer to any word of the principal sentence, the *ablative absolute* is used, that is, the nominative of the subordinate clause is put in the ablative, and the Participle made to agree with it in gender, number, and case ; thus,

If nature opposes, you will strive in vain.
Natura repugnante frustra niteris.

When spring approaches, the swallows return.
Vere appropinquante hirundines redeunt.

Shame being lost, all virtue is lost.
Pudore sublato omnis virtus tollitur.

Having crossed the river, we attacked the enemy.
Flumine trajecto hostem aggressi sumus.

Caninio consule scito neminem prandisse, nihil eo consule mali factum esse.[1] Curio ad focum sedenti magnum auri pondus Samnites attulerunt.

[1] See NOTE 3, p. 200,—and also foot-note to the example: Caninius fuit mirifica vigilantia, etc., § 199, II.

Regina apum nonnisi migraturo agmine procedit. Id Carthaginem delatum ("and") publice comprobatum est. Perditis rebus omnibus ipsa virtus se sustentare potest. Risus interdum ita repente erumpit ut eum cupientes ("though," "even if") tenere nequeamus. Cæsar omnium remotis equis cohortatus suos prælium commisit. Defuncto Trajano Ælius Hadrianus creatus est princeps. Maximas virtutes jacere omnes necesse est, voluptate dominante. Darius Charidemum, maxime utilia suadentem ("though"), abstrahi jussit ad capitale supplicium.

Notes on the Participial Construction.

Note 1.—The English phrases *by me, by thee, by him, by us,* etc., which arise from the change of the active voice into the passive, are in the Participial construction left untranslated ; as,

> After Alex. had subdued India, he returned to Babylon.
> A. returned to B., after India had been subdued [by him].
> *Alexander India subacta Babylonem rediit.*

Note 2.—When a verb wants the corresponding Participle, the Participial construction cannot be used. Thus we may say : *Cæsare adveniente,* "Cæsar arriving," or "at Cæsar's arrival ;" but we cannot say : *Cæsare advento,* "Cæsar having arrived," or "after Cæsar's arrival," because *advenio,* being intransitive, does not admit of a personal passive. Instead of *Cæsare advento,* we must therefore say : *cum Cæsar advenisset.*—For the same reason we cannot say : *Alexandro decesso,* "after Alexander's death,"—*Sylla fautus a multis,* "Sylla being favored by many,"—*Socrates quæsitus,* "Socrates being asked,"—*Cato egregie impositus a Milone,* "Cato being most beautifully deceived by Milo," etc., but we must say : *cum Alexander decessisset ; cum Sylla plurimi faverent ; cum ex Socrate quæreretur* or *quæsitum esset ; cum Catoni egregie imposuisset Milo.*

Note 3.—When *sum, esse,* is the verb of the subordinate clause, it is left out (there being no Present or Perfect Participle of *sum*). In this case the Predicate noun or adjective supplies the place of the Participle. E. g., "When the skies are serene, it seldom thunders," *Cælo sereno raro tonat.*

> *Cicerone consule,* under C.'s consulship, lit., C. being consul.
> *Herode rege,* in the reign of Herod, lit., Herod being king.
> *Te auctore,* by thy suggestion, lit., thou being the adviser.
> *Nobis invitis,* in spite of us, lit., we being unwilling.
> *Scipione duce,* under Scipio's command, lit., Sc. being the leader.
> *Me inscio,* without my knowledge, lit., I being ignorant of.
> *Hannibale vivo,* in H.'s lifetime, lit., H. being alive.
> *Teste Polybio,* according to the testimony of P., lit., P. being voucher.
> *Deo teste,* in God's presence, lit., God being witness.

Note 4.—The particles *velut, quasi,* and *tamquam,* "as if," are a l w a y s,—*etsi, licet quamquam,* and *quamvis,* s o m e t i m e s, retained in the Participial construction. E. g., "You live as if you were to live forever ;" *Vivitis tamquam semper victuri. Antiochus securus admodum de bello Romano erat, tamquam non transituris in Asiam Romanis.*—*Cæsarem milites, quamvis recusantem, ultro in Africam sunt secuti. Cæsar decumanos adire non cunctatus est, quamquam deterrentibus amicis.*

NOTE 5.—When the connective "and" is followed by "would," the verb following is frequently rendered by the Participle in *urus*. E. g., *Librum misi exigenti tibi, missurus* ('and I would have sent it') *esti non exegisses. Dedit mihi quantum maxime potuit, daturus amplius* ('and he would have given still more') *si potuisset. Jure interfectum Clitum Macedones decernunt, sepulturá quoque prohibituri, ni rex humari jussisset.*—(☞ This use of the Partic. in *urus* belongs chiefly to the writers of the silver age.)

NOTE 6.—When of two subordinate clauses connected by "and," one only admits of the Participial construction, the connective "and" may be omitted, but the introductory conjunction as, since, when, etc., must be expressed in the clause which does not admit of the construction. E. g., "As there was an irritation on both sides and the people had become emboldened, the senate dared, etc." *Irritatis utriusque partis animis, quum plebi animus accessisset, patres ausi sunt*, etc.

When both clauses admit of the Participial construction, the connective *et* is sometimes expressed and sometimes omitted. It should always be omitted, when one of the two Participles is an ablative absolute, the other not; as, "The Carthaginians killed Regulus after they had cut off his eyelids and tied him to the scaffold," *Carthaginienses Regulum resectis palpebris illigatum in machina necaverunt.*—When both Participles are ablatives absolute, *et* may be expressed or omitted; as, "Xerxes, having bridged the Hellespont and tunnelled Mount Athos, marched across the sea," *Xerxes Hellesponto juncto (et) Athone perfosso, mare ambulavit.*

NOTE 7.—The prepositions before, after, till, from, on account of, when placed before a verbal noun, are expressed by *ante, post, ad, ob, propter, de,* respectively, with the Partic. Perfect, when an action or event already completed is spoken of,—and with the Partic. in *dus,* when an action is conceived as yet to be performed. E. g., "Before (after) the birth of Christ," *Ante (post) Christum natum.* "From the building of Rome," *Ab urbe condita.—Scipio propter Africam domitam Africanus est appellatus. Bellum Turentinum ob violatos* ('on account of an insult offered to') *legatos Romanorum ortum est. Regulus de permutandis captivis Romam missus est.*

The preposition "after," before a verbal noun, is more commonly rendered by the simple Participle; as, "After the expulsion of the kings," *Regibus exactis,* though also *post reges exactos.*

NOTE 8.—The English "without" before a participial noun is variously rendered into Latin:

(a) By a Participle with *non, nemo, nullus, nihil.* E. g., "Without fixing any day," *Nulla præstituta die;* "Without paying any regard to," *Nulla habita ratione.—Quam multa non expectata* (without being expected) *eveniunt! Athenienses non rogati* (without being asked) *auxilium ferebant. Id etiam me tacente* (without my telling you) *intelliges. Me non sentiente,—nullo salutato* (without my knowing, without saluting anybody) *abiit. Lacrimæ cadunt nolentibus nobis* (without our willing it). *Compressi tuos nefarios conatus, nullo tumultu publice concitato. Multorum te oculi et aures non sentientem speculabuntur atque custodient.*

(b) By *quin* with the Subjunctive, when the preceding sentence is negative; as, *Timoleontem mater nunquam aspexit quin eum fratricidam impiumque compellaret* (without calling him).

When after a negative sentence, "without" is equivalent to "unless," it is expressed by *nisi* with either the Subjunctive or the participial construction. E. g., *Nunquam accurate eleganterque Latine scribes nisi perlectis* (without having read) *optimis scriptoribus,* or *nisi perlegeris optimos scriptores. Cæsar exercitum nunquam per insidiosa itinera duxit, nisi perspeculatus* (without having previously examined) *locorum situs.*

(c) By adjectives,—especially negative adjectives with the prefix *in*, as *inscius, invitus, insomnis, iniquus*, etc. E. g., "He does nothing without consulting me," *Nihil agit me inconsulto.*—"Without our knowing," *Nobis insciis.*—"Without having finished," *Infecto labore.*—"To spend the night without being able to sleep," *Noctem insomnem ducere.*—"Without violating one's conscience," *Salva fide.*—"Without complaining," *Æquo (haud iniquo) animo.*

d) Sometimes by a substantive, an adverb, or a conjunction; as, "Without hesitating," *Sine ulla dubitatione.*—"Without suspecting any thing," *Sine ulla suspicione.*—"Without fearing," *Sine metu*, or *confidenter.*—"Without shedding tears," *Sine lacrimis* or *siccis oculis.*—"Without thinking, reflecting," *Imprudenter, temere.*—"*Multi poetæ admirantur nec tamen intelligunt* (without understanding them).—*Malim esse vir bonus nec videri* (without seeming one), *quam videri nec esse* (without being so).—*Quidam litteris* (ita) *se tradunt ut nihil possint ex his ad communem afferre usum* (without being able to produce ....).

Note 9.—The verbs *volo, nolo, malo, cupio*, and *oportet*, are often construed with the Perfect, instead of the Infinitive, in order to express the thing which one has in view, as already completed. E. g., *Illud te admonitum volo. Omnes rempublicam defensam conservatamque volumus. Vobis omnibus me excusatum volo. Miser est qui patriam exstinctam cupit.*

Note 10.—*Habeo*, with the Perfect Partic. of verbs denoting k n o w l e d g e, etc., is sometimes used instead of the simple Perfect of these verbs; as, *Illud cognitum* (*perspectum, perceptum, comprehensum, exploratum, statutum, constitutum, deliberatum*) *habeo*, instead of *Illud cognovi, perspexi, comprehendi*, etc.—E. g., *Compertum habeo* (— bene scio), *milites, verba virtutem non addere. Cæsar perfidiam Æduorum perspectam habebat. Siculi ad meam fidem, quam habent spectatam jam et diu cognitam, confugiunt. An quisquam potest probare quod perceptum, quod comprehensum, quod cognitum non habet ?*
Similar constructions are : *urbem obsessam tenere, pecunias collocatas habere, domitas habere libidines*, etc.

Note 11.—The Perfect Participle of verbs *sentiendi* and *declarandi* (§ 101) sometimes stands by itself in the ablative absolute, the clause following being considered as the subject of the Participle. Ablatives of this kind are: *audito, cognito, comperto, explorato, nuntiato, edicto*, and a few more. E. g., *Alexander audito* (instead of *cum audivisset*) *Darium appropinquare cum exercitu, obviam ire constituit. Hannibal cognito* (instead of *cum cognovisset*) *insidias sibi parari, fuga salutem quæsivit.*—Even the ablative neut. of adjectives sometimes supplies the place of an ablative absolute; e. g., *Multi adnantes navibus, incerto præ tenebris* (quum *incertum esset*) *quid peterent aut vitarent, fæde interierunt.*

Note 12.—In the construction of the ablative absolute, two Participles belonging to the s a m e subject-ablative, are to be avoided. Thus we may say: *Quum Pompeius Strabo, de cælo tactus, mortuus esset*, etc.,—or, *Quum Regulus, prælio captus, Carthaginem esset abductus*, etc.,—but we should say neither: *Pompeio de cælo tacto mortuo*, nor *Regulo prælio capto Carthaginem abducto.*

CHAPTER VII.

PARTICLES.

1. Adverbs.—2. Prepositions.—3. Conjunctions.

I. ADVERBS.

GOVERNMENT OF ADVERBS.

Satis eloquentiæ, sapientiæ parum.

§ 222.—Adverbs of quantity govern the genitive. Such are, *sat, satis*, enough; *parum*, too little; *abunde, affätim*, abundantly; *nimis*, too much; as, "Enough (of) eloqnence, but too little wisdom."

Affatim est hominum, quibus negotii nihil est. Cæsar dicebat, se potentiæ gloriæque abunde adeptum. Nimis insidiarum adhibent. Multis in locis parum virium veritas habet. In isto juvene animi satis, auctoritatis parum est. Sat habet fautorum semper, qui recte facit.

NOTE 1.—Here is to be noticed the phrase *quoad (— quantum) ejus fieri potest* or *quoad ejus facere possum*, "as far as this is possible,"or "as far as I can,"—where the genitive *ejus* refers to the preceding clause. E. g., *Quoad ejus fieri potest, præsentiæ tuæ desiderium meo labore minuitur. Tu velim non intermittas, quoad ejus facere poteris, scribere ad me.*

NOTE 2.—The adverbs of place, *ubi, ubinam, ubique, ubicunque, usquam, nusquam, unde, hic, huc, eo, quo, quoquo, aliquo, quocunque*, are often, for the sake of emphasis, construed with the genitives *gentium, terrarum, locorum;* as, "Where on earth (or in the world) are we? *Ubinam gentium sumus?—Quo terrarum abiit? Vir bonus, ubicunque terrarum erit, diligetur. Quo gentium aufugiam, nescio. Rhodum aut aliquo terrarum migrandum est. Quæris quod nusquam est gentium. Abes longe gentium*," "you are greatly mistaken."—*Minime gentium*, "by no means."
In the phrases *postea loci*, 'afterwards;' *interea loci*, 'in the mean time;' *adhuc locorum*, 'until now,' the genitive seems to be superfluous.—*Hic loci, hoc loci, eo* (or *eodem*) *loci*, and *quo loci*, stand sometimes for *hoc loco, eo loco*, and *quo loco*.
The adverbs *huc, eo, quo*, in the sense of "to this degree," are construed with other genitives also; as, *Eo insolentiæ furorisque processit. Vide quo amentiæ progressus sis. Eo miseriarum pervenimus. Huccine rerum* ('to that state of things') *venimus?*

NOTE 3.—*Pridie* and *postridie* take both the genitive and accusative; as, *Pridie (postridie) ejus diei. Pridie (postridie) Calendas* or *Calendarum. Pridie insidiarum, Postridie nuptias. Pridie Nonas Junias litteras tuas accepi.*

The adverbs *propius* and *proxime* take commonly the accusative ; as, *Officium meum esse putavi exercitum habere quam proxime hostem :*—sometimes the dative, too ; as, *Quam proxime potest hostium castris castra communit.*

☞ The interjections *en* and *ecce*, Lo! behold! are usually construed with the nominative ; as, "Here I am," *En ego! En nova rixa! Ecce litterae tuae! Ecce Homo!*—*Ecce* is used, in poetry only, with the accusative of a pronoun ; as, *Ecce me! Eccum adest,* "behold, there he is!"—*Eccum quem quaerebam!* Thus the forms *eccam, eccillum, eccillam, eccos,* etc.

With *vae* and *hei*, the dative is used ; as, *Vae victis! Hei mihi!*

Heu and *pro* (*proh*) take both the accusative and vocative ; the accusative, in exclamations of wonder or grief ; the vocative, in direct address ; as, *Heu me miserum! cur senatum cogor, quem laudavi semper, reprehendere?*—*Proh deûm hominumque fidem!* —*Heu pietas, heu prisca fides! Pro sancte Jupiter! Pro dii immortales!*

PARTICULARS ABOUT THE USE OF ADVERBS.

§ ▩.—1. Distinction between *plus, magis, amplius,* and *potius.*

PLUS, "more," is used in respect of quantity, measure, value ; as, *Apud me argumenta plus quam testes valent. Vos et decem numero, et, quod plus est, Romani estis. Tantum et plus etiam mihi debet. Quam molestum est uno digito plus*[1] *habere!*

MAGIS, "more," is the comparative of action or quality,—it shows that a quality exists in a higher degree ; as, *Nemo fuit magis severus nec magis continens. Hoc magis est verisimile.*—*Magis virtute quam dolo contendunt. Nec me meae miseriae magis excruciant quam tuae.*

☞ *Plus*, in general, is used where in the positive *multum* would stand ; and *magis*, where *valde.*—In certain connections it is indifferent whether we use *plus* or *magis* ; as, *aliquem plus* or *magis amare, diligere.*

AMPLIUS, "more," "longer," "further," is used of extent in time and number ;—it denotes addition without comparison ; as, *Amplius sunt sex menses. Milites amplius horis quatuor fortissime pugnaverunt. Duo haud amplius millia peditum urbem ingressi sunt. Quid vis amplius?*

POTIUS, "more," "rather," "sooner," denotes choice between two objects or actions. (*Magis* attributes only a higher degree to one of the objects compared, whereas *potius* actually prefers it.) E. g., *Perpessus est omnia potius quam conscios indicaret. Nec vero imperia expetenda, ac potius non accipienda interdum.*

2. The adverb *quî* is often used instead of *quomodo* ; as, *Nos Deum, nisi sempiternum, intelligere quî possumus? Deus falli quî potest? Quî potest esse in ejusmodi trunco* ("blockhead") *sapientia?*

3. *Fortasse* and *forsitan* (poet. *forsan*) signify "perhaps."—*Forte* means "by chance," "accidentally :" but, when preceded by *ne, si, nisi, num,* it also acquires the meaning of "perhaps." E. g., *Si quis vestrum, judices, forte*

---

[1] a finger too much.

miratur.—Forsitan is generally used in sentences the nature of which requires the Subjunctive; e. g., *Forsitan aliquis dicat.*

4. *Nec vero, nec enim, nec tamen,* or *neque vero, neque enim, neque tamen,* are frequently used at the beginning of a sentence instead of *non vero, non enim, non tamen.* E. g., *Menti nihil est tam inimicum quam voluptas : nec enim libidine dominante temperantiæ locus est. Alcibiades magnam amicitiam sibi cum quibusdam regibus Thraciæ pepererat : neque tamen a caritate patriæ potuit recedere.*

5. As *nec (neque) non* often stands for *et non,* so Latin writers frequently use

nec ullus	*for*	et nullus,
nec quisquam	"	et nemo,
nec quidquam	"	et nihil,
nec unquam	"	et nunquam,
nec usquam	"	et nusquam ;

as, " Many pretend to know every thing, and yet know nothing," *Multi omnia se simulant scire, nec quidquam sciunt. Impedit consilium voluptas, nec ullum cum virtute habet commercium. Horæ cedunt et dies et menses et anni, nec præteritum tempus unquam revertitur.*

6. In translating " I don't know whether," " I am not sure that," by *haud scio (nescio, dubito) an,* if there is a " not," omit it in Latin : if there is no " not," put in *non.* Also translate " anybody" by *nemo,* " any" by *nullus,* " any thing" by *nihil,* " at any time or ever" by *nunquam,* and " anywhere" by *nusquam.*—Such is the practice of Cicero and his contemporaries. (Compare § 107, 2.)—E. g., " I don't know whether I should not prefer Thrasybulus to all," *Dubito an Thrasybulum primum omnium ponam.*[1]—" I am not sure that there is any happier man," *Haud scio an nullus sit beatior vir.*[2]—" I don't know whether, wisdom excepted, any thing better than friendship has been given by the gods to man," *Haud scio an excepta sapientia nihil melius amicitiâ homini sit a diis datum.*

7. The English " I say (will, order) that none, that no, that nothing, that never,"—is generally expressed in Latin by *nego (nolo, veto)* with *quisquam, quidquam, ullus, unquam.* E. g., *Negavit se unquam* (for *dixit se nunquam*) *talia vidisse. Vetuit quidquam* (for *jussit nihil*) *per fraudem fieri. Stoici negant quidquam* (for *dicunt nihil*) *esse bonum nisi quod honestum sit.*

When the verbs *nego, nolo, veto,* are followed by a second clause, the latter is introduced by *neque,* when it is negative, and by *et (que, atque),* when it is affirmative. E. g., *Illi vero obsides daturos se negabant neque* (and that they would not) *portas Consuli præclusuros. Plerique negant Cæsarem in conditione mansurum postulataque*[3] (and that) *hæc ab eo interposita esse, quo minus quod opus esset ad bellum, a nobis pararetur.*

8. Two negatives in the same sentence are equivalent to an affirmation.

---

[1] Or, I am inclined to prefer Th. to all. [2] Or, I am inclined to think that there is no happier man, or There is perhaps (probably, most likely) no happier man. [3] the same as *dicuntque postulata hæc,* etc.

Thus *non ignoro, non nescio, non sum inscius, non me fugit, non me præterit,* are equivalent to *probe scio ; non minimum,* to *multum ; non imperitissimus,* to *valde peritus ; non inferior,* to *par* or *superior ; non possum non,* to *cogor* or *debeo ; nec non,* to *et ; ne non,* to *ut ; neque vero non,* to *et vero ; neque tamen non,* to *et tamen,* etc. E. g., *Corporis dignitas non minimum commendat. Id indigne ferebant, neque tamen non patiebantur. Qui mortem in malis ponit, non potest eam non timere. Non potest non beatissimus esse, cui nihil deest. Neque vero non* (and in truth) *fuit apertum, si Conon non fuisset, Agesilaum Asiam Taurotenus regi fuisse erepturum.*

When a negative is followed by *ne-quidem, neque-neque, nec-nec,* or *neque-neque,* the first negative is not destroyed, but *ne-quidem* is then equivalent to *vel* ("even") and *neque-neque* to *aut-aut.* E. g., *Nunquam te ne minima quidem in re offendi,* "I never offended you even in the least."—*Urbes sine hominum coetu non potuissent nec ædificari nec frequentari. Nihil est illo mihi nec carius nec jucundius. Cæsar negat neque honestius neque tutius quidquam mihi esse* (— dicit nihil mihi esse neque . . . .) *quam ab omni contentione abesse.*

☞ *Ne non, ne nullus, ne nemo,* after the Imperative *vide,* "consider," must be rendered by "whether," or "that not—that no one." E. g., *Credere omnia quæ dicuntur vide ne non sit necesse ;* "Consider whether it be necessary to believe every thing," i. e., "remember that it is not necessary, etc."—*Vide ne nulla sit divinatio ;* "Consider whether such a science exists at all."

9. The particle *non,* placed before *nemo, nullus, nihil, nunquam,* renders the affirmation indefinite and incomplete ; but placed after them, definite and complete. Thus,

non nemo	means	*some one,*		nemo non	means	*every one,*
non nulli	"	*some,*		nullus non	"	*every one,*
non nihil	"	*something,*		nihil non	"	*every thing,*
non nunquam	"	*sometimes ;*		nunquam non	"	*always ;*

as, *Nemo non benignus est sui judex. Nulli non ad nocendum satis virium est. Hannibal non nihil temporis tribuit litteris. Athenienses Alcibiadem nihil non efficere posse ducebant. Nunquam non honorificentissime eum appellabat.*

When *nihil non, nunquam non, nusquam non,* have an Infinitive inserted between them, they retain their negative meaning, and are equivalent to an indefinite affirmation ; as, *Nihil agere animus non potest,* "cannot do nothing," i. e., must do s o m e t h i n g.—*Ubi sunt mortui aut quem locum incolunt ? Si enim sunt, nusquam esse non possunt,* "they cannot be nowhere," i. e., they must be s o m e w h e r e.

10. *Tantum quod,* in the Classical language, means "just," "just then," "hardly," "scarcely ;" and *tantum quod non,* "only that not," "nothing is wanting but." E. g., *Tantum quod ex Arpinati veneram, cum mihi a te litteræ redditæ sunt. Tantum quod hominem non nominat,* "he almost mentions him by name."

Tantum non, in Livy, and in the later prose writers, often occurs in the sense of "almost," "very nearly ;" as, *Nuntii afferebant tantum non* (only not) *jam captam Lacedæmonem esse. Videt Romanos tantum non jam circumveniri a dextro cornu.*

11 Enumerations are usually made by means of the numeral adverbs *primum, deinde, tum, denique,* or *postremo ;* as, *Primum mihi videtur de genere belli, deinde de magnitudine, tum de imperatore deligendo esse dicendum. Primum docent Stoici esse deos, deinde quales sint, tum mundum ab his administrari, postremo consulere eos rebus humanis.*

II. PREPOSITIONS.

§ 224.—The fundamental signification of each preposition has been already given § 77. This signification, however, in various passages suffers various modifications, with which the pupil should be duly acquainted, in order to comprehend more fully the sense of such passages. The more important of these modifications are exhibited in the following paragraphs :

Prepositions with the Accusative.

§ 225.—AD, 1) " near," " at " " close by ;" e. g., *pugna ad Cannas, ad Trebiam, ad Trasimenum ; urbs sita ad mare ; habet hortos ad Tiberim, ad portas urbis ; negotium habere ad portum* (— in portu) ;—2) " to," " toward," " till ;" e. g., *ad meridiem spectans ; ad lucem, ad vesperam,* towards daybreak, evening ; *ad multam noctem,* till late at night ; *ad summam senectutem tragœdias fecit ; ad Alpes* (as far as) *processerat ;*— 3) " about," " nearly" (of numerals) ; e. g., *annos ad quadraginta natus ; ad quingentos capti sunt ;* and adverbially in the sense of *circiter : occisis ad hominum millibus octo ;*—4) " in comparison with ;" e. g., *nihil ad Persium ; nihil ad hunc hominem ; terra ad universi cœli complexum quasi puncti instar obtinet ;*—5) " at," " on" (of a fixed time) ; e. g., *præsto esse ad horam destinatam, ad diem constitutam ; ad diem solvere,* " to pay on the day fixed upon ;"—6) " according to," " after ;" *ad voluntatem loqui, non ad veritatem ; ad speciem* or *similitudinem alicujus rei ; ad modum, ad normam, ad exemplum, ad nutum ;*—7) " in respect of," " as to ;" e. g., *homo ad labores belli impiger, ad consilia prudens.*

Phrases : *Ad tempus,* " for some time ;" as, *perturbatio animi plerumque brevis est et ad tempus ; ad præsens,* for the moment ; *ad extremum, ad ultimum,* at last, at length ; *ad unum omnes,* all to a man, even to the very last man ; *ad verbum,* word for word, literally ; *ad nummum convenit,* it agrees to a cent ; *omnia ad assem perdidit,* to the last cent or farthing.—(☞ Translate " at most" by *summum,* not by *ad summum.*)

APUD, 1) " by," " close by," " near," " with ;" e. g., *Apud Ægos flumen Athenienses victi sunt ; horam et amplius apud me fuit ; apud me nihil valet hominum opinio ; apud matrem recte est,* things go well with the mother ; *rectissime sunt apud te omnia ;*— 2) " in presence of," " before ;" e. g., *apud judices, apud prætorem, apud senatum verba facere ;*—3) " in the house of," " in the works or writings of ;" e. g., *Fuisti apud Leccam illa nocte ; Neptolēmus apud Lycomēdem educatus est ; apud Xenophontem Cyrus negat ; apud Ciceronem legimus.*

CIRCA, CIRCUM, " around ;" as, *urbes circa Capuam ; multos canes circum* or *circa se habebat ; terra circum axem se convertit.—Mittere aliquem circum amicos, circum vicinos, circum insulas,* etc., means, " to send somebody around to one's friends, neighbors, to the surrounding isles.—CIRCA is used also of time, in the sense of " about," "toward;" e. g., *postero die circa eandem horam ; circa meridiem ; circa Nonas.*—In the sense of "concerning," it occurs only in the later prose ; as, *varia circum hæc opinio ; Tiberius circa deos negligentior fuit.*

CIRCITER, "about," occurs with the accusative of time ; as, *circiter horam octavam ; circiter Calendas Septembres.*—CIRCITER is more commonly used as an adverb, as, *diebus circiter quindecim ; ex omni copia circiter pars quarta armis erat instructa.*

CIS, CITRA, "on this side" (opp. to *trans* and *ultra*).—CIS is generally used of rivers and mountains ; as, *cis Rhenum, cis Taurum montem :* CITRA, also of other places ; as, *citra Rubiconem ; is locus est citra Leucădem.*—In later writers *citra* frequently occurs in the sense of *sine ;* as, *citra invidiam nominare ; plus usus sine doctrina, quam citra usum doctrina valet.*

CONTRA, 1) "against" (always in a hostile sense) ; as, *contra leges, contra naturam ; Belgæ olim contra Populum Romanum conjurarunt ;*—2) "over against," "opposite ;" as, *Insulæ Britanniæ unum latus est contra Galliam.*—*Contra*, adv., like *contrario*, means "on the contrary." ☞ *Econtra* is not Latin.

JUXTA, "beside," "close by ;" as, *juxta murum ; sepultus est juxta viam Appiam.*—Sometimes it means "next to," "immediately after" (of rank and estimation) ; e. g., *apud quos juxta divinas religiones fides humana colitur.*—In the sense of *secundum*, "according to," *juxta* is unclassical ; hence, *juxta Platonem, juxta Tacitum, juxta præceptum Themistoclis*, and similar expressions, should be avoided.
Juxta, taken adverbially, means "equally,". "in like manner ;" as, *litteris Græcis juxta atque Latinis eruditus ; juxta boni maliqus obtruncati sunt.*

OB, "an account of ;" as, *ob hoc ipsum*, for this very reason ; *ob commodum suum dixit.*—It sometimes occurs in the sense of *ante ;* as, *non mihi mors, non exilium ob oculos versantur.*

PER, 1) "through," "throughout," "all along," "all over ;" as, *erant duo itinera, unum per Sequanos, alterum per provinciam ; hospitaliter per domos invitati*, i. e., from house to house, in or throughout all the houses ; *milites fuga per proximas civitates dissipati ; per agros vagari ; religiones per manus traditæ*, from hand to hand ;—2) "during ;" e. g., *luscinia per totam noctem cantat ; per quatuor annos abfuit ; per quietem, per somnum, per idem tempus ;*—3) "through," i. e., by the means of (of persons) ; as, *per te salvus sum ; injurias per vos ulcisci statuerunt ; per me hoc didici*, by myself ;—4) "on account of," in such phrases as *per ætatem, per invaletudinem, per morbum gravem non potuit prœlio interesse ; per me licet*, as far as I am concerned, as to me ;—5) "by," in adjurations and exclamations ; as, *jurare per Jovem deosque penates ; per deos atque homines te oro ; per deos immortales !*
☞ *Per* is often used to express the manner in which a thing is done ; as, *per ludum ac jocum*, by play and joke ; *per litteras*, by letter ; *per scelus*, criminally ; *per injuriam*, unjustly ; *per insaniam*, in a fit of madness ; *per vices*, by turns ; *per iram*, in anger ; *per ordinem*, in order : *per speciem* or *similitudinem*, under the cloak or color of....

POST, "after," "behind," "since ;" e. g., *post meridiem, post tres annos ; post principia*, behind the first line ; *post me erat urbs, ante me silva ; post hominum memoriam*, within the recollection of ; *post natos homines*, since the creation, or from time immemorial.

PRÆTER, 1) "besides," i. e., together with, not to mention ; as, *præter auctoritatem etiam vires ad coercendum habet ;*—2) "besides," "except ;" as, *præter se neminem amat ; nec hominis quidquam in eo erat præter figuram et speciem ;*—3) "contrary o," " against ;" as, *præter spem, præter consuetudinem, præter opinionem, præter naturam, præter modum*, beyond measure ;—4) " before," " along" (implying the idea of passing by) ; as, *servi præter oculos Lollii pocula ferebant ;*—5) " before" (with the idea of distinction) ; as, *præter alios, præter omnes ; Aristides præter ceteros Justus est appellatus.*

PROPE, " near," *propius, proxime ;* as, *prope urbem, proxime pontem, propius montem. (Propius* and *proxime* take also the dative.)—*Prope* is sometimes followed by the ablative with *ab ;* e. g., *Tam prope a muris hostem habemus.*

PROPTER, " on account of," " owing to ;" as, *more propter brevitatem vitæ nunquam longe abest.* It is used also in the sense of *prope*, " near ;" as, *duo filii propter patrem cubantes ; propter rivum ambulaverunt.*

SECUNDUM, 1) " according to," " in conformity with ;" as, *secundum arbitrium tuum, secundum Platonem ; secundum naturam vivere ;*—2) " along ;" as, *legiones secundum flumen duxit ad urbem Gergoviam ; secundum mare iter facere ;*—3) " after," " immediately after," " next to ;" as, *secundum comitia ; vulnus secundum aurem ; secundum Deum homines hominibus maxime utiles esse possunt ; secundum te nihil mihi amicius salitudine ;*—4) " in favor of ;" as, *secundum te* (to thy advantage) *decrevit ; multa secundum causam nostram disputavit.*

Prepositions with the Ablative.

§ 226.—AB, 1) " from ;" as, *a prima ætate, a principio, ab infantia, a pueritia* or *a puero ; ingenuis artibus a pueris dediti sumus ; ab adolescentia* or *ab adolescentulo ; ab ortu et occasu solis ; a fronte et a tergo*, in front and in the rear ; *a dextro (sinistro) cornu ; a radicibus, a fundamento ;*—2) " from," " against ;" as, *se defendere a frigore, a calore, ab hostibus ; custodiunt templum ab Hannibale ;*—3) " as to," " with regard to ;" e. g., *mediocriter a doctrina instructus ; ab æquitatu firmus ; a matre tibi cognatus sum*, on the mother's side ;—4) " next to," " immediately after ;" as, *proximus a rege ; confestim a cæna, a funere, a prælio ;*—5) " in consequence of," " out of," " from ;" as, *a spe, ab ira, ab eadem animi fiducia ;*—6) denoting an office ; as, *alicui esse a manu*, an amanuensis ; *ab epistolis*, a secretary ; *a rationibus*, a keeper of accounts ; *a pedibus*, a footman, servant ;—7) denoting the followers of a school ; as, *a Platone, ab Aristotele, a Socrate* (sc. *profecti*).

☞ *Interire ab aliquo* is — *occidi ab aliquo ;* as, *interiit a paucis*, he fell by the hands of a few ; *facere, sentire, stare ab aliquo* — to side with some one, to be of his party.

DE, 1) " from," " down from," " from among," " out of ;" e. g., *de tecto cadere ; extorquere sicam de manibus ; homo de plebe ; unus de multis ; de meo, de tuo, de alieno, de publico* (sc. *sumptu*), at my (thy, etc.) expense ;—2) " just after" (of time) ; as, *statim de prandio, statim de auctione ; de nocte*, at night ; *de tertia vigilia ; de die*, in broad daylight ; *navigare de* ('in') *mense Decembri ;*—3) " after," " according to ;" as, *de more ; de suorum sententia ; de consilio meo ; de Dionysio sum admiratus*, as regards, as for, or concerning ;—4) " about," " on," " respecting ;" as, *cogitare, loqui, scribere de aliqua re ;*—5) sometimes in the sense of *ab* or *ex ;* as, *hoc puer de patre meo audivi.*

Phrases : *De industria*, purposely ; *de integro*, afresh ; *de improviso*, unawares ; *nosse aliquem de facie*, by his appearance ; *expectare, differre diem de die*, or *diem ex die* (but not *de die in diem*), to be waiting, to put off day after day.

EX, 1) " from," " out of ;" e. g., *ex Italia redierunt ; ex equo pugnare* or *colloqui :*

scribere ex itinere, on the road ; *ex fuga*, during flight ; *ex omni parte*, from all parts ; *ex superiore loco dicere* ; *ex aliquo audire, scire* ; *pendēre ex arbore* ;—2) "from," "ever since," "directly after ;" as, *ex illo die* or *tempore* ; *ex consulatu* (*ex dictatura*) *in Galliam profectus* ; *diem ex die*, from day to day, or day after day ;—3) "out of," "from among ;" as, *unus ex multis, unus e plebe* ;—4) "according to," "in accordance with ;" as, *ex testamento, ex lege, ex consuetudine, ex senatus-consulto* or *auctoritate* ; *vivere e natura* ;—5) "from," "on account of" (denoting cause) ; as, *laborare ex capite, ex oculis, e renibus, e pedibus* ; *perire ex vulneribus* ; *e via languere* ; *ex lassitudine dormire.*

Phrases : *Est e re mea, e re tua, e re nostra, e republica*, it is for my good or advantage, etc. ; *ex animo*, heartily, sincerely ; *ex sententia* or *voluntate*, according to one's wish ; *ex composito*, according to agreement ; *ex parte*, partly ; *ex æquo*, with equal right or advantage ; *ex adverso, e regione*, opposite ; *e longinquo*, from afar ; *ex propinquo*, close by ; *e contrario*, on the contrary ; *ex tempore*, this instant, forthwith ; *e vestigio*, on the spot ; *ex usu*, useful.

PRÆ, 1) "before," with *fero* (also *ago*) and a pronoun, as *pugionem præ se tulit*, he held before him ; *præ se agere gregem, armentum* ;—2) "in comparison with," "above or more than ;" e. g., *præ se omnes contemnit* ; *omnes præ illo parvi futuros existimo* ; *Athenæ præ ceteris urbibus Græciæ floruere* ;—3) "through," "on account of" (of preventive causes) ; e. g., *præ dolore loqui non potuit* ; *solem præ sagittarum multitudine non videbitis.*—☞ The phrase *præ se ferre* often signifies "to show," "display ;" as, *speciem boni viri præ se ferre* ; *animum altum præ se ferre.*

PRO, 1) "before," "in front of," "close by ;" e. g., *pro vallo, pro castris, pro oppido, pro templo* ; also "in," "upon," "from," as *pro tribunali edicere, pro suggestu pronuntiare, pro rostris dicere* or *laudare* ;—2) "in proportion to," "according to," "in conformity with ;" as, *pro multitudine hominum* ; *prælium atrox pro numero pugnantium* ; *pro magnitudine periculi* ; *pro tua humanitate, prudentia, sapientia* ; *agere pro viribus* or *pro virili parte*, according to one's power or capacity ; *pro tempore, pro temporibus, pro re* or *pro re nata*, according to circumstances or emergencies ; *pro portione*, in proportion ; *pro rata portione* or *pro rata parte*, in certain proportions, proportionally ; *pro mea, tua, sua, nostra, vestra parte*, for my part, etc. ; *pro se quisque*, every one for his part ; *pro eo ut, pro eo ac*, according as, e. g., *pro eo ac debui*, according to my duty ;—3) "for," i. e., instead of, just as much as ; e. g., *alicui esse pro patre*, to act as a father ; *esse* or *se gerere pro cive* ; *habere aliquid pro certo, aliquem pro amico*, to consider as ; *unus Plato est mihi pro centum millibus* ;—4) "for," i. e., for the benefit of ; e. g., *pugnare pro patria, pro libertate* ; *verba facere pro aliquo.*

☞ For the prepositions IN and SUB, see § 78.

III. Conjunctions.

§ 227.—Whatever was deemed essential to be known with regard to the signification, division, and use of the conjunctions, has been already stated either in the Elementary or in the Syntactical part of the Grammar. The following additional remarks, however, will not fail to be useful to the student.

1. The conjunctions *ac* and *atque* are generally used in the sense of "as" or "than," after *æque, juxta, pariter, perinde, pro eo, similiter, totidem, aliter,*

ntra, *secus, alius, contrarius, similis, talis ;* as, *Felicitate tua æque gaudeo ac : ipse. Non perinde atque ego putaram, res evenerat.* *Pro eo tibi ac mereris, ·atiam referent. Cum totidem navibus atque erat profectus, Athenas rediit. ┌on aliter loquor ac sentio. Omnia fere contra ac speravi, evenerant. Tuam ιlutem non secus ac meam tueor. Aliud mihi ac tibi videtur. Similis Romæ ιavor erat ac fuit bello Gallico. Hannibalem in suspicionem adduxerunt tam- uam alia atque antea sentire.*

2. The conjunction *et* sometimes stands for *etiam;* e. g., *Non errasti, mater, ιam et hic Alexander est. Adjuvare nos possunt non tantum ii qui sunt, sed t qui fuerunt.*

3. *Etsi* and *quamquam* (although) are sometimes used in absolute sentences ιn the sense of "yet," to correct a preceding statement ; e. g., *Quamquam quid 'oquor ?* "Yet, why do I speak ?"—*Do pœnas temeritatis meæ : etsi quæ fuit illa temeritas ?*

4. *Autem* is sometimes used in the sense of *quid ego dico ?* to correct an ex- pression just made use of ; as, *Inţelligis quam meum sit scire et curare quid in republica fiat ; fiat autem ? immo vero quid futurum sit. Ferendus tibi in hoc error meus, ferendus autem ? immo vero etiam adjuvandus.*

5. The disjunctives *aut, vel* (ve), and *sive* (seu) are thus distinguished :

AUT stands when things and expressions are so opposed to each other that if one is, the other is not; e. g., *Hic vincendum aut moriendum, milites, est. Quidquid enuntiatur, aut verum est aut falsum. Audendum est aliquid uni- versis aut omnia singulis patienda.*—*Aut* stands also in the restrictive sense of " at least," to connect something less important with something more im- portant ; e. g., *Eripe mihi hunc dolorem aut minue saltem. Profecto cuncti aut magna pars Siccensium fidem mutavissent.*

VEL is the Imperative from *velle,* as *fer* from *ferre.* It means " if you please," and implies that it is indifferent which of several things takes place. *Vel,* for the most part, distinguishes only single words, more rarely whole clauses ; and when it does so, it implies not diametrical opposition, but·only a slight distinction ; e. g., *Gallia vel Britannia bellum inferet* (i. e., one or the other, no matter which).—*Vel imperatore vel milite me utimini* (i. e., use me in any capacity you like).—*Proceres vel corrumpere vel corrigere mores civitatis possunt* (i. e., they can do which they please).—*Hæc vel ad odium, vel ad miseri- cordiam, vel omnino* (or in general) *ad animos judicum movendos utilissima sunt. Non sentiunt viri fortes in acie vulnera, vel si sentiunt, se mori malunt.*—*Vel* is often used in the sense of " or rather," to correct a preceding expression ; as *Peteres vel potius rogares. Stuporem hominis vel dicam pecudis videte. Valde me diligit, vel ut ἐμφατικώτερον dicam, valde me amat.*

VE (abridged from *vel*) unites single w o r d s ; as, *ter quaterve ; plus minusve. Ea esse dico quæ cerni tangive possunt* (i. e., either of the two will suffice.)

SIVE (*seu*) generally denote synonymes and expresses the e q u i v a l e n c e of words or clauses; e. g., *Pallas sive Minerva; Mars sive Mâvors; Danubia sive Ister.* *Sive—sive (seu—seu)* is commonly used when the English "either—or" is the same as "be it .... or be it," "be it that .... or that;" e. g., *Illo loco libentissime soleo uti sive quid mecum ipse cogito, sive aliquid scribo aut lego.*

SEU is common in poetry and late prose. Cicero uses it only in combination with *potius;* as, *Regie seu potius tyrannice.* *O fortunatum hominem qui ejusmodi nuntios seu potius pegasos habet!*

6. *Nisi*, after negatives and after questions implying a negative, is often used in the sense of "except" or "than," instead of *præter* or *præterquam;* e. g., *Nihil arbitramur expedire nisi* (or *præterquam*) *quod rectum honestumque sit.* *Quid est pietas nisi* (or *præterquam*) *voluntas grata in parentes?* *Quem unquam senatus civem nisi* (or *præter*) *me nationibus exteris commendavit!—* When no negative precedes, *præterquam* only or *præter* can stand; as, *Præda omnis præterquam hominum captorum* (or *præter homines captos*) *militi concessa est.*

The English "except that" is expressed indiscriminately by *nisi quod* and *præterquam quod*, even where no negative precedes. But when a purpose is implied, *nisi ut* must be used; e. g., *Mihi omnia eum eo sunt communia nisi quod* (or *præterquam quod*) *in philosophia vehementer ab eo dissentio.* *Nihil aliud ex hac re quæro nisi ut intelligas.*

After *nihil aliud,—nisi* as well as *quam* may follow, with this difference, however, that *nihil aliud nisi* means "nothing more than," and *nihil aliud quam,* "nothing else than;" e. g., *Bellum ita suscipiatur ut nihil aliud nisi pax quæsita videatur.* *Nihil aliud molitus est quam ut omnes civitates in sua teneret potestate.*

APPENDIX.

I. ELLIPSIS.

§ 228.—Ellipsis is the omission of some word or words which are essential to the grammatical construction of sentences, but which can be readily inferred from the context.

The following words are frequently omitted:

Nouns.

1. *Ædes* or *templum ;* e. g., *Ventum erat ad Vestæ. Senatus habitus est ad Apollinis.*

2. *Aqua,* as *calida, frigida ;* e. g., *Ex labore sudanti frigidæ potio perniciosissima est.*

3. *Caro,* as *agnina, bubula, canina, ferina, porcina ;* e. g., *Pœni a Dario canina vesci prohibebantur.*

4. *Castra,* as *æstiva, hiberna, stativa ;* e. g., *Tres legiones ex hibernis educit.*

5. *Febris,* as *tertiana, quartana ;* e. g., *Modo audivi quartanam a te discessisse.*

6. *Homo ;* e. g., *Boni sunt rari.*—Thus *amicus, civis, miles,* when they stand with a possessive pronoun; as, *Cognovi ex meorum omnium litteris. Hannibalem sui ejecerunt. Cæsar suos misit. Insequentes nostros, ne longius prosequerentur, Sulla revocavit.*

7. *Locus* and *manus;* e. g., *Non habeo quo confugiam. Ubi ad Dianæ veneris, ito ad dextram.*

8. *Partes,* in such phrases as *alicui primas dare, concedere, deferre ;* e. g., *Amoris erga me tibi primas defero,* "I give you the first place among those who love me."

9. *Prædium,* as *Tusculanum, Pompeianum ;* e. g., *Miraris quod me Laurentinum meum tantopere delectet.*

10. *Verba ;* e. g., *Ne multa, ne plura, quid plura,* sc. *verba dicam.—Ne multis* (sc. *verbis utar*), *Diogenes emitur.—Quid multa? sic mihi persuasi non posse esse animum mortalem.*

11. *Via ;* e. g., *Xerxes, qua sex mensibus iter fecerat, eādem minus diebus triginta in Asiam reversus est.*

Verbs.

§ 229.—1. *Dico, inquit, respondeo,* in quoting a person's words or opinion, and *facio,* in expressing our own opinion ; e. g., *Tum ille. Hic ego.—Capins olim : non omnibus dormio. Recte ille* (fecit) ; *melius hi* (fecerunt). *Nihil per vim unquam Clodius, omnia per vim Milo* (sc. fecit).

2. *Facio, flo,* after *nihil aliud quam, quid aliud quam, nihil præterquam ;* e. g., " They do nothing but laugh," or " they are merely laughing ;" *Nihil aliud quam rident.—Tissaphernes nihil aliud quam bellum comparavit. Per biduum nihil aliud quam steterunt parati ad pugnandum. Illa nocte nihil* (sc. fiebat) *præterquam vigilátum est.* ☞ This form of expression is found in Livy, Nepos, Curtius, etc. ; but it does not occur in Cicero.

3. *Oro, precor, obsecro,* in adjurations ; as, *Propera, per deos ; scis enim quantum sit in celeritate. Per ego vos deos patrios, vindicate ab ultimo dedecore nomen gentemque Persarum.*

4. *Pertinere,* " to concern ;" e. g., *Quid hoc ad me? Quid ad te? Quorsus hoc?* " What is that for ?"—*Recte an secus, nihil ad nos. Zaleucus sive fui sive non fuit, nihil ad rem. Quid ad Cæsarem, quid agat nostra Germania?*

5. *Quod* sometimes stands (especially in letters) for *quod attinet ad id quod,* " with regard to," " as regards the fact that ;" e. g., " With regard to what you write about your coming to see me, I wish you to remain there :" *Quod scribis te si velim, ad me venturam : ego vero te istic esse volo. Quod mihi de nostro statu gratularis : minime miramur te tuo opere lætari. Quod scribis te velle scire qui sit reipublicæ status : summa dissensio est. Quod scire vis, qua quisque in te fide sit et voluntate, difficile dictu est de singulis.*

6. *Scito, scitote,* or (in indirect Narration) *sciat, sciret,*—especially after *quod* in the sense of *quod attinet ad id quod ;* e. g., *Quod mihi Pompeiam uxorem tuam commendas,* (scito) *cum Sura nostro statim, tuis litteris lectis, locutus sum. Legationi Cæsaris Ariovistus respondit : quod sibi Cæsar denuntiaret, se Æduorum injurias non neglecturum,* (sciret) *neminem secum sine sua pernicie contendisse.*

7. *Quid? quod*—frequently occurs instead of *quid dicam de eo quod,* and may be rendered by " nay," " nay even," " moreover ;" e. g., *Quid, quod salus sociorum in periculum vocatur? Orpheus in animum meum sæpe incurrit : quid, quod earum rerum, quæ nunquam omnino fuerunt, neque esse potuerunt, ut Scyllæ, ut Chimœræ, præsto est imago.*

8. An Infinitive is often to be supplied in indirect Narration after relatives, where the verb, if it were repeated, would be put either in the Indicative or

ubjunctive, according as the writer wished to express his own sentiment or that of another; e. g., *Fateor me in ea parte fuisse qua te*, or *qua tu fuisti. Fatetur se in ea parte fuisse qua me*, or *qua ipse fuerim. Cumanos ejusdem conditionis, cujus Capuam, esse placuit*, or *cujus Capua esset.*

Particles.

§ 230.—1. The conjunction *ut* is sometimes omitted, when a clause precedes with *ne; e. g., Patres Conscripti legatos in Bythiniam miserunt, qui ab rege peterent ne inimicissimum suum secum haberet sibique dederet. Monere cœpit Porum ne ultima experiri perseveraret dederetque se victori.*—The conjunction *et, que*, or *atque*, may in such passages be rendered by "but."

2. In the formula *non modo non—sed ne-quidem* (or *sed vix*), the second *non* is sometimes expressed, and sometimes omitted.

Non is expressed, when each clause of the sentence has its own finite verb, or when the finite verb stands in the first, in case there should be but one, common to both. E. g., *Ego tibi non modo non irascor, sed ne reprehendo, quidem factum tuum. Ille non modo non præerat ulli negotio, sed etiam ne intererat quidem.—Horum summorum imperatorum non modo res gestas non antepono meis, sed ne fortunam quidem ipsam. Id non modo re prohibere non licet, sed ne verbis quidem vituperare.*

Non is omitted, when the sentence has but one finite verb, expressed in the second clause.—In English, either the first clause is introduced by "not only not," and the second by "but not even" "but scarcely;"—or the order of the clauses is inverted, and then the former introduced by "not even," the latter by "much less." E. g., *Vir bonus non modo facere, sed ne cogitare quidquam audebit, quod non honestum sit. Assentatio non modo amico, sed ne libero quidem digna est. Tales homines non modo sine cura quiescere, sed ne spirare quidem sine metu possunt. Camillorum, Fabriciorum, Curiorum virtutes non solum in moribus nostris, sed vix jam in libris reperiuntur.*

II. FIGURES OF SYNTAX.

§ 231.—Syntactical Figures are certain deviations from the ordinary connection and arrangement of words. They are by various Grammarians variously divided and subdivided. The author, for the sake of reference, has preferred to present them here alphabetically arranged.

1. ANACOLUTHON, when the latter part of a sentence does not correspond in construction with the former; as, *Dum hæc ita fierent, rex Juba, cognitis Cæsaris difficultatibus copiarumque paucitate, non est visum, dari spatium convalescendi. Unum hoc certe videor mihi verissime posse dicere tum quum haberet respublica Luscinos—*(thus far, indirect: what follows, direct) *et tum quum erant Catones,—tamen hujuscemodi res commissa nemini est.*

2. ANASTROPHE is an inversion of the natural order of words; as, *Ego si*

potero, faciam vobis satis. Atheniensibus exhaustis præter arma et naves, nihil erat super.—Transtra per et remos. Spem metumque inter.

3. ASYNDETON is the omission of connectives; as, *Abiit, excessit, evasit, erupit. Ostentas patientiam famis, frigoris, inopiæ omnium rerum. Equidem non deero: monebo, prædicam, denuntiabo, testabor semper Deos hominesque quid sentiam. Ex cupiditatibus odium, dissidia, discordiæ, seditiones, bella nascuntur.*

4. ENALLAGE is a change of words, or a substitution of one gender, number, case, person, tense, mood, or voice, of the same word for another; as, *Populus late rex,* for *regnans. Romanus prælio victor,* for *Romani victores. Hostis habet muros,* for *hostes habent muros. Nostrum istud vivere triste,* for *vita nostra. Omnia Ciceronis patent Trebiano,* for *omnia mea tibi patent. Rem vides quomodo se habeat,* for *vides quomodo se res habeat. Nosti Marcellum quam tardus sit,* for *nosti quam tardus Marcellus sit.*

5. EVOCATIO is a figure by which a verb in the first or second person, is joined to a noun or pronoun of the third person; as, *Quisque suos patimur manes. Hannibal peto pacem qui neque peterem nisi utilem crederem.*

6. HELLENISM, or GRECISM, is the use of Greek forms and constructions; as, *Pallada, Cyclopas,* for *Palladem, Cyclopes. Opaca locorum,* for *opaca loca. Os humerosque Deo similis,* for *ore humerisque. Desine querelarium,* for *a querelis. Dignus amari,* for *qui ametur. Ibit frenare cohortes,* for *frenatum.*

7. HENDIADYS is the expression of one idea by two substantives connected by *et (que)*, where one of the substantives stands in place of an adjective or a genitive; e. g., *Pateris libamus et auro,* for *pateris aureis. Ex tenebris et carcere procedere,* for *e tenebroso carcere. Jactari æstu et febri,* for *æstu febris. Redimitus floribus coronisque,* for *coronis e floribus factis. Devinctus necessitudine ac vetustate,* for *vetusta necessitudine. Veteranos coloniamque deducere,* for *coloniam veteranorum. Aliquid prodere ad memoriam posteritatemque,* for *ad memoriam posteritatis. Alicui inferre vim et manus,* for *violentas manus.*

8. HYPALLAGE is an interchange of constructions, and a transferring of attributes from their proper subjects to others. E. g., *Dare classibus Austros,* for *classes Austris. Vina quæ cadis onerarat Acestes,* for *quibus cados. Fontium gelidæ perennitates,* for *fontium gelidorum perennitates.*

9. HYSTERON PROTERON is reversing the natural order of the sense, by placing (of two ideas) that first which should be last; as, *Valet atque vivit,* for *vivit atque valet. Moriamur et in media arma ruamus. Incendere ac diripere urbes.*

10. PERIPHRASIS or CIRCUMLOCUTION is a circuitous mode of expression; as, *Teneri fœtus ovium,* for *agni. Non ætate confectis, non mulieribus, non infantibus pepercit,* for *nemini pepercit. Omnes memoriam consulatus tui, mores, faciem, denique ac nomen detestantur,* for *te. Quis sibi persuadeat esse aliquem humana specie et figura, qui tantum immanitate bestias vicerit, ut, propter quos*

anc suavissimam lucem aspexerit, eos indignissime luce privarit, for *quis credat sse hominem qui parentes suos occidere possit ?*

11. PLEONASM is using a greater number of words than is necessary to ex)ress the meaning; *Erant omnino itinera duo quibus itineribus domo exire pos-*ent. *Somnum ego hac nocte oculis non vidi meis. Sic ore locuta est. Tuus lolor humanus est is quidem, sed tamen moderandus.*

12. POLYSYNDETON is a redundancy of connectives ; as; *Post hunc maximam habere vim arbitrantur Apollinem, et Martem, et Jovem, et Minervam. Una Eurusque Notusque ruunt, creberque procellis Africus. Ex cupiditatibus odium, et dissidia, et discordiæ, et seditiones, et bella nascuntur.*

13. SYNCHYSIS is a confused and intricate arrangement of words ; as, *Saxa vocant Itali mediis quæ in fluctibus aras,* for *quæ saxa in mediis fluctibus Itali vocant aras. Pœne macros arsit dum turdos versat in igni,* for *pœne arsit dum macros turdos,* etc. *Non erit melius, inquit, nisi de quo consulimus, vocem misisse,* for *melius erit, non misisse vocem, nisi de quo consulimus.*

14. SYNESIS or *constructio ad sensum,* when the construction refers to the sense rather than to the precise nature of the words ; as, *Latium Capuaque agro multati sunt. Ubi illic est scelus* (where is that scoundrel) *qui me per-didit ? Incitabant Catilinam corrupti civitatis mores quos luxuria atque avaritia vexabant* (= *mores civium quos,* etc.).

15. TMESIS, or DIACOPE, is the separating of a compound word by the inter-position of another word ; as, *Septem subjecta trioni gens,* for *septentrioni. Quale id cunque est. Altera pars per mihi brevis videtur. Thais maximo te orabat opere, ut cras redires.*

16. ZEUGMA is the uniting of two substantives to a verb, which is applicable only to one of them ; as, *Jugurtha, pacem an bellum gerens periculosior esset, in incerto habebatur* (here *gerens* is applicable to *bellum* only, because *pacem gerere* is not said). *Magonem alii naufragio, alii a servis interfectum scriptum reliquerunt* (we say *naufragio perire,* but not *naufragio interfici*).

III. THE ROMAN CALENDAR.

§ 232.—The Romans did not reckon the days of the month in an uninterrupted series, as we do, from the first to the last. They dis-tinguished in every month three principal days : the *Calendæ, Nonæ,* and *Idus,*—from which they counted backward.

The *Calendæ* were always the first day of the month ; the *Nonæ* fell on the 5th, and the *Idus* on the 13th, except in March, May, July, and October, in which the *Nonæ* fell on the 7th, and the *Idus* on the 15th.—The day preceding the *Calendæ, Nonæ,* and *Idus,* was called *pridie* (i. e., *pridie ante*) *Calendas, Nonas, Idus.*

Our days.	March, May, July, October (31 days).	January, August, December (31 days).	April, June, September, November (30 days).	Febr. has 28 days (in leap-years 29).
1.	Calendis.	Calendis.	Calendis.	Calendis.
2.	VI. ⎫	IV. ⎫ ante	IV. ⎫ ante	IV. ⎫ ante
3.	V. ⎬ ante	III. ⎭ Nonas.	III. ⎭ Nonas.	III. ⎭ Nonas.
4.	IV. ⎬ Nonas.	Pridie Nonas.	Pridie Nonas.	Pridie Nonas.
5.	III. ⎭	Nonis.	Nonis.	Nonis.
6.	Pridie Nonas.	VIII. ⎫	VIII. ⎫	VIII. ⎫
7.	Nonis.	VII. ⎮	VII. ⎮	VII. ⎮
8.	VIII. ⎫	VI. ⎬ ante	VI. ⎬ ante	VI. ⎬ ante
9.	VII. ⎮	V. ⎭ Idus.	V. ⎭ Idus.	V. ⎭ Idus.
10.	VI. ⎬ ante	IV. ⎮	IV. ⎮	IV. ⎮
11.	V. ⎬ Idus.	III. ⎭	III. ⎭	III. ⎭
12.	IV. ⎮	Pridie Idus.	Pridie Idus.	Pridie Idus.
13.	III. ⎭	Idibus.	Idibus.	Idibus.
14.	Pridie Idus.	XIX. ⎫	XVIII. ⎫	XVI. ⎫
15.	Idibus.	XVIII. ⎮	XVII. ⎮	XV. ⎮
16.	XVII. ⎫	XVII. ⎮	XVI. ⎮	XIV. ⎮
17.	XVI. ⎮	XVI. ⎮	XV. ⎮	XIII. ⎮
18.	XV. ⎮	XV. ⎮	XIV. ⎮	XII. ⎮
19.	XIV. ⎮	XIV. ⎮	XIII. ⎮	XI. ⎮
20.	XIII. ⎮	XIII. ⎮	XII. ⎮	X. ⎮
21.	XII. ⎮	XII. ⎮	XI. ⎮	IX. ⎮
22.	XI. ⎬ ante Calendas (of the month following).	XI. ⎬ ante Calendas (of the month following).	X. ⎬ ante Calendas (of the month following).	VIII. ⎬ ante Calendas Martias.
23.	X. ⎮	X. ⎮	IX. ⎮	VII. ⎮
24.	IX. ⎮	IX. ⎮	VIII. ⎮	VI. ⎮
25.	VIII. ⎮	VIII. ⎮	VII. ⎮	V. ⎮
26.	VII. ⎮	VII. ⎮	VI. ⎮	IV. ⎮
27.	VI. ⎮	VI. ⎮	V. ⎮	III. ⎭
28.	V. ⎮	V. ⎮	IV. ⎮	Pridie Calendas Martias.
29.	IV. ⎮	IV. ⎮	III. ⎭	
30.	III. ⎭	III. ⎭		
31.	Pridie Calend. (of the month following).	Pridie Calend. (of the month following).	Pridie Calend. (of the month following).	

NOTE 1.—The names of the months are sometimes used substantively, as *pridie Nonas Februarii.*—The best writers, however, use them as adjectives, and make them agree with *Calendæ, Nonæ,* and *Idus ;* as, *Pridie Nonas Februarias. Calendis Sextilibus veni Syracusas. Ecce Calendis Juniis mutata omnia! Pridie Nonas Junias litteras tuas accepi. Ea mente discessi ut adessem Calendis Januariis.*

Before the time of the emperors, the month of July was called *Quintilis,* and the month of August, *Sextilis.*

NOTE 2.—In leap years (*anni intercalares*) the month of February had one day more ; but this intercalary day, instead of being added at the end of the month, as it is the custom in modern times, was inserted after the 23d of February, so that the 24th of Febr. was reckoned double, and was for this reason called *dies bisextus* (*bis sextus*), whence the leap year itself received the name *annus bisextus* or *bisextilis*.

Construction of time according to the Roman Calendar

§ 233.—1. ON WHAT DAY?—The question *when?* or *on what day?* is answered by the ablative when the day is one of the three principal days of the month; as, *Calendis, Nonis, Idibus.*—The day immediately preceding the *Calendæ, Nonæ,* and *Idus,* is expressed by *pridie* with the accusative, and sometimes, though more rarely, with the genitive; as, *pridie Calendas, pridie Nonas, pridie Idus, pridie Calendarum.*

The remaining days are expressed either (a) by the ablative: as, " He died on the 30th of Dec. ;" *Obiit die tertio ante Calendas Januarias,* and abridged, without *die* and *ante : Obiit tertio Calendas Januarias* (obiit III. Cal. Jan.);—or (b) by *ante diem* with the accusative; as, *obiit ante diem tertium Calendas Januarias* (obiit a. d. III. Cal. Jan.).

☞ The formula *ante diem* with the accusative, difficult as it is to be explained grammatically, was almost exclusively used by Cicero and Livy. The " *ante diem*" was treated as an indeclinable substantive to which, like to other substantives, various prepositions were prefixed: but, whatever the preposition prefixed might be, *ad, in, ab,* or *ex,* it was invariably followed by the accusative.

2. BY WHAT DAY?—The question *by* or *for what day?* is answered by the accusative with *in, ad, usque ad ;* as, *Capuam venire jussi sumus ad Nonas Februarias* (by the 5th of Febr.),—*ad pridie Idus Februarias* (by the 12th of Febr.),—*ad ante diem sextum Calendas Martias* (ad a. d. VI. Cal. Mart., by the 24th of Febr.). *Nos in Formiano esse volumus usque ad pridie Nonas Martias* (by the 6th of March). *Consul comitia in ante diem tertium Nonas Sextiles* (in a. d. III. Non. Sext., " he fixed the elections by an edict for the 3d of August) *edixit.*

3. FROM WHAT DAY?—The question *from what day?* is answered by the ablative with *ab* or *ex ;* as, *Ludi Antii futuri sunt a IV. ad pridie Nonas Maias* (from the 4th to the 6th of May). *De Quinto fratre nuntii nobis tristes venerant ex ante diem Nonas Junias* (= *ex* or *a Nonis Juniis*) *usque ad pridie Calendas Septembres* (from the 5th of June to the 31st of August).

NOTE.—The next day after the *Cal., Nonæ,* and *Idus,* may be expressed also by *postridie ;* as, *Postridie Calendas Maias,* the 2d of May ; *postridie Nonas Martias,* the 8th of March ; *postridie Idus Decembres,* the 14th of December.

Method of reducing Roman time to our own.

§ 234.—1. To reduce the *Calendæ,* add 2 to the number of days of the preceding month : from the sum subtract the given date, and the remainder will give you our date. Thus,

XII.	Cal. Febr.	Jan. has 31 days ;	$31 + 2 = 33$; $33 - 12 = 21$st of Jan.
VIII.	Cal. Mart.	Febr. has 28 days ;	$28 + 2 = 30$; $30 - 8 = 22$d of Febr.
XIII.	Cal. Jun.	May has 31 days ;	$31 + 2 = 33$; $33 - 13 = 20$th of May.
XVI.	Cal. Dec.	Nov. has 30 days ;	$30 + 2 = 32$; $32 - 16 = 16$th of Nov.

2. To reduce the *Nonæ* and *Idus*, add 1 to the number of the day on which the *Nonæ* or *Idus* fall : from the sum subtract the given date, and the remainder will give you our date. Thus,

III.	Non. Sept.	Non. on the 5th ;	$5 + 1 = 6$; $6 - 3 = 3$d of Sept.
VI.	Non. Oct.	Non. on the 7th ;	$7 + 1 = 8$; $8 - 6 = 2$d of Oct.
VII.	Idus Febr.	Idus on the 13th ;	$13 + 1 = 14$; $14 - 7 = 7$th of Febr.
VII.	Idus Jul.	Idus on the 15th ;	$15 + 1 = 16$; $16 - 7 = 9$th of Jul.

Method of reducing our time to Roman.

§ 235.—1. If the given date is between the *Calendæ* and *Nonæ*, add 1 to the day of the *Nonæ* ; if between the *Nonæ* and *Idus*, add 1 to the day of the *Idus* : from the sum subtract the date given, and the remainder will be the Roman date. Thus,

February	3d.	Non. on the 5th ;	$5 + 1 = 6$; $6 - 3 = $ III. Non. Febr.
July	2d.	Non. on the 7th ;	$7 + 1 = 8$; $8 - 2 = $ VI. Non. Jul.
October	10th.	Idus on the 15th ;	$15 + 1 = 16$; $16 - 10 = $ VI. Idus Oct.
December	9th.	Idus on the 13th ;	$13 + 1 = 14$; $14 - 9 = $ V. Idus Dec.

2. If the given date is between the *Idus* and the *Calendæ* of the month following, add 2 to the number of days in the month : from the sum subtract the date given, and the remainder will be the number of the *Calendæ* of the next month. Thus,

February	19th.	Febr. has 28 days ;	$28 + 2 = 30$; $30 - 19 = $ XI. Cal. Mart.
April	25th.	Apr. has 30 days ;	$30 + 2 = 32$; $32 - 25 = $ VII. Cal. Maias.
August	18th.	Aug. has 31 days ;	$31 + 2 = 33$; $33 - 18 = $ XV. Cal. Sept.
November	23d.	Nov. has 30 days ;	$30 + 2 = 32$; $32 - 23 = $ IX. Cal. Dec.

3. If the date is the day on which the *Calendæ, Nonæ*, or *Idus* fall, it is called *Caendæ, Nonæ*, or *Idus*, respectively : if it is the day before, it is called *pridie Calendas* (always of the month following), or *pridie Nonas, pridie Idus* (both of the same month).—Thus the 31st of Dec., is called *pridie Calendas Januarias*; the 6th of October, *pridie Nonas Octobres* ; the 14th of March, *pridie Idus Martias*.

PROSODY.

CHAPTER I.

§ 236.—PROSODY treats of the length, or quantity, of syllables and the laws of Versification.

A syllable, with respect to its quantity, is either short (ᵕ), long (–), or common (ᵕ̄).

A syllable is said to be common, when it may be used short or long, at the option of the poet.

GENERAL RULES.

A VOWEL BEFORE ANOTHER VOWEL.

(In Latin words.)

Vocalem breviant alia subeunte Latini.
Produc, ni sequitur r, *fio* et nomina quintæ,[1]
Quæ geminos casus *e* longo assumit in *ei ;*
Verum *e* corripiunt *fidĕi*que, *spĕi*que, *rĕi*que.
Ius commune est vati : producito *alius ;*
Alterius brevia. *Pompĕi* et talia produc.
Eheu produces semper, variabitur *ŏhe.*

§ 237.—Rule 1. A vowel before another vowel, a diphthong, or an h, is short ; as, *Dĕus, pĭæ, nĭhil.*

Stat medĭo virtus : medĭum tenŭere bĕati.
Quam felix pŭer est, virtus in quo antĕit annos. *Mur.*

Exc. 1. *Fĭo* has the *i* long in all its forms, except those in which the second vowel is followed by *r ;* as, *fĭunt, fĭebam, fĭam ;*—but *fĭeri, fĭerem,* etc.

Omnia jam fīent, fĭeri quæ posse negabam. *Ovid.*

---

[1] Read : *Produc, ni sequitur Rho, fio,* etc.

Exc. 2. The genitive and dative sing. of the fifth declension have the *e* long before *i ;* as, *diēi, speciēi.* But *e* is short in *spĕi,* ánd commonly, also, in *rĕi* and *fidĕi.*

Exc. 3. Genitives in *ius* have the *i* long in prose, but common in poetry: as, *uniūs, solīus, totīus.*—The genitive *alīus,* however, is always long, and *alterīus* always short.

Invidus alterīus marcescit rebus opimis. *Hor.*

Exc. 4. *Cāïus, Pompēïus, Vultēïus* (also Cājus, Pompējus, Vultējus), and the like, have the *a* and *e* before *i* long. Voc. *O Cāi, Pompēi, Vultēi.*—In *ŏhe* and *Dïana,* the first syllable is common ; in *ĕheu* it is long.

A VOWEL BEFORE ANOTHER VOWEL.

(In Greek words.)

Nomina Græcorum certa sine lege vagantur :
Quædam etenim brevibus, veluti *symphonïa,* gaudent.
At quædam longis, ceu *dïa, chorĕa, Thalïa,*
Darïus, Cytherĕa, āer, elegïa, platĕa,
Atque alia.   At *chorĕam* breviat *platĕam*que poeta.
Solvit et in geminas, veluti *Cytherēïa,* longam.

§ 238.—**Rule 2.**   Words of Greek origin generally retain their original quantity.   Accordingly

a) The first vowel is short in *Simŏis, Deucalïon, Pigmalïon, idĕa, sophïa, philosophïa, theologïa, etymologïa,* and others in *ia,* which, however, are pronounced by many with the accent on the penult.[1]   ☞ In *Academïa* the penult ought to be regarded as long.

b) The first vowel is long in *Agesilāus, Archelāus, Menelāus, Lāertes, Lāomedon, Lycāon, Trōas, Trōïus, Io, Amphīon, Arīon, Ixīon, Orion, Pandīon,* and, in general, in those words that are written in Greek with a diphthong (ει) ; as, *Æneas, Cytherēa, Galatēa, Medēa, Odēum, gynæcēum, Clīo, Arīus, Basilīus, Iphigenīa, Alexandrīa, Antiochīa, Seleucīa, bravīum,* and also in adjectives in *ēus,* formed from Greek proper names, as *Cytherēus, Pythagorēus, Pelopēus, Phœbēus, gigantēus,* etc.

c) The first vowel is common in *Malĕa, Nerĕïs, Dædalĕus,* and a few more.— *Chorĕa* and *platĕa* (from χορεία and πλατεῖα sc. ὀδός) have the *e* long in prose, but common in poetry, as *chorĕa, platĕa.*

---

[1]) *Idea, Andreas, sophia, philosophia, symphonia, euphonia, etymologia, theologia, orthographia, prosodia, categoria, homilia, Lucia, Archias, Ananias,* et alia, quamvis vocalem ante vocalem corripiant, tamen a c u t a penultimâ a multis viris doctis, more Græcorum, in soluta oratione pronunciantur : *Idéa, Andréas, Sophía,* etc.—Contra, in *comœdia, tragœdia, Urania, ecclesia,* et similibus, quæ pariter vocalem ante vocalem corripiunt, antepenultima acuta potius Latine efferri placuit. *F. Alvares.*

Sit Medēa ferox invictaque, flebilis Ino,
Perfidus Ixīon, Io vaga, tristis Orestes. *Hor.*

NOTE 1.—The long vowels ē and ī, when arising from *ei*, are sometimes resolved
into two syllables; as, *Cythereïa, elegeïa, Pelopeïus,* instead of *Cytherēa, elegīa,
Pelopēus.*

NOTE 2.—Greek genitives and accusatives in *eos* and *ea,* from nominatives in *eus,*
have the penult generally short,—but sometimes, also, long; as, *Idomenēos, Idome-
nēa, Ilionēa.*

DIPHTHONGS AND CONTRACTED SYLLABLES.

Omnis diphthongus contractaque syllaba longa est.
Præ rape præpositam vocali, dicque *praĕustus.*

§ 239.—Rule 3. Every diphthong and every contracted syllable is long ; as,
praēda, moëror, laûdo,—cōgo for *coago, mālo* for *magis volo, jūnior* for *juvenior,
flēram* for *fleveram.*

Jam coēlum terramque meo sine numine, venti,
Miscere et tantas aūdetis tollere moles ?
Quos ego .... Sed motos praēstat componere fluctus. *Virg.*

Exc. *Præ* before a vowel in composition is short, as *praĕaltus, praĕcunt,
praĕiens, praĕustus.*

POSITION.

Vocalis longa est si consona bina sequatur,
Aut duplex, aut *i* vocalibus interjectum.
Quadrĭjugus rapitur, *bĭjugus* conjungitur illi.

§ 240.—Rule 4. A vowel before two consonants, or before x, z, j, is long by
position ; as, *tĕrra, rĭxa, gāza, mājor.*

Pluribus intēntus minor ēst ad sīngula sēnsus.
Cōnscia mēns rēcti famæ mēndacia ridet. *Ovid.*
Dat veniam cōrvis, vēxat cēnsura colūmbas.

☞ A vowel is long by position, also, when a word ends in a consonant,
and the word following begins with a consonant: as, *Sĭt Medea ferox ; ăt
pius Æneas.*

Exc. The compounds of *jugum* have the *i* before *j* short ; as, *bĭjugus, trĭ-
jugus, quadrĭjugus.*

MUTE AND LIQUID

Contrahit orator, variant in carmine vates,
Si mutam liquidamque simul brevis una præibit :
At mutam et liquidam quoties ab origine longa
Præcedit, producta manet, ceu *mătris*, *arātrum*.
Utraque vocalem si consona juncta sequentem
Non ferit, anteiens brevis est, velut *ŏbruo*, nunquam.

§ 241.—Rule 5. A short vowel before a mute and liquid is common in poetry,
but always short in prose; as, *volŭcris*, *latĕbra*, *tenĕbræ* ; in prose always
volŭcris, *latĕbra*, *tenĕbræ*.

> Et primo similis volŭcri ; mox vera volūcris. *Ovid.*
> Nox tenĕbras profert: Phœbus fugat inde tenēbras. *Ovid.*

NOTE 1.—That a vowel before a mute and liquid be common in poetry, three
things are necessary : viz.,

a) That the vowel be short by nature, as in *tenĕbræ*, *intĕgri*, *lugŭbris :* for,
when the vowel is long by nature, as in *mātris*, *mūcro*, *salūbris*, it always
remains long, in prose and poetry.[1]

b) That the mute precede the liquid, as in *pătris*, *ăgros*, *Cўclops ;* otherwise
the vowel would be long by position, as in *pārtis*, *Ārgos*.

c) That both the mute and liquid belong to the same syllable, as in *ă-trox*,
lu-gŭ-bris, *pha-rĕ-tra ;* otherwise the preceding vowel would again be long by
position, as in *ăb-luo*, *ŏb-ruo*, *sŭb-levo*.

NOTE 2.—The rule concerning mute and liquid applies only to the liquids
l and *r*.—A mute followed by *m* or *n* in Latin words, makes the preceding
vowel long by position, as in *āgmen*, *āgnus*, *lignum*, *rēgnum*, *ĭgnavus*. This,
however, is not always the case in words of Greek origin, as *cўgnus*, *Tēcmessa*.

SPECIAL RULES.

PRETERITES OF TWO SYLLABLES.

Præterita assumunt primam dissyllaba longam :
Sto, do, scindo, fero, rapiunt *bibo, findo,* priores.
Abscĭdit, abscīdit, modulatur utrumque poeta.

§ 242.—Rule 6. Preterites of two syllables have the first syllable long; as,
vĕni, vīdi, vīci.

---

[1]) Whether a vowel be short or long by nature, must be ascertained from the examples of the poets, or from the " *Gradus ad Parnassum.*"

O Corydon, Corydon, quæ te dementia cēpit ?   *Virg.*
Multa tŭlit fēcitque puer, sudavit et alsit.   *Hor.*

Exc. The following have the first syllable short : *stĕti, dĕdi, scĭdi, tŭli, bĭbi, f'ĭdi,* from *sto, do, scindo, fero, bibo, findo.*

☞ *Abscĭdi* from *cædo* is long ; but *abscĭdi* from *scindo,* short.

REDUPLICATING PRETERITES.

Præteritum geminans primam breviabit utramque,
Ut pario, *pĕpĕri :* vetet id nisi consona bina.

§ 243.—Rule 7. Reduplicating preterites have both the first and second syllables short, unless position prevent it.   Thus, *dĭdĭci, pĕpŭli, tĕtĭgi.*

Tityre, te patulæ cĕcĭni sub tegmine fagi.   *Virg.*
Quod pueri dĭdĭcere, senes dediscere nolunt.   *Hor.*

Exc. *Cado,* to fall, has *cĕcĭdi ; cædo,* to cut, *cĕcĭdi.*—In *cŭcŭrri, mŏmōrdi, pĕpērci, tŏtōndi,* and the like, the second is long by position.

Obstupuere animi gelidusque per ima cŭcūrrit
Ossa tremor.   *Virg.*

SUPINES OF TWO SYLLABLES.

Cuncta supina volunt primam dissyllaba longam :
At *reor* et *cieo, sero* et *ire, sino*que *lino*que,
Do; queo, et orta *ruo,* breviabunt rite priores.

§ 244.—Rule 8. Supines of two syllables have the first syllable long ; as, *vīsum, lūsum, mōtum.*

Huc ipsi pōtum venient per prata juvenci.   *Virg.*
In patulos lūsum pergamus, Tityre, campos.

Exc. The following have the first syllable short : *rătum, sătum, dătum, lĭtum, ĭtum, quĭtum, sĭtum,* from *reor, sero, do, lino, eo, queo, sino.*

NOTE 1.—*Ruo* has *rŭĭtum,* whence *rŭĭturus ;* but the compounds have *rŭtum,* as *dirŭtum, erŭtum, obrŭtum.*—*Cĭtum* from *cieo,* 2. has the first syllable short, but *cītum* from *cio,* 4. has the same syllable long ; hence we find *concĭtus* and *concĭtus, excĭtus* and *excītus.*

NOTE 2.—*Stātum* from *sto,* 1. is long, whence *stāturus, constāturus, obstāturus, præstāturus ;* but *stătum* from *sisto,* 3. is short, whence *stătus* (both noun and adj.), *stătio, stătua, stătuo, stătura, stăbilis, stăbulum, stătim.*

POLYSYLLABIC SUPINES.

Utum atumque trahunt polysyllaba cuncta supina.
De *vi* præterito semper producitur *itum*.
Cetera corripies in *itum* quæcunque supina.

245.—Rule 9. Polysyllabic supines in *utum, atum*, and *etum*, have the penultima long; as, *solūtum, argūtum, indūtum, amātum, delētum*.

Spectātum admissi risum teneatis amici. *Hor.*

Polysyllabic supines in *itum*, from preterites in *ivi*, likewise have the penultima long; as, *cupivi, cupītum ; petivi, petītum ; quæsivi, quæsītum ; condivi, condītum ;*—but those in *itum*, from preterites not in *ivi*, have the penultima short; as, *sonui, sonĭtum ; monui, monĭtum ; tacui, tacĭtum ; condidi, condĭtum.*

☞ *Recenseo* has *recensui, recensītum* and *recensum*.

DERIVATIVE WORDS.

Derivata patris naturam verba sequuntur.
Mŏbilis et *fōmes, lāterna* ac *rēgula, sēdes,*
Quamquam orta e brevibus, gaudent producere primam.
Corripiuntur *ărista, vădum, sŏpor,* atque *lŭcerna,*
Nata licet longis : usus te plura docebit.

§ 246.—Rule 10. Derivatives follow the quantity of their primitives: as, *pāternus* from *pāter ; māternus* from *māter ; salūbris* from *salūtis ; sanguĭneus* from *sanguĭnis ; judĭcium* from *judĭcis ; consĭlium* from *consŭlo ; pūnio* from *poēna ; ămor, ămicus, ămicitia, ămabilis,* from *ămo ; jūdex, jūdico, jūdicium, injūria,* from *jus, jūris ; lĕgere, lĕgerem, lĕgebam,* from *lĕgo ; lēgeram, lēgerim, lēgerunt, lēgisse,* from *lēgi.*

Sic vŏlo, sic jubeo : sit pro ratione vŏluntas. *Ter.*
Perge păti pătiens, pariet pătientia palmam.

Exc. The following derivatives deviate from the quantity of their primitives : *rex (rēgis), rēgina, rēgius, rēgula,* from *rĕgo ;*

lāterna	*from*	lăteo	sēdes	*from*	sĕdeo	hūmanus	*from*	hŏmo
tēgula	"	tĕgo	suspicio	"	suspĭcor	mŏbilis	"	mŏveo
fŏmes	"	fŏveo	măcero	"	măcer	sĕcius	"	sĕcus, etc.
ărista	*from*	āreo	sŏpor	*from*	sŏpio	săgax	*from*	săgio
ŏdium	"	ŏdi	dux, dŭcis	"	dŭco	mŏlestus	"	mŏles
lŭcerna	"	lūceo	vădum	"	vădo	quăter	"	quătuor, etc.

Ex bello redŭces iterumne ad bella redūces?
Tum cornix plena pluviam vŏcat improba vōce. *Virg.*

☞ The *i* is short in *fĭdes* and *perfĭdus,* but long in *fīdo, confīdo, diffīdo fīdus,* and *infīdus.*

COMPOUND WORDS.

Legem simplicium retinent composta suorum,
Vocalem licet aut diphthongum syllaba mutet.
Dejĕro sed *jūro* dat *pejĕroque; innŭba, nŭbo,*
Pronŭbaque; atque *hīlum, nihĭlum;* dat *semisŏpitus*
Sōpio; fatidĭcus fratresque a *dīco* creantur.
Participale *ambĭtum* ab *ĭtum* inter longa repone.

§ 247.—Rule 11. Compounds generally retain the quantity of their simples, though the stem vowel or diphthong be changed in composition; as, ăvus, *prŏdăvus;* nĕpos, *pronĕpos;* căvus, *concăvus;* brĕvis, *perbrĕvis;* ūtor, *abūtor;* nītor, *enītor;* sōlor, *consōlor;* rătus, *irrĭtus;* sătus, *insĭtus;* cădo, *occĭdo* ("to set"); caēdo, *occĭdo* ("to kill"); laēdo, *illīdo;* quaēro, *inquīro;* claūdo, *reclūdo;* aūdio, *obēdio;* faūces, *suffōco;* trux caēdo, *trucīdo.*

Confĭcuere omnes intentique ora tenebant. *Virg.*
Insĕquitur clamorque virûm stridorque rudentum. *Virg.*

☞ Particular attention should be paid to the following compounds: *exhālat, conclāmat, deprāvat, emānat, delĭbat, constĭpat, derīvat, evītat, investīgat, instīgat, irrĭtat, compōtat, deplōrat, elabŏrat, enōdat, immūtat, indūrat, refūtat, compāret, appāret, adrīdet, adrēpit, afflīgit, commūnit;—exŭrat, compŭrat, enŭtat, irrĭgat, allĭgat, devŏrat, comprŏbat, compŭtat, recŭbat, adjăcet, permănet, impĕdit, effŏdit, expŏlit, erŭdit.*

Exc. The following compounds change the long vowel of their simples into a short one: *dejĕro, pejĕro,* from *jūro; innŭba, pronŭba,* from *nūbo; agnĭtum, cognĭtum,* from *nōtum; nihĭlum* from *hīlum; semisŏpitus* from *sōpio;* and *causidĭcus, fatidĭcus, veridĭcus,* from *dīco.*
Connŭbium has the syllable *nu* generally short.—*Ambĭtus* (a participle) is long; but *ambĭtus* (a noun), and *ambĭtio, ambĭtiosus,* are short.
So also *oblītus* from *obliviscor;* but *oblĭtus* from *oblĭno.*

PREPOSITIONS IN COMPOSITION.

Longa *a, de, e, se, di,* præter *dĭrimo* atque *dĭsertus.*
Sit *re* breve; at *rĕfert,* a *res,* producito semper.
Corripe *pro* Græcum, produces rite Latinum.
Contrahe quæ *fundus, fugio, neptis*que *nepos*que,
Et *festus, fari, fateor, fanum*que crearunt.

Hisce *prŏfecto* addes, pariterque *prŏcella, prŏtervus,*
Atque *prŏpago* genus ; *prŏpago* protrahe vitis.

Corripe *ab* et reliquas, obstet nisi consona bina ;
Quæ sunt *ad* vel *in, ob, per, sub, super, anteque, circum.*

§ 248.—Rule 12. The prepositions *a, de, e, se, di,* are long in composition ;
as, *ămitto, dēduco, ērumpo, sēpono, dīmitto.* But *di* is short in *dīrimo* and
dīsertus.

Tergora dīripiunt costis et viscera nudant.   *Virg.*
Ut dēsint vires, tamen est laudanda voluntas.   *Ovid.*

Re is short by nature ; as, *rĕfero, rĕvoco, rĕdux.* But *re* is long in the im
personal verb *rēfert,* and whenever it is followed by two consonants or a *j ;* as,
rēsto, rēscribo, rēspondeo, rējicio, rējectus.—Before mute and liquid *re* becomes
common ; as, *rĕflecto, rĕcludo, rĕprimo, rĕfringo.*

Ingemuit, et duplices tendens ad sidera palmas,
Talia voce rĕfert : O terque quaterque beati !   *Virg.*

Nec rēfert dominos illic famulosne rĕquiras ;
Tota domus duo sunt : idem parentque jubentque.   *Ovid.*

Pro, in composition, is short in Greek words, but long in Latin ; as, *Prŏ-
pontis, Prŏmetheus, prŏlogus,—prōveho, prōmitto, prōpono.*

Exc. Pro is short in *prŏcella, prŏfari, prŏfano, prŏfanus, prŏfiteor, prŏficiscor,
prŏfecto, prŏfestus, prŏfugus, prŏfugio, prŏfundo, prŏfundus, prŏnepos,* and *prŏ-
neptis.*—In *prŏpago* (noun and verb) and *prŏpino,* pro is common.

Ab, ad, in, ob, per, sub, super, ante, and *circum,* are short in composition,
unless they be long by position ; as, *ăbhinc, ădhuc, ădoro, ĭneo, pĕrimo, sŭbigo,
supĕraddo, antĕcello, circŭmeo,*—but *ābduco, ădmitto, antēsto, circŭmdo.*

Quin ădeas vatem, precibusque oracula poscas.   *Virg.*
Nec frustra signorum ŏbitus speculamur et ortus.   *Virg.*

☞ In *dĕamo, dĕeram, dĕesse, dĕhisco, sĕorsim, prŏinde, prŏhibeo,*—*de, se,* and
pro, are short by Rule 1.

A, E, I, O, IN COMPOSITION.

Produc A semper composti parte priore :
At simul E, simul I, crebro breviare memento.
Nēquidquam produc, *nĕquando,* venĕfica, *nĕquam,*
Nēquaquam, nĕquis sociosque, *vidĕlicet* addes.
Idem masculeum produc et *sĭquis, ibĭdem,*

Scilicet et *bīgæ, tibīcen, ubīque, quadrīgæ,*
Bīmus, tantīdem, quīdam, et composta-*diei.*
Compositi O breviant Græci : *Samŏthracia* testis ;
Sed *Minŏtaurus* pariterque *geŏmetra* longum est.
O Latium variat, producere namque *aliŏquin,*
Et *quandŏque ;* at *quandŏquidem* breviare solemus.

§ 249.—Rule 13. A at the end of the first part of a compound is long ;
E, generally short ; as, *trāno, trāduco, trādo ;—nĕque, nĕqueo, nĕfas, nĕfandus,*
nĕfarius, trĕcenti, and the compounds of *facio* and *flo,* as *calĕ-* (*madĕ-, rubĕ-,*
stupĕ-, tremĕ-, tumĕ-, and commonly also *patĕ-, putrĕ-, tepĕ-,* and *liquĕ-*) *facio.*

> Credebant hoc grande nĕfas et morte piandum. *Juv.*

Exc. A is short in *quăsi :* E is long in *nēve, nēdum, nēmo* (*ne homo*), *nēquis,*
nēquitia, nēquam, nēquaquam, nēquidquam, nēquando, vidēlicet, venēfica, sēde-
cim, and *sēmestris.*

I and Y at the end of the first part of compounds are generally short ; as,
bĭpes, bĭceps, trĭceps ; utĭque, undĭque, sĭquidem ; cornĭcen, fidĭcen, lyrĭcen,
tubĭcen ; carnĭvorus, dulcĭsonus, ignĭvomus, mortĭferus, sacrĭlegus, omnĭpotens,
vatĭcĭnor, signĭfico ; Eurȳpylus, Polȳdorus ;—but *Polȳxena* and *Polȳcletus.*

> Myrtea silva subest bĭcoloribus obsita baccis. *Ovid.*

Exc. I is long in the masculine *īdem* (neut. *ĭdem*), *sīquis, ĭbīdem, ubīque,*
utrobīque, utrīque, plerīque, bīgæ, quadrīgæ, scīlicet, īlicet, bīmus, trīmus, quad-
rīmus, tantīdem, quantīvis, quantĭcunque, tibīcen, lucrīfacio, and the compounds of *dies,* as *bīduum, trīduum, prīdie, postrīdie, merīdies, quotīdie.*
In *ubīvis, ubīlibet, ubīcunque,* and *ubĭnam,* the *i* is common.

O at the end of the first part of compounds is sometimes long, as in
aliŏquin, ceterŏquin, quandŏque, quŏminus, intrŏduco, retrŏversus,—and sometimes short, as in the particle *quŏque, quandŏquidem, hŏdie, duŏdeni.*

> Indignor, quandŏque bonus dormitat Homerus. *Hor.*

Note.—In words of Greek origin the *o* is long where it is written in Greek
with ω, as in *lagŏpus, geŏmetra, Minŏtaurus,*—and short where it is written
with ο, as in *philŏsophus, Areŏpagus, Carpŏphorus, Argŏnauta, Samŏthracia.*
In *Nicŏstratus, Philŏxenus,* and the like, the *o* is long by position : in *chirŏ-*
graphus, Hippŏcrene, it is common on account of mute and liquid.
U at the end of the first part of compounds is short ; as, *Trojŭgena, quad-*
rŭpes.—But it is long in *Jūpiter, jūdex, jūdicium ;* and common in *quadrŭplex,*
locŭples.

CHAPTER II.

INCREMENTS.

The word INCREMENT, in Prosody, means an increase of syllables.

There are two kinds of increments : viz., the increment of nouns and the increment of verbs.

I. THE INCREMENT OF NOUNS.

§ 250.—A noun is said to increase when in any of its cases, it has more syllables than in the nominative singular; as, *pax, pacis ; sermo, sermonis.*

The number of increments in nouns is equal to the number of its additional syllables.

If a word has but one increment, it is the penult; if it has two increments, the antepenult is called the first, and the penult the second increment; and if it has three, the syllable before the antepenult is called the first, the antepenult the second, and the penult the third increment.

☞ The last syllable of a word, be it a noun or a verb, is never regarded as an increment.

INCREMENTS OF THE FIRST TWO DECLENSIONS SING.

Casibus obliquis vix crescit prima : secunda
Corripit incrementa ; tamen producit *Ibĕri.*

§ 251.—The first declension has no increment, except among the poets, in the old genitive form in *aï,* where the *a* is long ; as, *aulāi, aquāi, pictāi,* instead of *aulæ, aquæ, pictæ.*

The increments of the second declension sing. are short ; as, *vir, vĭri; miser, misĕri ; satur, satŭri.*—But *Iber* and *Celtiber* have *Ibĕri* and *Celtibĕri.*

Ite domum satŭræ, venit Hesperus, ite capellæ.   *Virg.*

INCREMENTS OF THE THIRD DECLENSION SING.

A.

Nominis A crescens, quod flectit tertia, longum est.
Mascula corripies *al* et *ar* finita; simulque
Par cum compositis, *hepar* cum *baccare, nectar,*
Cum *väde mas* et *anas,* queis junge *läremque jubar*que.
A quoque et *as* Græcum breve postulat incrementum
S quoque finitum, si consona ponitur ante;
Et *dropax, anthrax, Atrax* cum *smilace, climax.*
His *Atacem, panacem, colacem, styracem*que *facem*que,
Atque *abacem, coracem, philacem* compostaque necte.

§ 252.—The increment A of the 3d declension sing. is long; as, *pax, pācis;*
Ajax, Ajācis; Syphax, Syphācis; calcar, calcāris; vectīgal, vectigālis.

> Rex erat Æneas nobis, quo justior alter
> Nec pietäte fuit, nec bello major et armis. *Virg.*

Exc. The increment A is short:
1.) In masculine proper names in *al* and *ar;* as, *Hannibal, Hannibālis;*
Cæsar, Cæsăris.

2.) In *par, păris,* and its compounds *compar, dispar,* and *impar;* also in *sal,*
sălis; vas, vădis; mas, măris; anas, anătis; hepar, hepătis; lar, jubar, bac-
car, and *nectar.*

> Dixit et in cœlum păribus se sustulit alis,
> Ingentemque fuga secuit sub nubibus arcum. *Virg.*

3.) In Greek words in *a* and *as;* as, *thema, themătis; lampas, lampădis;*
Pallas, Pallădis.

> Scribimus indocti doctique poemăta passim. *Hor.*

4.) In words in *s* with a consonant before it; as, *trabs, trăbis; Arabs, Ară-*
bis;—and also in the words *fax, climax, abax, Atax, colax, corax, dropax, pan-*
ax, anthrax, Atrax, smilax, styrax, and *Arctophylax.*

> Jamque făces et saxa volant, furor arma ministrat. *Virg.*
> Vela damus vastumque cava trăbe currimus æquor. *Virg.*

E.

E crescens numero breviabit tertia primo:
Verum protrahitur genitivus in *enis, Iber*que,

Ver, halex, locuples, hæres, mercesque, quiesque,
Lex, vervex, halec, seps, plebs, rex: insuper adde
El peregrinum : *er* et *es* Græcum, *æthĕre* et *aëre* demptis.

§ 253.—The increment E of the 3d declension sing. is short ; as, *grex, grĕgis;*
nex, nĕcis; pes, pĕdis; teres, terĕtis; Ceres, Cerĕris; iter, itinĕris.

Salve sancte parens, iterum salvete recepti
Nequidquam cinĕres, animæque umbræque paternæ!   *Virg.*

Exc. The increment E is long:
1.) In *Iber, Ibēris,* and in words that make the genitive in *enis;* as, *ren, rēnis;*
Siren, Sirēnis ; attagen, attagēnis. But *hymen* makes *hymĕnis.*

2.) In the words *ver, locuples, hæres, merces, quies, lex, rex, plebs, vervex,*
seps, and *halec.*

Quidquid delirant rēges, plectuntur Achivi.   *Hor.*

3.) In foreign names in *el ;* as, *Daniel, ēlis ; Raphael, ēlis ; Israel, ēlis.*

4.) In Greek words in *es* and *er;* as, *magnes, magnētis; tapes, tapētis; crater,*
cratēris ; soter, sotēris.—But *æther* and *aër* increase short, as *æthĕris, aëris.*

I.

Corripiet pariet crescens I tertia primo
In numero : at Græcum patrium producit in *inis,*
Gryps, vibex, Nesis, lis, Dis, glis, addito *Samnis.*
Ix produc : breviato *histrix* cum *fornĭce, varix,*
Coxendix, chœnixque, Cilix, natrixque calixque ;
Adde et *Eryx* et *onyx, nix pixque salixque filixque,*
Sardonўchis, calўcis, larĭcis: fit Bebrycis anceps,
Sed brevibus junges, in *gis* cum patrius exit.
Mastix, mastīgis ; coccyx, coccўgis amabit.

§ 254.—The increment I of the 3d declension sing. is short ; as, *stips, stĭpis;*
remex, remĭgis; iter, itĭneris; anceps, ancĭpĭtis ; chalybs, chalўbis ; chlamys,
chlamўdis.

Gutta cavat lapĭdem non vi, sed sæpe cadendo.   *Ovid.*
Flumĭna jam lactis, jam flumĭna nectaris ibant,
Flavaque de viridi stillabant ilice mella.   *Ovid.*

Exc. Tho increment I is long:
1.) In genitives in *inis* and *ynis* from words of Greek origin ; as, *delphin, del-*
phĭnis ; Phorcyn, Phorcўnis ; Salamis, Salamīnis.

2.) In the words *gryps, grȳphis; Dis, Dītis; lis, lītis; glis, glīris; vibex
vibīcis; Nesis, Nesīdis; Samnis, Samnītis*, and *Quiris, Quirītis.*

> Noctes atque dies patet atri janua Dītis. *Virg.*

3.) In words in *ix;* as, *felix, felīcis; bombyx, bombȳcis; perdix, perdīcis;
pernix, īcis; coturnix, īcis.*—But the following in *ix* increase short : *nix, nĭvis;
Phryx, Phrȳgis; strix, īgis; Styx, ȳgis; Japyx, ȳgis; Onyx, ȳchis; Sardonyx,
ȳchis,* together with *pix, calix, larix, natrix, salix, varix, Cilix, phœnix, coxendix,
Eryx, filix, fornix, histrix,* and the proper names *Ambiorix, Biturix, Vercinge-
torix,* and the like.

· O.

O crescens numero producimus usque priore.
O parvum in Græcis brevia, producito magnum.
Corripitur genitivus *oris,* quem neutra dedere :
Os, ōris, mediique gradus sed protrahe casus,
Ut *melius.* Brevibus dantur *memor, immemor, arbor,*
Et *lepus* et πούς compositum, *bos, compos* et *impos :*
Adde his *Cappadŏcem, Allobrŏgem,* cum *prœcŏce, scrobs, ops :*
Verum produces *Cercops, hydropsque, Cyclopsque.*

§ 255.—The increment O of the 3d declension sing. is long ; as, *sol, sōlis,
dos, dōtis; vox, vōcis; lepor, lepōris; nepos, nepōtis.*

> Gaudia principium nostri sunt sæpe dolŏris.
> In silvis lepŏres, in verbis quære lepōres.

Exc. The increment O is short :
1.) In the words *memor, immemor, arbor, lepus, bos, compos,* and *impos;* in the
compounds of πούς, as *tripus, polypus, Œdipus;*—also in *Cappadox, Allobrox,
prœcox,* and in words in *s* with a consonant before it, as *scrobs, ops, inops,
Æthiops, Cecrops,* and *Dolops.*—But *Cyclops, Cercops,* and *hydrops* increase
long : *Cyclōpis, Cercōpis, hydrōpis.*

> Strata jacent passim sua quaque sub arbŏre poma. *Virg.*

2.) In genitives in *oris* from words of the neuter gender ; as, *pecus, ŏris;
decus, ŏris; ebur, ŏris; marmor, ŏris.*—But *os, ōris,* and all comparatives increase long ; as, *melior, meliōris.*

> Tempŏra labuntur tacitisque senescimus annis. *Ovid.*
> Video meliŏra proboque :
> Deteriŏra sequor. *Ovid.*
> Sic oculos, sic ille manus, sic ōra ferebat. *Virg.*

3.) In Greek proper names in *or;* as, *Actor, Castor, Hector, Nestor,* and in
rhetor.

4.) In words of Greek origin in ων, ονος ; as, *canon, aëdon, Iason, sindon, Amæon, Philemon* :—but those in ων, ωνος, increase long ; as, *agon, Oïmon, Conon, Dion, Solon, Laco, Plato, Zeno, Hiero,* and also *Tros, heros,* and *Mīnos* (gen., *ŏis*).—In *Orīon* and *Ægæon,* the increment *o* is common.

5.) In Gentile names in *ones*, as *Macedŏnes, Saxŏnes, Lingŏnes, Teutŏnes, Vascŏnes, Vangiŏnes.*—But the following are long: *Eburōnes, Burgundiōnes, Suessiōnes,* and *Vettōnes.*—*Brittōnes* has the *o* common.

U.

U brevia incrementa feret : sed casus in *udis,*
Uris et *utis,* ab *us* recto producitur, et *fur,*
Lux, frux ; sed brevis *intercusque pecusque Ligus*que.

§ 256.—The increment U of the 3d declension sing. is short ; as, *dux, dŭcis ; crux, crŭcix ; nux, nŭcis ; redux, redŭcis.*

Si canimus silvas, silvæ sint Consŭle dignæ.   *Virg.*
Lumina volvit obitque trŭci procul omnia visu.   *Virg.*

Exc. The increment U is long :   .
1.) In genitives in *udis, uris,* and *utis,* from nominatives in *us ;* as, *palus, ūdis ; incus, ūdis ; tellus, ūris ; virtus, ūtis.*—But *pecus, Ligus,* and *intercus,* increase short : *pecŭdis, Ligŭris, intercŭtis.*

Terra viros urbesque gerit silvasque ferasque
Fluminaque et nymphas et cetera numina rūris.   *Ovid.*

2.) In the words *fur, fŭris ; lux, lūcis ; Pollux, ūcis ;* and (*frux*) *frūgis.*

Quid domini facient, audent cum talia fūres ?   *Virg.*

PLURAL INCREMENTS OF NOUNS.

§ 257.—A plural increment exists in the genitive and dative plural, when either of these cases contains more syllables than the ablative singular ; as, *musâ, musarum ; servo, servorum ; pede, pedibus ; re, rerum, rebus.*

Pluralis casus, si crescit, protrahet A, E,
Atque O ; corripies I, U ; verum excipe *bŭbus.*

§ 258.—The plural increments A, E, and O, are long ; I and U, short ; as, *quārum, hārum ; rērum, rēbus ; hōrum, quōrum : ŏvĭbus, trĭbus ; trĭbŭbus, lacŭbus.*—☞ *Bŭbus* (for *bovibus*) is long.

Et jam summa procul villārum culmina fuma.
Majoresque cadunt altis de montĭbus umbræ.   *Virg.*

II. The Increment of Verbs.

§ 259.—A verb is said to increase when in any of its parts, it has more syllables than in the 2d pers. sing. of the Present Indic. Active.

The number of increments in verbs is equal to the number of its additional syllables: the last syllable, however, as has already been observed, is never regarded as an increment.

In determining the increments of deponent verbs, an active voice may be supposed. Thus, for example, the increments of *reor, tueor, nitor,* and *molior,* are regulated by the supposed standards *res, tues, nitis,* and *molis :*

rĕ-bar, tu-ĕ-bă-mur, ni-tĕ-rĕ-mĭ-ni, mo-lĭ-ĕ-bă-mĭ-ni.

A.

A crescens produc : *do* incremento excipe primo.

§ 260.—The verbal increment A is long; as, *stābam, stābāmus, regāmur, audiebāmini.*

Donec eris felix, multos numerābis amicos. *Ovid.*
Incidit in Scyllam qui vult vitāre Charybdim. *Virg.*

Exc. A is short in the first increment of *do;* as, *dăre, dăte, dăbam, dăbo, dăbāmus, dăbāmini.*

E.

E quoque producunt verba increscentia. Verum
Corripiunt *e* ante *r,* ternæ dūo tempora prima :
Sed *rēris* vel *rēre* datur penultima longis.
Sit brevis *e,* quando *ram, rim, ro,* adjuncta sequuntur ;
Et *bĕris* atque *bĕre* in verbis breviato futuris.
Corripit interdum *stĕtĕrunt dĕdĕrunt*que poeta.

§ 261.—The verbal increment E is long; as, *flēbam, rēbar, monērem, monērē mini, regēris* (Fut. Ind. Pass.), *venērunt.*

Jamque quiescēbant voces hominumque canumque
Lunaque nocturnos alta regēbat equos. *Ovid.*

Exc. The increment E is short :
1.) Before *r* in the Present and Imperfect of the 3d conjugation · as, *regĕre, regĕrem, regĕris, regĕrer, regĕrēmur.* But *e* before *r* is long in the ending *rēris,* as *regĕrēris, loquĕrēris.*

2.) Before *ram, rim, ro,* throughout ; as, *venĕram, venĕrim, venĕro.* (☞ *Mī-ram, flĕrim, flĕro,* and the like, are long by Rule 3

> Nondum cæsa suis, peregrinum ut visĕret orbem,
> Montibus in liquidas pinus descendĕrat undas.   *Ovid.*

3.) In the Future ending *bĕris* or *bĕre;* as, *amabĕris* or *amabĕre, monebĕris* or *moncbĕre.*

> Tu cave defendas quamvis mordebĕre dictis.   *Ovid.*

I.

Corripit I crescens verbum : producitur *ivi*
Præteritum; sed *ĭmus* breviatur.   Deme *velĭmus,*
Nolĭmus, sĭmus, quæque hinc composta dabuntur,
Et quodvis quartæ incrementum I protrahe primum.
Ri conjunctivi possunt variare poetæ.

§ 262.—The verbal increment I is short; as, *regĭmus, amabĭmus, monebĭmĭni, audiebamĭni.*

> Nitĭmur in vetitum semper cupĭmusque negata.   *Ovid.*
> Vincĭmus ferro, ferro quos vincĭmus hostes.
> Scindĭtur incertum studia in contraria vulgus.   *Virg.*

Exc. The increment I is long :

1.) In the penult of Perfects in *ĭvi;* as, *petīvi, quæsīvi, audīvi,*—but *ĭmus* (of the plural) is short ; as, *petīvĭmus, quæsīvĭmus, audīvĭmus, amavĭmus.*

2.) In the first increment of the fourth conjugation (except *ĭmus* of the Perfect, as just remarked).   Thus, *ībam, ībĭtis, īte, subīmus, sentīmus, venīmus, reperīmus;*—but *sensĭmus, venĭmus, reperĭmus* (Perf.).—In *audĭunt, audĭatis, audĭebar,* etc., the *i* is short by Rule 1.

3.) In *nolīto, nolīte; nolīmus, nolītis; velīmus, velītis; malīmus, malītis; sīmus, sītis; possīmus, possītis; prosīmus, prosītis; intersīmus, intersītis; adsīmus, adsītis,* etc.

☞ The I in *rimus* and *ritis* of the Perfect Subj. and the Fut.-Perfect seems to be common in poetry, as *fecerĭmus, fecerĭtis* and *fecerīmus, fecerītis.* In prose : *Ne sermonem des auditoribus,* says the learned F. Alvarez, *consuetudini regionis servies.*

O, U.

O incrementum produc ; U corripe semper :
Cuncta sed U longum reddent tibi verba futuri.

§ 263.—The verbal increment O is long ; U, short ; as, *scitōte, habetōte; sŭmus, possŭmus, prosŭmus, adsŭmus, supersŭmus, volŭmus, nolŭmus, malŭ-*

ius.—But U is long in the Participles in *urus,* as *futūrus, factūrus, peritūrus, entūrus.*

> Nos numerus sŭmus et frŭges consumere nati. *Hor.*
> Ventūræ memores jam nunc estōte senectæ. *Ovid.*

CHAPTER III.

I. QUANTITY OF PENULTS.

§ 264.—1. Patronymics in *ades* and *ides* (those in *ides* from εύς and ης excepted) shorten the penult; as, *Æneădes, Scipiădes ; Priamĭdes, Hectorĭdes*—but *Atrīdes, Pelīdes, Heraclīdes,* from *Atreus, Peleus, Hercules* ('Ατρεύς, Πηλεύς, 'Ηρακλῆς).

> Quis genus Ænĕadûm, quis Troiæ nesciat urbem? *Virg.*
> Hinc procul Æsonĭden, procul hinc jubet ire ministros. *Ovid.*

Patronymics in *aïs, eïs,* and *oïs,* commonly lengthen the penult; as, *Ptolemāïs, Ænēïs, Latōïs.*—*Thebăïs* is short; *Nerēïs,* common.

2.—Substantives in *ina* for the most part lengthen the penult; as, *carīna, culīna, farīna, gallīna, medicīna, piscīna, pistrīna, pruīna, resīna, sagīna, sentīna, spīna, sutrīna, textrīna, tonstrīna, vagīna,* etc.—But the following are short: *fiscĭna, fuscĭna, femĭna, lamĭna, machĭna, pagĭna, sarcĭna, trutĭna.*

> Eripit interdum, modo dat medicīna salutem. *Ovid.*
> Torquet nunc lapidem, nunc ingens machĭna tignum. *Hor.*

3.—Substantives in *aca, ica,* and *uca,* generally lengthen the penult; as, *cloāca, formīca, lectīca, lorīca, Nasīca, vesīca, urtīca, festūca, verrūca, lactūca,* etc.—But the following are short: *brassĭca, fabrĭca, pedĭca, mantĭca, pertĭca, scutĭca, tunĭca.*

> Nunc gruibus pedĭcas et retia ponite cervis. *Virg.*
> Et tunĭcæ manĭcas et habent redimicula mitræ. *Virg.*

4.—Adjectives in *acus, icus, idus,* and *imus,* usually shorten the penult; as, *Ægyptiăcus, aromatĭcus, maledĭcus, acĭdus, arĭdus, avĭdus, cupĭdus, calĭdus, callĭdus, perfĭdus, invĭdus, gelĭdus, frigĭdus, lepĭdus, finitĭmus, legitĭmus,* etc.—But the following are long: *opācus, amīcus, aprīcus, inimīcus, mendīcus, pudīcus, fīdus, infīdus, opīmus, īmus,* and *primus.*

> Accipiunt inimīcum imbrem rimisque fatiscunt. *Virg.*
> O lux Dardaniæ, spes O fīdissima Teucrûm! *Virg.*

5.—Adjectives in *ulus* shorten the penult; as, *bibŭlus, credŭlus, garrŭlus, patŭlus, querŭlus.*

Adjectives in *ilis*, derived from verbs, likewise, shorten the penult ; as. *agĭlis, docĭlis, facĭlis, flebĭlis, fertĭlis, fusĭlis, habĭlis, mobĭlis, nobĭlis, utĭlis,*—but those derived from nouns, lengthen the penult; as, *anīlis, civīlis, herīlis, hostīlis, puerīlis, juvenīlis, virīlis, senīlis,* to which must be added : *exīlis, subtīlis. Aprīlis, Quintīlis, Sextīlis.*

> Et semel emissum volat irrevocabĭle verbum.   *Virg.*
> Inde senīlis hiems tremŭlo venit horrida passu.   *Ovid.*

6.—Adjectives in *inus* lengthen the penult ; as. *agnīnus, anatīnus, anserīnus, arietīnus, asinīnus, canīnus, caprīnus, cervīnus, equīnus, ferīnus, leporīnus. lupīnus, taurīnus, viperīnus ; bīnus, trīnus, quīnus ; collīnus, marīnus, vicīnus; matutīnus, repentīnus, vespertīnus ; divīnus, genuīnus, clandestīnus, intestīnus, adulterīnus, festīnus, libertīnus, inopīnus, inquilīnus, supīnus, Alexandrīnus, Latīnus, Venusīnus.*—But *inus* is short in *cedrĭnus, fagĭnus, oleagĭnus, crocĭnus, hyacinthĭnus, adamantĭnus, smaragdĭnus, corallĭnus, crystallĭnus, bombycĭnus, elephantĭnus ; crastĭnus, diutĭnus, pristĭnus, serotĭnus, perendĭnus.*

> Instar montis equum divīna Palladis arte
> Ædificant, sectāque intexunt abjete costas.   *Virg.*

§ 265. NOTE.—The quantity of a syllable may not unfrequently be ascertained either by *Composition* (i. e.; using compound words) or *Subtraction* (i. e., dropping some syllable).

For this end change the given word by either of these methods into a trisyllable, but so that the syllable in question may occupy the place of the penult. If then the penult has the accent, you may infer with certainty that the syllable whose quantity you seek, is long : if otherwise, it is short. Thus we find

1.) By Composition, that in the words *sanitas, gratissimus, scribuntur, sumendus, ponentis, clamantes,* the first syllable must be long, because we know that the trisyllabic compounds *insānus, ingrātus, adscrībo, consūmo, compōno, exclāmo,* have the accent on the penult,—and on the contrary that in the words *super, decem, probus, rego, capio, habeo, sequor,* the first syllable must be short, because we know the trisyllabic compounds *insŭper, undĕcim, imprŏbus, cŏrrĭgit, accĭpit, prŏhĭbet, cŏnsĕquor,* have the accent on the antepenult.—In like manner we find

2.) By Subtraction, that in the words *rescribēntis, remiseritis, valetudo, ingratissimus, amicitia, consumentis,* the second syllable must be long, because we know that the kindred trisyllables *rescrībo, remīsi, valēre, ingrātus, amīcus, consūmo,* have the accent on the penult,—and on the contrary that in the words *militĭbus, cognitio, sedulitas, sanguineus, compulerant, corrigerent,* the second syllable must be short, because we know the corresponding trisyllables *milĭtis, cognĭtus, sedŭlus, sanguĭnis, compŭli, corrĭgo,* have the accent on the antepenult.

II. Quantity of Final Syllables.

The Quantity of final syllables is known partly by position, as *prudēns, felix;* partly by diphthongs, as *musae, pennae;* partly by special rules.

Final A.

A finita dato longis : *ită* corripe semper,
Ejă, quiă, et casus omnes ; sed protrahe sextum.
Productis Graecos casus adjunge vocandi.

§ 266.—A final is long; as, *amă, circă, contră, extră, frustră, posteā,*[1] *triginta,* etc.

Tu vită quidquid tibi non est vită salusque.
Signă te, signă ; temere me tangis et angis.[2]

Exc. A final is short :

1.) In *eiă, ită, quiă,* the adverb *pută* and the names of letters, as *alphă, betă, gammă.*

2.) In all the cases,—the ablative sing. and Greek vocatives from nominatives in *as* (gen. *œ* or *antis*) excepted ; as, *rosă, regnă, temporă, leviă, majoră.* But *rosă, eă, illă* (Ablat.); *O Æneā, Pallā, Atlā!*—Greek vocatives from nominatives in *es* have either *ĕ* or *ă;* as, *O Atridĕ* or *Atridă! O Thyestĕ* or *Thyestă!*

Mitto tibi navem prorā puppique carentem.[3]
Et quamquam sub aquă, sub aquă quoque rană coaxat.

Final E.

Corripe E; sed primæ quintæque vocabula produc,
Atque *famĕ, cetĕ, tempĕ, fermĕque ferĕque:*
Adde *doce* similemque modum et monosyllaba, præter
Encliticas ac syllabicas. *Benĕ* cum *malĕ* demptis
Cetera produces adverbia cuncta secundæ.

§ 267.—E final is short ; as, *natĕ, fugĕ, pœnĕ, sinĕ, nempĕ.*

Omnĕ tulit punctum qui miscuit utilĕ dulci. *Hor.*
Heu fugĕ, natĕ dea, teque his, ait, eripĕ flammis. *Virg*
Tityrĕ, dum redeo, brevis est via, pascĕ capellas. *Virg.*

---

[1]) Short (*posteă*) according to some : but in reality long. [2]) This verse can be spelled backwards. [3]) i. e., n(AVE)m, the *n* being the *prora;* the *m,* the *puppis* of the word *navem,* — "I send you (an AVE, or) my best respects."

Exç. E final is long

1.) In the cases of the first and fifth declensions: as, *epitomē, Culliopē, rē, diē*, with their compounds *quarē, hodiē, pridiē,*—and also in *famē, ferē, ohē,* and the contract plural nouns *cetē, melē, Tempē.*

2.) In the Imperative sing. act. of the 2d conjugation, as *salvē, vidē, valē.*— But *cavĕ* has the *e* final common.

3.) In monosyllables, as *mē, tē, sē, nē* (conj.),—the enclitics *quĕ, vĕ, nĕ,* and the syllabic additions *ptĕ, cĕ, tĕ,* excepted.

> Tu nĕ cedĕ malis, sed contra audentior ito.   *Virg.*
> Semper honos nomenquĕ tuum laudesquĕ manebunt.   *Virg.*

4.) In adverbs derived from adjectives of the 2d declension; as, *probē, latē, longē, valdē.*—But *benĕ, malĕ, infernĕ, supernĕ,* and adjectives of the 3d decl., used adverbially, have the final *e* short, as *sublimĕ, suavĕ, facilĕ, difficilĕ.*

FINAL I.

> I produc: brevia *nisī* cum *quasī*, Græcaque junge.
> Jure *mihī* variare, *tibī*que *sibī*que solemus.
> Corripies *ibi, ubi,* melius, dissyllabon et *cui.*

§ 268.—I final is long; as, *classī, fierī, utī, Mercurī.*

> Rixantur multī de lana sæpe caprina.   *Hor.*
> Frigidus, O puerī! fugite hinc, latet anguis in herba.   *Virg.*

Exc. I final is short:

1.) In *nisĭ* and *quasĭ.*

2.) In Greek neuters, as *gummĭ, sinapĭ, molŷ;*—in Greek datives and vocatives, as *Palladĭ, Paridĭ, Thetidĭ, Daphnidĭ—Alexĭ, Tethŷ, Parĭ, Amaryllĭ,*—and in plural datives in *si,* as *heroisĭ, Dryasĭ, Troasĭ.*

Contracted Greek datives, and the datives of proper names in *es* (gen. *is*), which follow in Greek the first declension, have final *i* and *y* long; as, *Socratī, Demosthenī, Achillī, Tethŷ* (Σωκράτεϊ, Ἀχιλλέϊ, Τηθύϊ, etc.),—*Orestī, Pyladī* (from Ὀρέστης, *ov,* etc.).

☞ I final is common in *mihĭ, tibĭ, sibĭ,* and *ubĭ.*—*Cui,* as a dissyllable, has final *i* generally short.—*Uti* seems to be uncertain: most prosodians make it long.

Of the compounds of *ibi, ubi,* and *uti,* the following should be noticed: *velutī, ibīdem, ubīque,* always long: *ubīcunque,* common; *necubĭ, sicubĭ, utĭnam,* and *utĭque,* always (*ubĭnam* generally) short.

> Si fueris Romæ, Romano vivito more:
> Si fueris alibi, vivito sicut ibi.

Final O.

O datur ambiguis : Græca et monosyllaba longis,
Ergŏ, verŏ, immŏ, ternus sextusque secundæ,
Atque *adeŏ*, atque *ideŏ*, atque adverbia nomine nata.
Dant brevibus *modŏ* cum sociis, *egŏ* et *octŏ*, poetæ.

§ 269.—O final is common, though more frequently long than short ; as,
Polliŏ, Scipiŏ, Carthagŏ.

> Quandŏ conveniunt Catharina, Camilla, Sibylla,
> Sermonem faciunt et ab hoc, et ab hac, et ab illa.[1]

> Ottŏ tenet mappam, madidam mappam tenet Otto.[2]
> Horrendum et dictu videŏ mirabile monstrum. *Virg.*

Exc. 1. O final is long :
1.) In monosyllables ; as, *O, dŏ, stŏ, prŏ*, and in Greek words written with ω,
as, *Androgeŏ, Athŏ, Inŏ, echŏ, Cliŏ, Sapphŏ.*

2.) In the dative and ablative sing. of the 2d declension ; as, *somnŏ, vinŏ,
læto*,—and in adverbs derived from adjectives, as *falsŏ, rarŏ, subito.*

Exc. 2. O final is short in *citŏ, egŏ, octŏ, modŏ, dummodŏ, quomodŏ, postmodŏ*,
and generally also in *duŏ, illicŏ, immŏ, sciŏ, nesciŏ*, and *cedŏ*, in the sense of
dic or *da*.

☞ The shortening of O final in verbs is very rare in the writers of the Augustan age. It gradually became more common with the later writers, such as
Juvenal, Lucan, Martial, etc.

> Rure morans quid agam, respondeŏ pauca rogatus :
> Prandeŏ, potŏ, canŏ, ludŏ, lavŏ, cœnŏ, quiescŏ. *Mart.*

Final U, B, D, T.

U · semper produce : B, D, T, corripe semper.

§ 270.—U final is long : B, D, T, final are short, unless position or contraction prevent it. E. g., *diū, manū, Panthū ;—ăb, ăd, illŭd, amăt.* But *ăst, haŭd,
amănt, obĭt*, (for *obiĭt*), *ăt pius Æneas.*

> Regis ăd exemplum totus componitur oris. *Hor.*
> Quidquĭd ĭd est, timeo Danaos et dona ferentes. *Virg.*
> Vos exemplaria Græca
> Nocturna versate manū, versate diurna. *Hor.*

---

[1] Imitation of woman's garrulity.   [2] This verse can be read and spelled backwards.

FINAL C, L, M.

C longum est : varium *hic* pronomen : corripe *donec*
Et *nec : fac* pariter malunt breviare poetæ.
Corripe L ; at produc *sal, sol, nil,* multaque Hebræa.
M vorat ecthlipsis,—prisci breviare solebant.

§ 271.—C final is long, L final short, and M final, when followed by a vowel, is elided with the vowel before it. Thus, *ăc, dĭc, dūc, sĭc, illūc ; semĕl, simŭl, procŭl, Consŭl ; monstr' horrend' ingens,* instead of *monstrum horrendum ingens.*

> Omnibus hoc viti*um* est cantoribus, inter amicos
> Ut nunqu*am* inducant animum cantare rogati,
> Injussi nunquam desistant. *Hor.*

Exc. 1. C final is short in *nĕc, donĕc,* and *fŭc.—Hic,* the pronoun, is common, but more frequently long than short ; *hic,* the adverb, is always long.—*Hŏc,* the nom. neut. sing. is occasionally found short in the comic poets.

Exc. 2. L final is long in *săl, sŏl, nĭl,* and in Hebrew names, as *Danĭēl, Nabăl, Isrăēl.*

FINAL N.

N longum est Græcis pariter pariterque Latinis.
En brevia quod format *ĭnis* breve : Græca secundæ,
Jungimus et quartum, si sit brevis ultima recti.
Forsitan, in, forsan, tamen, an, viden', adjice curtis.

§ 272.—N final is long ; as, *ēn, nōn, sĭn, rēn ; Titān, Sirēn, Delphīn ; Sōlōn, agōn (ων); Circēn, Anchisēn, Æneān ; Athōn, Androgeōn ; chalybōn, Georgicōn.*

> Cum semel effluxit, nōn est revocabilis hora. *Ovid.*
> Nōn opibus virtus, sed opes virtute parantur. *Mur.*

Exc. N final is short :

1.) In substantives in *en, -ĭnis ;* as, *nomĕn, flumĕn, lumĕn,* and in the words, *ăn, ĭn, forsăn, forsĭtăn, tamĕn, attamĕn,* and *vidĕn'* for *videsne ?*

> Naturam expellas furca, tamĕn usque redibit. *Hor.*
> Monstrum horrendum, informe, ingens, cui lumĕn ademtum. *Virg.*

2.) In Greek nominatives in *on* (ον) of the 2d declension ; as, *Iliŏn, Peliŏn ;*—in Greek accusatives of any declension, if the ultima of the nominative is short ; as, *Maiăn, Iphigeniăn ; Rhodŏn, Delŏn ; Parĭn, Daphnĭn ;*—and in Greek plural datives in *in,* as *Arcasĭn, Troasĭn,*

Final R.

R breve : sed longum est *far, par* cum pignore, *ver, Nar,*
Cur, fur, cum Græcis quibus est genitivus in *eris ;*
Addito *Iber ;* sed *cor* melius breve, *Celtiber* anceps.

§ 273.—R final is short; as, *vĭr, sempĕr, precŏr, Cæsăr, Hectŏr, turtŭr.*

> Dum juga montis aper, fluvios dum piscis amabit,
> ` Dumque thymo pascentŭr apes, dum rore cicadæ,
> Sempĕr honos nomenque tuum laudesque manebunt. *Virg.*

Exc. R final is long :
1.) In *cŭr, fŭr, făr, păr* with its compounds *compār, dispār,* and *impăr, vĕr,*
Ibĕr, Năr and *lăr.*

> Ædificare casas, plostello adjungere mures,
> Ludere păr impăr, equitare arundine longa,
> Si quem delectat barbatum, amentia verset. *Hor.*

2.) In Greek words in *er, -eris ;* as, *sotĕr. cratĕr (-ĕris) ; aĕr, æthĕr (-ĕris).*

Final AS.

AS produc : breve *anas ;* Græcorum tertia quartum
Corripit, et rectum per *ădis* si patrius exit.

§ 274.—AS final is long ; as, *făs, nefăs, terrās, Æneās, Pallās (-antis).*

> Credebant hoc grande nefās et morte piandum. *Juv.*
> O curās hominum, O quantum est in rebus inane ! *Pers.*

Exc. AS final is short .
1.) In *anăs,* and in Greek words in *as, -ădis ;* as, *Arcăs, lampăs, Pallăs.*

2.) In Greek accusatives plur. of the 3d declension ; as, *Troăs, delphinăs,*
heroăs, Cyclopăs.

Final ES.

ES quoque produces : breviat sed tertia rectum,
Cum patrii brevis est crescens penultima : *pes* bino
Excipitur, *paries, aries, abies*que *Ceres*que.
Corripe et *es* de *sum,* et *penes,* et pluralia Græca.

§ 275.—ES final is long , as, *spēs, diēs, locuplēs, vidēs, audiēs, Anchisēs.*

Regia, crede mihi, rēs est succurrere lapsis. *Ovid.*
Apparent rari nantēs in gurgite vasto. *Virg.*
Noctēs atque dies patet atri janua Ditis. *Virg.*

Exc. ES final is short :

1.) In words in *es* of the 3d declension, which increase short in the genitive ; as, *dĭvĕs, equĕs, hospĕs, pedĕs, milĕs, sospĕs.*—But long are : *ariēs, pariēs, Cerēs,* and *pēs* with its compounds *bipēs, tripēs, sonipēs, quadrupēs.*

Vivitur ex rapto, non hospĕs ab hospite tutus. *Ovid.*

2.) In *penĕs* and *ĕs* from *sum,* with its compounds *potĕs, prodĕs, abĕs, obĕs, subĕs.*

3.) In Greek neuters, as *cacoēthĕs, hippomanĕs,* and in Greek nominatives and vocatives of the 3d declension ; as, *lampadĕs, rhetorĕs, Amazonĕs, Troĕs, heroĕs,* etc.

Compulerantque greges Corydon et Thyrsis in unum :
Ambo florentes ætatibus, Arcadĕs ambo. *Virg.*

NOTE 1. *Hæresēs, phrasēs, crisēs,* and the like, being derived from nouns in *ις, -εως,* and consequently contracted from *εις,* are long.

NOTE 2.—Proper names in *es* (from *ης, εος*), as *Demosthenes, Diogenes, Socrates, Pericles,* have the final *es,* long in the nominative, but short in the vocative.

FINAL IS.

Corripias *IS* et *YS:* plurales excipe casus ;
Glis, sis, vis, verbum ac nomen, *nolis*que *velis*que ;
Audis cum sociis ; quorum et genitivus in *inis,*
*Entis*ve, and *itis* longum, producito semper.

§ 276.—IS final is short ; as, *apĭs, inquĭs, digerĭs, bĭbis, Tethÿs, Itÿs.*

Hei mihi qualis erat ! quantum mutatus ab illo ! *Virg.*
Stulte, quid est somnus, gelidæ nisi mortĭs imago ? *Ovid.*
Tantæ molĭs erat Romanam condere gentem ! *Virg.*

Exc. IS final is long :

1.) In all plural cases ; as, *virīs, armīs, musīs, nobīs, vobīs, omnīs, urbīs* (for omneis, urbeis).

Quam multa in silvīs avium se millia condunt ! *Virg.*

2.) In the 2d pers. sing. of the Present Ind. Act. of verbs belonging to the 4th conjugation ; as, *audīs, sentīs, nescīs, fīs, abīs, redīs, perīs, subīs.*

3.) In nouns that have in the genitive long *-ĭnis*, *-ĭtis*, or *-entis;* as, *Salamĭs, nis ; Samnĭs, ĭtis; līs, lītis; Simoĭs, entis.*

> Grammatici certant et adhuc sub judice lis est.   *Hor.*

4.) In the words *glĭs, vĭs* (verb and noun), *velĭs* and *sĭs,* with their compounds, *quamvĭs, quivĭs, utervĭs; nolĭs, malĭs; adsĭs, absĭs, prosĭs, possĭs,* etc.; and in the adverbs *forĭs, gratĭs, ingratĭs, imprimĭs.*

> Imbellis tota est : caput exime,—vīs erit illi.[1]

☞ The ending *ris* of the Fut. Perfect and Perfect Subj. is common ; as, *dederĭs, fecerĭs.*

> Vilis adulator si dixeris : *æstuo,* sudat.   *Juv.*

FINAL OS.

Vult *OS* produci : *compos* breviatur et *impos,*
*Os*que, *ossis;* Græcorum et neutra, et cuncta secundæ
Addicta Ausonidûm, Græcus genitivus et omnis.

§ 277.—OS final is long ; as, *ōs* (*oris*), *virōs, nepōs, custos;* *Trōs, herōs, Minōs, Androgeōs,* and others that are written with ω.

> Ōs homini sublime dedit cœlumque tueri
> Jussit et erectōs ad sidera tollere vultus.   *Ovid.*

Exc. OS final is short :
1.) In *ŏs* (*ossis*), *exŏs, compŏs,* and *impŏs,* and the Greek neuters *Argŏs, chaŏs, melŏs,* and *epŏs.*
2.) In Greek nominatives of the 2d declension, which are written with *o* ; as, *Delŏs, Rhodŏs, Tyrŏs, Tenedŏs,* and in Greek genitives of the 3d declension, as *Arcadŏs, Orpheŏs, Tethyŏs.*

> Smyrna, Rhodos, Colophon, Salamin, Chiŏs, Argŏs, Athenæ :
> Orbis de patria certat, Homere, tua.

FINAL US.

US breve ponatur : produc monosyllaba, quæque
Casibus increscunt longis, et nomina quartæ,
Excepto recto et quinto, et quibus exit in untis
Patrius, et conflata e πούς, contractaque Græca
In recto ac patrio, et venerandum nomen JESUS.

---

[1] *Ovis, o-vis.*

§ 278.—US final is short; as, *littŭs, improbŭs, imŭs, scindimŭs, intŭs.*

> Fraxinŭs in silvis pulcherrima, pinŭs in hortis,
> Populŭs in fluviis, abies in montibŭs altis.   *Virg.*

> Tityrŭs hinc aberat[1]: ipsæ te, Tityre, pinus,
> Ipsi te fontes, ipsa hæc arbusta vocabant.   *Virg.*

Exc. US final is long:

1.) In monosyllables; as, *plūs, rūs, thūs, mūs,* and in words that increase long in the genitive; as, *salūs, tellūs, palūs.*

> Haud procul hinc stagnum, tellūs habitabilis olim.   *Ovid.*

2.) In the genitive sing. and in the nom., acc., and voc. plur. of the 4th declension.   But the nom. and voc. sing. are short.

> Hic situs est Phaeton, currūs auriga paterni.   *Ovid.*

3.) In the compounds of πούς; as, *tripūs, Melampūs,* and when *us* is contracted from οος, as in *Opūs, Pessinūs,* and *Amathūs* (all three G. -untis); *Panthūs, echūs, Cliūs, Inūs, Sapphūs.*

> Est Amathūs, est celsa mihi Paphos atque Cythera.   *Virg.*

4.) In the sacred Name of our Lord and Redeemer; as,

> Dic, JESUS infans circa cur viderit agmen
> Pastorum primum?—scilicet AGNUS erat.

CHAPTER IV.

VERSIFICATION.

FEET. METRE. VERSE.

§ 279.—Poems are composed of verses; verses, of feet; and feet, of syllables.

A FOOT is a combination of two or more syllables of a certain quantity.   Feet are divided into simple and compound.

----

[1]) See § 284.—1.

A simple foot consists of two or three syllables ; a compound foot, of four.

SIMPLE FEET.

(of two syllables.)

Spondee	— —	Trochee	— ◡
Pyrrhic	◡ ◡	Iambus	◡ —

(of three syllables.)

Molossus	— — —	Bacchīus	◡ — —
Tribrach	◡ ◡ ◡	Antibacchīus	— — ◡
Dactyl	— ◡ ◡	Amphibrach	◡ — ◡
Anapaest	◡ ◡ —	Amphimăcer	— ◡ —

COMPOUND FEET.

Choriambus	— ◡ ◡ —	Diiambus	◡ — ◡ —
Antispast	◡ — — ◡	Ditrochee	— ◡ — ◡
Smaller Ionic	◡ ◡ — —	Dispondee	— — — —
Greater Ionic	— — ◡ ◡	Proceleusmatic	◡ ◡ ◡ ◡
First Pæon	— ◡ ◡ ◡	First epitrit	◡ — — —
Second Pæon	◡ — ◡ ◡	Second epitrit	— ◡ — —
Third Pæon	◡ ◡ — ◡	Third Epitrit	— — ◡ —
Fourth Pæon	◡ ◡ ◡ —	Fourth epitrit	— — — ◡

§ 280.—METRE, in a general sense, denotes a particular kind or species of verse. Thus we say—the *Dactylic, Iambic, Trochaic, Choriambic, Ionic* metre, according as the Dactyl, the Iambus, the Trochee, the Choriambus, or the Ionic, prevails.

We also say—the *Sapphic, Alcaic, Asclepiadic, Anacreontic* metre, after the name of some celebrated poet, who has employed a particular species of verse.

Metre, in a restricted sense, signifies either a single foot in a verse, or a combination of two consecutive feet, usually called a *Dipodia.*

In the Dactylic and Choriambic Metre, every single foot constitutes "a metre" or measure, so that a dactylic verse of six feet is called hexameter; of five, pentameter; of four, tetrameter, etc.

In the Iambic, Trochaic, and Anapæstic Metre, "a metre" or measure consists of two feet; hence, an Iambic verse of eight feet is called Iambus tetrameter; of six feet, trimeter; of four, dimeter.

§ 281.—A VERSE (στίχος) is a certain number of feet, arranged in a regular order and forming a line of poetry.

A *verse* that has the exact number of syllables requisite, is called *acatalectic:* if it lacks a syllable at the end, it is called *catalectic;* if two syllables, *brachycatalectic;* if it lacks a syllable at the beginning, *acephalous;* and if it has a syllable too much at the end, *hypercatalectic* or *hypermeter.*

RHYTHM. ARSIS. THESIS.

§ 282.—By *Rhythm* is meant a regular, alternate raising and lowering of the voice. The effort by which stress is laid upon a syllable, is called *ictus* or rhythmical accent.

A syllable which has the ictus or rhythmical accent, is said to be in the *arsis;* a syllable on which the voice sinks, in the *thesis.*

The natural place of the *arsis* is the long syllable of every foot: hence, in the iambus it falls on the second syllable; in the dactyl and trochee, on the first.—The spondee, in Iambic and Anapæstic Verse, has the arsis on the second syllable; but in Trochaic and Dactylic, on the first. Thus the tribrach, in the Iambic metre, has the arsis on the last syllable (‿ ‿ ◡́); but in the Trochaic, on the first (◡́ ‿ ‿).

CÆSURA. SCANNING. FIGURES.

§ 283.—The *Cæsura* is used by prosodians with reference either to whole verses or to single feet.

CÆSURA, with reference to whole verses, means such a division of the line into two parts as affords to the voice a short pause of rest in some convenient place, without injury to the sense or to the harmony of the verse. This cæsura is usually called the *cæsural pause,* and has its application chiefly in hexameter verses. Its place is for the most part after the arsis of the third foot, or in the thesis of that same foot. Sometimes, however, a different division is admitted. E. g,

Hectora quis nosset, | felix si Troia fuisset ? *Ovid.*
Infandum regina | jubes renovare dolorem. *Virg.*
Belli ferratos postes | portasque refregit. *Hor.*
Prima tenet | plausuque volat | fremituque secundo. *Virg.*

CÆSURA, with reference to single feet, is either masculine, feminine, or monosyllabic.

The cæsura is said to be *masculine* when, after a foot is completed, there remains a syllable at the end of a word to begin the next foot; *feminine,* when there remains a trochee ; and *monosyllabic,* when the first syllable of a foot is a monosyllable. E. g.,

Sub lace-|ris cre-|bro vir-|tus latet | aurea | pannis. *Mur.*
Sic abe-|unt rede-|untque me-|i vari-|antque ti-|mores. *Virg.*
Idem ego | sum, qui | nunc an | vivam, | perfide, | nescis. *Ovid.*

Scanning is dividing a verse into the feet of which it is composed.—To scan correctly, one must know not only the quantity of each syllable, but also the several poetical usages and licenses, called *figures* of prosody.

The following are the principal figures: *Synalœpha, Ecthlipsis, Synæresis, Diæresis, Systole, Diastole* or *Ectasis.*

SYNALŒPHA is a figure by which a vowel or diphthong is cut off at the end of a word when the following word begins with a vowel, a diphthong, or the letter *h*; as, *Dardanid' infensi, ub' ingens,* instead of *Dardanidæ infensi, ubi ingens.*

☞ *Synalœpha* never takes place in the particles *O, ah, vah, væ, hei, heu,* and *proh.*

> Conticuere omnes intentique ora tenebant. *Virg.*
>
> Rara avis in terris nigroque simillima cygno.

ECTHLIPSIS is a figure by which the consonant *m* together with the preceding vowel, is cut off at the end of a word, when the following word begins with a vowel, a diphthong, or an *h*. Examples are obvious.—Both Ecthlipsis and Synalœpha sometimes take place at the very end of a verse ; as,

> Omnia Mercurio similis vocemque colorem*que*
> Et crines flavos et membra decora juventæ. *Virg.*
>
> Jamque iter emensi turres ac tecta Latino*rum*
> Ardua cernebant juvenes murosque subibant. *Virg.*

SUNÆRESIS is a figure by which two syllables are contracted into one; as, *deinc, proin-de,* for *de-hinc, pro-in-de ; dee-ro, dee-ram,* for *de-e-ro, de-e-ram ; om-nia, au-reis,* for *om-ni-a, au-re-is ; anthac, sorsum,* for *antehac, seorsum ; vemens, prendo,* for *vehemens, prehendo ; vincla, repostum,* for *vincula, repositum ; caldior, porgite,* for *calidior, porrigite ; antire, antambulo,* for *anteire, anteambulo ; tenvis, genva,* for *tenuis, genua ; abjete, parjetes,* for *abiete, parietes,* etc.

> Sint Mæcenates : non dee-runt, Flacce, Marones. *Mart.*
>
> Genva labant, gelido concrevit frigore sanguis. *Virg.*
>
> Manet alta mente repostum
> Judicium Paridis, spretæque injuria formæ. *Virg.*

DIÆRESIS is a figure by which one syllable is divided into two ; as, *aurāï, aquāï, Nāïădes, sĭluœ, persoluisse, sŭbiectus,* etc., instead of *auræ, aquæ, Naïdes, silvæ, persolvisse, subjectus.*

> Flebilis indignos, elegēïa, solve capillos. *Ovid.*
>
> Aulāï in medio libabant pocula Bacchi. *Virg.*

SYSTOLE is a figure by which a syllable is shortened, which is otherwise long by nature or by position ; as, *stetĕrunt, dedĕrunt ; sŭbicit, ăbicit ; vidĕn', satin',* instead of *stetērunt, dedērunt, sŭbjicit, ābjicit, vidēsne, satĭsne.*

> Di tĭbi divitias dedĕrunt artemque fruendi. *Hor.*
>
> Obstupui stetĕruntque comæ et vox faucibus hæsit. *Virg.*

DIASTOLE or Ectasis is a figure by which a syllable naturally short is made long. This figure occurs chiefly in proper names and in words compounded with *re;* as, ˉ*Italia,* ˉ*Arabia,* from ˘*Italus,* ˘*Arabs;* rĕligio, rĕliquia. rĕperi, rĕtuli (also written rĕlligio, rĕlliquiæ, rĕpperi, rĕttuli), instead of rĕligio, rĕliquiæ, rĕperi, rĕtuli.

> Ibitis ˉItaliam portusque intrare licebit. *Virg.*
>
> Hanc tibi Prīamides mitto, Ledæa, salutem. *Ovid.*

§ 284.—Besides the above-mentioned licenses, the following two are also to be noticed :

1.) That a syllable naturally short is occasionally made long when it falls in the arsis, that is, when it is cæsural ; as,

> Desine plura puĕr, et quod nunc instat, agamus. *Virg.*
>
> Luctus ubique, pavŏr et plurima mortis imago. *Ovid.*

2.) That a long vowel or diphthong, in the cæsural syllable, occasionally remains unelided and is even made short when it falls in the thesis ; as,

> Et succus pecorī et lac subducitur agnis. *Virg.*
>
> Te Corydon, ˘O Alexi ; trahit sua quemque voluptas. *Virg.*
>
> Ter sunt conatī imponere Peliŏ Ossam. *Virg.*

DACTYLIC METRE.

Dactylic Hexameter.

§ 285.—The *Hexameter,* as its name imports, consists of six feet. Of these, the first *four* may be either dactyls or spondees ; the *fifth* must regularly be a dactyl ; the *sixth,* a spondee.

1.	2.	3.	4.	5.	6.
— ◡ ◡	— ◡ ◡	— ◡ ◡	— ◡ ◡	— ◡ ◡	— ≃
— —	— —	— —	— —		

> Tītўrĕ, | tū pătŭ-|læ rĕcŭ-|bāns sŭb | tĕgmĭnĕ | fāgī
>
> Sīlvē-|strēm tĕnŭ-|ī Mū-|sām mĕdĭ-|tārĭs ă-|vēnā. *Virg.*

NOTE 1.—Sometimes the fifth foot of a hexameter is a spondee instead of a dactyl : but in this case, there is generally a dactyl in the fourth foot and a word of four syllables at the end of the verse. Such lines are called *spondaic* verses. E. g.,

> Cara deûm soboles, magnum Jovis incrementum. *Virg.*
>
> Constitit atque oculis Phrygia agmina circumspexit. *Virg.*

NOTE 2.—The hexameter is called also the *heroic verse*, because this kind of verse has been chosen by the epic poets to celebrate the achievements of distinguished heroes. The hexameter is used, moreover, in didactic and satyric compositions.

Rules for the structure of hexameters.

§ 286.—1. Every well-formed hexameter should have a least one masculine cæsura, if possible, on the third foot.—Lines with only one cæsura either on the second or fourth foot, are in general for want of melody to be rejected.— Lines without any cæsura at all, are destitute of poetical beauty and harmony, and scarcely differ from common prose. Of this kind are the following lines :

> Nuper | quidam | doctus | cœpit | scribere | versus.
> Aurea | scribis | versus, | Juli, | maxime | vatum.
> Sparsis | hastis | late | .mpus | splendet et | horret.

When a verse has two cæsuras, they are either on the 2d and 3d feet, or on the 3d and 4th, or on the 2d and 4th.—When a verse has three cæsuras, they are generally on the 2d, 3d, and 4th feet ; as,

> Ode-|runt hila-|rem tri-|stes, tri-|stemque jo-|cosi. *Hor.*

2. Every hexameter ought to end with a dissyllable or trisyllable, as *ŭtĭlĕ | dŭlcī, ĭrrĕpă-|răbŭlĕ | tēmpŭs, rānă cŏ-|āxāt, fŭrĭ-|ōsă cŭ-|pĭdō,* and the like.—Monosyllables should never be placed at the end of a line, except (*a*) when another monosyllable precedes ; (*b*) when the verse ends with *est*, and the word before it suffers elision ; (*c*) when the poet wishes to express something harsh and rough, or something which is quite unexpected. Thus,

> Principibus placuisse viris non ultima laus est. *Hor.*
> Pauca loqui puero sed tempestiva, decorum est. *Mur.*
> Parturiunt montes, nascetur ridiculus mus. *Hor.*
> Sternitur exanimisque tremens procumbit humi bos. *Virg.*

3. Too many monosyllables or polysyllables in succession should be avoided. The following lines are, in this respect, faulty :

> Contur-|baban-|tur Con-|stanti-|nopoli-|tani
> Innume-|rabili-|bus | sollici-|tudini-|bus.

4. The beauty and elegance of Hexameter Verse depend chiefly on a happy and expressive combination of dactyls and spondees, and on a judicious use of the cæsura. Thus beautifully Virgil :

> Vertitur interea cœlum et ruit Oceano nox,
> Involvens umbra magna terramque polumque
> Myrmidonumque dolos : fusi per mœnia Teucri
> Conticuere : sopor fessos complectitur artus.

And again :

>Incubuere mari, totumque a sedibus imis
>Una Eurusque Notusque ruunt, creberque procellis
>Africus, et vastos volvunt ad littora fluctus.
>Eripiunt subito nubes coelumque diemque
>Teucrorum ex oculis : ponto nox incubat atra.
>Intonuere poli et crebris micat ignibus aether,
>Praesentemque viris intentant omnia mortem.

Sometimes, however, the poet exceeds in dactyls, when he wishes to express *quickness* of motion, *vivacity*, or *joy*. Thus the dactyls in the following lines from Virgil, in which he respectively describes a courser at full speed, and a pigeon hastening to her nest, both suggest and imitate the gallop of the horse, and the rapid flight of the bird :

>Quadrupedante putrem sonitu quatit ungula campum.

>   Mox aëre lapsa quieto
>Radit iter liquidum, celeres neque commovet alas.

On the other hand, he exceeds in spondees, when he wishes to express *slowness* of motion, *majesty*, or *grief*. Thus Virgil by a succession of spondees describes the slow and measured stroke of the Cyclops in forming the thunder :

>Illi inter sese magna vi brachia tollunt
>In numerum, versantque tenaci forcipe massam ;

The majesty of the tempest king :

>   Hic vasto rex Æolus antro
>Luctantes ventos tempestatesque sonoras
>Imperio premit....;

The grief at the loss of Anchises :

>Amissum Anchisen flebant, cunctaeque profundum
>Por tum aspectabant flentes....;

And again the sadness of Æneas :

>Atque haec ipse suo tristi cum corde volutat,
>Aspectans silvam immensam et sic voce precatur.

5. Elisions should be neither too harsh nor too frequent ; nor should they take place at the very beginning of a line, especially between monosyllables, as in the following line from Virgil :

>Si ad vitulam spectes, nihil est quod pocula laudes.   *Virg.*
>Quodsi in eo spatio atque ante acta aetate fuere.   *Lucr.*

6. Two successive feminine cæsuras in the second and third feet should be avoided, because they give the verse a flippant, cantering air. Still more uncouth and inelegant are those lines in which the feminine cæsura runs throughout ; as,

> Ergo magisque magisque viri nunc gloria claret.
>
> Sole cadente juvencus aratra reliquit in arvis.

7. The words of a line should be so disposed of as not to render the sense obscure and puzzle the reader. Of this kind are the following lines :

> Dico poeta bonum quem carmen fecit Homerum.[1]
>
> Omnia principium, musæ, Jovis ab Jove plena.[2]

8. If rhyme is to be avoided in prose, it is not less so in poetry. Hence verses like the following should not be imitated :

> Hac sunt in fossa Bedæ Venerabilis ossa.
>
> Contra vim mortis non est medicamen in hortis.
>
> Mensibus erratis ad solem ne sedeatis.
>
> Post cœnam stabis, passus aut mille meabis.

9. The too frequent repetition of the same letter or syllable ought likewise to be avoided. Hence the following lines are so severely censured :

> O fortunatam natam me Consule Romam !   *Cic.*
>
> O Tite, tute, Tati, tibi tanta tyranne tulisti.   *Auct. ad Her.*
>
> Africa terribili tremit horrida terra tumultu.   *Enn.*

In a playful style, however, the repetition of the same letter or syllable may be tolerated, and, not unfrequently, the repetition may even prove agreeable, as in the following lines :

> Perge pati patiens, pariet patientia palmam.

> Si qua sede sedes et erit tibi commoda sedes,
> Illa sede sede, nec ab illa sede recede.

The same may be remarked of the following distich, which is said to have thus originated.—A youth, gifted with uncommon poetical talent, happened, for some crime or other, to be sentenced to death. The unfortunate offender appealing for mercy, his prince, in consideration both of his age and abilities, promised to spare his life if he could, on the instant, compose a Latin distich, every word of which should begin with the same letter. The youth, in awful suspense between fear and hope, after a moment's pause, produced the following beautiful lines :

> Flos fueram factus, florem fortuna fefellit :
> Florentem florem florida Flora fleat.

---

[1] *Poeta, quem dico Homerum, bonum carmen fecit.*   [2] *Ab Jove principium, musæ, Jovis omnia plena.   Virg.*

Dactylic Pentameter.

§ 287.—The *Pentameter* (so called from the number of its feet) is composed of two dactyls or spondees and a long cæsural syllable, followed by two dactyls and another long or short syllable, which, with the foregoing cæsural syllable, constitutes the fifth foot.

The Pentameter is commonly used as an appendage to a hexameter. Both together are termed a *distich* (from δίς, " twice," and στίχος, " a verse"); and a collection of such distichs is called an *elegy* or elegiac poem, because they were originally employed on mournful subjects.

(First hemistich.)			(Second hemistich.)		
— ⌣ ⌣	— ⌣ ⌣	—	— ⌣ ⌣	— ⌣ ⌣	⌒
— —	— —				

Principiis obsta, sero medicina paratur,
    Quūm mălă | pĕr lŏn-|gās | īnvălŭ-|ĕrĕ mŏ-|rās.

Pastor, arator, eques, pavi, colui, superavi,
    Cāprās, | rūs, hŏ-|stēs, | frŏndĕ, lī-|gŏnĕ, mă-|nū.[1]

Est avis in silva nigro vestita colore:
    Sī cŏr | sūstŭlĕ-|rīs, | rēs ĕrīt | ālbă nī-|mīs.[2]

LUSUS ECHŪS.

Hæc Bethleemitæ pastoris verba referre
    Audita est echo, quæ juga montis habet.
Quis natus? dixit: *Natus!*—Patrisne Judæi?
    Illa: *Dei.*—Verusne est homo? dixit: *homo.*
Atque hic idem nonne Deus remanet? *manet.*—Estne
    Ut Pater omnipotens? retulit illa: *potens.*
Hunc quid de cœlis duxit? *lis duxit.*—At istam
    Dic utrum vincet? *vincet,* et ipsa refert.
Litis erat radix longæva? *Eva.*—An mala? *mala.*
    Anne gula hoc potuit[3]? Illa refert: *potuit.*
An puer hic fiet magnus? quæ reddidit: *Agnus.*
    Ipse ait hoc? *ait hoc.*—Cur ita clamat? *amat.*
Is majus nostro numquid dare possit amori?
    Reddidit illa nihil quam gemebunda: *mori.*
Hoc faciet? *faciet.*—Moriens? *oriens!*—Deus ille?
    Hæc: *ille.*—Est forsan causa tua? *ausa tua.*
Diligere hunc ergo par est super omnia Christum?
    Istum.—Nonne Deum? dixit: *Eum,*—et tacuit.

---

[1] By this distich allusion is made to Virgil's Eclogues (*Pastor pavi capras fronde*), Georgics (*Arator colui rus ligone*), and Æneid (*Eques superavi hostem manu*). [2] *Cornix,* cor—nix. [3] See § 284.—1.

Rules for the structure of pentameters.

§ 288.—1. At the beginning of a pentameter, a dactyl followed by a spondee is preferable to a spondee followed by a dactyl.

2. Neither hemistich should end with a monosyllable. If, now and then, a monosyllable happen to be at the end of the first hemistich, it should be preceded either by another long monosyllable, or by a word of two short syllables, such as *sĭnĕ*, *măgĭs*, and the like; e. g.,

> Idem ego sum qui nunc an vivam, perfide, nescis,
> Cura tibi dē quo | quærere nulla fuit. *Ovid.*

> Atque ita te tacitus quærenti plura legendum
> Ne quod non ŏpŭs est | forte loquare, dabis. *Ovid*

An exception, however, is made when the monosyllable at the end of either of the hemistichs is the verb *est*, and the word going before suffers elision. (☞ In the first hemistich, the word before *est* may be either a dissyllable or a polysyllable; but in the second hemistich, it should always be a dissyllable.) E. g.,

> Nihil opŭs est, dixit, certamine, Romulus, ullo:
> Magna fides avium est, | experiamur aves. *Ovid.*

> Dic, age, dic aliquam quæ te mutaverit iram:
> Nam nisi justa tua est, | justa querela mea est. *Ovid.*

3. Those pentameters are reckoned the best which end with a dissyllable, especially with a dissyllabic noun, pronoun, or verb, such as *ăqua*, *dŏlor*, *sŏnus*, *dĕus*, *mănu*, *dŏmo*, *căput*,—*mĭhi*, *mĕo*, *tŭo*,—*ĕrat*, *ĕris*, *vĭdes*, *pŏtes*, *rĕfert*, *dĕdi*, *tŭli*, and the like.

4. Elisions should take place as rarely as possible, especially in the second hemistich, and never in the last dactyl, except in the case of *est*, when it ends the verse, and is preceded by a dissyllable, as in the foregoing line: "*Nam nisi justa tua est, justa querela mea est.*"

IAMBIC METRE.

§ 289.—The *Iambic* Metre, so called from the iambus, of which it was originally composed, consists either of 4, 6, or 8 feet, and is accordingly either Iambus dimeter, Iambus trimeter, or Iambus tetrameter. In the odd places—that is, in the first, third, and fifth feet—there may be an iambus, a tribrach, spondee, dactyl, or anapæst; in the even places—that is, in the second and fourth feet—the long syllable of the iambus is sometimes resolved into two short ones, and thus the tribrach obtained admission.—At the end of the verse, a pyrrhic may be used instead of an iambus.

☞ Horace did not use this kind of metre, except in combination with verses of a different kind.

1. Iambic dimeter acatalectic.

(First metre or dipod.)		(Second metre or dipod.)	
1.	**2.**	**3.**	**4.**
◡ —	◡ —	◡ —	◡ ≃
◡ ◡ ◡	◡ ◡ ◡	◡ ◡ ◡	
— —		— —	
— ◡ ◡		— ◡ ◡	
◡ ◡ —		◡ ◡ —	

Several of the sublime hymns in the public service of the Catholic Church are composed in this metre. The following lines form the commencement of two of those beautiful hymns:

Salutis humanæ sator,
JESU, voluptas cordium,
Orbis redempti conditor
Et casta lux amantium, etc.

Vexilla regis prodeunt,
Fulget crucis mysterium,
Qua vita mortem pertulit
Et morte vitam protulit, etc.

2. Iambic trimeter acatalectic.

(First metre or dipod.)		(Second metre or dipod.)		(Third metre or dipod.)	
1.	**2.**	**3.**	**4.**	**5.**	**6.**
◡ —	◡ —	◡ —	◡ —	◡ —	◡ ≃
◡ ◡ ◡	◡ ◡ ◡	◡ ◡ ◡	◡ ◡ ◡	◡ ◡ ◡	
— —		— —		— —	
— ◡ ◡		— ◡ ◡		— ◡ ◡	
◡ ◡ —		◡ ◡ —		◡ ◡ —	

Bĕā-|tŭs ĭl-|lĕ, quĭ | prŏcūl | nĕgŏ-|tĭĭs;
Ut pris-|ca gens | morta-|lium,
Pătĕr-|nă rū-|ră bŏ-|bŭs ĕx-|ērcĕt | sŭĭs,
Solu-|tus om-|ni fœ-|nore, etc. *Hor.*

The Iambic trimeter is often called the "*senarius*," from the number of feet of which the line is composed. When a line consists entirely of Iambusses, it is called a *pure* Iambic line; but when other feet, besides the iambus, enter into it, a *mixed* Iambic.

By prefixing one metre to the common iambic trimeter, the latter is changed into the Iambic tetrameter or "*octonarius*," which species of verse was used especially by the Latin comic writers.

TROCHAIC METRE.

§ 290.—The *Trochaic* Metre, so called from the trochee, its principal foot, is generally composed of either four or eight feet. In the odd places, it admits a tribrach; but in the seventh foot, a trochee only. In the even places, besides the tribrach, the spondee also, the dactyl, and anapæst are admitted.

The most common trochaic verse is the *octonarian* or tetrameter catalectic. It has the cæsural pause uniformly after the fourth foot, and is from its grave and sonorous character admirably adapted for hymns.

Trochaic tetrameter catalectic.

1.	2.	3.	4.	5.	6.	7.	8.
— ◡	— ◡	— ◡	— ◡	— ◡	— ◡	— ◡	≖
◡ ◡ ◡	◡ ◡ ◡	◡ ◡ ◡	◡ ◡ ◡	◡ ◡ ◡	◡ ◡ ◡		
	— —		— —		— —		
	◡ ◡ —		◡ ◡ —		◡ ◡ —		
	— ◡ ◡		— ◡ ◡		— ◡ ◡		

Pange | lingua | glori-|osi || laure-|am cer-|tami-|nis,
Et su-|per cru-|cis tro-|phæo || dic tri-|umphum | nobi-|lem,
Quali-|ter Re-|demptor | orbis || immo-|latus | vice-|rit. *S. Aug.*

Trochaic dimeter catalectic.

§ 291.—The Trochaic dimeter catalectic, which some prosodians consider and scan as an Iambic dimeter acephalous, admits in the second place the spondee, dactyl, and anapæst. But Horace, in the few lines he left us of this metre, uniformly employed the trochee.

THE LYRIC METRES OF HORACE.

§ 292.—A poem which contains one kind of verse only, is called carmen *monocŏlon;* a poem which contains two kinds, *dicŏlon;* and a poem which contains three kinds, *tricŏlon.*

When in a poem, after the second verse, the first returns, it is called *distrŏphon;* when after the third, *tristrŏphon;* when after the fourth, *tetrastrŏphon.*

The several verses which occur before the first line returns, are called a *stanza* or *strophe.*

§ 293.—1. ALCAIC (*carmen tricolon tetrastróphon*). The Alcaic strophe con-
sists of four lines. The first two are greater Alcaics, so called from the poet
Alcæus. The third is an iambic dimeter hypermeter, and the fourth a Minor
Alcaic.

```
⏑— | ⏑— |  —  | —⏑⏑ | —⏑⏘
⏑— | ⏑— |  —  | —⏑⏑ | —⏑⏘
   ⏑— | ⏑— | —— | ⏑— | ⏘
   —⏑⏑ | —⏑⏑ | —⏑ | —⏘
```

2. SAPPHIC (*carmen dicólon tetrastróphon*). The Sapphic strophe consists
of three Sapphic verses, invented by the poetess *Sappho*, and one Adonic.

```
—⏑ | —— | —⏑⏑ | —⏑ | —⏘
—⏑ | —— | —⏑⏑ | —⏑ | —⏘
—⏑ | —— | —⏑⏑ | —⏑ | —⏘
                    —⏑⏑ | —≍
```

3. ASCLEPIADIC (*carmen monocólon*). The Asclepiadic Metre consists of
one verse, invented by the poet *Asclepiades*.

```
—— | —⏑⏑— | —⏑⏑— | ⏑≍
                or
—— | —⏑⏑ | — | —⏑⏑ | —⏑⏘
```

4. ASCLEPIADIC-GLYCONIC (*carmen dicólon tetrastróphon*). This metre
consists of three Asclepiadic lines and one Glyconic, invented by the poet *Glyco*.

```
—— | —⏑⏑— | —⏑⏑— | ⏑≍
—— | —⏑⏑— | —⏑⏑— | ⏑≍
—⏜ | —⏑⏑— | —⏑⏑— | ⏑≍
        —— | —⏑⏑— | ⏑≍
```

5. ASCLEPIADIC-PHERECRATIC-GLYCONIC (*carmen tricolon tetrastró-*
phon). It consists of two Asclepiadics, one Pherecratic, so called from the poet
Pherecrátes, and one Glyconic.

```
—— | —⏑⏑— | —⏑⏑— | ⏑≍
—— | —⏑⏑— | —⏑⏑— | ⏑≍
    —— | —⏑⏑— | ≍
        —— | —⏑⏑— | ⏑≍
```

6. GLYCONIC-ASCLEPIADIC (*carmen dicōlon distrŏphon*). This metre consists of two verses—the first, a Glyconic; the second, an Asclepiadic.

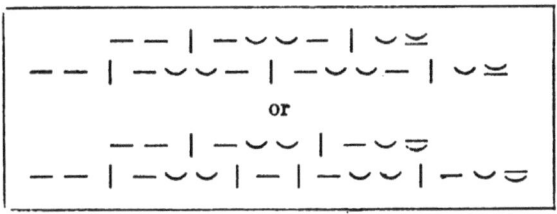

7. IAMBIC TRIMETER (*carmen monocōlon*). See § 289.—2.

8. One IAMBIC TRIMETER and one **IAMBIC DIMETER** (*carmen dicolon distrŏphon*). See § 289.—2 and 1.

9. One IAMBIC DIMETER acephalous and one **IAMBIC TRIMETER** acatalectic (*carmen dicolon distrŏphon*).

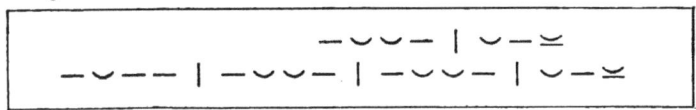

10. CHORIAMBIC PENTAMETER (*carmen monocōlon*). This line is made up of a spondee, three choriambi, and an iambus.

$$-\,- \mid -\,\smile\,\smile\,- \mid -\,\smile\,\smile\,- \mid -\,\smile\,\smile\,- \mid \smile\,\asymp$$

11. One CHORIAMBIC DIMETER and one **CHORIAMBIC TETRAMETER** (*carmen dicōlon distrŏphon*). ☞ In the first foot of the second verse, Horace generally uses a second epitrit ($-\,\smile\,-\,-$) instead of a choriambus.

$$-\,\smile\,\smile\,- \mid \smile\,-\,\asymp$$
$$-\,\smile\,-\,- \mid -\,\smile\,\smile\,- \mid -\,\smile\,\smile\,- \mid \smile\,-\,\asymp$$

12. One HEXAMETER and one **DACTYLIC TETRAMETER** a posteriore (*carmen dicōlon distrŏphon*). The dactylic tetrameter *a' posteriore* consists of the last four feet of the hexameter.

$$=\,\smile\,\smile \mid =\,\smile\,\smile \mid =\,\smile\,\smile \mid =\,\smile\,\smile \mid -\,\smile\,\smile \mid -\,\asymp$$
$$=\,\smile\,\smile \mid =\,\smile\,\smile \mid -\,\smile\,\smile \mid -\,\asymp$$

13. One **HEXAMETER** and one **DACTYLIC TRIMETER** catalectic (*carmen dicōlon distrŏphon*). The dactylic trimeter consists of the last three feet of the hexameter.

14. One **HEXAMETER** and one **IAMBIC TRIMETER** (*carmen dicōlon distrŏphon*). See §§ 285 and 289.—2.

15. One **HEXAMETER** and one **IAMBICO-DACTYLIC** (*carmen dicōlon distrŏphon*).

16. One **ARCHILOCHIAN HEPTAMETER** and one **IAMBIC TRIMETER** catalectic (*carmen dicōlon distrŏphon*). The Archilochian heptameter is made up of a dactylic tetrameter a priori,—that is, of the first four feet of the hexameter, of which the fourth is always a dactyl,—and of a pure trochaic dimeter brachycatalectic.

§ 294.—Index to the Odes of Horace,
(From the Paris edition)
containing the first words of each, with reference to the synopsis of the Horatian metres, as exhibited in § 293.

RHYMING VERSIFICATION.

§ 295.—Towards the middle of the fifth century a new political order compelled the Latin races to admit into their language a great many words, borrowed from the conquerors. The pronunciation was altered, little attention paid to prosody, and the meters, which result from a skilful combination of long and short syllables, seemed to have lost their power. Then sprang up a new poetical system, not grounded, as that of the ancients, on the quantity, but on the number of syllables : the harmonious blending of sounds became the chief object of poetry, and, at a still later period, symmetry called forth the modern rhyme. Part of the "*Jesu dulcis memoria*" and the whole of the "*Dies iræ*"—two sacred songs that have acquired a well-deserved celebrity, are subjoined as examples of rhyming versification. The easy flow and sweetness of the former make us almost forget Anacreon ; while the short, majestic lines of the latter so powerfully impress the mind, that they can scarcely be matched by the sublimest numbers of Horace.

JESU DULCIS MEMORIA.

(Attributed to St. Bernard.)

Jesu dulcis memoria,
Dans vera cordis gaudia,
Sed super mel et omnia
Ejus dulcis præsentia.

Nil canitur suavius,
Nil auditur jucundius,
Nil cogitatur dulcius,
Quam Jesus Dei filius.

O Jesu, spes pœnitentibus,
Quam pius es petentibus,
Quam bonus te quærentibus,
Sed quid invenientibus?

Nec lingua valet dicere,
Nec littera exprimere,
Expertus potest credere,
Quid sit Jesum diligere.

Jesu rex admirabilis
Et triumphator nobilis,
Dulcedo ineffabilis,
Totus desiderabilis.

Quando cor nostrum visitas,
Tunc lucet ei veritas,
Mundi vilescit vanitas
Et intus fervet charitas.

Jesu, decus Angelicum,
In aure dulce canticum,
In ore mel mirificum,
In corde nectar cœlicum.

Qui te gustant, esuriunt;
Qui bibunt, adhuc sitiunt;
Desiderare nesciunt,
Nisi Jesum, quem diligunt.

O Jesu mi dulcissime,
Spes suspirantis animæ,
Te quærant piæ lacrimæ
Te clamor·mentis intimæ.

Quocunque loco fuero,
Mecum Jesum desidero:
Quam lætus cum invenero,
Quam felix cum tenuero!

Jesum omnes agnoscite,
Amorem ejus poscite;
Jesum ardenter quærite,
Quærendo inardescite.

Te nostra, Jesu, vox sonet,
Nostri te mores exprimant,
Te corda nostra diligant,
Et nunc et in perpetuum. Amen.

DIES IRÆ.

(Immortalized by Mozart's Requiem.)

Dies iræ, dies illa
  Solvet sæclum in favilla,
  Teste David cum Sibylla.

Quantus tremor est futurus,
  Quando Judex est venturus,
  Cuncta stricte discussurus!

Tuba mirum spargens sonum
  Per sepulchra regionum,
  Coget omnes ante thronum.

Mors stupebit et natura,
  Cum resurget creatura,
  Judicanti responsura.

Liber scriptus proferetur,
  In quo totum continetur,
  Unde mundus judicetur.

Judex ergo cum sedebit,
  Quidquid latet, apparebit:
  Nil inultum remanebit.

Quid sum miser tunc dicturus,
  Quem patronum rogaturus,
  Cum vix justus sit securus?

Rex tremendæ majestatis,
  Qui salvandos salvas gratis,
  Salve me, fons pietatis.

Recordare, JESU pie,
  Quod sum causa tuæ viæ,
  Ne me perdas illa die.

Quærens me sedisti lassus,
  Redemisti crucem passus :
  Tantus labor non sit cassus.

Juste judex ultionis,
  Donum fac remissionis,
  Ante diem rationis.

Ingemisco, tamquam reus,
  Culpa rubet vultus meus ;
  Supplicanti parce, Deus.

Qui Mariam absolvisti,
  Et latronem exaudisti,
  Mihi quoque spem dedisti.

Preces meæ non sunt dignæ :
  Sed tu bonus fac benigne,
  Ne perenni cremer igne.

Inter oves locum præsta,
  Et ab hœdis me sequestra,
  Statuens in parte dextra.

Confutatis maledictis,
  Flammis acribus addictis,
  Voca me cum benedictis.

Oro supplex et acclinis,
  Cor contritum quasi cinis,
  Gere curam mei finis.

Lacrimosa dies illa,
  Qua resurget ex favilla,
  Judicandus homo reus.

Huic ergo parce, Deus :
  Pie JESU Domine,
  Dona eis requiem. Amen.

READING LESSONS.

DIALOGUES.

1. *On God.*

Pater. Filius.

P. Quid putas, fili mi, si consideras hæc prata, hos flores, has arbores; si conspicis fruges in agris, pisces in aquis, aves in aëre, solem in cœlo: num hæc omnia casu fortuito orta sunt? *F.* Hoc credere non possum. *P.* Unde igitur omnia habent originem? *F.* A Deo qui conditor est omnium rerum. *P.* Recte, fili mi! Deus auctor est cœli, solis, lunæ, et siderum; ignis, aëris, aquæ et terræ; hominum, bestiarum, quadrupedum, avium, piscium, ceterarumque animantium; plantarum, fruticum, et arborum; marium et fluminum; montium ac vallium; lapidum et metallorum. Unde igitur nosti, Deum esse? *F.* Ex innumeris ejus operibus.

2. *On rising.*

Vivianus. Paulus.

V. Heus, heus, Paule, expergiscere! tempus est surgere. Audisne? *P.* Non audio. *V.* Ubi ergo habes aures? *P.* In lecto. *V.* Hoc video. Sed quid facis adhuc in lecto? *P.* Quid faciam?—dormio. *V.* Dormis? et loqueris tamen mecum. *P.* Saltem volo dormire. *V.* Nunc autem non est tempus dormiendi, sed surgendi. *P.* Quota hora est? *V.* Septima. *P.* Quando tu surrexisti e lecto? *V.* Jam ante duas horas. *P.* Num sorores jam surrexerunt? *V.* Jam pridem. *P.* Sed Ludovicus certe adhuc jacet in lecto. *V.* Erras. Quum expergefacerem eum, statim reliquit nidum suum. *P.* Mox igitur surgam.

3. *On writing.*

Leonardus. Henricus.

L. Quid agis, Henrice? *H.* Scribo, ut vides. *L.* Quid scribis? *H.* Versus quos præceptor dictavit. *L.* Ostende, quæso, scripturam. *H.* Aspice. *L.* Videris mihi nimis festinanter scripsisse. *H.* Scribo interdum melius.

L. Cur igitur nunc tam male scribis? *H.* Desunt mihi bene scribendi adju
menta. *L.* Quænam? *H.* Bona charta, bonum atramentum, bona penna.
Hæc enim charta, ut vides, misere diffundit litteras; atramentum est aquo-
sum et pallidum; penna mollis et male parata. *L.* Cur ista omnia non
mature providisti? *H.* Pecunia mihi deerat et nunc etiam deest. *L.* Tibi
aliquid pecuniæ commodabo, ut meliorem chartam resque ceteras tibi emere
possis. *H.* Benevolentiam tuam gratus agnosco.

4. *On ink.*

Julius. Augustus.

J. Habesne bonum atramentum, amice? *A.* Habeo. *J.* Visne mihi dare
aliquantulum? *A.* Eho! non habes? *J.* Equidem habeo, sed eo non possum scribere. *A.* Cur non? *J.* Quia nimis spissum est. *A.* Porrige
vasculum tuum; ego tibi infundam. *J.* Ecce, infunde. Vah, quam liqui-
dum est! Sed admodum decôlor esse videtur. *A.* Satis nigrum evadet,
modo bene miscueris. *J.* Feci, et probe miscui. *A.* Nunc fac periculum et
scribe aliquid. *J.* Dicta mihi sententiam aliquam. *A.* Græcam mavis, an
Latinam, an Anglicam? *J.* Dicta Latinam. *A.* Scribe: *Experientia est
optima rerum magistra.* *J.* Scripsi. *A.* Nunc expecta dum scriptura bene
desiccata sit. Jam vide quam nigra sit. *J.* Sic est. *A.* Ergo experientia
tua magistra fuit.

5. *On letter-writing.*

Daniel. Philippus.

D. Quid legis, Philippe? *P.* Epistolam. *D.* Quis scripsit? *P.* Frater
meus. *D.* Unde? *P.* Parisiis. *D.* Quo die? *P.* Die Mercurii. *D.* Quando
accepisti? *P.* Hac ipsa hora. *D.* Quis attulit? *P.* Nescio. *D.* Nescis?
Quis tibi eam dedit? *P.* Auriga quidam misit mihi e deversorio. *D.* Quid
tibi scripsit frater? *P.* Longum est enarrare omnia, necdum totam perlegi:
litteras ipsas tibi ostendam post prandium. *D.* Id mihi pergratum erit.
Quando rescribes? *P.* Fortasse perendie. *D.* Tum saluta eum meo nomine.
Nosti enim quantopere eum semper amaverim. *P.* Hoc probe scio. *D.* Ergo
epistolam mecum communicabis? *P.* Ut promisi.

6. *On repetition.*

Fredericus. Carolus.

F. Quid agis, Carole? *C.* Repeto pensum hesternum. *F.* Tenesne memoria? *C.* Propemodum. Et tu num recitare poteris? *F.* Vereor ut possim.
C. Visne repetamus una? *F.* Libentissime. Sed quomodo rem instituemus?
C. Audiamus alter alterum. *F.* Cur autem repetimus hodie quæ pridie
didicimus? *C.* Quia præceptor nos sic facere jubet? *F.* Id satis scio; sed
cur jubet? *C.* Ut memoriam exerceamus; nam quo diligentius pensum
repetimus, eo melius tenemus. Incipe igitur et recita. *F.* Atqui tuum est
potius incipere. *C.* Quid ita? *F.* Quia me invitasti. *C.* Incipiam igitur.
Tu vero attente audi ut moneas si quid peccaverim.

7. *On playing.*

Conradus. Godofredus. Otto.

C. Veni, Godofrede! veni Otto! venite ambo! *G.* Quo tandem? *C.* In aream; præceptor enim nos jussit ludere. *O.* Quid hic narrat? *C.* Quod certissimum est et quod ipsi a ceteris commilitonibus mox audietis. *G.* Ludant sane alii, quantum voluerint: ego non ludam. *O.* Nec mihi animus est ludendi. *C.* Quare autem? *G.* Malo repetere lectiones meas quam ludendo tempus perdere. *C.* Num hoc est tempus perdere, si corpus exercemus ad valetudinem conservandam? *O.* Tu corpus exerce: ego vero describam quæ præceptor dictavit. *C.* Ohe! quam morosos habeo condiscipulos! *G.* Sibi quisque serit, sibi metit. *C.* At præceptor nos ludere jusssit. *O.* Mentiris! Debebas dicere eum permisisse ut ludamus, non autem jussisse. Nemo enim ad ludum cogitur. *C.* Valete, ego ludam.

8. *Funny talk.*

Andreas. Mauritius. Rudolphus.

A. Salve, mi Mauriti! *M.* Gratias ago, mi Andrea! Quid affers? *A.* Meipsum. *M.* Sic rem haud magni pretii huc attulisti. *A.* Atqui magno constiti patri meo. *M.* Credo pluris quam quisquam te æstimet. *A.* Sed Rudolphus estne domi? *M.* Nescio. Pulsa fores ejus et videbis. *A.* Heus! Rudolphe, num domi es? *R.* Non sum. *A.* Impudens! non ego audio te loquentem? *R.* Immo tu es impudens. Nuper ancillæ vestræ credidi, te non esse domi, cum tamen esses; et tu non credis mihi ipsi. *A.* Æquum dicis; par pari retulisti. *R.* Equidem, ut non omnibus dormio, ita non omnibus sum domi. Nunc vero adsum. *A.* Sed tu mihi videris cochleæ vitam agere. *R.* Quid ita? *A.* Quia perpetuo domi latitas, nec unquam prorepis. *R.* Foris mihi nihil est negotii. *A.* At serenum cœlum nunc invitat ad deambulandum. *R.* Verum est. Si ergo deambulare lubet, per horulam te comitabor; nam toto hoc mense pedem porta non extuli. Vocabo Mauritium ut una nobiscum eat. *A.* Placet. Sic enim jucundior erit deambulatio.

9. *The sluggard.*

Maximilianus. Guilielmus.

M. Hodie te conventum volebam, Guilielme; sed negabaris esse domi. *G.* Non omnino mentiti sunt. Tibi quidem non eram, sed mihi tum eram maxime. *M.* Quid isthoc ænigmatis est? *G.* Dormiebam. *M.* Quid ais? atqui jam præterierat octava, quum sol hoc mense oriatur ante quartam. *G.* Per me quidem soli liberum est oriri vel media nocte, modo mihi liceat ad satietatem usque dormire. Nullus enim somnus suavior est quam post exortum solem. *M.* Qua tandem hora soles e lecto surgere? *G.* Inter quartam et nonam. *M.* Satis amplum spatium! Vix unquam vidi hominem te magis prodigum. *G.* At mihi parsimonia potius videtur; interim enim nec candelas absumo, nec vestes detero. *M.* Præpostera sane parsimonia. Aliter sentiebat ille philosophus qui rogatus quid esset pretiosissimum, respondit, tempus.

10. *Continued.*

G. Sed dulce est dormire. *M.* Quid potest esse dulce nihil sentienti? Verum reputa, quæso, quantum eruditionis tibi parare possis quatuor illis horis quas somno intempestivo perdere soles. Nosti proverbium : Aurora musis amica. Nunquam enim alacrior est animus hominis quam matutino tempore, nec unquam feliciores in litterarum studiis progressus facere possumus. Quid suspiras, Guilielme? *G.* Vera profecto prædicas et vix a lacrimis mihi temperare possum quum cogito quantam fecerim jacturam. *M.* In id igitur incumbe ut futuro tempori parcas; nec nimio te dedas somno. Septem enim horas dormisse adulto homini, bene valenti, sufficit. *G.* Vereor ut possim ; nam consuetudo est altera natura, ac difficillimum est ea relinquere, quibus diu assuevimus. *M.* Initio quidem, sed eam molestiam brevi tempore vinces, et tum tibi ipse sero licet gratulaberis mihique gratias ages qui monuerim.

11. *Invitation to dinner.*

Gustavus. Stephanus.

G. Salve multum, jucundissime Stephane! *S.* Salve et ipse, humanissime Gustave! Quid agis? *G.* Ego nonnihil habeo quod tibi succenseam. *S.* Quid ita? quid admisi sceleris? *G.* Quod me plane negligis meque tam raro revisis. *S.* Verum hoc non mea culpa accidit. Dabis veniam occupationibus meis per quas mihi non licet te quoties cupio revisere. *G.* Ita demum tibi ignoscam, si hodie apud me cœnes. *S.* Haud iniquas pacis leges præscribis, Gustave. Libentissime veniam. *G.* At cave me deluseris. *S.* Hac in re non fallam. Sed heus tu! cave quidquam paraveris præter quotidiana. *G.* Cavebo et satis frugali cœna te excipiam. At tu vide, omnes curas tuas et quidquid hilaritati officiat, domi relinquas. *S.* Ita fiet. Explicabimus frontem nosque jucunditati dabimus. Numquid aliud vis? *G.* Fac ad quintam horam adsis. *S.* Adero. Interea vale.

12. *On hunting.*

Paulus. Theophilus. Vivianus. Ludovicus. Bernardus.

P. Trahit sua quemque voluptas: mihi placet venatio. *T.* Placet etiam mihi; sed ubi canes, ubi venabula, ubi casses? *P.* Valeant apri, ursi, cervi, et vulpes! nos insidiabimur cuniculis. *V.* At ego laqueos injiciam locustis. *T.* Ego ranas captabo. *B.* Ego papiliones venabor. *T.* Difficile est sectari volantia. *B.* Difficile, sed pulchrum ; nisi pulchrius esse ducis sectari lumbricos aut cochleas, quia carent alis. *L.* Equidem malo insidiari piscibus; est mihi hamus elegans. *B.* Sed unde parabis escam? *L.* Lumbricorum ubivis magna est copia. *B.* Sed plerique pisces delicatioris et elegantioris sunt palati quam ut esca tam vulgari capiantur. *T.* Tu vide, Ludovice, possisne imponere piscibus; ego ranis facessam negotium. *L.* Quomodo? reti? *T.* Non; sed arcu. *L.* Novum piscandi genus. *T.* At non injucundum. Videbis et fatebere. *V.* Quid, si certemus nucibus? *P.* Nuces pueris relinquamus; nos grandiores sumus. *V.* Et tamen nihil adhuc aliud quam pueri sumus. *P*: Sed quibus decorum est ludere nucibus, iisdem non indecorum est equitare in arundine longa. *V.* Tu igitur præscribito lusus genus; sequar quocunque vocaveris. *P.* Et ego futurus sum omnium horarum homo.

13. *The traveller.*

Ferdinandus. Eugenius.

F. Salve, mi Eugeni! *E.* Tu quoque salve, mi Ferdinande! *F.* Quomodo vales ex tam diuturno itinere? *E.* Optime, ut vides. *F.* Vehementer gaudeo te rediisse incolumem. Ubinam fuisti tot annis? quas terras peragrasti. *E.* In Anglia fui, in Gallia et Italia. *F.* Quasnam Italiæ urbes vidisti? *E.* Imprimis commoratus sum Genuæ, Florentiæ, Venetiis, Neapoli, et Romæ. Postea Bononiam vidi, Patavium, et Mediolanum; in singulis autem hisce urbibus tantum aliquot menses commoratus sum. *F.* Quid autem novi vidisti in tot locis celeberrimis? *E.* Fere omnia mihi nova videbantur; sed longum est omnia enarrare. *F.* Dic saltem quomodo urbs nostra tibi visa sit post tam longam absentiam? *E.* Omnia mutata sunt. Quam repente res hominum mutantur! Vix decem annos abfueram, et non secus omnia admirabar ac somnians ille Epimenides, cum esset expergefactus.

14. *Continued.*

F. Quænam ista est fabula? *E.* Narrant historici de Epimenide quodam Cretensi, qui deambulandi gratia solus urbe egressus, quum subita pluvia compellente in quandam speluncam ingressus obdormisset, nescio quot annos perpetuos somnum continuarit. *F.* Quid narras? Isthoc est mentiri! Sed perge, quæso. *E.* Epimenides igitur somno solutus e spelunca prodit, circumspicit, mutata videt omnia, silvas, flumina, ripas, arbores, agros. Accedit ad urbem; percontatur, manet illic aliquamdiu, neque novit quemquam, neque a quopiam agnoscitur. Alius hominum cultus, mutatus sermo, diversi mores. Nec miror hoc Epimenidi post tot annorum spatium evenisse, quum mihi idem propemodum evenerit qui nonnisi paucos annos abfuerim. *F.* Jam te diutius detinere nolim; alio tempore multa mihi narrabis. Vale, Eugeni carissime! *E.* Vale.

15. *A promenade.*

Pater. Filius.

P. Paululum deambulaturus sum et tu me comitaberis, fili mi! *F.* Quonam ibimus, pater carissime? *P.* In agros. Segetem lustrabimus. *F.* Qua vero via? hacne lata, an illa semita? *P.* Per semitam ibimus; nam hæc lata via nondum satis sicca est. *F.* Verum ista semita angusta est et lubrica. *P.* Noli timere. Simulac post illam maceriam venerimus, latior fiet atque expeditior. *F.* O quam serenum et mite cœlum! *P.* Audisne alaudam canentem? *F.* Audio, sed non video. *P.* Alauda magis auribus percipitur quam oculis. Sed hic sursum tolle vultum, et eam videbis. *F.* Jam video. Puncti instar est; adeo pusilla apparet. *P.* Nunc pervenimus ad collem, mi fili! ex quo immensa panditur planities. Ascendamus igitur. *F.* O præclarum prospectum! *P.* Hic urbem nostram vides et fluvium flexuosis anfractibus labentem, ad dexteram campos patentissimos, ad sinistram montes silvis vestitos, et vineas amœnissimas.

16. *Continued.*

F. Istic ovium gregem conspicio. Ubi est opilio? *P.* Illic sub arbore consēdit. *F.* Nulline ei canes sunt? *P.* Nonne eos vides prope opilionem cubantes? *F.* Timeo ne me mordeant. *P.* Non est quod timeas; non te lædent. Sed illuc verte oculos. Videsne cervum ramosis ornatum cornibus? *F.* Quam præstanti est forma! Hic leporem video currentem. Quos ille saltus facit! *P.* Est animal timidissimum. *F.* Sed quis ille vir est, viridi indutus veste? *P.* Venator est. *F.* Habet secum duo canes venaticos. *P.* Hi semper venatorem sequuntur, cum sint ad venandum necessarii. *F.* Video hominem pauperem, nobis appropinquantem. Nos allocuturus videtur esse. Ibo ei obviam, ut si forte ope nostra egeat, preces ejus præveniam. *P.* Bene facis, fili mi, ito! *F.* Non erat mendicus, sed viator, qui me, ut viam sibi monstrarem, rogabat. *P.* Monstrastine brevissimam? *F.* Monstravi, ut aberrare non possit. *P.* Sed jam redeamus, satis jam ambulatum est. Eamus per hanc silvulam; hac via citius domum veniemus. *F.* Visne præcedam? *P.* Præcede.

17. *Missed lessons.*

Theodorus. Augustus.

A. Hodiene demum rure rediisti? *T.* Hodie, paulo ante prandium *A.* Atqui dixeras te modo biduum ibi mansurum. *T.* Ita fore sperabam et pater sic prædixerat. *A.* Quid igitur obstitit, quominus citius redieris? *T.* Mater me detinuit. *A.* Cur te tam diu retinuit? *T.* Ut ipsam redeuntem comitarer. *A.* Quid vero agebas interea? *T.* Colligebam fructus cum rusticis nostris. *A.* Quos fructus? *T.* Quasi ignoti tibi sint fructus serotīni: pira, mala, juglandes, castaneæ. *A.* Jucundum sane negotium! Sed interim quinque aut sex scholarum fructus tibi periit. *T.* Hoc valde doleo: sed omnibus viribus enītar ut damnum quodammodo resarciam. *A.* Quid facies? *T.* Describam omnia quam diligentissime. *A.* Sed non omnia satis intelliges. *T.* Tum tu mihi aderis et explicationem præceptoris mecum communicabis. *A.* Quanto præstitisset, ipsum audire magistrum! *T.* Multo sane præstitisset; sed cum hoc mihi non contigerit, nec mea culpa factum sit, non habeo quod me accusem. *A.* Recte dicis. Sed frater nos vocat ad cœnam. *T.* Intremus igitur.

15.

Carolus. Eugenius.

C. Audi amice! *E.* Quid vis? *C.* Visne mecum ire in hortum principis? *E.* Quid illic aspectu jucundum videbimus? *C.* Varias et pulchras arbores, herbarum et florum miram varietatem, amœnissimas ambulationes, fontes salientes plurimasque statuas. *E.* Cœli serenitas nos invitat, et tempus vacat. Paululum modo expecta, dum vestem mutaverim. Jam paratus sum. Num hortus longe hinc abest? *C.* Non admodum longe. Nunquamne in eo fuisti? *E.* Nunquam. *C.* Ecce porta! Intremus! *E.* Præi, ego sequar. *C.* Videsne ambulationem pulcherrimam? hic ad dextram taxorum duplicem seriem? *E.* Et hæ statuæ, quam artificiose sculptæ sunt!

Continued.

E. Ubi autem est fons saliens? *C.* Mox videbis. *E.* Jam video. Vah, quam alte aquas ejaculatur! *C.* Hic xystus est, in quo, cum pluit, inambulant, ne imbre madescant. *E.* Quænam sunt hæ arbores, in cistis ligneis positæ? *C.* Sunt citri et ficus. Ambulemus paulisper in hoc pomario. *E.* O locum amœnissimum! quot areŏlæ, pulcherrimis floribus consïtæ! *C.* Illic topiarii filiolus florum fasciculum colligit. Illum, credo, tibi offeret. *E.* Ego vero sorori meæ feram. Gratissimum id ipsi futurum scio. *C.* Sed munusculum aliquod puerulo dandum est. *E.* Sane! ejusmŏdi dona gratis accipere turpe esset. *C.* Nullus est sensus, qui hic non aliqua voluptate afficiatur. Quæ colorum varietas! qui cantus avium! quam grati odores! Et quid mollius hac ipsa aura, quæ salutari spiritu corpus refrigerat et vires reficit. Non solum corpus, sed etiam animus noster exhilaratur hujusmodi amœnitatibus. *E.* Verum est, quod dicis. Sed fructus isti me cœnæ commonefaciunt. Invitatus sum a Sempronio. *C.* Redeamus igitur.

16.

Gustavus. Ferdinandus.

G. Audisne ventum vehementer flantem? *F.* Audio. *G.* Nonne melius nobiscum ageretur, si omnis ventus et tristis illa hiems a terris nostris abesset? *F.* Non est ita; istæ res valde utiles sunt. *G.* Cuinam rei? *F.* Venti purgant aërem vaporibus minus salubribus et ne pestiferis impleatur vaporibus, impediunt. *G.* Audio. Sed quid hiems prodest? *F.* Terræ aliisque rebus vires reddit, quas per æstatem amiserunt. Nonne arbores, si perpetuo solis calore crescere et fructus ferre cogerentur, brevi tempore interirent? *G.* Unde autem fit, ut hieme terra gelu concrescat et flumina glacie indurentur? *F.* Hiberno tempore radii solis obliquius feruntur ad eam terræ partem, ubi hiems est, ideoque longe minorem vim habent calefaciendi. Huc accedit quod per hiemem noctes longiores sunt, dies autem breviores.

Continued.

G. Attamen satius foret, si perpetuo vere frueremur. *F.* Erras. Ver perpetuum tibi et mihi omnibusque tandem tædio foret. *G.* Hoc vix crediderim. *F.* Omnis voluptas rerum varietate nititur. Res quamvis pulcherrima et jucundissima tandem tædio fit, si ea perpetuo utimur. Cogita quam suavis sit sanitas corporis iis, qui gravi morbo laborarunt, et quam parvi æstimetur ab iis qui nunquam ægrotarunt. *G.* Quid autem dicis de tonitribus? Nonne optandum esset, ut nunquam fulmina, nunquam tonitrua nos terrērent? *F.* Etiam fulmina et tonitrua sunt necessaria; terram enim fertiliorem reddunt noxiosque vapores consumunt. Deus etiam ea quæ terribilia nobis videntur, commodi nostri causa fecit. *G.* Non stulte loqueris. Video Deum res omnes sapientissime instituisse.

17.

Julius. Augustus.

J. Quid facis, Auguste? Cave tibi, obsecro. *A.* Quid mihi cavebo? *J.* Ne in morbum incidas tua ipsius culpa. *A.* Qua ex causa? *J.* Ex nimia lusus intemperantia. *A.* Unde adparet periculum? *J.* Quia totus æstuas, totus sudore mades. *A.* Recte et in tempore admónes; profecto non sentiebam. *J.* Desiste, si me audis. *A.* Libentissime tibi morem gero. Quis enim respuat tam fidele consilium? *J.* Deterge faciem et vestj te celeriter, ne subitum frigus contrahas. Omnis enim subita mutatio periculosa est. *A.* Habeo tibi gratiam, Juli, nam vere morbis sum obnoxius. *J.* Tanto magis debes cavere. *A.* Istud probe scio, et parens uterque me monet sæpissime. Sed quid agam? natura proni sumus in nostram perniciem. *J.* O mi Auguste! non est voluptati serviendum, sed temperantia valetudini consulendum. Jam satis bene indutus es. Nunc suadeo ut domum redeas. *A.* Vale, suavissime Juli, monĭtor amicissime!

NARRATIVES AND ANECDOTES.

1.

Sutor quidam corvum instituerat, ut Augustum his verbis salutaret : Ave, Cæsar, victor, imperator! Quoties autem corvus hanc salutationem recitare noluerat, sutor indignabundus dixerat: Oleum et operam perdidi. Tandem avem obtulit Augusto. Qui cum audiret corvi salutationem : Satis, inquit, domi salutatorum talium habeo. Tum corvus addidit: *Oleum et operam perdidi.* Risit Augustus, emique avem jussit, quanti nullam adhuc emerat.

2.

Marcus Piso, orator Romanus, ne interpellaretur, servis præceperat, ut ad interrogata tantum responderent, nec quidquam præterea dicerent. Evenit ut Clodium qui tum magistratum gerebat, ad cœnam invitari juberet. Hora cœnæ instabat ; aderant ceteri convivæ omnes ; solus expectabatur Clodius. Piso servum, qui convivas vocare solebat, aliquoties emisit ut videret, num veniret. Vesperascente jam cœlo, quum adventus ejus desperaretur, Piso servo : Dic, inquit, num forte non invitasti Clodium ?—Invitavi, respondit ille.—Cur ergo non venit ?—Quia venturum se negavit. Tum Piso : Cur id non statim dixisti ?—Quia id non sum abs te interrogatus.

3.

Puer quidam, cui interdictum erat ne quid cibi inter cœnandum peteret, quum se prætermissum videret, nonnihil salis posuit in orbe. Interrogatus quare id faceret: Hoc, inquit, sale aspergam carnem quam accepturus sum.

4.

Quum medicus celeberrimus omnes artis suæ vias ad levandum Frederici Secundi, Borussiæ regis, morti jam vicini, morbum frustra tentasset, atque hic vultu indignanti et impatienti ex ipso quæsisset: Tune jam multis iter ad inferos maturasti? ille, qui regem breviter et acute sibi responderi velle probe intelligeret: Non tam multis, quam tu, rex.—Atque hoc ei responsum non displicuisse vultu tum prodidisse dicitur.

5.

Hugo Grotius, quum esset inimicorum machinis in custodiam conjectus, identidem arcam librorum, sibi ab uxore missam in carcerem, recepit. Hos libros quum perlegisset, in eadem arca repositos ad uxorem referri jussit, quæ eam novis libris onustam ad Grotium remittere solebat. Tandem uxor consilium cepit, hac ratione mariti ex custodia liberandi. Suasit ei ut se ipsum in hac arca componi pateretur. Obsequutus est Grotius, et custodum diligentiam, quippe qui libros more consueto e carcere efferri putarent, fefellit.

6. *Demosthenes and the judges.*

Demosthenes causam orans quum judices parum attentos videret: Paullisper, inquit, aures mihi præbete; rem vobis novam et jucundam narrabo. Quum aures arrexissent: Juvenis, inquit, quispiam asinum conduxerat, quo Athenis Megăram profecturus uteretur. In itinere quum sol ureret, neque esset umbraculum, deposuit clitellas et sub asino consedit, cujus umbra tegeretur. Id vero agaso vetabat, clamans, asinum locatum esse, non umbram asini. Alter quum contra contenderet, tandem in jus ambulant. Hæc locutus Demosthenes, ubi homines arrectis auribus auscultantes vidit, abiit. Tum revocatus a judicibus rogatusque ut reliquam fabulam enarraret: Quid, inquit, de asini umbra libet audire? causam hominis de vita periclitantis non audietis?

7. *The silly critic.*

Sunt qui vel mundi opificem sapientissimum reprehendere audeant. Quum quidam cucurbitam grandiorem tenui in caule humi jacentem videret: Hem! inquit, non in caule tenui, sed in alta quercu ego eam suspendissem. Abire deinde, et sub quercu aliqua obdormiscere. Qui quum dormiret, ventus glandes innumeras a quercu decutere, quarum aliqua nasum hominis vehementius tetigit. Expergefactus ille quum sanguinem e naso profluentem cerneret: Quid, inquit, si hæc cucurbita fuisset, vix equidem viverem amplius. Deum profecto sentio sapientissime atque optime mundum disposuisse.

8. *Remarkable sayings.*

Thales interrogatus, hominumne facta Deum fallerent, *ne cogitata quidem*, respondit.—Idem rogatus quid maxime commune esset hominibus, *Spes*, respondit; *hanc enim illi quoque habent qui nihil habent aliud.*—Socrates in pompa quum magna vis auri argentique ferretur: *Quam multa non desidero*, inquit.—Epictetus interrogatus quis esset dives? *Cui*, inquit, *satis est, quod habet.*—Rutilius Rufus, homo justissimus, quum amici cujusdam injustis precibus resisteret isque indignabundus dixisset: Quid ergo amicitia tua mihi prodest, si quod rogo, non facis? *Immo,* inquit, *quid mihi tua, si propter te aliquid inhoneste facturus sum?*

9. *The boaster put to the trial.*

Homo quidam reversus in patriam, unde aliquot abfuerat annos, ubique gloriabatur jactabatque præclara sua facinora. Inter alia narrabat in insula Rhodo saliendo se vicisse optimos in hac exercitatione artifices. Ostendebat etiam spatii longitudinem, quam præter se nemo potuisset saltu superare, cujus saltus testes se habere universos Rhodios dicebat. Tum unus ex adstantibus: Heus tu, inquit, si vera narras, nihil opus est istis testibus. Hic Rhodum esse puta, hic salta.

10. *Funny stories.*

Geminorum frater alter mortuus erat. Quidam igitur obvius vivo: Tune, inquit, mortuus es an frater tuus?

Vir quidam nobilis in littore maris ambulabat. Occurrit homo importunus ejusque latus percutiens: Non ego, inquit, cuilibet fatuo decedere soleo. At ego soleo, inquit alter et decessit.

Vir quidam verberibus castigavit servum maxime ob pigritiam. Cur me percutis, hic clamare cœpit, nihil enim feci. Atqui propter hoc ipsum, respondit herus, te percutio, quod nihil fecisti.

11.

Quidam flumen trajecturus, equo insidens navem conscendit. Quum quis causam percontaretur: Festino, inquit.

Homo quidam stolidus audiverat corvos amplius ducentos annos vivere. Hoc igitur, verumne esset, exploraturus, pullum corvinum in cavea inclusum alere cœpit.

Puer quidam passeres in arbore conspicatus, clanculum subrepsit et linteo substrato arborem quassavit, passeres excepturus.

12.

Agaso quidam, quum asinis suis identidem numeratis sensisset unum numero abesse, iratus accusare vicinos furti cœpit, oblitus, se illi asino insidēre, quem amissum arbitrabatur.

Stolidus stolido obviam factus: Audivi, inquit, te mortuum esse.—At me vivum adhuc et spirantem vides, respondit alter. Verum, inquit ille; sed qui mihi hoc dixit, te fide dignior est.

Hominem jocosum stolidus quidam interrogavit: Cur, quæso, inquit, sol qui occidentem versus occidere solet, semper tamen ab oriente resurgit? Respondit alter, solem eadem semper via recurrere post occasum, sed cerni non posse redeuntem, obstante scilicet noctis caligine.

13.

Græcus quidam Augusto e Palatio descendenti, honorificum aliquod epigramma porrigere solebat spe præmii. Id quum sæpe frustra fecisset, Augustus eum deterriturus breve epigramma sua manu exaratum Græculo advenienti obviam misit. Ille, dum legeret, laudabat, et tum voce, tum vultu gestuque mirabatur. Deinde ad sellam accessit qua Cæsar ferebatur, paucosque ex crumena denarios protraxit, quos Cæsari daret, dixitque, se plus daturum fuisse, si plus habuisset. Omnes risere; Cæsar autem dispensatorem vocari et Græco satis magnam pecuniæ summam numerari jussit.

14.

Lysimăchus inter duces Alexandri illustri genere, sed longe magis virtute quam genere clarus erat. Cum Alexander Callisthěnem philosophum miserandum in modum omnibus membris truncasset et insuper cum cane in cavea inclusum circumferri jussisset, Lysimachus, qui philosophum audire atque ex ejus ore virtutis et sapientiæ præcepta percipere solitus erat, venenum ei dedit remedium calamitatum. Quod adeo ægre tulit Alexander, ut Lysimachum leoni objici juberet. Sed quum leo impetum fecisset in eum,

Lysimachus manum amiculo involutam in os leonis immersit arreptaque lingua feram exanimavit. Quod quum nuntiatum regi esset, admiratio iræ successit, carioremque Lysimachum habuit propter tantam constantiam.

15.

Ad P. Scipionem Africanum visendum, cum in villa prope Liternum versaretur, plures prædonum duces eodem tempore forte convenerant. Quos cum Scipio ad vim faciendam venisse putaret, præsidia domesticorum disposuit omnique modo domum defendere statuit. Prædones, hoc viso, arma statim abjecerunt januæque appropinquantes clara voce exclamarunt se non vitæ ejus hostes, sed virtutis admiratores venisse; conspectum et congressum tanti viri quasi cœleste aliquod beneficium se expetere: proinde securus spectandum se præberet. Tum Scipio januas reserari ac prædones intromitti jussit. Qui quum januam tamquam aram aliquam aut delubrum venerati essent, cupide Scipionis dextram comprehenderunt atque osculati sunt. Mox positis ante vestibulum donis, quæ deorum numini consecrari solebant, læti, quod Scipionem videre contigisset, ad naves suas recesserunt. Tanta hujus viri admiratio etiam apud abjectissimos fuit homines.

16.

Antisthenes discipulos hortabatur ut sedulo operam darent sapientiæ. Pauci obtemperabant. Itaque indignatus dimisit omnes. Inter hos Diogenes erat. Qui quum magna discendi cupiditate incensus ad Antisthenem ventitare pergeret nec discedere vellet, Antisthenes tandem minatus est se caput ejus percussurum esse baculo quem manu gestare solebat. Non recessit Diogenes, sed animo obstinato: Percŭte, inquit, si ita placet. Ego tibi caput præbebo, neque tam durum fustem invenies, quo me a tuis disputationibus abigas. Antisthenes tam cupidum doctrinæ discipulum admisit eumque maxime adamavit.

17.

Athenis olim fuit vir quidam, nomine Timon, qui in universum hominum genus odium conceperat. Is aliquando prodiit in concionem. Quod cum præter consuetudinem faceret, magna omnium expectatio fuit, quidnam afferret. Tum ille e suggestu, in quem ascenderat: Athenienses, inquit, est mihi ficus quædam, e qua jam multi sponte se suspenderunt. Quoniam autem in area illa ædes exstructurus sum, priusquam ficum cædo, monere vos volui, ut si quis de suspendio cogitet, quam maxime properet.

18.

Fuerunt olim duo pictores celeberrimi, quorum alter Zeuxis, Parrhasius alter appellatus est. Hi aliquando de arte certabant. Zeuxis uvas pinxerat atque sic erat imitatus naturæ veritatem, ut aves ad tabulam advolarent, quasi veræ essent uvæ. Tum Parrhasius tabulam attulit, in qua linteum pinxerat. Zeuxis deceptus pictum linteum verum habuit, sub quo pictura occultaretur. Quum igitur diutius morari videretur Parrhasius, Zeuxis flagitabat ut tandem linteum removēret ostenderetque picturam. Tum vero quum intellexisset errorem, palmam Parrhasio detulit ingenuo pudore, quoniam ipse aves fefellisset, Parrhasius autem ipsum artificem.

19.

Diogenes interroganti cuidam, quanam ratione posset optime ulcisci inimicum : Si te ipsum, inquit, probum et honestum virum præstiteris.— Cum Græci, qui Asiam incolebant, Persarum regem ex more Magnum appellarent, Agesilaus : Num, inquit, ille me major est, si non est justior et temperantior?—P. Scipio dicere solebat, nunquam se minus otiosum esse, quam quum otiosus, nec minus solum, quam quum solus esset. Magnifica vero vox et magno viro ac sapiente digna!—Solon, Atheniensium legislator, cum interrogaretur, cur nullum supplicium constituisset in eum qui parentem necasset : Quia neminem, inquit, hoc facturum esse puto.—Diogenes lucernam accensam circumferens clarissima luce in foro ambulabat, quærenti similis. Rogantibus quid ageret? Hominem, inquit, quæro.

20.

Marcus Cato puer in domo avunculi sui, Drusi, tribuni plebis, educabatur. Apud quem cum socii de civitate impetranda convenissent, et Quintus Poppedius, Marsorum princeps, eum rogaret ut socios apud avunculum adjuvaret, constanti vultu respondit, non facturum se. Iterum deinde et sæpius rogatus, in proposito perstitit. Tunc Poppedius puero in altissimam ædium partem sublato minatus est, se eum inde dejecturum, nisi precibus obtemperaret. Sed Cato ne hac quidem re ab incepto depelli potuit. Ita Poppedio vox illa expressa est : Gratulemur nobis, socii, hunc esse tam parvum : quo senatore ne sperare quidem civitatem liceret. Sic ea constantia, quam postea per totam vitam ostendit, jam in puero Catone apparuit.

FABLES.

1.

Vulpes, extrema fame coacta, uvam appetebat, ex alta vite dependentem. Quam quum summis viribus saliens attingere non posset, tandem discedens: Nondum matura est, inquit; nolo acerbam sumere.—Sic sæpe homines, quæ facere non possunt, verbis elevant.

2.

Asinus ægrotabat famaque exierat eum cito esse moriturum. Cum igitur lupi canesque venissent ad eum visendum, quærerentque ex filio, quomodo pater ejus se haberet, ille per ostii rimulam respondit: Melius quam velletis.

3.

Opiliones aliquot, cæsa atque assata ove, convivium agebant. Quod quum lupus, qui prædandi causa forte stabula circumibat, videret, ad opiliones conversus: Quos clamores, inquit, et quantos tumultus vos contra me excitaretis, si ego facerem, quod vos facitis? Tum unus ex iis: Hoc interest, inquit: nos quæ nostra sunt comedimus; tu vero aliena furaris.

4.

Rapuerat caseum corvus atque, ut comederet illum, in celsa arbore consedit. Quo conspecto, vulpes avida casei, accurrit eumque blande astuteque aggreditur: O corve, inquit, quam pulchra es avis, quam speciosa! Te decuit esse avium regem. Sane omnes aves regiis virtutibus antecederes, si vocem haberes. His corvus laudibus inflatus, ut vocem ostenderet clamorem edidit, sed simul, aperto rostro, caseum amisit. Hunc vulpes statim arripuit atque irridens dixit: Heus, corve! Nihil tibi deest præter mentem.

5.

Formica sitiens quum ad fontem descendisset ut biberet, in aquam cecidit nec multum abfuit quin misera periret. Columba quædam, in arbore sedens, misericordia tacta, ramulum in aquam injecit. Hunc assecuta est formica eique innatans mortem effugit. Paulo post adfuit auceps, qui columbæ insidiabatur. Formica, ut piæ columbæ opem ferret, ad aucupem arrepsit et tam vehementer eum momordit ut arundines præ dolore abjiceret. Columba, strepitu arundinum territa, avolavit ac periculo incolumis evasit. —Juva et juvabere; raro beneficium perit.

6.

Vulpes, asinus et leo venatum iverant. Ampla præda facta, leo asinum illam partiri jubet. Qui quum singulis singulas partes poneret æquales, leo eum correptum dilaniavit et vulpi negotium partiendi tribuit. Illa astutior leoni maximam partem apposuit, sibi vix minimam reservans particulam. Tum leo subrīdens ejus prudentiam laudare et, unde hoc didicerit, interrogare cœpit. Et vulpes: Hujus me, inquit, calamitas docuit, quid minores potentioribus debeant.

7.

Leo annis confectus morbum finxit. Ut eum viserent, plures bestiæ ad ægrotum regem venerunt, quas ille protinus devoravit. Sed cauta vulpes procul ante speluncam stabat, regem salutans. Leo rogavit, cur non intraret? Quia, inquit, multa intrantium vestigia video, sed nulla exeuntium.

8.

Asinus sale onustus fluvium transiit et titubans in aquam decidit. Quum surgeret, onus non nihil levatum esse sensit; sal enim in aqua delicuerat. Qua re gavisus, quum postea spongiis onustus ad fluvium accederet, speravit, si rursus collaberetur, fore ut onus fieret levius. Quare de industria lapsus est. Spongiis autem madefactis exsurgere nequivit ideoque oneri succumbens misere in aqua periit.

9.

Serpens ingenti saxo oppressus rogavit virum illac iter facientem, ut a se onus amoliretur, pollicitus, se illi ingentem thesaurum daturum esse si hoc faceret. Quod cum vir iste fecisset, non modo promissa non solvit, sed hominem occidere conatus est. Dum contendunt, accidit ut vulpes transiret. Quæ arbitra electa: Non possum, inquit, tantas lites componere, nisi videro prius, quomodo serpens saxo oppressus fuerit. Cum igitur vir serpenti saxum iterum imposuisset, vulpes astuta: Ingratum animal, inquit, sub saxo relinquendum esse censeo.

10.

Lupus et agnus, siti compulsi, ad eundem rivum venerant. Superior lupus, longe inferior agnus stabat. Tunc improbus latro jurgii causam quærens: Cur, inquit, aquam mihi bibenti turbulentam fecisti? Agnus perterritus: Quomodo, inquit, hoc facere possum; aqua a te ad me decurrit. Lupus, veritate rei repulsus: Sex menses abhinc, inquit, mihi maledixisti. Illo tempore, respondit agnus, equidem nondum natus eram. Hercle igitur, inquit lupus, pater tuus de me male locutus est, atque ita correptum agnum dilaniat.

11.

Cervus cum vehementer sitiret, ad fontem accessit, suaque in aquis imagine conspecta, cornuum magnitudinem et varietatem laudabat, crura vera ut gracilia et exilia vituperabat. Haec cogitanti supervenit leo. Quo viso in fugam se conjicit cervus et leoni longe præcurrit. Quamdiu in planitie erat, nullum ei ab hoste imminebat periculum. Ubi vero ad nemus venit opacum, inter dumeta cornibus adhærescens, quum celeritate pedum uti non posset, captus et dilaniatus est. Tum moriturus: O me desipientem, inquit, cui ea displicerent, quæ me servarunt, placerent autem, quæ me perdiderunt!

12.

Senex quidam ligna in silva ceciderat et, fasce in humeros sublato, domum redire cœpit. Quum autem defatigatus esset et onere et itinere, deposuit ligna, et senectutis inopiæque miserias secum reputans, clara voce invocavit mortem ut se ab omnibus malis liberaret. Mox adfuit mors quid vellet interrogans. Tunc senex perterritus: Nihil volo, inquit, nisi ut hunc fascem lignorum humeris meis imponas.

13.

Duo amici iter unâ faciunt. Occurrit in itinere ursus, quo conspecto alter eorum illico arborem conscendit sicque periculum evitat; alter vero, quum meminisset, bestiam illam cadavera non attingere, humi se prosternit animamque continet, se mortuum esse simulans. Accedit ursus, contrectat jacentem, os suum ad hominis os auresque admovet atque, cadaver esse ratus, discedit. Quum postea socius quæreret, quidnam ei ursus dixisset in aurem, respondit: Monuit ne amicum esse mihi unquam persuaderem, cujus fidem adverso tempore non fuissem expertus.

14.

Mures, in pariete cavo commorantes, diu contemplabantur felem, quæ capite demisso et tristi vultu placide recumbebat. Tunc unus ex iis: Hoc animal, inquit, admodum benignum et mite videtur esse. Quid, si alloquar et familiaritatem cum illo contraham? Quæ cum dixisset et propius accessisset, a fele captus et dilaceratus est.

15.

Sturnum, qui ex urbe aufugerat, cuculus interrogavit: Quid dicunt homines de cantu nostro? quid de luscinia? Sturnus: Maximopere, inquit, omnes cantum ejus laudant. Quid de alauda? Permulti, respondit sturnus, hujus quoque cantum laudibus extollunt. Et quid de coturnice dicunt? Non desunt, qui voce ejus delectentur. Quid tandem, rogat cuculus, de me judicant? Hoc, inquit sturnus, dicere nequeo; nusquam enim tui fit mentio. Iratus igitur cuculus: Ne inultus, inquit, vivam, semper de me ipse loquar.

16.

Cani perpingui occurrit forte lupus macie confectus. Quum inter se salu-
tassent, lupus: Unde, inquit, sic nites? aut quo cibo tam pinguis factus es?
Ego, qui longe fortior sum, fame pereo. Canis respondit: Eádem tibi erit
fortuna, si domino par officium præstabis. Quodnam? inquit ille. Custos
ut sis liminis et noctu domum a furibus tuearis. Tum lupus: Ego vero, inquit, paratus sum; nunc enim patior frigora et imbres, in silvis oberrans.
Quanto facilius est sub tecto vivere et largo satiari cibo!—Veni ergo mecum.—Dum procedunt, aspicit lupus collum canis catena detritum. Unde
hoc, amice? Nihil est.—Dic, quæso!—Quia acer sum, me interdiu alligant,
ut quiescam et noctu alacrior sim. Vesperi me solvunt. Tunc vagor ubi
lubet. Ultro mihi afferunt panem, de mensa sua dat ossa dominus, frusta
dat familia.—Age vero, si quo abire vis, estne tibi abeundi licentia?—Non
semper.—Vale, respondit ille, et fruere ista felicitate tua, quam mihi laudas.
Equidem regnare nolo, si libertate carendum est.

17.

Cædebat quidam ligna juxta fluvium. Laboranti excïdit secûris et in
flumine demersa est. Tum ille, inops consilii, in ripa assïdens, deflere fortunam suam et misere lamentari cœpit. Mercurius autem, cum querelas
illius cognovisset, hominis miseritus, ex aqua emersus, ei retulit secûrim,
non eam quidem, quam amiserat, sed auream, hominemque interrogavit,
hæccine esset, quam perdidisset. Cum suam illam esse negaret, Mercurius
alteram argenteam extulit; sed quum ne hanc quidem agnosceret lignator,
ferream postremo protulit, quam lætus homo suam esse dixit. Qua probitate delectatus deus, omnes secûres homini donat.

18.

Ranæ olim regem a Jove petivisse dicuntur. Quarum ille precibus commotus trabem ingentem in lacum dejecit. Ranæ sonitu perterritæ primum
refugerunt, deinde vero, trabem in aqua natantem conspicatæ magno cum
contemptu in ea consederunt aliumque regem novis clamoribus expetive-
runt. Tum Jupiter, ut ranarum stultiam puniret, hydrum illis misit, a quo
plurimæ captæ misere perierunt. Tum sero stolidarum precum ranas pœni-
tuit.

19.

Circum leonem dormientem lascive discurrebant musculi, quorum unus
in dorsum ejus insiluit. Captus autem a leone experrecto excusavit impru-
dentiam gratiasque se ei habiturum esse pollicitus est, si vitæ parceret.
Leo, etsi erat ira commotus, ignovit tamen musculo precanti, et tam con-
temtam bestiolam dimisit incolumem. Paulo post incautius prædam vestï-
gans leo in laqueos incïdit, quibus adstrictus rugïtum maximum edidit.
Accurrit musculus, cernensque vinculis detentum, qui sibi dudum vitam

petenti concesserat, arrepsit ad laqueos eosque corrosit. Hoc modo quum leonem periculo liberasset: Tibi, inquit, ludibrio eram, quasi nullum vicissim beneficium præstare possem; nunc scias, etiam murem gratias referre posse.

20.

Lupus moribundus vitam ante actam perpendebat. Malus quidem fui, inquit, neque tamen pessimus. Multa male feci, fateor, sed multum etiam boni perpetravi. Agnus aliquando balans, qui a grege aberraverat, jam prope ad me accesserat, ut facile devorare possem; sed parcebam illi. Eodem tempore convicia ab ove quadam in me jactata æquissimo ferebam animo, licet a canibus nihil mihi metuendum esset.—Atque hæc omnia ego testari possum, inquit vulpes. Probe enim rem memini. Nimirum tum temporis accidit, cum os illud devoratum in faucibus tuis hæreret, ad quod extrahendum gruis opem implorare cogebaris.

21.

Societatem inierunt leo, capra et ovis. Præda autem, quam ceperant, in quatuor partes divisa, leo: Prima, inquit, mea est, quia sum leo, vobis longe præstantior. Tollam etiam secundam, quam meretur robur meum. Tertia debetur egregio labori meo. Quartam qui tangere voluerit, is sciat mecum sibi negotium futurum esse. Sic improbus totam prædam solus abstulit.

22.

Mendax et verax simul iter facientes forte in simiorum terram venerant. Quos quum unus e turba, qui se regem simiorum fecerat, vidisset, teneri eos jussit, ut audiret, quid de se homines dicerent. Simul jubet omnes adstare simios longo ordine dextra lævaque, sed sibi poni thronum, ut hominum reges quondam facere viderat. Tum homines in medium adductos rogat: Qualisnam vobis esse videor, hospites? Respondit mendax: Rex videris esse maximus. Quid hi, quos mihi vides astantes? Hi comites tui sunt, hi legati et militum duces. Simius, mendacio laudatus, munus dari adulatori jubet. Tum ad veracem simius: Et qualis tibi esse videor? et quales illi, qui mecum sunt? Vir verax: Verus, inquit, tu es simius, et simii omnes illi, qui tui similes sunt. Tum rex iratus dentibus et unguibus eum dilacerari jussit.

23.

Ferunt quodam in conventu bestiarum tam belle saltasse simium, ut omnium sententia rex crearetur. Hunc vulpes superbientem videns, dixit simio, quum regnum ipsi obtigisset, se non amplius celare velle, quæ magnopere, ut resciceret, regis interesset. Quid id esset, simio interroganti, thesaurum respondit sibi a patre suo esse indicatum, defossum in solitudine, qui jam optimo jure regis esset. Eamus igitur, inquit simius, ut effodiamus. —Cave tibi, inquit vulpes, nam ego sæpe audivi, hanc rem periculo non carere.—Nihil, inquit simius, periculi est; an tu, obsecra, times? Eamus modo, inquit vulpes. Diu ambo in silvis vagantur. Tandem venerunt ad laqueos sub fruticibus ad capiendas bestias absconditos. Tum vulpes: Hic, inquit, thesaurus obrŭtus est. Simius festĭnans neque ullo modo sibi cavens statim capitur ac laqueis implicitus vulpem suppliciter orat, ut sibi succurrat. Hæc vero: Regem, inquit, attingere non audeo; ceteroquin ars saltandi regnum non merebatur.

24.

Rusticus moriturus, cum relinquere filiis suis divitias non posset, animos illorum ad studium diligentis agrorum culturæ et ad laboris assiduitatem excitare voluit. Arcessit igitur illos ad se atque ita alloquitur: Filii mei, quo modo res meæ se habeant, videtis; quidquid autem per omnem vitam reservavi, hoc in vinea nostra quærere poteritis. Hæc cum dixisset, paulo post moritur senex. Filii in vinea patrem alicubi thesaurum abscondisse arbitrantes, arreptis ligonibus universum vineæ solum effodiunt. Thesaurum quidem nullum inveniunt, terram vero fodiendo adeo fertilem reddiderunt, ut vites uberrimum fructum ferrent.

25.

Agitata vulpes a canibus, longo spatio confecto, devenit tandem ad casulam, ante quam lignator findebat stipitem quernum. Ad eum supplex confugit, orans, ut sibi latebras aliquas demonstraret, in quibus, dum venatores præteriissent, occultaretur. Ille, misericordia motus, suam casulam jubet subire. Postea recordatus animantem illam esse nocentem, nec tamen manifeste prodere supplicem ausus, venatoribus vulpem persequentibus et, num vulpem vidisset, percontantibus, verbis quidem se vidisse negabat, sed manu oculisque casulam suam indicabat. Sed venatores, non animadverso indicio, celeriter discedunt. Vulpes, quæ omnia audierat et viderat, non ita multo post de casula progressa, insalutato lignatore abiit. Quod quum ille ægre ferret et cum vulpe expostularet, astutum animal: Libenter, inquit, tibi gratias agerem, si cum oratione tua manus et oculi non discrepassent· linguam tuam laudo, sed manus tibi præcisas et oculos effossos velim.

EXTRACTS FROM CICERO.

1.

Cum rex Pyrrhus populo Romano bellum ultro intulisset, cumque de imperio certamen esset cum rege generoso ac potente, perfüga ab eo venit in castra Fabricii, eique est pollicitus, si præmium sibi proposuisset, se, ut clam venisset, sic clam in Pyrrhi castra rediturum et eum veneno necaturum. Hunc Fabricius reducendum curavit ad Pyrrhum ; idque factum ejus a senatu laudatum est. (*De Offic.* III. 22.)

2.

Laudabo sapientem illum, Biantem, ut opinor, qui numeratur in septem ; cujus cum patriam Prienen cepisset hostis, ceterique ita fugerent, ut multa de suis rebus secum asportarent, cum esset admonitus · a quodam, ut idem ipse faceret : Ego vero, inquit, facio ; nam omnia mea porto mecum (*Parad.* I. 1.)

3.

Socrates quum esset ex eo quæsitum, Archelaum Perdiccæ filium, regem Macedōnum, qui tum fortunatissimus haberetur, nonne beatum putaret. Haud scio, inquit, nunquam enim cum eo collocutus sum. Ain' tu ? an aliter id scire non potes ?—Nullo modo.—Tu igitur ne de Persarum quidem rege magno dicere potes, beatusne sit ?—An ego possim, inquit, quum ignorem quam doctus sit, quam vir bonus ?—Quid ? tu in eo sitam esse vitam beatam putas ?—Ita prorsus existimo : bonos beatos, improbos miseros.— Miser ergo Archelaus ?—Certe, si injustus. (*Tuscul. Quæst.* V. 12.)

4.

Duodequadraginta annos tyrannus Syracusanorum fuit Dionysius, cum quinque et viginti natus annos dominatum occupavisset. Qua pulchritudine urbem, quibus autem opibus præditam, servitute oppressam tenuit civitatem ! Atqui de hoc homine a bonis auctoribus sic scriptum accepimus, summam fuisse ejus in victu temperantiam, in rebusque gerendis virum acrem et industrium ; eundem tamen maleficum natura et injustum. Ex quo omnibus, bene veritatem intuentibus, videri necesse est miserrimum. (*Tuscul. Quæst.* V. 20.)

5.

Xenocrates, cum legati ab Alexandro quinquaginta ei talenta attulissent, quæ erat pecunia temporibus illis, Athenis præsertim, maxima, abduxit legatos ad cœnam in Academiam : iis apposuit tantum, quod satis esset, nullo apparatu. . Cum postridie rogarent eum, cui numerari juberet : Quid ?

vos hesterna, inquit, cœnula non intellexistis, me pecunia non egere? Quos quum tristiores vidisset, triginta minas accepit, ne aspernari regis liberalitatem videretur. (*Tuscul. Quæst.* V. 32.)

6.

Æschines, cum propter ignominiam judicii cessisset Athenis, et se Rhodum contulisset, rogatus a Rhodiis, legisse fertur orationem illam egregiam quam in Ctesiphontem contra Demosthenem dixerat: qua perlecta, petitum est ab eo postridie ut legeret etiam illam, quæ erat contra a Demosthene pro Ctesiphonte edita: quam cum suavissima et maxima voce legisset, admirantibus omnibus: Quanto, inquit, magis admiraremini, si audissetis ipsum! (*De Orat.* III. 56.)

7.

Cum Hannibal, Carthagine expulsus, Ephesum ad Antiochum venisset exsul, invitatus est ab hospitibus ut Phormionem quendam philosophum andiret; cumque se non nolle dixisset, locutus esse dicitur homo copiosus aliquot horas de imperatoris officio et de omni re militari. Tum, cum ceteri qui illum audierant, vehementer essent delectati, quærebant ab Hannibale, quidnam ipse de illo philosopho judicaret. Hic Pœnus non optime grœce, sed tamen libere respondisse fertur, multos se deliros senes sæpe vidisse, sed qui magis, quam Phormio, deliraret, vidisse neminem. Neque mehercule injuria. Quid enim arrogantius aut loquacius fieri potuit, quam Hannibali, qui tot annos de imperio cum populo Romano omnium gentium victore certasset, Græcum hominem, qui nunquam hostem, numquam castra vidisset, nunquam denique minimam partem ullius publici muneris attigisset, præcepta de re militari dare? (*De Orat.* II. 18.)

8.

Roges me quid aut quale sit Deus, auctore utar Simonide; de quo cum quæsivisset hoc idem tyrannus Hiero, deliberandi causa sibi unum diem postulavit. Cum idem ex eo postridie quæreret, biduum petivit. Cum sæpius duplicaret numerum dierum, admiransque Hiero requireret cur ita faceret: Quia quanto, inquit, diutius considero, tanto mihi res videtur obscurior. (*De Nat. Deor.* I. 22.)

9.

Dionysius tyrannus ipse indicavit, quam esset beatus. Nam quum quidam ex ejus assentatoribus, Damocles, commemoraret in sermone copias ejus, opes, majestatem dominatus, rerum abundantiam, magnificentiam ædium regiarum, negaretque unquam beatiorem quemquam fuisse: Visne igitur, inquit, O Damocle, quoniam hæc te vita delectat, ipse eandem degustare et fortunam experiri meam? Quum se ille cupere dixisset, collocari jussit hominem in aureo lecto strato pulcherrimo textili stragulo, magnificis operibus picto: abacosque complures ornavit argento auroque cælato. Tum ad mensam eximia forma pueros delectos jussit consistere eosque nutum illius intuentes, diligenter ministrare. Aderant unguenta, coronæ ; incendebantur odores, mensæ conquisitissimis epulis exstruebantur. Fortunatus sibi Damocles videbatur. In hoc medio apparatu Dionysius fulgentem gladium e lacunari seta equina aptum demitti jussit, ut impendēret illius beati cervicibus. Itaque nec pulchros illos ministratores aspiciebat Damocles, nec plenum artis argentum, nec manum porrigebat in mensam : jam ipsæ defluebant coronæ : denique exoravit tyrannum ut abire liceret, quod jam beatus nollet esse. (*Tuscul. Quæst.* V. 21.)

10.

Lysandrum Lacedæmonium dicere aiunt solitum, Lacedæmonem esse honestissimum domicilium senectutis : nusquam enim tantum tribuitur ætati, nusquam est senectus honoratior. Quin etiam memoriæ proditum est, cum Athenis, ludis, quidam in theatrum grandis natu venisset, in magno consessu locum ei a suis civibus nusquam datum ; cum autem ad Lacedæmonios accessisset, qui legati cum essent, in loco certo consederant, consurrexisse omnes, et senem illum sessum recepisse. Quibus cum a cuncto consessu plausus esset multiplex datus, dixisse ex iis quendam, Athenienses scire quæ recta essent, sed facere nolle. (*De Senect.* XVIII.)

11.

Sic existimabam nihil homines aliud Romæ, nisi de quæstura mea, loqui. Frumenti in summa caritate maximum numerum miseram : negotiatoribus comis, mercatoribus justus, municipibus liberalis, sociis abstinens, omnibus eram visus in omni officio diligentissimus : excogitati quidam erant a Siculis honores inauditi. Itaque hac spe decedebam, ut mihi populum Romanum ultro omnia delaturum putarem. At ego, cum casu diebus iis, itineris faciendi causa, decedens e provincia, Puteolos forte venissem, cum plurimi et lautissimi solent esse in iis locis ; concidi pæne, cum ex me quidam quæsisset, quo die Roma exissem, et num quid in ea esset novi : cui cum respondissem, me ex provincia decedere : Etiam mehercules, inquit, ut opinor, ex Africa. Huic ego jam stomachans fastidiose : Imo ex Sicilia, inquam. Tum quidam, quasi qui omnia sciret : Quid ? tu nescis, inquit, hunc Syracusis quæstorem fuisse ?—Quid multa ? destiti stomachari, et me unum ex iis feci, qui ad aquas venissent. Sed ea res haud scio an plus mihi profuerit, quam si mihi tum essent omnes congratulati. (*Orat. pro Plancio ;* 26. 27.)

12.

Annibalem Cœlius scribit, cum columnam auream, quæ esset in fano Junonis Laciniæ, auferre vellet, dubitaretque utrum ea solida esset an extrinsecus inaurata, perterebravisse ; cumque solidam invenisset, statuisse tollere : ei secundum quietem visam esse Junonem prædicere ne id faceret, minarique, si id fecisset, se curaturam ut eum quoque oculum, quo bene videret, amitteret ; idque ab homine acuto non esse neglectum. Itaque ex eo auro, quod exterebratum esset, buculam curasse faciendam, et eam in summa columna collocavisse. (*De Divinat.* I. 24.)

13.

Fuit Spartiatarum gens fortis, dum Lycurgi leges vigebant : e quibus unus, quum Perses hostis in colloquio dixisset glorians : Solem præ jaculorum multitudine et sagittarum non videbitis ; In umbra igitur, inquit, pugnabimus.—Esto : fortes et duri Spartiatæ ; magnam habet vim reipublicæ disciplina. Quid ? Cyrenæum Theodorum, philosophum non ignobilem, nonne miramur ? cui quum Lysimachus rex crucem minaretur : Istis quæso, inquit, ista horribilia minitare purpuratis tuis : Theodori quidem nihil interest, humine, an sublime putrescat.—Leges Lycurgi laboribus erudiunt juventutem, venando, currendo, esuriendo, sitiendo, algendo, æstuando. Spartæ vero pueri ad aram sic verberibus accipiuntur, ut multus e visceribus sanguis exeat : nonnunquam etiam, ut, cum ibi essem, audiebam, ad necem : quorum non modo nemo exclamavit, sed ne ingemuit quidem. (*Tuscul. Quæst.* I. 42, 43 ; II. 14.)

14.

L. Manlio, cum dictator fuisset, M. Pomponius, tribunus plebis, diem dixit, quod is paucos sibi dies ad dictaturam' gerendam addidisset ; criminabatur etiam, quod Titum filium, qui postea est Torquatus appellatus, ab hominibus relegasset, et ruri habitare jussisset. Quod quum audivisset adolescens filius, negotium exhiberi patri, accurrisse Romam et cum prima luce Pomponii domum venisse dicitur : cui quum esset nuntiatum, quod illum iratum allaturum ad se aliquid contra patrem arbitraretur, surrexit e lectulo, remotisque arbitris, ad se adolescentem jussit venire. At ille, ut ingressus est, confestim gladium destrinxit, juravitque se illum statim interfecturum, nisi jusjurandum sibi dedisset, se patrem missum esse facturum. Juravit hoc coactus terrore Pomponius : rem ad populum detulit ; docuit cur sibi causa desistere necesse esset ; Manlium missum fecit ; tantum temporibus illis jusjurandum valebat. (*De Offic.* III. 31.)

15.

Sophocles ad summam senectutem tragœdias fecit : quod propter studium cum rem familiarem negligere videretur, a filiis in judicium vocatus est ; ut, quemadmodum nostro more male rem gerentibus patribus bonis interdici solet, sic illum, quasi desipientem, a re familiari removerent judices. Tum senex dicitur eam fabulam, quam in manibus habebat, et proxime scripserat, Œdipum Coloneum recitasse judicibus, quæsisseque, num illud carmen desipientis videretur : quo recitato sententiis judicum est liberatus. (*De Senect.* VII.)

16.

Cum duo quidam Arcades familiares iter una fecissent et Megaram venissent, alterum ad cauponem devertisse ; ad hospitem, alterum : qui ut cœnati quiescerent, concubia nocte visum esse in somnis ei qui erat in hospitio, illum alterum orare ut subveniret, quod sibi a caupone interitus pararetur ; eum primo perterritum somnio surrexisse ; dein quum se collegisset, idque visum pro nihilo habendum esse duxisset, recubuisse ; tum ei dormienti eundem illum visum esse rogare, ut, quoniam sibi vivo non subvenisset, mortem suam ne inultam esse pateretur : se interfectum in plaustrum a caupone esse conjectum et supra stercus injectum ; petere, ut mane ad portam adesset, priusquam plaustrum ex oppido exiret. Hoc verò somnio eum commotum, mane bubulco præsto ad portam fuisse ; quæsisse ex eo, quid esset in plaustro ; illum perterritum fugisse ; mortuum erūtum esse ; cauponem, re patefactā, pœnas dedisse. (*De Divin.* I. 27.)

17.

In itinere quidam proficiscentem ad mercatum quendam et secum aliquantum nummorum ferentem, est consecutus : cum hoc, ut fere fit, in via sermonem contulit ; ex quo factum est ut illud iter familiarius facere vellent : quare quum in eandem tabernam devertissent, simul cœnare et in eodem loco somnum capere voluerunt. Cœnati discubuerunt ibidem. Caupo autem quum illum alterum, videlicet qui nummos haberet, animadvertisset, noctu, postquam illos arctius jam, ut fit, ex lassitudine dormire sensit, accessit : et alterius eorum, qui sine nummis erat, gladium propter appositum e vagina eduxit, et illum alterum occidit, nummos abstulit, gladium cruentatum in vaginam recondidit, ipse sese in lectum suum recepit. Ille autem, cujus gladio occisio erat facta, multo ante lucem surrexit, comitem illum suum inclamavit semel et sæpius : illum somno impeditum non respondere existimavit : ipse gladium et cetera quæ secum attulerat, sustulit, solus profectus est. Caupo, non multo post, conclamavit hominem esse occisum, et, cum quibusdam deversoribus, illum qui ante exierat consequitur : in itinere hominem comprehendit, gladium ejus e vagina educit, reperit cruentum, homo in urbem ab illis deducitur ac reus fit. (*De Invent. Rhetor.* II. 4.)

18.

Acerrimo studio tenebar ; quotidie et scribens, et legens, et commentans, oratoriis tamen exercitationibus contentus non eram. Juris civilis studio multum operæ dabam ; quumque princeps academiæ Philo cum Atheniensium optimatibus, Mithridatico bello, domo profugisset Romamque venisset, totum ei me tradidi, admirabili quodam ad philosophiam studio concitatus ; in quo hoc etiam commorabar attentius, quod rerum ipsarum varietas et magnitudo summā me delectatione retinebat. Eodem anno etiam Moloni Rhodio Romæ dedimus operam, et actori summo causarum, et magistro. Ego vero, hoc tempore omni, noctes et dies in omnium doctrinarum meditatione versabar. Eram cum Stoico Diodoto, qui quum habitavisset apud me, mecumque vixisset, nuper est domi meæ mortuus : a quo, cum in aliis rebus, tum studiosissime in dialectica exercebar, quæ quasi contracta et adstricta eloquentia putanda est. Huic ego doctori et ejus artibus variis atque multis ita eram tamen deditus, ut ab exercitationibus oratoriis nullus dies vacuus esset.—Commentabar declamitans (sic enim nunc loquuntur) sæpe cum M. Pisone, et cum Q. Pompeio, aut cum aliquo quotidie ; idque faciebam multum etiam latine, sed græce sæpius : vel quod græca oratio plura ornamenta suppeditans, consuetudinem similiter latine dicendi afferebat, vel quod a Græcis summis doctoribus, nisi græce dicerem, neque corrigi possem, neque doceri. Itaque prima causa publica, pro Sext. Roscio dicta, tantum commendationis habuit, ut non ulla esset, quæ non digna nostro patrocinio videretur.—(*De claris Orat.* 89, etc.)

19.

Nunc, quoniam totum me videris velle cognoscere, complectar nonnulla etiam, quæ fortasse videantur minus necessaria. Erat eo tempore in nobis summa gracilitas et infirmitas corporis: procerum et tenue collum: qui habitus et quæ figura non procul abesse putatur a vitæ periculo, si accedit labor et laterum magna contentio. Eoque magis hoc eos, quibus eram carus, commovebat, quod omnia sine remissione, sine varietate, vi summa vocis et totius corporis contentione dicebam. Itaque quum me amici et medici hortarentur ut causas agere desisterem, quodvis potius periculum mihi adeundum, quam a sperata dicendi gloria discedendum putavi. Sed, quum censerem remissione et moderatione vocis, et commutato genere dicendi, me et periculum vitare posse, et temperantius dicere, ut consuetudinem dicendi mutarem, ea causa mihi in Asiam proficiscendi fuit. Itaque cum essem biennium versatus in causis, et jam in foro celebratum meum nomen esset, Roma sum profectus. Cum venissem Athenas, sex menses cum Antiocho, veteris academiæ nobilissimo et prudentissimo philosopho, fui ; studiumque philosophiæ nunquam intermissum, a primaque adolescentia cultum et semper auctum, hoc rursus summo auctore et doctore renovavi.—(*De claris Orat.* 89.)

20.

Aiunt T. Cœlium quendam Tarracinensem, hominem non obscurum, quum cœnatus cubitum in idem conclave cum duobus adolescentibus filiis isset, inventum esse mane jugulatum. Quum neque servus quisquam reperiretur, neque liber, ad quem ea suspicio pertineret; id ætatis autem duo filii propter cubantes ne sensisse quidem se dicerent: nomina filiorum de parricidio delata sunt. Quid postea? erat sane suspiciosum: neutrum sensisse? ausum autem esse quemquam se in id conclave committere, eo potissimum tempore, quum ibidem essent duo adolescentes filii, qui et sentire et defendere facile possent? Erat porro nemo, in quem ea suspicio conveniret. Tamen quum planum judicibus esset factum, aperto ostio dormientes eos repertos esse, judicio absoluti adolescentes et suspicione omni liberati sunt. Nemo enim putabat quemquam esse, qui quum omnia divina atque humana jura scelere nefario polluisset, somnum statim capere potuisset: propterea quod qui tantum facinus commiserunt, non modo sine cura quiescere, sed ne spirare quidem sine metu possunt.—(*Orat. pro Rosc. Amer.* 28.)

21.

Narrat Xenophon, Cyrum minorem, regem Persarum, præstantem ingenio atque imperii gloria, cum Lysander Lacedæmonius, vir summæ virtutis, venisset ad eum Sardis eique dona a sociis attulisset, et ceteris in rebus comem erga Lysandrum atque humanum fuisse et ei quendam conseptum agrum, diligenter consitum ostendisse. Quum autem admiraretur Lysander et proceritates arborum et directos in quincuncem ordines, et humum subactam atque puram, et suavitatem odorum qui afflarentur e floribus: tum dixisse, mirari se non modo diligentiam, sed etiam solertiam ejus, a quo essent illa dimensa atque descripta; et ei Cyrum respondisse: Atqui ego omnia ista sum dimensus, mei sunt ordines, mea descriptio; multæ etiam istarum arborum mea manu sunt satæ. Tum Lysandrum intuentem ejus purpuram, et nitorem corporis, ornatumque Persicum multo auro, multisque gemmis dixisse: Recte vero te, Cyre, beatum ferunt, quoniam virtuti tuæ fortuna conjuncta est.—(*De Senect.* XVII.)

22.

Quid potest esse tam apertum, tamque perspicuum, cum cœlum suspeximus, cœlestiaque contemplati sumus, quam esse aliquod numen præstantissimæ mentis, quo hæc regantur? Quod qui dubitet, haud sane intelligo cur non idem, sol sit, an nullus sit dubitare possit. Quid enim est hoc illo evidentius? Quod nisi cognitum comprehensumque animis haberemus, non tam stabilis opinio permaneret, nec confirmaretur diuturnitate temporis, nec una cum seculis ætatibusque hominum inveterare potuisset. Etenim videmus ceteras opiniones fictas atque vanas diuturnitate extabuisse. Quis enim Hippocentaurum fuisse, aut Chimæram putat? Quæve anus tam excors inveniri potest, quæ illa, quæ quondam credebantur apud inferos portenta, extimescat? Opinionum enim commenta delet dies: naturæ judicia confirmat.—(*De Nat. Deor.* II. 2.)

23.

Præclare Aristoteles: "Si essent," inquit, "qui sub terra semper habitavissent, bonis et illustribus domiciliis, quæ essent ornata signis atque picturis, instructaque rebus iis omnibus, quibus abundant ii qui beati putantur, nec tamen existent unquam supra terram: accepissent autem fama et auditione esse quoddam numen et vim deorum: deinde aliquo tempore, patefactis terræ faucibus, ex illis abditis sedibus evadere in hæc loca quæ nos incolimus atque exire potuissent: cum repente terram, et maria cœlumque vidissent, nubium magnitudinem, ventorumque vim cognovissent, aspexissentque solem, ejusque tum magnitudinem pulchritudinemque; tum etiam efficientiam cognovissent, quod is diem efficeret toto cœlo luce diffusa; cum autem terras nox opacasset, tum cœlum totum cernerent astris distinctum et ornatum, lunæque luminum varietatem tum crescentis, tum senescentis, eorumque omnium ortus et occasus, atque ratos immutabilesque cursus: hæc quum viderent, profecto et esse deos, et hæc tanta opera deorum esse arbitrarentur."—Atque hæc quidem ille.

Nos autem tenebras cogitemus tantas, quantæ quondam eruptione Ætnæorum ignium finitimas regiones obscuravisse dicuntur, ut per biduum nemo hominem homo agnosceret; quum autem tertio die sol illuxisset, tum ut revixisse sibi viderentur. Quod si hoc idem ex æternis tenebris contingeret, ut subito lucem aspiceremus: quænam species cœli videretur! Sed assiduitate quotidiana, et consuetudine oculorum, assuescunt animi: neque admirantŭr, neque requirunt rationes rerum earum quas semper vident: proinde quasi novitas nos magis, quam magnitudo rerum, debeat ad exquirendas causas excitare.—(*De Nat. Deor.* II. 37.)

24.

Quis hunc hominem dixerit, qui quum tam certos cœli motus, tam ratos astrorum ordines, tamque omnia inter se connexa et apta viderit, neget in his ullam inesse rationem, eaque casu fieri dicat, quæ quanto consilio gerantur, nullo consilio assequi possumus? An, quum machinatione quadam moveri aliquid videmus, ut sphæram, ut horas, ut alia permulta, non dubitamus quin illa opera sint rationis; cum autem impetum cœli admirabili cum celeritate moveri vertique videamus, constantissime conficientem vicissitudines anniversarias, cum summa salute et conservatione rerum omnium, dubitamus quin ea non solum ratione fiant, sed etiam excellenti quadam divinaque ratione? Licet enim jam, remota subtilitate disputandi, oculis quodammodo contemplari pulchritudinem rerum earum, quas divina providentia dicimus constitutas.—(*De Nat. Deor.* II. 38.)

25.

Esse præstantem aliquam æternamque naturam, et eam suspiciendam admirandamque hominum generi, pulchritudo mundi, ordoque rerum cœlestium cogit confiteri.

Firmissimum hoc afferri videtur, cur deos esse credamus, quod nulla gens tam sit fera, nemo omnium tam sit immanis cujus mentem non imbuerit deorum opinio. Multi de diis prava sentiunt: id enim vitioso more effici solet: omnes tamen esse vim et naturam divinam arbitrantur. Nec vero id collocutio hominum aut consensus effecit: non institutis opinio est confirmata, non legibus. Omni autem in re consensio omnium gentium, lex naturæ putanda est.—(*De Divin.* II. 72.—*Tusc. Quæst.* I. 13.)

26.

Hic ego non mirer esse quemquam, qui sibi persuadeat corpora quædam solida atque individua vi et gravitate ferri, mundumque effici ornatissimum et pulcherrimum ex eorum corporum concursione fortuita? Hoc qui existimat fieri potuisse, non intelligo cur non idem putet, si innumerabiles unius et viginti formæ litterarum vel aureæ, vel qualeslibet, aliquo conjiciantur, posse ex his in terram excussis annales Ennii, ut deinceps legi possint, effici: quod nescio an ne in uno quidem versu possit tantum valere fortuna. Isti autem quemadmodum asseverant, ex corpusculis non colore, non qualitate aliqua, non sensu præditis, sed concurrentibus temere atque casu, mundum esse perfectum? vel innumerabiles potius in omni puncto temporis alios nasci, alios interire? Quod si mundum efficere potest concursus atomorum, cur porticum, cur templum, cur domum, cur urbem non potest, quæ sunt minus operosa, et multo quidem faciliora? Certe ita temere de mundo effutiunt ut nunquam admirabilem cœli ornatum suspexisse videantur.—(*De Nat. Deor.* II. 37.)

bus picto: abacosque complures ornavit argento auroque cælato. Tum ad mensam eximia forma pueros delectos jussit consistere eosque nutum illius intuentes, diligenter ministrare. Aderant unguenta, coronæ; incendebantur odores, mensæ conquisitissimis epulis exstruebantur. Fortunatus sibi Damocles videbatur. In hoc medio apparatu Dionysius fulgentem gladium e lacunari seta equina aptum demitti jussit, ut impendēret illius beati cervicibus. Itaque nec pulchros illos ministratores aspiciebat Damocles, nec plenum artis argentum, nec manum porrigebat in mensam: jam ipsæ defluebant coronæ: denique exoravit tyrannum ut abire liceret, quod jam beatus nollet esse.

15. *Socrates and Xenophon.*

Xenophonti in angiportu obviam venit Socrates. Qui quum videret adolescentem vultu admodum specioso atque verecundo, porrecto baculo vetuit, ne præteriret. Ut constitit, Socrates eum interrogavit, ubinam venderentur, quæ essent necessaria variis civium usibus. Ad quæ quum expedite respondisset Xenophon, percontatus est, ubinam boni ac probi homines fierent. Quum autem adolescens responderet, id se nescire, Socrates: Sequere igitur me, inquit, et disce. Ex eo tempore Xenophon cœpit esse Socratis auditor et bonus probusque factus est.

LETTERS.

1.

M. T. C. Terentiæ Suæ S. P. D.—In Tusculanum nos venturos putamus aut Nonis, aut postridie: ibi fac ut sint omnia parata. Plures enim fortasse nobiscum erunt, et ut arbitror, diutius ibi commorabimur. Labrum, si in balneo non est, fac ut sit: item cetera, quæ sunt ad victum, et ad valetudinem necessaria. Vale.

2.

M. T. C. Terentiæ Suæ S. P. D.—Si vales, bene est: ego valeo. Redditæ mihi tandem sunt a Cæsare litteræ satis liberales: et ipse opinione celerius venturus esse dicitur. Cui utrum obviam procedam, an hic eum expectem, cum constituero, faciam te certiorem. Tabellarios mihi velim quamprimum remittas. Valetudinem tuam cura diligenter. Vale.

3.

M. T. C. Tironi S. P. D.—Omnia a te data mihi putabo, si te valentem videro: summa cura expectabam adventum Menandri, quem ad te miseram. Cura si me diliges, ut valeas, et cum te bene confirmaris, ad nos venias. Vale.

4.

Cicero S. D. Terentiæ.—Quod nos in Italiam salvos venisse gaudes, perpetuo gaudeas velim. Sed perturbati dolore animi, magnisque injuriis, metuo ne id consilii ceperimus, quod non facile explicare possimus. Quare, quantum potes, adjuva. Quid autem possis, mihi in mentem non venit. In viam quod te des hoc tempore, nihil est: et longum est iter, et non tutum: et non video, quid prodesse possis, si veneris. Vale. D. prid. Nonas Novembres. Brundusio.

5.

CICERO S. D. TIRONI.—Non queo ad te, nec lubet scribere, quo animo sim affectus: tantum scribo, et tibi et mihi maximæ voluptati fore, si te firmum quam primum videro. Tertio die abs te ad Alyziam accesseramus. Is locus est citra Leucadem stadia CXX. Leucade aut te ipsum, aut tuas litteras a Marione putabam me accepturum. Quantum me diligis, tantum fac ut valeas, vel quantum te a me scis diligi. Nonis Novemb. Alyziâ.

6.

CICERO S. D. TIRONI.—Tertiam ad te hanc epistolam scripsi eodem die, magis instituti mei tenendi causa, quia nactus eram, cui darem, quam quo haberem, quid scriberem. Igitur illa: quantum me diligis, tantum adhibe in te diligentiæ. Ad tua innumerabilia in me officia adde hoc, quod mihi erit gratissimum omnium: cum valetudinis rationem, ut spero, habueris, habeto etiam navigationis. In Italiam euntibus omnibus ad me litteras dabis, ut ego euntem Patras neminem prætermitto. Cura, cura te, mi Tiro. Cum non contigit, ut simul navigares, nihil est, quod festines: nec quidquam cures, nisi ut valeas. Etiam atque etiam vale.

7.

CICERO PAPIRIO PÆTO S.—Heri veni in Cumanum: cras ad te fortasse. Sed cum certum sciam, faciam te paulo ante certiorem. Etsi M. Ceparius, cum mihi in silva Gallinaria obviam venisset, quæsissemque quid ageres, dixit te in lecto esse, quod ex pedibus laborares. Tuli scilicet moleste, ut debui: sed tamen constitui ad te venire, ut et viderem te, et viserem, et coenarem etiam. Non enim arbitror, coquum etiam te arthriticum habere. Expecta igitur hospitem cum minime edacem, tum inimicum coenis sumptuosis. Vale.

8.

CICERO S. D. MEMMIO.—Aulum Fusium, unum ex meis intimis, observantissimum, studiosissimumque nostri, eruditum hominem, et summa humanitate, tuaque amicitia dignissimum, velim ita tractes, ut mihi coram recepisti. Tam gratum mihi id erit, quam quod gratissimum. Ipsum præterea summo officio, et summa observantia tibi in perpetuum devinxeris. Vale.

9.

CICERO S. D. CÆLIO.—Marco Fabio, viro optimo et homine doctissimo, familiarissime utor, mirificeque eum diligo, cum propter summum ingenium ejus summamque doctrinam, tum propter singularem modestiam. Ejus negotium sic velim suscipias, ut si esset res mea. Novi ego vos magnos patronos: hominem occidat oportet, qui vestra opera uti velit. Sed in hoc homine nullam accipio excusationem. Omnia relinques, si me amabis, cum tua opera Fabius uti volet. Ego res Romanas vehementer expecto et desidero: in primisque, quid agas, scire cupio: nam jam diu propter hiemis magnitudinem nihil novi ad nos afferebatur. Vale.

10.

CICERO S. D. TREBATIO.—Quam sint morosi qui amant, vel ex hoc intelligi potest. Moleste ferebam antea te invitum istic esse: pungit me rursus, quod scribis esse te istic libenter. Neque enim mea commendatione te non delectari facile patiebar; et nunc angor, quidquam tibi sine me esse jucundum. Sed hoc tamen malo, ferre nos desiderium, quam te non ea, quæ spero, consequi. Cum vero in C. Matii, suavissimi doctissimique hominis, familiaritatem venisti, non dici potest quam valde gaudeam: qui fac ut te quam maxime diligat. Mihi crede, nihil ex ista provincia potes, quod jucundius sit, deportare. Cura ut valeas.

11.

CICERO S. D. CORNIFICIO.—Sex. Aufidius et observantia, qua me colit, accedit ad proximos; et splendore equiti Romano nemini cedit. Est autem ita temperatis moderatisque moribus, ut summa severitas summa cum humanitate jungatur. Cujus tibi negotia, quæ sunt in Africa, ita commendo, ut majore studio, magisve ex animo commendare non possim. Pergratum mihi feceris, si dederis operam, ut intelligat, meas apud te litteras maximum pondus habuisse. Hoc te vehementer, mi Cornifici, rogo. Vale.

12.

CICERO S. D. SERVIO SULP.—Asclapone Patrensi, medico, utor valde familiariter: ejusque cum consuetudo mihi jucunda fuit, tum ars etiam, quam sum expertus in valetudine meorum: in qua mihi cum ipsa scientia, tum etiam fidelitate benevolentiaque satisfecit. Hunc igitur tibi commendo; et a te peto, ut des operam, ut intelligat diligenter me scripsisse de sese, meamque commendationem usui magno sibi fuisse. Erit id mihi vehementer gratum. Vale.

13.

CICERO S. D. ACILIO.—Cn. Octacilio Nasone utor familiarissime; ita prorsus, ut illius ordinis nemine familiarius. Nam et humanitate ejus, et probitate in consuetudine quotidiana magnopere delector. Nihil jam opus est expectare te, quibus eum verbis tibi commendem, quo sic utar, ut scripsi. Habet is in provincia tua negotia, quæ procurant liberti, Hilarus, Antigonus, Demostratus: quos tibi, negotiaque omnia Nasonis non secus commendo, ac si mea essent. Gratissimum mihi feceris, si intellexero, hanc commendationem magnum apud te pondus habuisse. Vale.

tuis rebus capio, maxime scilicet consolatur spes, quod valde suspicor fore, ut infringatur hominum improbitas et consiliis tuorum amicorum, et ipsa die, qua debilitantur cogitationes et inimicorum et proditorum. Facile secundo loco me consolatur recordatio meorum temporum, quorum imaginem video in rebus tuis. Nam etsi minore in re violatur tua dignitas, quam mea salus afflicta sit; tamen est tanta similitudo, ut sperem, te mihi ignoscere, si ea non timuerim, quæ ne tu quidem unquam timenda duxisti. Sed præsta te eum, qui mihi a teneris (ut Græci dicunt) unguiculis es cognitus. Illustrabit (mihi crede) tuam amplitudinem hominum injuria. A me omnia summa in te studia officiaque expecta: non fallam opinionem tuam. Vale.

16.

Cicero T. Furfano Proc. S. D.—Cum Aulo Cæcina tanta mihi familiaritas consuetudoque semper fuit, ut nulla major esse possit: nam et patre ejus, claro homine, et forti viro, plurimum usi sumus: et hunc a puero, quod et spem mihi magnam afferebat summæ probitatis, summæque eloquentiæ, et vivebat mecum conjunctissime, non solum officiis amicitiæ, sed etiam studiis communibus, sic semper dilexi, ut nullo cum homine conjunctius viverem. Nihil attinet me plura scribere; quam mihi necesse sit ejus salutem et fortunas, quibuscunque rebus possim tueri, vides. Reliquum est, ut cum cognoverim pluribus rebus quid tu et de bonorum fortuna, et de Reipublicæ calamitatibus sentires, nihil a te petam, nisi ut ad eam voluntatem, quam tua sponte erga Cæcinam habiturus esses, tantus cumulus accedat commendatione mea, quanti me a te fieri intelligo. Hoc mihi gratius facere nihil potes. Vale.

17.

Cicero L. Culleolo Proc. S. D.—Quæ fecisti Lucceii causa, scire te plane volo, te homini gratissimo commodasse: et cum ipsi, quæ fecisti, pergrata sunt, tum Pompeius, quotiescunque me videt (videt autem sæpe), gratias tibi agit singulares. Addo etiam illud, quod tibi jucundissimum esse certo scio, me ipsum ex tua erga Lucceium benignitate, maxima voluptate affici. Quod superest, quamquam mihi non est dubium, quin, cum antea nostra causa, nunc jam etiam tuæ constantiæ gratia mansurus sis in eadem ista liberalitate: tamen abs te vehementer etiam atque etiam peto, ut ea, quæ initio ostendisti, deincepsque fecisti, ad exitum augeri et cumulari per te velis. Id et Lucceio, et Pompeio valde gratum fore, teque apud eos præclare positurum confirmo et spondeo. De republica, deque his negotiis cogitationibusque nostris perscripseram ad te diligenter paucis ante diebus, easque litteras dederam pueris tuis. Vale.

18.

Cicero Dolabellæ Suo S. D.—Vel meo ipsius interitu mallem litteras meas desiderares, quam eo casu, quo sum gravissime afflictus: quem ferrem certe moderatius, si te haberem. Nam et oratio tua prudens et amor erga me singularis multum levaret. Sed quoniam brevi tempore, ut opinio nostra est, te sum visurus, ita me affectum offendes, ut multum a te possim juvari; non quod ita sim fractus, ut aut hominem me esse oblitus sim, aut fortunæ succumbendum putem, sed tamen hilaritas illa nostra et suavitas, quæ te præter ceteros delectabat, erepta mihi omnis est. Firmitatem tamen et constantiam, si modo fuit aliquando in nobis, eandem cognosces quam reliquisti. Quod scribis prœlia te mea causa sustinere, non tam id laboro, ut, si qui mihi obtrectent, a te refutentur, quam intelligi cupio, quod certe intelligitur, me a te amari: quod ut facias te etiam atque etiam rogo, ignoscasque brevitati mearum litterarum; nam et celeriter una futuros nos arbitror, et nondum satis confirmatus sum ad scribendum. Vale.

19.

CICERO S. D. MARCELLO.—Etsi nihil erat novi, quod ad te scriberem, magisque litteras tuas jam expectare incipiebam, vel te potius ipsum: tamen cum Theophilus proficisceretur, non potui nihil ei litterarum dare. Cura igitur, ut quam primum venias. Venies enim, mihi crede, spectatus, neque solum nobis, id est, tuis, sed prorsus omnibus. Venit enim mihi in mentem, subvereri interdum, ne te delectet tarda decessio. Quod si nullum haberes sensum, nisi oculorum, prorsus tibi ignoscerem, si quosdam nolles videre; sed cum leviora non multo essent, quæ audirentur, quam quæ viderentur; suspicarer autem, multum interesse rei familiaris tuæ, te quamprimum venire, idque in omnes partes valeret, putavi, ea de re te esse admonendum. Sed, quoniam quod mihi placeret, ostendi, reliqua tu pro tua prudentia considerabis. Me tamen velim, quod ad tempus te expectemu. certiorem facias. Vale.

20.

CICERO S. P. D. TIRONI SUO.—Paulo facilius putavi posse me ferre desiderium tui: sed plane non fero; et quamquam magni ad honorem nostrum interest quamprimum ad urbem me venire, tamen peccasse mihi videor qui a te discesserim: sed quia tua voluntas ea videbatur esse, ut prorsus, nisi confirmato corpore, nolles navigare, approbavi tuum consilium: neque nunc muto, si tu in eadem es sententia: sin, posteaquam cibum cepisti, videris tibi me posse consequi, tuum consilium est. Marionem ad te eo misi, ut aut tecum ad me quamprimum veniret; aut, si tu morarere, statim ad me rediret. Tu autem hoc tibi persuade, si commodo valetudinis tuæ fieri possit, nihil me malle quam te esse mecum: sin intelliges opus esse te Patris convalescendi causa paulum commorari, nihil me malle quam te valere. Si statim navigas, nos Leucade consequere: sin te confirmare vis, et comites et tempestates et navem idoneam ut habeas, diligenter videbis. Unum illud, mi Tiro, videto, si me amas, ne te Marionis adventus et hæ litteræ moveant. Quod valetudini tuæ maxime conducet, si feceris, maxime obtemperabis voluntati meæ. Hæc pro tuo ingenio considera. Nos ita te desideramus, ut amemus: amor, ut valentem videamus, hortatur; desiderium, ut quamprimum. Illud igitur potius. Cura ergo potissimum ut valeas; de tuis innumerabilibus in me officiis, erit hoc gratissimum. Tertio Nonas Novembris. Vale.